COLLEGE WRITING SKILLS

Jason Przhodka
104 Alumni Towers
4114

Jason Przhodka
104 Alumni Towers
4114

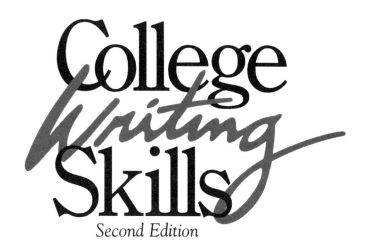

College Writing Skills

Second Edition

Peder Jones

Jay Farness
Northern Arizona University

COLLEGIATE PRESS

Preface

College Writing Skills teaches, through precept and practice, those skills essential to success in college writing. A glance at the table of contents will show that we construct a framework of rhetoric—work in paragraph and essay—around disciplined study of sentences and words. In this way the book combines the most important features of current and traditional approaches to college English. Our overall aim, however, is to present a limited number of skills and techniques which, when mastered, will enable the beginning college writer to compose clear and effective sentences, paragraphs, and brief essays.

The book emphasizes practice: it emphasizes student writing rather than students reading about writing. Accordingly, we have provided more than 450 sets of exercises and an additional 102 optional workshop activities, all of which require the student's active participation. These exercises embody our belief that practice—practice in forming ideas, practice in getting ideas out of one's head and onto paper, practice in finding the most effective way to say something, practice in avoiding or correcting errors in grammar, mechanics, and usage—is crucial to developing one's writing skills.

Equally important, of course, is an understanding of the basic terms and concepts that all successful writers employ. This book presents those principles in simple and concise form, gives examples of applications, and then offers exercises in which students develop facility with structures and concepts. The variety of lessons and exercises helps students work through conscious acts of writing toward the assurance and spontaneity that mark most students' mastery of spoken English.

Students begin work in the book by studying, developing, and writing paragraphs, and the book, throughout its sentence, word, and essay sections, returns to and reinforces paragraph writing skills. This emphasis on paragraph writing reflects the widely held view that the paragraph is a composition in miniature. Moreover, experience has shown us that the paragraph is the most accessible unit of language for classroom discussion and study and that paragraph writing can cultivate rhetorical sense even in students busy with work on sentence or word difficulties.

For the sake of consistency and practicality, our approach and terminology are essentially traditional. We must nevertheless acknowledge numerous debts to recent work in language study and rhetoric, including strategies developed in the teaching of English as a second language. Such new ideas and techniques are reflected, for instance, in this book's development of sentence skills through use of grammar frames, in its emphasis on *doing* writing, in its strengthening of reading and thinking skills as the by-product of the teaching of writing, in its use of familiar situations and relevant subject matter—whole language—as lesson content.

Finally, we are happy to express our gratitude to colleagues and friends for their professionalism, their help, and their good wishes. In particular, we thank Bryan Short, Sharon Crowley, and a superb composition faculty at Northern Arizona University for its exemplary dedication to a great public work. We also thank Jayne de Lawter, Anne Hilles, Mark Messer, Keith Muscutt, Adrian Sanford, Barry Sherman, and especially Paul Mann.

P. J.
J. F.

Contents

UNIT ONE *Writing Paragraphs*

UNIT TWO *Writing Sentences*

UNIT THREE *Choosing Words*

UNIT FOUR   *Composition Writing*

Writing Paragraphs

Putting Your Thoughts to Work

A. HARNESSING THE POWER OF NEGATIVE THINKING

Language is so complex and the human being's capacity for language is so immense that scientists are continually awed by the ordinary speech—your speech—that they must interpret. Nature and culture seem to have adapted human beings for nothing so well as for language use. By age four, when our physical and mechanical movement is still imperfect, we have already mastered the grammar and many of the codes of our native language.

True, a child's vocabulary is limited like its world, and the child will continue to study the tricky and uncertain corners of grammar throughout the school years and beyond. But even a four-year-old composes sentences and thus shows a very impressive mental and verbal skill. For the sake of illustration, suppose only one simple sentence pattern (the four-year-old actually knows several): adjective-noun-verb-adverb ("Big balls bounce high"). And suppose a child's vocabulary is limited to fifty adjectives, fifty nouns, fifty verbs, and fifty adverbs (the average child's vocabulary is actually far larger and more complex). We then face this many possible utterances from this child:

$$50 \times 50 \times 50 \times 50 = 6{,}250{,}000$$

This imaginary child controls and can produce millions of possible, meaningful utterances even before starting kindergarten!

Most of your sentences are longer and more complex, involving many more word choices than this simple example. Actually you have *billions* of possible sentences at your disposal when you speak or write. Linguists—scientists of language—assert that you regularly combine and utter sentences never before spoken in the history of the universe. Your amazing linguistic skill makes this inventiveness routine.

Scientists face the enormous challenge of understanding and explaining the language talents of human beings. But the rest of us have only to use and develop these talents, which indeed are among nature's greatest gifts to our species.

The vast majority of college students have the motivation, ambition, and good sense to invest in and work at their strongest talents, including their impressive linguistic talents. Even students who may not have sufficiently worked up their writing skills are fluent speakers, able thinkers, skeptical listeners, and sensible readers; they are sophisticated users of a complex instrument they have spent a lifetime mastering.

So what happens when the typical student comes face to face with a writing task? The

3

typical student lets loose his or her verbal and mental skills, but not always in the most effective direction. Strange to say, many college students—many people, really—use (and waste) their finest verbal and rhetorical powers persuading themselves that they cannot possibly do an assignment, that they have nothing to say, that the assignment is totally unjust.

EX 1–1   For fun, test the truth of this observation by jotting down on a separate sheet of paper answers to the question "Why can't I write an essay?" Let your experience, your memory, and your imagination help you come up with as many answers as you can.

These familiar roadblocks may have appeared in some form on your list: *I don't know what to write; I can't discipline myself to sit down and write; I'm a terrible speller, and I never know where to put commas.* You probably included some personal favorites as well.

EX 1–2   Now, as you perhaps expected, this game can be made harder and more productive with a slight change in the question: "Why *can* I write an essay?" Once again, jot down as many answers as possible.

If this question stymies you more than the first, go back to your answers to the first question (EX 1–1). By turning those answers around, you may find that your weaknesses are also, or are really, strengths. Suppose one of your answers was "I don't know spelling." If you reflect for a minute, you will probably see that you *know* much more spelling than you *don't know.* If you misspell ten words in a 500-word composition, haven't you also correctly spelled 490 words? In what other activity do you bat so close to 1.000? This reasoning may seem a little silly, but it's not nearly so silly as your telling yourself, after so many years of practice, that you don't know English well enough to write a successful paper. See if you can't apply such positive thinking to the other answers you wrote to the first question and thereby use them to answer the second question (EX 1–2).

There is a trick in this procedure. *If* you *can't* answer the first question, *then* there's no reason you cannot write essays. But *if* you *can* answer the first question, *then* you are already well on the way to composing an essay: an essay *on* the first question, on the difficulties of essay writing.

EX 1–3   On another sheet of paper, write an essay of 150–200 words on either of the following topics:
Why I Can't Write an Essay
Why I Can Write an Essay

B. PLAYING GAMES BEFORE WRITING SERIOUSLY

Finding ideas and writing about them often involve the use of such schemes to bypass our mental blocks and detour around memory lapses. Each of us knows so much; yet we often leave our brains idling in neutral, claiming we do not know enough to write. After a while we believe our alibis. To get moving, we must trick, tease, or cajole stored information out of our minds. We seem to do this best in action, not in thought. We don't do all the thinking *before* we start writing. We think *in* language or writing; thought comes *with* writing. We are better language users than we are pure thinkers. So when in doubt, write. After all, when you use language, you use your best, your most practiced and developed, human skills.

This view of language and writing has led many teachers and students to an appreciation of "freewriting"—writing nonstop off the top of one's head, sheer writing—as a way of stimulating expression. Freewriting—on almost any subject—can help remind you that English is as fundamentally yours as the air you breathe, that language is your medium to use and benefit from, as water is to a fish.

EX 1–4   Try some freewriting on another sheet of paper. Pretend you are a fish swimming in a river of language. Write—nonstop—what you see and feel in there.

You can channel freewriting by using some playful procedures to help you tease or trick ideas out of a temporarily closed or lazy brain. Then later, by reading or studying what you have written, you can follow cues or leads for further writing.

EX 1–5   Play this descriptive game. Write a sentence or two about what you are experiencing at this moment through each of your senses. Make each statement as vivid and precise as you can.

1. *Hearing* _____

_____

_____

_____

2. *Touching* _____

_____

_____

_____

3. *Smelling* _____

_____

_____

_____

4. *Tasting* _____

_____

_____

_____

5. *Seeing* _____

_____

_____

_____

Taking messages from the senses and converting them to precise statements on paper is not just the province of poets. Chemists, anthropologists, theater critics, and political analysts, among others, must also be able to express their sensory impressions in writing.

EX 1-6   On a separate sheet of paper, list two college courses that you plan to take later this year or next year. Next to each course name, write two or three sentences telling which sense or senses you will have to employ in the course work and in what ways you will use them.

You may have noted, for example, that vision is important in most types of research. The ability to see what is there and to describe it accurately in writing is a valuable skill.

EX 1-7   This freewriting game requires a partner. Look at your partner carefully. Describe your partner's costume (clothes, jewelry, hairstyle—all the elements of appearance that a person can, within limits, alter at will). Proceed with this description from bottom to top, one sentence per item; do this on another sheet of paper.

C. SCRIBBLING INSIGHTS AND INSULTS: JOURNAL WRITING

Many people believe journal writing to be the best of all freewriting activities. If you have never kept a journal, now may be a good time to try one; the joys, surprises, crises, and occasional absurdities of college life make for great journal entries. If you have unsuccessfully tried to keep a journal, perhaps you were trying to create the wrong kind of journal for your personality. A daily entry—a diary—is not necessary (though it is a good idea to date each entry you do make). In fact, most journals are really scrapbooks of freewriting: sometimes spontaneous scribblings, sometimes expressive writing according to various procedures. Don't the names of the journal-writing games listed below tickle your fancy just a little bit?

- imaginary dialogue
- outrageous comparison
- fake love letters
- if I could make myself invisible . . .
- New Year's resolutions
- the world's greatest party
- the world's worst party
- your thrilling moments in sports or theater or dance
- the Insult Hall of Fame

If one of these ideas seems like something you could write an interesting paragraph about, why not give it a try? (This is not an assignment—just an invitation.)

A freewriting premise can help you explore fact as well as fancy. Here is a page of a writer's journal that on this particular day turns out to read very much like the classic "diary" entry.

> Question: What is the most memorable thing that happened to you yesterday? When you close your eyes, what particular vision of yesterday do you see in your mind's eye?
>
> My father and I played golf in the rain yesterday. Actually the rain varied between big, pelting drops and a fine, annoying, wind-driven mist. The mist was light enough so that my father could turn to me and say, "See? It's letting up." *That's* what I see in my memory. I didn't want to play in such weather, but golf is my father's passion, and I hadn't seen him in more than a year. He had counted on this outing. Besides, if he wasn't going to chicken out,

neither was I. So we both got very wet. But later, when the sun finally came out, everything dried out but my shoes. His were rubber; mine were leather. Today, my shoes are still wet, but that's another story.

EX 1-8   Write quick answers to these questions on a separate sheet of paper.

1. What do you like about the journal entry above? What particular features of it would you praise if the writer came around looking for a little encouragement?
2. What parts of this experience can you relate to? What could most people sympathize with?
3. What would you be interested in hearing more about from this writer? How might he expand this paragraph? What could he follow it up with?

Here is another paragraph about a memorable event, but this one is not so effective as the first. The question remains: What is the most memorable thing that happened to you yesterday? When you close your eyes, what particular vision of yesterday do you see in your mind's eye?

Yesterday I went grocery shopping, and I was so clumsy wheeling a cart through the store that I knew I was in for a bad day. After I paid, as I left the store with my arms full of groceries, a kid came running into me and I dropped them.

EX 1-9   Imagine that this experience has happened to you and that these words are your words. How might you revise this paragraph to improve its effectiveness? Where might you enliven it by adding important or interesting information? On another sheet of paper, rewrite the paragraph to make it more memorable.

Now look over your paragraph again. Have you made the experience easier *to see* in your mind's eye? Have you, unlike the original writer, *shown* as well as *told*? For instance, how exactly were you *clumsy* in the store? How exactly did the kid come running into you? How exactly did the groceries drop, and where did the dozen eggs end up? How exactly did you feel? How did the kid seem to feel? Use your imagination! Go back and make the changes that will bring this incident to life.

EX 1-10   Now try writing your own show-and-tell paragraph. The question remains: What is the most memorable thing that happened to you yesterday? When you close your eyes, what particular vision of yesterday do you see in your mind's eye? Write your paragraph on another sheet of paper.

EX 1-11   Many well-written descriptions say something—in or between the lines—about human behavior or human nature. Such stories have "morals." Write the "moral" (theory, rule of life, or principle) that each paragraph seems to illustrate. One sentence should be enough for each.

1. the paragraph about the golf game
2. your paragraph about the grocery accident
3. your paragraph about yesterday's incident

D. FINDING SOMETHING TO ARGUE ABOUT

Freewriting with varying degrees of freedom, while it seems quite different from a long, authoritative college paper, actually resembles formal writing in many ways. In both kinds of writing, you are thinking in language, you are showing what you know and can say, you are expressing yourself, you are declaring your curiosity, your ambition, your talents, your imagination; you are discovering and tapping your enormous resources as a genius of language in defiance of all temporary mental blocks, and you may be working up material that could be shaped, supplemented, and polished into a finished paper.

The fact is that if you truly have nothing to say, you are a new species and should report immediately to a testing laboratory. Your future and academic career are assured. If you simply *think* you have nothing to say, however, you are experiencing an ordinary crisis in motivation, letting yourself be intimidated by life and by the weighty responsibilities thrust upon your talents. When you are at a loss for something to say, go back to questions of value (something is good or bad, useful or useless, beautiful or ugly, just or unjust) or go back to subjects you have feelings about (things you like, things you dislike). Or go back to freewriting. Or use this workbook and its games and techniques. If you are honest with yourself, you will discover that you hold some arguable opinion about something, perhaps about almost everything.

With our usual skepticism, let's test this claim that you have an opinion about something. Here is the challenge: find and express an opinion about some current concern in the local environment—your campus, its services, its lifestyles and routines. Here is an example of such an opinion:

> I think the campus parking rules are very unfair. You have to park far away, pay too much, and cope with overcrowded lots. The other day, for instance, I had to deal with a parking officer who gave me a ticket for parking in an unmarked space, when I had no other choice in a packed-full lot. The officer told me to appeal the ticket to the parking director or pay the fine. I don't have time to park, let alone hassle bureaucrats and red tape. If I appeal, I miss class. If I miss class, I flunk out. If I flunk out, my parking problems are over. Some solution! Something should be done. I lose more respect for rules and regulations every time I have to deal with these local authorities.

EX 1-12   Now it's your turn. The question is, "What do you think about X?" For X, substitute some current concern of yours—a topic similar to "campus parking" in the example. Write your paragraph on a separate sheet of paper.

E. BECOMING MORE THAN A LONE VOICE

Suppose we called in an outside observer or some impartial judge to decide the merits of the parking complaint or to appraise the merits of the opinion you have just expressed. Even though in writing this paragraph (EX 1-12) you've become an *author*, can you see why your views may not seem *authoritative*? What are the obvious weaknesses of the parking paragraph—perhaps shared by your paragraph—that might prevent an impartial judge from remedying the situation described?

One potential weakness of the "campus parking" paragraph is its lack of facts to support its opinion. But let us postpone this matter of facts for a while to explore another potential weakness of the campus parking paragraph: its point of view is quite *personal*, too personal to accomplish its implied purpose of publicizing and spreading the argument. The writer refers to "I," "me," and "my" more than a dozen times in a few sentences. And yet the mention of "you" in the second sentence suggests that the problem is not merely *personal*, that it affects many others besides the writer. So here the *personal* viewpoint needlessly restricts the force and extent of the opinion. One person's problem, unfortunately, is relatively easy to ignore, but if the problem is widespread, common to many people, and in this sense *impersonal*, then the complaint carries more weight. When it speaks for many good but aggrieved citizens, a complaint is more authoritative. Our impartial judge should hear our arguments as representative of this public, not as uniquely personal.

To bring out the real weight and importance of our opinion—if many people share it, it is *our* opinion, not *my* opinion—the writer should try to convey more impersonal authority, less personal viewpoint.

Study this revision of the campus parking paragraph.

> The parking rules on this campus are very unfair. Students have to park far away, pay too much, and cope with overcrowded lots. Students are given tickets for parking in unmarked spaces when all lots are completely full and they have no place else to park. Unsympathetic officers only refer students to appeal procedures or to the cashier's window at the police office. Most students don't have the money to pay the fines. Nor do they have the time to hassle bureaucrats and red tape. If students appeal, they miss class. If they miss class, they flunk out. If they flunk out, their parking problems are over. Some solution! Something should be done. Students lose more respect for campus rules and local authorities every time they are victimized by these parking regulations.

EX 1-13   Briefly describe what the writer did to the original campus parking paragraph to make it sound more authoritative.

_____

_____

_____

Notice that impersonality does not remove personality and style; it only alters them. Even though they are now impersonal, for instance, this paragraph's last six sentences are still quite striking. And notice, too, that this enhanced authority has come about even though the paragraph still lacks another important source of authority: factual evidence or support.

The transformation of this sample paragraph suggests that you can write about most subjects either personally or impersonally. In personal writing, you and your personal experience dominate the writing because your point of view is first-person (I, me, myself), and your writing becomes very particular and limited in appeal—limited to those who know and respect you or to those interested in what you, in particular, have to say. In impersonal writing, by contrast, you and your experience remain for the most part offstage. When you draw on personal feelings, opinions, or experiences—and you always do—you generalize them and frame them in the third person (students, Americans, baseball fans). Your writing is now broader in its appeal; you write for those who care about students, America, or baseball, not just for those interested in you.

EX 1-14   Now it's your turn again. On another sheet of paper, revise your opinion paragraph (EX 1-12) for the impartial judge by making it more impersonal and more authoritative.

Much formal writing and most college writing—in science, in sociology, in history, in philosophy—is impersonal in the special sense you have just studied: impersonal, *not* inhuman. Think this way about impersonal writing: unless you're the President, few people will care what you personally think about the energy crisis. Instead they will want to know what they should think about the crisis and why. To write for them, you should write impersonally and objectively, citing arguments, circumstances, and facts. Let your voice be representative of impersonal reason. Of course, this is impersonal reason *as you see it*, the best approximation to impersonal reason that anyone can manage. That you are writing about *your* informed opinion *goes without saying*.

Does this mean that every time you pick up a pen or pencil as an undergraduate, you should write in an impersonal voice? Probably not; in fact, to get thoughts and ideas flowing, you may find it very helpful *first* to write personally, *then later* to edit and polish for authority.

Look at this paragraph, written as a first step toward a paper exploring the role of corporations in America today.

> To me, some corporations are just rotten. They make all this money and tear up the land and produce junk and plastic. I think they should be outlawed unless they start showing some concern for the land and the people. They don't show any now, as far as I can see.

Notice how such paragraphs become the *opposite* of persuasive: they so lack authority that they become arguments *for* the things they claim to be *against*. Most people sympathize with the objects or victims of purely *personal* attacks, even when such attacks touch on valid public arguments. This writer has alluded to excessive profits ("all this money"), pollution ("tear up the land"), and shoddy products ("junk and plastic"). Yet the paragraph as written is unlikely to increase readers' concern about these problems.

EX 1-15   In the blanks below, write two or three sentences specifying what should be done to the paragraph about corporations to make it authoritative.

_____

_____

_____

_____

_____

One more word on impersonality: don't be intimidated by it; impersonality makes communication possible. Your individual viewpoint and uniqueness *do* count for something in impersonal writing, but within the larger context of what you have in common with other people. To communicate with other people, you must keep an eye on your similarities with them as well as your differences from them. And similarities are always there; they only need to be allowed to surface. Don't you really mislead a reader, after all, by stressing "I think," "I believe," and "in my opinion" when in fact your views are shared by hundreds, even millions of like-minded people? Make your voice their voice. Show individuality in the choices you make when it comes to style, diction, and nuance of thought; these choices subtly show your personality, much as your choice of clothes or cosmetics does.

F. WRITING WITH A PURPOSE IN MIND

Imagine that you are invited to a formal banquet. To perform there with confidence, you might have to study a little the proper use of all the spoons and forks; nevertheless, the experience you have gained eating at a table daily, using silverware, observing the mealtime customs of our society, makes this new study more an adjustment than an overhaul of manners. Think where you would be at such a banquet if your previous mealtime experiences consisted solely of eating wild fruits and nuts right off the trees! Formal writing resembles this formal banquet. Formal writing is one of many instances of your use of the English language. While its conventions and strategies offer different challenges from ordinary language use, formal writing does have much in common with conversational English. This workbook will give you practice in the *how* of formal writing. But, to a great extent, you will be responsible for choosing the *when*. Formal writing when an informal approach is called for can be as awkward as informal writing in a formal situation—as inappropriate as eating with your fingers at a sit-down dinner.

EX 1-16   Essay questions require the use of formal language; this has become a convention, perhaps because formal language indicates a seriousness of purpose and a dedication to scholarship. Advertisements, in contrast, depend on conversational English to communicate effectively with readers.

Study the essay answer and the ad copy below. You will note that the writer of each has chosen an improper degree of formality. On another sheet of paper, rewrite each so that its level of formality is more appropriate.

Essay Question: In a few sentences, what are the basic characteristics of a falcon?
Essay Answer: The falcon. You've never seen a bird quite like this one: twenty inches of streamlined dynamite! Fast. Graceful. A hunter that knows what it wants, and goes for it! This raptor is *awesome* on its power dives—streaking toward a flying target at speeds of 175 mph and more! How can you recognize a falcon? Look for the distinctive notched beak. Where can you find one? They're widely distributed throughout the world. In fact, there's probably one or more varieties in the wild skies near you right now! But look fast. By the time your eyes cross that falcon's flight path, it'll probably be out of sight!

Purpose: Write a paragraph about the 1983 Osprey that makes this auto sound exciting.
Ad Copy: The 1983 Osprey is a four-passenger car. It has a fuel-injected four-cylinder engine with a horsepower rating of 95. Its top speed is approximately 110 miles per hour. The EPA mileage estimates for this automobile are 26 city and 38 highway. The city figure should be used for comparison; actual highway mileage figures will probably be less.

Purpose and degree of formality, you can see, are closely related. A writer must always keep in mind what is to be accomplished by a particular piece of writing.

EX 1-17   Take a moment to think about the purposes of communication—a subject concerning which you have many, many years or experience. Complete the list of answers to the question below.

Question: Why do people communicate with one another?

1. *to discover or learn*   5. _____
2. *to persuade*   6. _____
3. _____   7. _____
4. _____

EX 1-18   Try to think of an ordinary conversational situation to illustrate each of the purposes you listed in EX 1-17. In the blanks below, identify a situation that goes with the purpose listed in the corresponding blank in EX 1-17.

1. *people on a committee discussing ways to raise funds*

2. _____

3. _____

4. _____

5. _____

6. _____

7. _____

EX 1-19   Now that you have analyzed types of oral communication, try classifying the following written items according to purpose.

Draw a line from each item in the left-hand column to the appropriate purpose listed in the right-hand column.

a letter to a newspaper editor	to entertain
a love letter	to inform
a magazine ad	to share feelings
a *National Lampoon* article	to express an opinion
a dictionary entry	to persuade
a poem	to motivate to buy
a news story	to define

You may have noticed that several items in EX 1-19 could be matched with more than one purpose: a newspaper's news articles must inform *and* entertain readers if the paper is to stay in business; a satirical article may seek to express an opinion as well as entertain. The effective writer keeps in mind *all* the things that a given piece of writing is intended to accomplish.

Let's narrow our focus a little. Against this background of communication for a purpose, think about the writing you will be doing in college.

EX 1-20   What kinds of writing do students typically perform in college?

1. *workbook responses*   6. _____

2. _____   7. _____

3. _____   8. _____

4. _____   9. _____

5. _____   10. _____

Do you have a clear sense of the purposes of these kinds of writing? Can you specify, for instance, why you write essay exams? This issue and others relating to purposes of writing will be taken up in the remainder of this chapter.

G. EMPLOYING FACTS TO ACHIEVE A PURPOSE

As you know, most course work—the essay exam included—has for one of its purposes your need to prove yourself, to compete, to show off what you have learned in the course. But in most courses you show off not *yourself*, but *what* you know, not your *personality* so much as *objective or impersonal* facts, skills, experiences, concepts, or ideas. These facts, concepts, and ideas help make your work authoritative; they give your work the weight it needs to hold its own in a crowd; they help give you the voice you need in order to be heard among many voices.

This emphasis on what you know, not on you, is hard but helpful to remember when you are tempted to take a test or paper score *personally*. College and its classes, like most public institutions, are more concerned with what we share than with what is uniquely mine or thine. In this way, public institutions allow and respect personal privacy and freedom.

To help yourself appreciate the importance of facts to fair play and persuasion, consider this problem in communication: Two drivers have been involved in an auto accident. Fortunately, no one has been seriously hurt, but the collision has badly damaged both cars. Whoever ends up being judged at fault will probably see a painful increase in his insurance rate. On a state department of motor vehicles accident report form, one driver writes the following report:

> *Name*: John Fisher
> *Describe in your own words what happened.*
>   I was on my way home on June 3, 1982, in the city of Minneapolis, Minnesota. It was about six o'clock in the evening, and I needed to buy some gasoline for my Chevrolet before getting on Circle Freeway. Approaching the overpass on Oregon Avenue, I saw an open Standard station on the left, and I prepared to make a left turn across the three oncoming traffic lanes. These lanes were clear of oncoming traffic when I began my turn. As I started across the lanes, however, some children ran across the gas station driveway. I had to slow and stop my car until the children on the sidewalk had crossed the driveway. Before these children had cleared the sidewalk, I saw a large yellow sedan come speeding down the freeway offramp on to Oregon Avenue. The driver was traveling very fast—at least fifty miles an hour, in my estimation. Apparently, he didn't see me, because he didn't slow down until he screeched his brakes and slammed into me.

Before long, another accident report is filed; this one comes from the second driver.

> *Name*: L. T. Green
> *Describe in your own words what happened.*
>   I was on my way home from a hard day's work, minding my own business, not breaking any laws, making good time, relaxing with the radio, when this guy suddenly pulls across the road in front of me. I don't know what he thought he was doing. But I couldn't stop in time and I hit him. It was his fault all the way.

If you were a police officer reviewing these reports to try to determine who was at fault, what would you decide? Which driver makes a better case for himself?

EX 1-21   As you know, first impressions can be deceiving. If you study the first driver's statement more critically, for instance, what potential problems for his insurance company can you find there? Identify some of the problems in a brief paragraph; write this on another sheet of paper.

The second driver may lose his case in this imaginary example, not because of his driving (he did, after all, have the right of way), but because of his inability to report the accident fully, factually, and accurately from his point of view.

EX 1-22   Reconstructing the accident from these two paragraphs, can you rewrite the second driver's report to make it more competitive with the first driver's report? Write this improved report on another sheet of paper; copy the two lines below to begin the report.

Name: L. T. Green
Describe in your own words what happened.

EX 1-23   Now that you have seen some of the pitfalls of reporting the facts, write a report of your own as concisely, accurately, factually, and effectively as you can. Drawing on your experience, choose some accident or perhaps some dispute—a quarrel with a roommate over some event, for instance—that might be decided by an impartial judge to whom you are appealing. Present *your* view of the incident or issue fairly and fully. Use another sheet of paper to write this report.

H. SEPARATING FACTS FROM FALSEHOODS AND OPINIONS

The disagreement about the auto accident centers on an event, on something that happened. A single set of facts can be put forth to describe what actually did happen. In theory, the only area for dispute should be *what the facts mean*—specifically, who is at fault in this particular accident.

Of course people do dispute facts, if given half a chance. With regard to an event such as the traffic accident, this may be due to viewpoint: different people can see events differently from different points of view. The sun, for instance, really does *seem* to us on earth to revolve around the earth. The possibility of disagreement makes full and careful treatment of relevant facts all the more important. A person may also dispute the facts for selfish reasons. A person in the wrong in a disagreement stands to benefit if he or she can hide, confuse, or alter the facts of the matter.

Facts, by definition, are confirmable through observation. Opinions, in contrast, are personal interpretations of facts. Opinions can be supported but not proved. The ability to separate fact from opinion is virtually a survival skill—for college students, for consumers, for voters, for clerks and for executives, for judges and for would-be superstars.

EX 1-24   How are your survival skills today? Mark *F* beside each item below that concerns a matter of *fact*. Mark *O* beside each item that concerns a matter of opinion.

_____ 1. the day the first manned space shuttle flew into space

_____ 2. the reason the space shuttle program was started

_____ 3. the amount of money NASA (National Aeronautics and Space Administration) was budgeted last year

_____ 4. the amount of money NASA should be budgeted next year

_____ 5. the success of the U.S. space program

_____ 6. the name of the President who has done most for the space program

I. USING "THE FIVE *W*s AND *H*" AS GUIDES

A traditional, important freewriting procedure focuses on the precise description of such an event as our auto accident. This journal-writing procedure actually fills the journals every day, the journals we call "newspapers." You too can use this procedure—the answering of six specific questions—to help you elicit and express important information, the sort of information essential to many forms of communication. When reporting a news event, the reporter tries to answer these questions about it: Who? What? Where? When? Why? How? The reporter whose story answers all of these questions that apply to a situation has, we say, *covered* the news event; such *adequate coverage* makes the reporter's audience—and editors—believe in the reporter's authority.

Notice how the first driver in our imaginary accident has adequately covered the story as he sees it:

Who?   First driver, John Fisher
What?   Was struck by second driver, L. T. Green
Where? Near the Standard station at the Oregon Avenue–Circle Freeway overpass, in Minneapolis, Minnesota
When?   About 6:00 P.M., June 3, 1982
Why?   Because L. T. Green, the second driver, failed to slow down to avoid an ordinary hazard
How?   By driving into Fisher's automobile, while Fisher was stopped for pedestrians

EX 1-25   Look back at your revision of the second driver's report. Does it satisfy the standards of news *coverage*? Show how you have answered the journalist's six questions. Write phrases from your report in the appropriate blanks.

Who?   _____

What?   _____

Where? _____

When?   _____

Why?   _____

How?   _____

If you were able to answer accurately, you should be able to notice how Green's case has been strengthened. He now appears much less likely to be judged at fault than he did when the original two reports were compared.

EX 1–26   Now test the report of your own accident or dispute from EX 1–23 to see whether you successfully covered the key facts of the matter.

Who?   _____

What?   _____

Where? _____

When?   _____

Why?   _____

How?   _____

The "lead" or first paragraph of news stories regularly includes brief answers to all of these questions. When a question can't be answered definitively—in the case of crimes by unknown persons, for example—the reporter will explain his lack of an answer. Here is a report of the Fisher-Green accident as it might have appeared in a newspaper:

> A two-car accident yesterday evening near the Oregon Avenue–Circle Freeway interchange resulted in substantial property damage, but no serious injuries. A car driven by John Fisher, 36, of Circle City, was struck while making a left turn by a car driven by L. T. Green, 34, also of Circle City. Police are investigating the cause of the collision, but as yet have issued no citations.

Notice that the reporter does not definitively explain *why* the accident occurred, since accounts differ. This determination is left to the police investigation, and the police may ultimately let the court decide.

Since much of your authority as a writer and much of your success as a college student depend on your ability to produce, develop, and work adequately with facts, working on some further exercises should be well worth your time. Notice that the concern here is not *memorizing* facts; rather, it is choosing and using facts to *cover* an event or topic adequately.

Here is an assortment of facts concerning the invention of the common match, facts that can be developed and arranged into an effective, informative paragraph with the use of the reporter's list of questions.

> *The facts:* Stockton-on-Tees, England; England during the Industrial Revolution; matches better than flint and steel; John Walker, a chemist, the inventor; the year 1827; houses in England heated mostly with coal; England not yet very democratic; one day Walker happened to scrape a rough surface with a stick coated in potash and antimony; we still use the friction match to this day.

With the help of the 5 *W*s and the *H*, a writer can separate key facts from trivial or irrelevant information.

Who?   John Walker, a chemist
What?   Invented the friction match
Where? Stockton-on-Tees, England
When?   1827
Why?   People needed a convenient source of fire
How?   By accidentally striking a rough surface with a stick coated in potash and antimony

A brief but complete story, as if for a newspaper, results from this procedure.

> A lucky accident produced the convenient source of fire we know as the friction match. John Walker, a chemist in Stockton-on-Tees, England, invented this match in 1827 by accidentally striking a rough surface with a stick coated in potash and antimony. When the stick burst into flame, Walker had struck the first match.

Here is another assortment of facts, followed by another report. But notice that the reporter's use of the facts is considerably less effective than in the above example.

> *The facts:* Bikini swimsuit invented; first modeled by a French dancer; she received 50,000 fan letters because of publicity; 1946; made of cotton; named after American A-bomb test at Bikini Atoll in July, 1946; the designer thought his bikini was as profound in its way as the atomic bomb; French designer Louis Reard; Bikini the name of a Pacific atoll used for A-bomb testing in 1940s and 1950s.

A researcher has brought these notes back from the library, having done a good job of information gathering. But now our researcher turns writer and writes the following:

> The bikini was invented in France in 1946. A French dancer first modeled it and she became an instant celebrity. The bikini has become ever more popular in ensuing years.

EX 1–27 What important information concerning the invention of the bikini has this report omitted? Using the who-what-where-when-why-how series of questions, supply the missing information and expand and revise the paragraph. Do this on another sheet of paper.

Notice how such *adequate coverage* of key points imparts authority to your paragraphs, whether or not your style is elegant, your words are fancy, and your punctuation is exactly correct.

EX 1–28 Now try working up a paragraph of your own from the following collection of facts, facts of the sort you might have gathered in a trip to the library. As before, some of these facts are relevant, while others are not. Select the significant facts and combine them into a coherent paragraph.

> *The facts:* Padlock invented; inventor Joseph Bramah, Yorkshire, England; first lock virtually impossible to pick; people could at last safely lock up valuables; lock was iron, fist-sized, barrel-shaped; in nineteenth century an American locksmith was able to pick the lock without a key—good old American know-how, even though it took him a month's work; "key" to this lock's success was the nearly half-billion combinations of cylinder alignments that a would-be lockpicker had to deal with; invented 1784; many modern padlocks are easy to pick.

WORKSHOP

1. Begin a journal. If possible, purchase a bound notebook or hardbound blank-page book for this purpose. As a first step, write a paragraph explaining to yourself what you think your journal should be like. Write in your journal either on a regular schedule or whenever you have something to say.

2. Choose one of the journal freewriting games listed on page 6. Play this game in your journal or on blank sheets of paper.

3. Think of a person you see often on campus but do not know personally. Describe this person in two ways. First write a paragraph describing this person's appearance from top to bottom; use the instructions for EX 1–7 as a guide. Then write a paragraph about this person using the five *W*s and the *H* as a guide; explain *who* this person is, *when* you see him or her, *where* you see him or her, *what* this person is doing when you see him or her, *why* you have noticed this person, and *how* someone could recognize him or her. Compare the two paragraphs.

4. Think of an amazing or ridiculous occurrence on campus—one that would make an entertaining movie scene.
   a. Write one or two paragraphs describing it using a personal voice, as you would in writing a letter to a friend.
   b. Write about the scene impersonally, as if you were describing it to a movie producer who wished to recreate it.
   c. Write about it in a brief news article that could be published in the campus newspaper.

5. Decide what is your most valuable possession. Prepare to sell it.
   a. Write a brief classified ad, describing this item simply, stating your asking price, and giving the information a prospective buyer needs in order to respond.
   b. Write an enticing ad for this item that could be posted on a campus bulletin board.

6. Find an article on the invention of the paper clip (Walter Hunt invented it), roller skates (Dr. James L. Plimpton was the creator of the first pair), the automobile heater (Augusta Rogers devised this), or any other ingenious and useful device. Write a brief paragraph giving adequate coverage to the key points concerning this invention. You may need to do some library research before you begin writing.

Building Paragraphs: Key Concepts and Skills

A. DEVELOPING A PARAGRAPH FROM AN IDEA

The paragraph is a unit of meaning and organization. To be effective, a paragraph should be organized around a single controlling idea or purpose. The length of a paragraph varies with the number of sentences required to discuss the main idea.

As a rule, to write a good paragraph, you need to be able to *develop* an idea or topic. Effective communication requires more than just the mention of a topic; the intention of a writer must be made clear to readers, just as in conversation the intention of a speaker must be made clear to listeners. Suppose, for instance, that someone walks up to you, looks you in the eye, and utters the word "Copernicus." How are you likely to respond? Maybe with impatience, maybe with apprehension, but certainly with bewilderment. You need more information before you can interpret the speaker's intention. If the speaker really has something to say, he or she will have to develop "Copernicus" further to communicate that intention. And if the speaker does not say anything more, you will have every right to ignore the message.

Here are two ways a speaker might develop a puzzling word into a meaningful sentence:

a. "Copernicus changed people's ideas about the solar system."
b. "Copernicus was the name I needed to remember during the history test, but couldn't."

In some cases, a single sentence develops an idea or topic well enough to convey an intention to an audience. Sentence *b* above is an example of a sentence that could stand alone in some circumstances and give the listener enough information to understand the speaker's intention. But more often a sentence answers some questions while raising others. Consider the following statement.

"I hypnotized a salamander on television once."

A person hearing this would probably not let the speaker stop without some additional explanation. Here are some of the questions a listener might ask:

How did you hypnotize the salamander?
How did you know it was hypnotized?
What did it do when it was hypnotized?
Which program were you on?
When was it shown?

Can you hypnotize any salamander, or do you have to work with several before you find one that can be hypnotized?

Why would anyone want to hypnotize a salamander?

I don't believe you; did you really hypnotize a salamander on television?

EX 2–1   What further questions might a listener or reader ask after encountering each of the following sentences? (Don't hesitate to ask even silly questions.)

1. Copernicus changed people's ideas about the solar system.

_____
_____
_____
_____

2. Many factors pulled Texas away from Mexico.[1]

_____
_____
_____
_____

3. He was not really disappointed to find Paris so empty.[2]

_____
_____
_____
_____

4. In great secrecy, on a private airstrip about fifty miles southwest of New York, Aereon 7 got ready to fly.[3]

_____
_____
_____
_____

5. The Greeks made their gods in their own image.[4]

_____
_____
_____
_____

[1] Samuel Eliot Morison, *The Oxford History of the American People, II.*
[2] F. Scott Fitzgerald, "Babylon Revisited."
[3] John McPhee, *The Deltoid Pumpkin Seed.*
[4] Edith Hamilton, *Mythology.*

Look at sentence 1 again and at the questions you formulated about it. Several points in this sentence, while not confusing, do not fully communicate concepts. For instance, what is a "solar system" exactly? Can a writer assume that most readers do not need this term to be defined for them? Actually, sentence 1 packs in several points that deserve development. It *implies* that more will be said about the topic it introduces. By repeating a technique you have practiced before, you can see how much *implication* a sentence like sentence 1 can carry, and you can practice developing some of those implications. What you will be doing is expanding a sentence into a group of sentences organized around a single controlling idea —that is, expanding a sentence into a paragraph.

EX 2–2   On another sheet of paper, write a paragraph about Copernicus beginning with the sentence "Copernicus changed people's ideas about the solar system." Use the technique of *who-what-when-where-why-how* and any of the following miscellaneous facts to develop a paragraph that tells who Copernicus was. (Reading a brief encyclopedia article about Copernicus may help you get the facts straight before you begin writing.)

FACTS ABOUT COPERNICUS AND HIS TIME
- Studied church law, medicine, astronomy at leading European universities during the Renaissance.
- Born and lived most of his life in Poland.
- Believed that the sun stayed in the center of the universe and that planets revolved around the sun.
- The Renaissance (c. 1400–c. 1650) was a historical period during which people's renewed interest in thought, learning, and science caused many beliefs and prejudices of the Dark Ages to be overturned.
- Before Copernicus, most people believed the sun orbited the earth.
- No telescope available to Copernicus to allow for verification of theory.
- Copernicus published theories and observations that influenced later researchers who had more data and better instruments, like the telescope.
- Galileo, in the century after Copernicus, was able to study the planets through a telescope.
- Copernicus also believed that the earth spun on an axis.

B. WRITING TOPIC SENTENCES

A sentence like "Copernicus changed people's ideas about the solar system" is customarily called a *topic sentence*. It states in a sentence the main point, intention, or purpose of the paragraph. The balance of the paragraph develops, and relates to, that statement of the topic. The topic sentence often, but not always, appears at the beginning of a paragraph.

EXAMPLES OF TOPIC SENTENCES
The 1981 Major League Baseball players' strike threw the media into a tizzy. How would newspapers lure readers into the sports section, with no games to describe, no strategic moves to analyze? How would TV networks draw large numbers of viewers to sit docilely for two-hour stretches three or more times a week? How would radio and TV newscasters break the ominous hum of international confrontations, domestic economic problems, street violence, and natural disasters? Between the tennis blurbs and the golf drone, sportscasters sounded notes of desperation. Advertisers wanted those viewers, those readers. If the media could not

deliver them in proper numbers, then the sponsors would not come across with the advertising expenditures that are the media's lifeblood. Advertisers pay for numbers. Excuses, in advertising as in baseball, count for nothing.

A janitor pulls a sensitive memo out of a wastebasket, and its contents wind up on page one of a daily newspaper a week later. A desperate competitor beats the sanitation truck to a successful corporation's trash bin and filches copies of memos about a new product. Three thousand defective pairs of designer jeans ticketed for destruction wind up instead in bargain stores—and result in a near-fatal blow to the expensive product's image. *The need for the services of firms such as Confidential Destruction Inc., a Maine corporation, has become quite apparent to many corporate managers in recent times.* [This introductory paragraph has its topic sentence at the end rather than at the beginning.]

EX 2-3   Underline the topic sentence in each paragraph below.

1. In a very cold, moist cloud, a minuscule crystal forms around a speck of dust. The crystal then grows rapidly: thousands of molecules of water vapor link themselves to its frozen structure. More droplets of supercooled water evaporate near the crystal, and more vapor for the crystal's growth is produced. After perhaps ten minutes of building itself, the crystal is large enough to fall from its cloud. But the crystal is not alone; thousands of other crystals have been developing nearby. As the crystal moves through the crowded cloud, it knocks into other crystals, which in turn bump others. Tiny fragments produced during these collisions become the nuclei of new frozen crystals. Gravity eventually does force the large crystals to leave the cloud and fall to earth. It is ironic that we call the products of this process by collective names: *snow, snowfall, snowflakes*; for each flake is one of a kind, having its own singular history and thus its own crystalline structure.

2. Calculator manufacturers have done an excellent job of marketing the small mathematical marvels during the past decade. Now, however, they must confront the problem of how to sell more calculators to people who already own one or two or three. Their answer appears to be written in black and white: the new generation of small calculators print their computations on paper tape, as well as flashing them in liquid-crystal colors. The advantages of such calculators are significant. People working problems involving several numbers will no longer have to calculate a second time to be sure they have entered all numbers correctly; they can simply check the printout against the data. Also, important calculations can be saved for future reference or sent elsewhere to be used by others. Taking the printing calculator off the desk and placing it into the engineer's or homemaker's or manager's hand should result in increased efficiency, wiser decision making, and less duplication of effort, not to mention several profitable years for calculator manufacturers.

3. Thomas Wentworth Higginson served as colonel of the first black regiment in America and wrote an excellent book about his experiences. Higginson had been an ardent champion of freedom for black Americans during the years before the eruption of the Civil War. Having enlisted in the Union Army, he welcomed the opportunity to recruit a regiment of slaves to fight for the cause of individual liberty. The regiment, being the first of its kind, was watched closely by friend and foe. Although few of Higginson's troops had received any education or had had much experience as free individuals, most of them

proved to be capable and courageous soldiers. Higginson himself earned a reputation as a fine leader during the war, and he subsequently gained recognition as a social and military historian by writing *Army Life in a Black Regiment.*

EX 2-4   Each of the two paragraphs below needs a topic sentence. Write an appropriate topic sentence in each blank.

One college student, Brett Johnson, decided that custom-printed caps could become even hotter items than printed T-shirts. He pushed his low-cost, high-visibility items to the point where, at last report, he was projecting a half-million dollars in gross sales for the year. Two other students, Debbie Laster and Chris Fontana, put into practice what they were learning in hotel management school. They established a fast-food restaurant off campus—"Munchies"—that featured home-baked goodies. They made it pay off well enough to entertain thoughts of franchising.

In late June 1981, the staff of a hotel in Johannesburg, South Africa, was shocked to discover that thieves had made off with, of all things, the world's largest orange. This 5.51-pound fruit, recently certified by the Guinness Book of World Records as the world's largest, had been on display in the hotel. The hotel manager was unable to come up with an explanation of why someone would want to steal the huge orange. "There has been no ransom demand," he told reporters.

C. KEEPING THE PARAGRAPH FOCUSED

All sentences in a paragraph should develop its main idea. If information does not really develop or relate to the paragraph's topic sentence, then it is irrelevant; it does not belong in the paragraph.

EXAMPLE OF A PARAGRAPH WITH IRRELEVANT SENTENCES

Where should a person put extra money nowadays? Some suspicious individuals still stuff money into mattresses or other domestic hideaways. Although this allows for some safety and ready access, it puts the capital at the mercy of inflation, which shrinks its value at a heartbreaking rate. Money market funds pay high interest, but are not insured. Certificates of deposit pay high interest and are insured, but require a high initial investment and are not liquid. *High interest rates have severely hurt the construction industry during the past few years.* Regular savings accounts do not pay enough interest to combat the effects of inflation. Common stocks yield dividends and the promise of capital gains, but they can quickly lose value as well. Precious metals historically have had value even in the worst of times, but they pay no dividends and present storage problems. Land is a speculative investment, and usually requires annual tax payments during the time it is held. *During the Great Depression banks failed, many stocks became almost worthless, and land values in most areas decreased dramatically.* In truth, though, who wouldn't rather worry about where to invest extra money than worry about where to borrow enough money to get by?

EX 2-5   Two sentences in the paragraph below do not belong. Cross out these sentences.

The Kolyma is an arctic region in the Soviet Union; during Josef Stalin's regime, a number of concentration camps were established in this frozen wilderness to hold work battalions of political prisoners. Among those sent to the Kolyma was Eugenia Ginzburg; she was one of millions of Soviet citizens picked up in mass arrests during the 1930s. Ginzburg has given us a vivid look at the lives of those condemned to the Kolyma in her book *Within the Whirlwind*, which has recently been translated into English and published. More quality translations of foreign works are available today than were available twenty years ago. She writes of women cutting trees in -50°F weather, of people hacking through frozen soil in search of gold, of chronic malnutrition, of ragged clothing and rampant tuberculosis, and of forced marches in blizzards. Alexander Solzhenitsyn has also written about the grim conditions in arctic and subarctic Soviet prison camps during the Stalin era. But although Ginzburg's story is one of people's inhumanity toward others, it reflects the sparks of hope that she and others were able to keep alive in the darkest of times.

D. DEVELOPING A PARAGRAPH FROM A TOPIC SENTENCE

A ratio or proportion may help show how a paragraph is similar to but more complex than a sentence.

$$\frac{\text{subject}}{\text{sentence}} \cong \frac{\text{paragraph topic sentence}}{\text{paragraph}}$$

That is to say, the subject's role in a sentence is similar to the topic sentence's role in a paragraph.

A writer develops a subject—"Copernicus"—into a sentence—"Copernicus changed people's ideas about the solar system"—and then develops this topic sentence into a full, explicit paragraph. If the writer successfully develops and arranges supporting sentences, he or she will inform readers, not confuse them with such short, mysterious utterances as "Copernicus" spoken all by itself.

EX 2–6   Following are some possible topic sentences. Proceed as you did in EX 2–1: ask further questions of these sentences from the standpoint of an average audience. Point up with questions the single words or short phrases that demand further explanation or development.

1. As Europe emerged from the Dark Ages into the light of the Renaissance, people came to believe more and more in witchcraft and black magic.

   _____

   _____

   _____

   _____

2. The ancient Greeks associated natural violence and catastrophe with particular divine beings.

   _____

   _____

   _____

   _____

3. Queen Elizabeth I of England used her intelligence and toughness to overcome the sixteenth-century prejudice that women were vastly inferior to men and unfit to rule.

_____

_____

_____

_____

4. When asked what he did during the French Revolution's Reign of Terror, the Count of Sieyès said, "I survived."

_____

_____

_____

_____

EX 2-7   Test the questions you wrote in EX 2-6. First, would answers to the questions you have asked *be relevant* to the main point of these topic sentences? Second, would answers to these questions *adequately* explain or elaborate the main point? Cross out any questions that do not satisfy these criteria. Substitute a more relevant or adequate question for each one you cross out.

Paragraphs built with answers to questions such as those you now have written in EX 2-6 would be *relevant* and *adequately developed*. Each paragraph would effectively develop and communicate its main intention or topic.

E. BEING SPECIFIC

In many cases, the most effective way to develop an idea is to *specify* it. This interesting word may help you see the value of development. By writing a more detailed paragraph on Copernicus, you *specified* his achievement; you provided relevant *specifics*, or details. You also answered the question, "What's *special* about Copernicus?" What is *special* about Copernicus, what is *specific* to him, is what he in particular did. If a writer merely answered the question "What is special about Copernicus?" by saying, "He was a famous astronomer," the answer would be inadequately developed, since there have been many other famous astronomers, like Galileo. The writer needs to specify, "Copernicus was an astronomer famous for arguing that the earth circles the sun," something that Galileo, whose *specialty* was the telescope, was not so famous for.

The word *specify* has another interesting property in addition to being kin to all these words—*specialty, specific, special. Specify* was formed long ago from a Latin word meaning "to see," so *specify* also shows itself in *spectacles* and *spectaculars*, in *speculations* and *specters*, in *prospectors* and *inspectors. Specification*, in short, can help a reader or listener really *see* your point, not just hear it. *Specifics* energize the imagination, offer spectacles to the mind's eye, show as well as tell. Notice how the following sample paragraph opens with a paragraph topic sentence that tells, but doesn't really show. But then notice how the paragraph develops *specifics* that show you the intention of the first sentence.

EXAMPLE OF A PARAGRAPH WITH SUPPORTING SPECIFICS

Scientific or empirical fact often overturns the hasty judgments of our senses. The two steel rails of the railroad track seem to intersect in the distance, but they do not. Sticks half immersed in water seem to bend, but do not. Dry ice seems to vanish before our eyes. Mirage effects lay down pools of water across the highway that disappear as we approach. The sun seems to fly across the sky as a satellite of our earth. Who says seeing is believing?

Such specifics as you see in this paragraph are an important feature of vivid exposition—of lively writing or speaking that leaps right into an audience's imagination to share the work of communication. Writing without such appeals to imagination is like riding a bike only up-hill or sailing only into the wind.

EX 2-8   Consider this sample paragraph with an eye to improving it.

The ancient Greeks associated natural violence and catastrophe with particular divine beings. When something bad or unexpected occurred, these Greeks held one or another of their gods responsible. Bad weather was the specialty of one god; plague and disease were the specialty of another.

The writer of this paragraph does go part of the way toward developing the topic sentence with specifics. Note the mention of divine "specialties." Still, the paragraph does not develop, focus on, and drive home its intention as successfully as it might. Here is some miscellaneous information on the topic to help you repair this paragraph. Not all of it will be of use to you.

- Poseidon, nicknamed "the earthshaker," was the Greek god of earthquakes.
- Artemis was goddess of the hunt, but also of sudden or quiet death.
- Apollo, twin brother of Artemis, was nicknamed "the destroyer" for the plagues he sent, like that at the beginning of the *Iliad*, the famous story about the Trojan War.
- Zeus hurled thunderbolts; trees struck by lightning became holy places.
- Zeus's sacred tree was the oak, perhaps because it was so big and so readily struck by lightning.
- The god Pan was thought responsible for *panics*.
- Dionysus was the Greek god of emotions and vitality.

Rewrite the paragraph so its supporting sentences become more specific and vivid. Do this on another sheet of paper.

EX 2-9   Following is a topic sentence on a subject most people have some familiarity with. Develop relevant specifics to convey the intention of the sentence adequately; then compose a vivid paragraph incorporating those specifics. Observe this rule of thumb: a full, substantial, reasonably developed paragraph should run from four to ten sentences; it should be short enough for you to control and develop easily, but long enough to say what it must and to assure your audience of your authority on the topic. Write your paragraph on another sheet of paper.

Topic sentence: In English, pronunciation is not necessarily a guide to the correct spelling of a word.

EX 2-10   Check the paragraph you wrote in EX 2-9. Have you adequately developed and specified the point? Has your development stayed relevant to the point? Could you fairly *test* your audience on the paragraph topic? If you notice any sentences that could make their points more clearly, revise them on your draft. If the entire paragraph could be raised to excellence through rewriting, do this on another sheet of paper.

F. WRITING EFFECTIVE GENERAL STATEMENTS

Like the subject and predicate of a sentence, the topic sentence and development of a paragraph make a nicely balanced couple. Very often, this is a balance between the *general* and the *specific*, between *generalization* and *specification*. Developing paragraphs often involves the discipline of specifying, but the writing of paragraph topic sentences often involves the knack of writing general statements that fit the information you have to share.

EXAMPLES OF EFFECTIVE TOPIC SENTENCES THAT MAKE GENERAL STATEMENTS
- *To provide some basic information on Greek mythology:* The ancient Greek religion was *pantheistic*, holding that all natural things are infused with divinities.
- *To explain why people go to the movies:* Going to the movies has always been more a social event than participation in an art form.
- *To discuss how electronic communication is changing our democracy:* Advances in electronics are rapidly changing American political processes.

EX 2-11   The italicized topic sentence in each paragraph below is not an effective generalization of what is said in the paragraph. In the blanks following each paragraph, write a more effective general statement that would make a good topic sentence for the paragraph.

People don't really understand our universe. The distance across our galaxy is approximately 100,000 light years. This means that, traveling at 186,000 miles per second, light would take 100,000 years to cross it. Our galaxy contains thirty times as many stars—thirty times as many suns—as there are people on earth. But there are also about thirty times as many *galaxies* as there are people on earth.

_____

_____

Frail and sickly as a youth and afflicted with poor eyesight, Theodore Roosevelt eventually became one of our greatest Presidents. Roosevelt spent two years roughing it in the Dakota Territories. He worked as a cowhand, rode fence, and even tracked thieves hundreds of miles cross country. Even as President he continued such strenuous activities as boxing regularly in the White House gym. In 1912, an assassin's bullet seriously wounded Roosevelt, who nevertheless insisted on making a campaign speech before seeking treatment for his deep chest wound. And he was famous for his vigorous hunting and camping tours—some, like his Brazilian trek of 1913, extremely hazardous and physically grueling. Throughout his life Roosevelt remained committed to physical culture; he demonstrated to Americans that a strong will and a program of vigorous exercise can enable even a weak person to become quite strong.

_____

_____

EX 2-12   The following paragraph needs a fitting topic sentence. Study the specifics in the paragraph before writing an appropriate generalization to introduce those specifics.

_____

_____

They use sonic echoes to pinpoint landscape features, objects, and food underwater. Whales also use sound to communicate practical information to other whales; they do this by means of elaborate phonic and musical emissions, which range over a wide sound frequency well adapted to their incredibly sensitive hearing. The lack of clear vision, sense of taste, and sense of smell apparently does not inhibit whales, because their keen hearing brings them almost all the sensory information they require.

G. MAKING SENTENCES AND PARAGRAPHS FLOW

Successful paragraphs *flow* from one sentence to the next. The paragraph *coheres*; it sticks or hangs together in an acceptably logical way. One of the writer's most convenient ways of ensuring flow and coherence involves use of *transitions*. English speakers automatically use many kinds of transitions, unconsciously responding to the need for flow and continuity.

EXAMPLE OF THE USE OF TRANSITIONAL WORDS
Galileo helped to establish the telescope as a tool of science. *He* used *it* to observe craters and mountains on the moon.

The italicized words are pronouns that refer back to words mentioned in the previous sentence. These references weave two sentences together, so that the second seems to follow coherently and logically from the first.

Certain transitional words and phrases—*for instance, moreover, however, generally*—can make an especially helpful contribution to paragraph coherence by giving gentle directions to readers.

EXAMPLE OF THE USE OF A TRANSITIONAL PHRASE TO GUIDE READERS
Galileo helped to establish the telescope as a tool of science. He used it, *for instance*, to observe craters and mountains on the moon.

Transitional words and phrases can direct the flow of a paragraph or series of paragraphs in many subtle ways, but for expository writing the following four kinds of transition are most useful:

↓ *specification*, pinning down—*for example, specifically*
↑ *generalizing*, overviewing—*in general, on the whole*

→ *continuation*, straight-ahead flow—*and, also*

↩ *turnaround*, reversed flow—*but, however*

Let us examine more closely these common types of transitions between sentences. A second sentence may continue the thought of the sentence that precedes it:

→ Whales emit sounds with astonishing versatility. *And* they *also* hear with unequaled sensitivity.

Experiment with your options by omitting *and*, then *also*, then both *and* and *also*. Which result do you prefer?

It is also easy to think of a situation in which a second sentence reverses the thrust of the preceding sentence:

↩ Whales hear with unequaled sensitivity. *But* they have very poor senses of sight and smell.

↩ Copernicus believed that the earth circled the sun. Most authorities, *however*, believed that the earth was the stationary center of the universe.

EX 2-13   Supply suitable transitional words in the following blank spaces. Choose between words that indicate continuing flow—such as *and, also, in addition, furthermore*—and words that signal reversed flow—such as *but, however, nevertheless*.

1. Some say that the Greeks destroyed Troy in order to recover Helen, who had left her Greek husband for a Trojan lover. _____ others say Helen never went to Troy.

2. Pronunciation is not necessarily a guide to the correct spelling of a word. _____ spelling is no sure guide to the correct pronunciation of a word.

3. Galileo's discoveries outraged scholarly astronomical opinion. They _____ stirred the anger of religious and political authorities.

4. Sixteenth-century Englishmen warned against the folly of female rule. _____ Queen Elizabeth I governed with admirable resourcefulness.

As a third possibility, a second sentence may specify or pin down the claim of the preceding sentence:

→ Whales are the earth's largest creatures. The female blue whale, *for instance*, can weigh 150 tons.

Fourth, a second sentence may generalize the point or points made in the sentence that precedes it:

↑ Whales are nearly blind, suicidally loyal to injured or diseased companions, and ruthlessly hunted with all the tricks of twentieth-century human technology. *On the whole*, it's a wonder they have survived at all.

Each of these four kinds of transitions gives the reader a signal about the nature of the next point to be made. Such signals discreetly guide a reading and ensure successful flow from one point to the next.

EX 2-14   Complete the following paragraphs by supplying suitable transitional words or phrases in the blank spaces. Choose among *all four* possibilities you have just studied.

PARAGRAPH 1

Scientific fact often overturns the hasty judgments of our senses.

_____ the two steel rails of the railroad track seem to intersect in the

distance, but do not. _____ sticks half immersed in water seem to
bend, but do not. The sun seems to fly across the sky as a satellite of our earth.

_____ these phenomena make one wonder whether what appears is
what is real.

PARAGRAPH 2

Theodore Roosevelt proved to be an exceptionally popular, personable chief

executive. _____ like many other successful politicians, he was oppor-
tunistic rather than consistent; in other words, he managed to work both sides

of the street. _____ he won the Nobel Peace Prize for helping to end

the Russo-Japanese War of 1905. _____ he frequently struck warlike
poses by threatening other nations—in Asia, South America, North Africa—with
invasion by the U.S. fleet. He was the first President to invite a black person—

Booker T. Washington—to the White House. _____ he was also partly
responsible for unfairly discharging 170 black infantrymen after a racial incident

in 1906. _____ he championed the American wilderness, setting mil-

lions of acres aside for preservation; _____ he led large, political,
widely publicized hunting and camping expeditions into the wild—expeditions
that helped to perpetuate highly questionable ideas of wilderness use and preser-

vation. _____ Roosevelt, like other Presidents, appears to deserve a
measure of historical criticism as well as our patriotic applause.

PARAGRAPH 3

The first scientific thinkers of the ancient world sought principles other than
gods to explain reality. Some postulated primary physical elements.

_____ Thales in Asia Minor believed water to be the core element of
all things. Others believed in more abstract principles. One of these was Anaxi-
mander, a Greek, who believed things to "owe a debt" to the "unbounded" or
infinite. Still others seemed to believe in both concrete and abstract principles.

_____ Heraclitus, a Greek from Ephesus, refers in his fragmentary writ-

ings to fire as the core element of everything. _____ he also mentions

logos, or "proportion," as the key to reality. _____ such variety of
opinion and speculation foreshadows genuine scientific inquiry and disagreement.

H. USING TRANSITIONS TO ORDER EVENTS

Most people understand an event more easily by seeing it happen than by reading about it. An eyewitness usually has a good idea of *when* and *where* each phase of the event happened, since he or she was present in that time and space. A reader, in contrast, normally has no sense of time and space other than what the writer provides. To make clear a sequence of occurrences the writer must specify what happened *first*, what happened *next*, what happened *then*, and what *finally* happened. To make clear the spatial relationships involved in an event, the writer must describe fixed points or specific areas and use locational terms such as *near*, *above*, *in back of*, and *fifty feet beyond* to place events in some frame of reference.

EXAMPLE OF WORDS EMPHASIZING THE SEQUENCE OF EVENTS

The three-year-old showed no fear of the water. *First* she pulled herself up onto the diving board. *Then* she walked out to the edge and hollered, "Watch me jump!" *Next* she leaped out into space with a gleeful screech. Her mother took hold of the child just after she hit the surface and guided her toward the edge of the pool; she *then* let the child swim unassisted for a few strokes. *Finally* the mother gave the child a gentle push to the edge and helped her clamber out to begin the process *once again*.

EX 2-15 On another sheet of paper, rewrite the following paragraph. Make it easier for readers to follow by adding words that give a sense of the order of events, such as *first, the next step, after that*, and *last*.

It is not difficult to replace unsatisfactory, poorly placed car radio speakers with quality speakers mounted for excellent sound quality. Borrow, rent, or buy a power drill and a hole cutter the diameter of your speakers. Unsnap the protective panels on your doors. Spot the hole positions where no metal framework will interfere. Resnap the panels and drill the two holes. Drill four small mounting holes for each speaker and place the clip nuts in position. Attach speaker wires to each speaker and feed wires through the holes, behind the protective panels, and out between the panel and the frame at the bottom front corner of each door. Mount the speakers on the doors by screwing a sheet metal screw into each clip nut. Cut the wires to the old speakers and solder or splice the new speaker wires to the wires from the radio or tape player. Test the speakers.

I. REVIEWING CHAPTER CONCEPTS

This chapter has described some of the ways the paragraph can bridge the distance between the sentence and the composition—the distance between basic sentence skills that most people have and the composition skills that most people need to work hard at. The chapter has pointed out that the work of the general statement—the *topic sentence* of a paragraph—is to state explicitly the paragraph's message or intent; but the topic sentence should also imply ideas and information for the paragraph to develop and pin down.

Paragraphs may develop the intention of the topic sentence by *specifying, exemplifying, detailing*, or *illustrating the generalization*. These similar ways of *showing* as well as *telling* help to make writing vivid. Effective transitional words and phrases, meanwhile, help to make paragraphs coherent and to channel the flow of writer's and reader's thoughts.

By studying and practicing the techniques of paragraph building, you can improve and extend your command of them. After all, you *speak* paragraphs often, though perhaps not with as much regularity, sureness, and control as you would like. Here is an analogy on behalf of study and practice:

Most people unknowingly put spin on tennis balls, baseballs, golf balls, or billiard balls; they are haphazardly using the physics of spin that becomes a real power when it is practiced and controlled by the masters of these sports.

Can you explain how this analogy might apply to your writing?

EX 2-16   In the summary paragraphs above, you will find some form of each of the following words. Many of these words are abstract—you can't see or touch what they name—and are therefore somewhat difficult to understand and remember. Nevertheless, because these words can help you to learn, think, and talk about writing and reading, they deserve to be studied. Underline the words or their related forms in the preceding paragraphs. Then, in the blanks next to each word below, write a definition or explanation that would help a friend or classmate understand these terms. After your explanation, list in parentheses any other forms of the work you can think of.

EXAMPLE: *adequacy*—saying enough, in enough detail, about a topic to inform or persuade an audience (*adequate, adequately*)

1. *specify* _____

_____

2. *example* _____

_____

3. *generalization* _____

_____

4. *topic* _____

_____

5. *coherent* _____

_____

6. *imply* _____

_____

7. *explicit* _____

_____

8. *illustrate* _____

_____

9. *vividness* _____

_____

10. *transition* _____

_____

WORKSHOP

1. Make one of the mysterious utterances below the subject of an effective topic sentence. Then write a paragraph that includes the topic sentence and develop what the topic sentence implies. You may have to do some research before you begin writing.

Michelangelo	Stravinsky
Diaghilev	Keats
Queen Victoria	Zapata

2. Find three of the following items in a daily newspaper or a magazine.
   - a personality feature
   - an editorial
   - an account of an event
   - an obituary
   - a letter to the editor

   Select at random a paragraph near the middle of each. Find the topic sentence in each of these paragraphs.

3. Some possible topic sentences appear below. Proceed as you did in Ex 2–1: ask further questions of these sentences from the standpoint of a member of an average audience. Point up with questions the single words or short phrases in each sentence that require further explanation or development.
   a. Athamas, the mythical ruler of Boeotia, married a phantom named Nephile who had been created by Zeus.
   b. Because of his physical and emotional makeup, Jonathan Swift was more inclined to bully than to flatter.
   c. When the Malayan mantis senses danger, it can change its body colors from its usual pink, purple, white, and green to the colors of the orchid on which it is settled.

4. The topic sentence below is on a subject you should be familiar with. Develop a list of specifics to convey the intention of the sentence adequately, and then compose a vivid paragraph incorporating these specifics.

   Topic sentence: One type of television commercial first attempts to make viewers feel that they have a personal problem or need and then presents a particular product as the obvious answer to the problem or need.

5. a. Find a lengthy expository paragraph in a textbook. List each transitional word or phrase that appears in the paragraph.
   b. Find an article about a political uprising, such as the continuing conflict in Northern Ireland. Choose a paragraph that describes a sequence of actions. List each transitional word you find in the paragraph.

6. Find a paragraph you have written that could benefit from revision. This can be from any paper you have written this year. Rewrite the paragraph; as you do so, ask yourself these questions:
   - Does this paragraph contain a clear, concise topic sentence?
   - Are the implications of the topic sentence developed with specifics?
   - Do all sentences in the paragraph relate to the topic sentence?
   - Are transitions used to help the reader gain a clear sense of what is being said?

   Note that you will seldom make all these kinds of corrections in a single paragraph. Nevertheless, trying out a number of possibilities can help you to discover a better way of saying what you want to say.

Choosing Methods of Paragraph Development: Part One

3

A. CONSIDERING STRATEGIES

By looking at the paragraph from the outside in, you have now seen some of its complexity. You have seen that a paragraph is a whole composed of such differently functioning parts as the topic sentence, specifics, and transitions. But paragraph writing is multiple in another sense, as you look from the inside out, toward different communicating purposes, toward different questions you need to answer. In this respect a writer is like a traveler who takes different vehicles and routes depending on his or her destination and reasons for travel.

Writers and speakers naturally adapt different strategies or methods of development to suit different aims. To describe *what* the solar system is will send your writing off in a different direction from a discussion of *how* the solar system came about. The *content* of these two paragraphs will differ, and so in some ways will their *form*: one will *describe a thing*; the other will *narrate a process*.

In this chapter and the next you will study and practice some of the most common and most helpful ways writers can develop paragraphs to satisfy different topics and purposes.

B. DEVELOPING A PARAGRAPH BY LISTING SPECIFICS

First, suppose a writer has some general statement or claim to convey to an audience. Perhaps the writer can most easily drive home the point simply by *listing* evidence or specifics.

EXAMPLE OF A PARAGRAPH THAT LISTS EVIDENCE

Elizabeth I was one of the most successful and popular of all British monarchs, for a number of reasons. First, she took a country on the verge of civil war and united it both by appealing to the patriotism of her people and by consolidating her power. Second, she renewed and reestablished the state church. Third, she fostered foreign commerce and colonization. Fourth, she encouraged the domestic economy through laws dealing with labor, currency, and poverty. And fifth, she outmaneuvered England's many foreign enemies—Spain, France, Scotland, the Vatican—in a series of sometimes shrewd, sometimes downright sneaky promises, plots, and alliances.

The numbers in this sample paragraph show you how closely this account resembles a simple list. And yet this simple method of listing proves quite effective for conveying the reasons for the queen's success. Such paragraphs are complex—yoking several parts and points together—but this does not mean they are difficult to write, provided you have your information and your wits about you.

Study these three sorts of lists, each of which can be a powerful method for conveying a claim or generalization:

A. List of facts
B. List of typical instances or examples
C. List of reasons or arguments

The sample paragraph about Elizabeth I seems closest to type C: the writer has listed *reasons* for regarding her as a successful and popular ruler.

EX 3-1   Which kind of listing strategy—A, B, or C—would best suit a paragraph written to develop each of the following generalizations? Write the appropriate letter in the blank next to each topic sentence.

EXAMPLE: __*B*__ A volcanic eruption can disrupt the economy of an entire region.

1. _____ Capital punishment should be reintroduced nationwide.

2. _____ Alaska is the largest state in the United States.

3. _____ Movies have become more lurid and violent in recent years.

4. _____ The National League plays better baseball than the American League.

5. _____ College should be shortened by a year.

6. _____ The U.S. owns a larger arsenal than the U.S.S.R.

7. _____ Insects may one day conquer the earth.

8. _____ Modern science has not dispelled our superstitiousness.

Since opinions about the best kind of list may vary somewhat, be ready to justify or explain your preferences.

When scientists graph data, they cannot plot lines with fewer than two points, nor planes with fewer than three. In fact, the more points they have, the surer they can be of their figures. A scientist need not, of course, mark every point—only enough points to establish a probable pattern. Similar rules of thumb apply in listing points in a paragraph. Cite enough points to be clear and convincing, but not so many that your paragraph becomes repetitive or tedious. If the writer had cited only one or two points on behalf of Queen Elizabeth, the sample paragraph would have been much less convincing and authoritative.

EX 3-2   Here is a general statement followed by a list of specifics. By wisely selecting among the specifics, develop a paragraph that is convincing and authoritative without being repetitive or boring. If you detect some choppiness in your paragraph, polish it with some transitions. Write your paragraph on another sheet of paper.

Topic sentence: Don Quixote, the "Man of La Mancha," became one of the world's most famous story characters largely because he could not tell the difference between what was real and what was make-believe.

- He destroyed a puppet show trying to save a lady puppet in distress.
- He stole a barber's basin, thinking it to be an enchanted helmet.
- He read many fantasy stories of knights in armor, but believed them to be true histories.
- He mistook a roadside inn for a lord's magnificent castle.
- His shrewd squire Sancho Panza often took advantage of his master's weakness.
- He was once trampled by a herd of pigs that he thought was an army.
- The book is filled to almost a thousand pages with absurd, whimsical adventures.
- He once mistook a flock of sheep for an army.
- He mistook a Basque servant for a wicked knight.
- He attacked windmills, believing they were wicked giants.
- He believed his lady Dulcinea had been transformed into a sweating peasant.
- Don Quixote's story was popular even in its author's lifetime.

Listing paragraphs work best when the elements listed are more or less *parallel*—all reasons or all examples or all facts, not a mixture of the three. Such mixtures, reflecting a writer's indecision about paragraph strategy, can confuse readers, as in this promising but flawed paragraph.

EXAMPLE OF A LISTING PARAGRAPH WITH NONPARALLEL ELEMENTS
Achilles was the most celebrated Greek hero of the ancient world for both his strengths and weaknesses. His story shows how Greeks liked to mingle the joy of triumph with the sadness of fate, loss, and tragedy. First, his being the hero of Homer's *Iliad*, the most influential Greek book, is one reason for his popularity. Second, he was famous for invulnerability, except for the "Achilles' heel" by which his mother held him when she dipped him in magic waters. Third, the legends say Achilles dressed in women's clothes, as a favor to his mother, to avoid the draft for the Trojan War. Fourth, Achilles showed his strength of character when fate offered him a choice between a long, peaceful life and a short, glorious one: he chose fame, but at the price of death. Only Achilles could beat the Trojan hero Hector, and when Achilles temporarily withdrew from battle, the Trojans began to win. And last, Achilles has in fact been the world's most famous hero for 3,200 years.

EX 3-3   Here are a few additional points that the writer chose not to use; you may find some of them helpful in rewriting and improving this paragraph.

The *Iliad* concerns a feud between a pouting Achilles and the Greek general Agamemnon; Achilles was a mortal, though the son of the sea-goddess Thetis; he was killed from a distance by the archer Paris, who shot him in the heel; Achilles was the greatest of all the heroes at Troy for courage, strength, and self-control; Achilles killed Hector; the Greeks won the Trojan War despite Achilles' death.

On another sheet of paper, rewrite the paragraph about Achilles, editing and selecting from the information provided. In particular, try to list or specify more clearly and directly the hero's strengths and weaknesses.

EX 3-4   Now try writing a listing paragraph on your own. On another sheet of paper, write a paragraph citing reasons in answer to one of these questions:

- Why has a significant proportion of the public lost confidence in its high schools?
- Why do people *really* come to college?

Try to make your reasons and your paragraph as exact and as vivid as you can. Remember that you can draw on your own views and experiences, if you generalize from them sensibly and if you frame your writing impersonally.

EX 3-5   Develop another listing paragraph, this time by citing examples—enough interesting, relevant examples to convey the truth of your claim.

> *Topic sentence:* Even though our modern, scientific world is nearing the eve of the twenty-first century, we encounter many instances of superstitiousness every day.

C. ANSWERING THE QUESTION "WHAT?"

Think of another set of paragraph strategies clustered around the question "What?" When writers must identify, define, describe, or classify something, they are in effect answering *what* something is: *What is a solar system? What is a paragraph? What does "repression" mean? What kinds of science courses must students take to satisfy degree requirements? What sort of day have you had?*

In fact, when developing a composition, every writer should have an impish "what"-questioner perched at his or her ear to raise constant questions about the explicitness and clarity of words or concepts mentioned in the composition: *What* do you mean by "stereotype?" Do you really expect your audience to know *what* a "writ of *habeas corpus*" is? *What kind* of "repression" are you referring to? This impish questioner can help a writer detect and work through knotty or weak spots in the presentation.

The questioner can further help by guiding you to and through another strategy of paragraph development with which you present key terms, important things, and necessary distinctions successfully. Study these three sorts of paragraph development with which to answer the "what"-questioner:

- Definition
- Description
- Classification or Division

Each of these strategies aims at clarifying and explaining some *what*—some term or concept (definition); some person, place, or thing (description); some set of related terms, ideas, or things (classification or division). The remaining sections of this chapter will give you practice in these three strategies for writing paragraphs.

D. WRITING A PARAGRAPH OF DEFINITION

Definition customarily aims at distilling the essence of a term or concept so that you and your readers can communicate on common ground. Some terms or phrases, like *free enterprise*, have so vague a meaning that writers cannot assume, no matter how familiar these words, that readers grasp the writers' intended meanings. Other terms, like *repression, mystery, bias,* even *schooner,* have multiple meanings that can confuse a writer's intended meaning unless he or she stops to define or clarify terms.

You can judge the value of definition to the competent user of English from the popularity of the dictionary—our storehouse of definitions as well as of pronunciations, spellings, and word roots. A dictionary is also a fine place for you to begin your reply to the "what"-questioner.

Suppose that you are writing a paper on energy production and conservation and that you confront the term *dynamo*, but you are unsure of its meaning or how to pass on this meaning to your readers. You wisely consult a good dictionary. It might tell you that *dynamo* is sometimes just another word for *generator*; sometimes it more precisely refers to a "generator that supplies direct current." Dictionary writers try to supply a definition that places a term—here, *dynamo*—in the class or set to which it belongs—here, the class or set of *generators*. Further, these dictionary writers try to *specify* what is *special* about the term—how it differs from other members of its class or set. In our example, the dynamo resembles other generators except that it produces *direct current* rather than *alternating current.* For many readers this definition may still be obscure or incomplete; that problem will be addressed after the following exercise.

EX 3-6   Practice your definitional thinking on the following list of terms. In the first blank, try to name the class to which the term belongs. Then in the next blank, try to specify how the term differs from other members of its class. Work from your own resources, but if you get stuck, consult a dictionary.

EXAMPLE: veal	*meat*	*of a young calf*
1. convertible	_____	_____
2. monarchy	_____	_____
3. freeway	_____	_____
4. condominium	_____	_____
5. professor	_____	_____
6. misdemeanor	_____	_____
7. wrath	_____	_____
8. bicycle	_____	_____
9. magazine	_____	_____
10. mascara	_____	_____

Research into *dynamo* led to a "a generator producing direct current." But perhaps you do not know what *generator* refers to or what *direct current* is. If you do not, you have run up against a limitation of the dictionary: its conciseness, its brief, tightly packed definitions that often explain hard words with other words almost as hard. (This limitation is one strong argument against opening papers with such strategies as "Webster defines *liberty* as . . . ." Because they often fail to develop definitions clearly and fully, the writers of Webster's and of other dictionaries are not the most effective writers of definitional paragraphs.) If you do not know what *generator* or *direct current* means, you must explore the dictionary further until you have established the meaning of *dynamo* to your satisfaction. You might learn, for instance, that a *generator* is "a machine that converts mechanical energy to electrical energy" and that *direct current* refers to the flow of electricity or electrons in a circuit or electrical path in only one direction, unlike the *alternating current* produced by most generators, which alternates the direction of electrical flow with each half-turn of the generator shaft.

Having researched the problem to a point of reasonable completeness, you can shape your facts into a paragraph that defines *dynamo.* Let's suppose you are writing for an average high-school-educated audience. (If you were writing for engineers, this paragraph of definition would probably not be needed.)

> A dynamo is a source of electrical power. Like a generator, it converts mechanical energy—ordinary push-and-pull energy—to electrical energy, electricity. But unlike a generator, which alternates its flow of electricity to produce the alternating current we use in our houses, the dynamo produces a direct current, the kind of current we use in our cars.

EX 3-7   Here is a definitional paragraph that lacks both precision—careful focus on a particular term (on its class and its difference from other members of its class)—and explicitness (development or specification of all difficult words). Study this paragraph with an eye to revising and rewriting it.

> Even though the word *ensign* may make one think of a navy officer, the more important meaning of *ensign* is the flag. You may have seen such a flag flown by the armed forces on their sea-and-air mobile units. It must have been interesting to design the special insignia that goes on the flag to represent the branch of the armed forces that the vehicle or unit belongs to. Actually, the flag and the title of the navy officer are probably connected. Back in the old days, when the military carried flags into battle, the ensign carried the ensign. If you doubt the emotion attached to a flag in battle, recall the famous photograph of the flag-raising on Iwo Jima in World War II—a widely published picture that inspired many statues and a postage stamp.

Supply a tighter focus to the definition of *ensign*; eliminate distracting and irrelevant information; clarify or pin down some of the writer's vague words or phrases. Write your revision of this paragraph on another sheet of paper.

EX 3-8   Using your dictionary for research and reference, write brief paragraphs (three to seven sentences) answering the following requests for definition. Aim your definitions at a high-school-educated audience. Where words have more than one sense (more than one numbered definition in the dictionary), choose the first modern sense that the dictionary lists. This first entry usually gives the most common or most important meaning of a word.

1. What is a *bishop?* _____

_____

_____

_____

_____

_____

_____

2. What is an *omelette?* _____

_____

_____

_____

_____

_____

_____

3. What is *corduroy?* _____

_____

_____

_____

_____

_____

4. What is a *schooner?* _____

_____

_____

_____

_____

_____

_____

5. What is a *hero*? _____

_____

_____

_____

_____

_____

_____

6. What is *magic*? _____

_____

_____

_____

_____

_____

_____

E. RECOGNIZING DENOTATION AND CONNOTATION

Work with the dictionary will usually give you a word's *denotation*, the strict and literal definition of a term. The dictionary will tell you, for instance, that a *rose* is a shrub or vine of the genus *Rosa*, with prickly stems, compound leaves, and variously colored, often fragrant flowers. But the dictionary largely overlooks the feelings, impressions, or images that we regularly associate with many words—like *rose* or *hero* or *magic*. We associate the *rose*, for example, with positive ideals of beauty, delicacy, hope, the attainment of quests or desires; furthermore, the *rose* figures in the symbolism of most of the great Western religions. These regular associations of a word make up its *connotation*, its value in our culture. For example, despite similar denotations, *desire* has a favorable or positive value, while *lust* has an unfavorable or negative value.

EX 3-9 Mark the connotations of the following terms as *favorable* (+), *unfavorable* (–), or *neutral* (0).

1. _____ greed   2. _____ dinner   3. _____ flexibility

_____ thrift   _____ banquet   _____ tolerance

_____ miserliness   _____ orgy   _____ permissiveness

4. _____ flower   5. _____ beast   6. _____ arrogant

_____ plant   _____ animal   _____ proud

_____ weed   _____ lion   _____ dignified

Often a definition of a loaded, or highly connotative, word like *magic* is incomplete without some mention of the feelings, impressions, or images that the word regularly conveys. (*Regularly* here means that there is a standard of connotation: most members of a language community share similar feelings about terms.) The connotation of a word like *rose* is much harder to learn than its denotation; the denotation is the tip of a verbal iceberg extending deep down into the seas of social and cultural feeling, belief, and prejudice. Fortunately, native speakers of a language have spent their whole lives learning important connotations. You learn connotation in the same, almost natural way you learn most of the rules, values, and ideals of your culture.

EX 3–10   Next to each of the following words, list with as much precision as you can the important feelings, impressions, qualities, or images we associate with it.

EXAMPLE: lion   *courage, nobility, grace, loyalty, power, kindness*

1. star _____

2. snake _____

3. child _____

4. noon _____

5. eagle _____

Here is a sample paragraph of definition that tries to cover both the denotation and the connotation of a difficult but important word. (Note how italics indicate when the word is used merely *as a word* and not to refer to the thing. In your writing, use underlining for words as words.)

> People in our society have never really been quite sure how to value *ambition*. Ambition is generally held to be a strong desire to achieve something, usually in the areas of government, business, or the military. So why should such desire make people feel unsure or uneasy? Don't parents and schools habitually urge children to succeed and achieve? Of course. But *ambition* often carries the flavor of a desire *too* strong, for achievements *too* grandiose, so that other desires and ideals play second fiddle to success at any cost. George Patton, Howard Hughes, and Richard Nixon were all ambitious people; but we now regard their desires for glory as excessive, as causes of their failures as well as of their successes. In our democracy we seem caught between ambition as an expression of freedom or social mobility and ambition as a route to one person's undemocratically lording it over another. Parents and teachers want children to practice their talents, to strive, to compete, but they do not want them to be ruthless, overeager, on the make; they want their children to be ambitious without being, well, ambitious.

Here is another paragraph of definition that does not pay enough attention to the connotation of words. Study the paragraph and the words to see how the writer missed an important chance to develop and pin down this interesting subject effectively.

> It is interesting to think about the different words people use for deliberately missing school classes. In the old days, if you deliberately missed class, you were *truant* in the eyes of the authorities—what the dictionary calls "absent without leave or permission, especially from school." Students themselves have used other words—verbs—which focused on the deed, not on the person doing the deed. These words—*playing hooky, skipping, cutting, ditching*—all carry different views of *truancy*, the student's view as opposed to the institution's view, different views that are interesting to reflect on.

EX 3-11   On another sheet of paper, expand and rewrite this promising paragraph by paying further attention to the connotations of words it tries to define.

EX 3-12   On another sheet of paper, write a paragraph of definition for one of the following terms; this paragraph should include reference to both the denotation and the connotation of the term. If necessary, use your dictionary to research the denotation and your classmates to research the connotation.

tycoon	rock 'n roll	computer
politician	bureaucracy	boogie

F. WRITING A PARAGRAPH OF DESCRIPTION

Frequently when writers face "what" questions, it is not a term or concept they aim to clarify. Often it is some particular person, place, or thing—the dynamo I ran last summer, the schooner owned by the Naval Academy, or the mythical hero Achilles. In these cases the abstract, intellectual slant of definition does not really suit a writer's purpose. A writer wants to produce something more vivid, more immediate, something closer to experience—a kind of paragraph development that we will call *description*. Description thrives on detail; unlike definition, which addresses the intellect, description most strongly appeals to the memory and imagination. And since more people are imaginative than are intellectual, you can imagine the value of such description.

Another helpful way of conceiving the difference between definition and description is this: the dictionary is a book of definitions; the encyclopedia is a book of descriptions. Here is a brief list that shows the swing from the definition of a term to the description of a thing:

Denotation of a Term	*Description of a Thing*
general, universal	detailed, particular
conceptual	perceptual
intellectual	imaginative, memorable

These poles include two interesting and, at the college level, fairly common clusters of words, so you may find them worth your study and reflection.

Here is a sample descriptive paragraph; it describes a thing, not a term. Notice how it strives for perceptible detail, how it tries to engage your imaginative participation.

Coffee is a developed taste, both in the bean and in the drinker, but once you have the habit, coffee becomes a total sensory experience. The robust smell of coffee—fresh roasted, fresh ground, redolent of tropical earth—is probably the coffee drinker's greatest delight next to its peculiar, rich, musty range of flavors, flavors that the bitter bean lacks till it is roasted. Even the touch of coffee—whether of the polished, beadlike bean in the fingers or of the loamy texture of the grounds—is pleasant and oddly soothing. So is the sight of the fine, dark-brown liquid. And if you doubt that coffee has a compelling sound, remember those commercials that romanticized the sound of the percolator as music to a coffee drinker's ears. This complete sensory envelopment, admittedly with the help of a little caffeine, brings about the coffee drinker's well-known exhilaration and satisfaction with the first cup of the day.

Notice how this paragraph draws on a freewriting strategy—an inventory of the five senses—to develop its description of the pleasures of coffee.

The following paragraph overlooks some of the requirements of effective description: its need of detail, of thoroughness, of vividness. Study this description with an eye to revising it.

> Most people know the typical lawyer from movies, television, or books. The typical lawyer wears typical lawyer's clothes, talks typical lawyer's language, and carries the typical lawyer's briefcase, which gets its name from the "briefs" it holds. He inhabits typical lawyer's surroundings. The only person he seems to be really nice to is the judge. He is a very verbal person and has trouble just listening. But he knows his rights, so you had better treat him right.

EX 3-13   Develop, expand, and improve the preceding paragraph to make it more vivid and descriptive. Write your revised version on another sheet of paper.

The previous paragraph exemplified a wonderful descriptive technique. It treated a type or stereotype, something that exists only in the mind, as though it were a real thing existing in the world. This technique, by making one stand for many, lets you draw on the directness, vividness, and force of the particular while still covering or treating a general class or set.

EX 3-14   On another sheet of paper, write a paragraph describing one of the following. Use your memory and imagination to reflect on, pin down, and develop information for the "type" you select. Some humor or exaggeration, provided it is not vicious or irrelevant, can help drive home the point of the description.

- the typical textbook
- the typical college class
- the typical day of a college student
- the typical college date
- the typical upperclassman or upperclasswoman

G. WRITING A PARAGRAPH OF CLASSIFICATION OR DIVISION

Sometimes the best answer to a "what" question is several parallel or related answers. Someone asks, "What movies are especially vital and inventive these days?" And you feel compelled to answer, "Three kinds are particularly effective: romances, horror-mysteries, and science-fiction fantasies." When applied to paragraph development, this way of responding is termed *classification* or *division*. It is a method of development that analyzes—literally, "breaks down"—a complex thing into its related parts or parallel features. Here are some other examples of classification or division in response to questions:

Q.: What sort of person goes into politics?
A.: Actually, there are two sorts: the statesman and the politician.

Q.: What is knowledge?
A.: Knowledge is, obviously, different things to different people, but generally it seems to be (1) skill, (2) intelligence, or (3) wisdom.

Q.: What is a definition?
A.: A definition can aim at denotation, connotation, or both; the intention of the writer will determine the nature of the definition.

Here is a sample paragraph developed according to a strategy of classification:

> Knowledge is highly prized among all people, at least in some of its several forms. The value of knowledge is easiest to see when it takes the form of skill or know-how. Knowing how to build a house, repair a car, or write a business letter or law brief is certainly worth something in our society. Less clearly valuable is knowledge in the form of simple intelligence, particularly all the quickness of mind, all the information and booklore, all the impractical curiosity that intelligent people have developed almost in spite of themselves. True, such knowledge as this can occasionally lead to wondrous discoveries; but when it produces boredom, impatience, or intolerance, it is clearly not of much value. Finally, most people recognize wisdom as a form of knowledge—the knowledge that people acquire the hard way as the result of life experience. This knowledge is probably not good for much more than respect, since it was not available for use when it was most needed. It is by making mistakes for lack of knowledge that we acquire wisdom—knowing our limits as human beings—as a sort of consolation prize.

The following paragraph fails to divide and classify explicitly, and so it seems contradictory and confusing:

> Because of the variety of styles used by painters over the centuries, painting is a difficult art to comprehend. For a long time, the classic painters beautifully represented the world in portraits, landscapes, and still lifes. Admittedly some of these paintings seemed a little unrealistic in their use of color and lighting. But lately it is hard to see anything in paintings. They have become networks of lines or masses of colors or tangles of texture. Sometimes, however, I do sort of grasp this dance of unrealism, this stress on *form* rather than on *content*. Recent art often reminds me of still another kind of painting: ancient or primitive painting. This painting sometimes just decorates or ornaments places or things; sometimes it depicts people, gods, or things for the sake of worship or magic. Nowadays a person is supposed to be able to appreciate all this as painting, but with so many choices it's hard to know what real painting is.

EX 3–15 Improve the preceding paragraph by imposing a clear scheme of classification on its material and by eliminating any distracting or irrelevant comments. Write your revised version on another sheet of paper.

EX 3–16 Develop schemes of classification for each of the following topics. Humorous or playful schemes may suit some topics; serious schemes may best suit others. A helpful question to ask yourself after writing a particular scheme of classification is this: Does this scheme *adequately cover* the topic?

EXAMPLE: College classes *lecture, seminar, laboratory, workshop, studio, discussion section*

1. College exams _____

_____

_____

_____

_____

2. Excuses for absence from class _____

_____

_____

_____

_____

3. Factors determining physical attractiveness _____

_____

_____

_____

_____

4. Leisure activity of college students _____

_____

_____

_____

_____

5. Success _____

_____

_____

_____

_____

EX 3-17   Develop one of your foregoing schemes of classification into an effective paragraph, complete with relevant specifics and explanation. Again, be sure your system of classification allows for adequate coverage and exploration of your topic.
Write your paragraph on another sheet of paper.

WORKSHOP

1. Freewrite the following lists.
   - List five pet peeves.
   - List the five worst things that have happened to you.
   - List five things that many people fear but you do not.
   - List five achievements that illustrate your talents.
   - List five foods you like most.
   - List five other lists you would be interested in making.

2. Another use of the listing strategy occurs in paragraphs of evaluation where you itemize
   important strengths or weaknesses, advantages or disadvantages, pros or cons. Try such a
   list with these topics:
   - advantages and disadvantages of blue jeans

- advantages and disadvantages of the bicycle as a form of transportation
- advantages and disadvantages of studying in the library
- advantages and disadvantages of blind dates
- advantages and disadvantages of *paperback* books

3. Convert one of your lists from exercise 2, above, into a paragraph or composition: adopt a stance pro *or* con (*not* both) and itemize the arguments or considerations. Cite items contrary to your stance first; then develop your preferred items more fully. Thus if you think blind dates are, on the whole, a bad idea, briefly mention arguments *for* blind dates *before* discounting those arguments and dwelling on arguments *against* blind dates.

4. Develop the paragraph you wrote in EX 3–11 into a fuller, longer composition on different views of *truancy*.

5. *Dynamo* is a word that can also refer to a person. Write a paragraph developing the similarity between the machine and some human dynamo you know.

6. Write a paragraph defining the word *mystery* and distinguishing it from *magic*.

7. Take a short descriptive paragraph from the encyclopedia and, for fun, enliven it with more descriptiveness, stronger language and vividness, more style. This is easiest if you select a paragraph from an article on a subject you know something about: an article on your home town or home state, on the country or continent of your nationality, on your hobby, on your prospective major.

8. List as many human stereotypes as you can think of (stereotypes familiar from jokes, cartoons, situation comedies, advertisements, and other media that flatten or pigeonhole people). Some examples to get you started: the stereotype of the politician, of the housewife, of the cheerleader, of the small-town sheriff.

9. Develop one of your stereotypes listed in exercise 8, above, into a descriptive paragraph or composition. You might divide or classify this description into (a) what the stereotype looks like, (b) how the stereotype talks or behaves, (c) in what places or with what people the stereotype can be found, and (d) what equipment the stereotype regularly owns (the biker's Harley-Davidson, for instance).

Choosing Methods of Paragraph Development: Part Two

4

This chapter presents additional strategies for developing successful paragraphs and offers practice in these various strategies. Their variety reflects the variety of human language and intelligence, and it makes for lively, interesting writing. Matching the right strategy or form to your purpose often also proves the key to getting the paragraph out of your head and onto the paper.

A. DEVELOPING A NARRATIVE PARAGRAPH

Narration is storytelling; to narrate is to tell a story, to give an account of something that happened in time. Your learning to ride a bicycle, the Civil War truce signing at Appomattox, the strange life of Arthur Rimbaud—all these subjects are candidates for narration. In contrast, why the Edsel failed, what Keynesian economics is, and what sort of people go into real estate are all questions that have no special need of time sequence.

Commonly a narration, story, or anecdote emphasizes *before* and *after*; it establishes a situation and then changes it. The narration's impact comes in the turn of events that brings an audience from the earlier moment to the later moment. Many jokes and tall tales are in fact successfully planned and paced narratives. Here is one such humorous tale from the folklore of the southern United States.

> There once were a husband and wife who did nothing but argue, a problem the husband blamed on his wife's stubbornness and contrariness. One day a neighbor approached the husband as he was chopping wood and told him that his wife had fallen into the creek and drowned. "Show me where," said the husband. The neighbor showed him, and the husband immediately headed off upstream to look for his wife's body. "Where are you going?" asked the neighbor. "Gonna find that hard-headed woman," said the husband; "she always did run against the current."

EX 4–1   The following traditional joke is disorganized and uneven. Using your own intuitive sense of a good story, rewrite the paragraph to improve its narration and enhance its effectiveness. Do this on another sheet of paper.

> Sam Jones died. There once was a cowboy who had the unpleasant responsibility of reporting this death to Mrs. Jones. He did it in a characteristic way. This cowboy was famous—aren't they all?—for his typical cowpoke's tough, unemotional, laconic manner. She was rocking on her porch as he rode up. He said, "Howdy, Widow Jones!" "Widow Jones!" she exclaimed. Then she said, "I'm no widow!" Then the cowboy said, "Betcha twenty dollars you are."

EX 4–2   Now tell your own joke or anecdote—not a riddle, but some joke that seems to have elements of a story ("Once there were . . ."). Write it on another sheet of paper.

A joke or funny anecdote is not quite a narrative paragraph, however. To become such a paragraph, the anecdote needs a "topic sentence": the point or moral or generalization that the anecdote illustrates. The moral of the first husband-wife tale might stress how predictable people are or how people let their expectations of other people get the better of their common sense. Here is a possible topic sentence that could be used to lead into that story: "Some people become so frozen into a relationship that nothing can change their habits or attitudes toward the other person. Southerners tell a folktale that illustrates this point."

EX 4–3   Write a topic sentence capturing the possible point of

1. the cowboy story (EX 4–1)

_____

_____

2. your story in EX 4–2

_____

_____

B. MAKING A POINT THROUGH NARRATION

Splicing a moral or generalization—the topic sentence—and a narrative illustration of it yields the classic form of expository narrative paragraph. You have backed into this form through the joke partly to discover how keen a sense of narrative—at least of jokes and funny anecdotes—you may already have. This narrative sense is now ready to go to work in other language situations.

Of course, not all stories or narratives are humorous, though jokes are extremely popular with public speakers and writers ranging from preachers to politicians. Some narratives, like those of great moral or religious teachers, are parables or fables, simple fantasy tales told to make points about human behavior. Other narratives draw upon personal experience—sometimes humorous, sometimes quite sad or sobering—to make their points.

In each case, the development of the paragraph reflects change in time, from earlier to later. In one respect, organization is easy—first things first, last things last. In another respect, *pacing* is difficult, just as with jokes, since it is tempting to stray from the main line or plot of the story and spend time on irrelevant details. The economy, drama, and bite of the joke can thus be a useful guide to the tricky problem of pacing or timing of narrative paragraphs.

The following narrative paragraph successfully manages both point and pacing:

PACING OF A NARRATIVE PARAGRAPH

Despite the brevity, uncertainty, and squalor of life, the English people of Queen Elizabeth's time loved grace, elegance, and courtliness. Legend has made Sir Walter Raleigh a wonderful example of this courtliness. One day, as the queen walked the streets of London, she encountered a muddy ditch, the curse of a country without sewers or garbage collection. Before she could maneuver around the obstacle, Sir Walter stepped from the crowd, removed his luxurious cloak, and gallantly laid it across the mud. The queen passed dryshod. As she walked on, she called back, "Hark ye, Master Raleigh, see thou fail not to wear thy muddy cloak." Raleigh did wear it—proudly—and Elizabeth gratefully bought him a new, finer one. This incident never happened, but the British people's wish to believe and preserve it and repeat it as fact proves the point: the British love courtesy and always have.

Here is another paragraph that aims for narrative development, but this one loses effectiveness in irrelevant detail, long-windedness, and poor sentence sequence.

EXAMPLE OF A POORLY STRUCTURED NARRATIVE PARAGRAPH

Great genius does not always include the practical intelligence needed for day-to-day survival. For example, there was the ancient philosopher Thales, who lived in Asia Minor. The ancient world, by the way, was fond of illustrating this point about genius with a class of stories told against philosophers and deep thinkers, stories that made philosophers out to be quite stupid in actuality. Anyhow, Thales was supposed to be this great astronomer and investigator into the causes of things in the heavens and beneath the earth. For instance, he thought water was the first element of reality. Well, one day he went out to gaze at the heavens and to contemplate universal cosmic harmony. Maybe as he walked around he also made calculations concerning the solar eclipse he predicted. (Yes, legend says he was the first to predict one.) Anyhow, as he walked along with eyes raised, he tumbled headfirst into a stinking ditch and spent the night in a daze and a quagmire. Finally some farmers the next morning pulled him out, but he of course carried no money to reward them, so they almost threw him back in. Thales may have been smart enough to foresee the disappearance of the sun, but he wasn't alert enough to see an ordinary ditch.

EX 4–4   On another sheet of paper, revise, tighten, and rewrite the preceding paragraph.

EX 4–5   Develop, on another sheet of paper, your own narrative illustration of a general point from the following assortment of time-related statements about the ancient Greek folk hero Sisyphus. Before you begin to write, determine what moral your story will illustrate. This will be your topic sentence.

- Sisyphus was once a famous, cunning, prosperous human being.
- He died unmourned and poorly honored by his wife.
- But those were his instructions to her.
- Actually Sisyphus died twice.
- Earlier in his life he tricked Death and tied him hand and foot. This deed enraged the immortal gods, especially Ares, the god of war, who was put out of business (no death, no war!).
- Ares released Death and turned him on Sisyphus.
- So Sisyphus instructed his wife to bury him badly.

- Dead, in Hades, Sisyphus complained to the lord of the underworld about his bad wife, asking permission to return briefly to bawl her out.
- Sisyphus returned to earth, loved his wife, and of course failed to return to Hades.
- You can't win.
- When he died the second time, Sisyphus was punished by the gods for his trickiness.
- They sentenced him to a menial task.
- He rolls the same boulder up the same hill forever; up he pushes, down it rolls, up he pushes.

In exposition—writing that seeks to convey information—narration usually exists for the sake of the general point it means to illustrate. A writer tells a story to drive home a moral or truth. But people also delight in stories for their own sake, regardless of moral or message. These two uses of narrative reflect two different writing purposes that you should strive to keep distinct. You don't want—and your audience probably doesn't want—your short composition to slip away from you and become a novel.

C. DEVELOPING A PARAGRAPH THAT EXPLAINS A PROCESS

Another very useful paragraph format also in a sense narrates things or events in sequence. Writers commonly refer to this development strategy as *process* writing, but most people also know it more familiarly in one of its forms as the "recipe." Process or recipe writing generally answers "how" questions: How does one bake bread, change a tire, operate a computer, or write a paragraph? Process writing is also a common and valuable strategy in technical accounts—say, from biology, physics, or chemistry laboratories. Describing the probable formation, in time or sequence, of the solar system, of the Grand Canyon, of the human fetus, of social groups, or of an ecosystem involves narrating a process. As with narration in the previous section, the organization of process writing is usually easily dictated by sequence: you mix dough before you knead it; you knead it before you bake it.

Here is a sample process paragraph. Study its sequences and transitions. Notice how the custom of general topic sentence followed by specifics still applies.

EXAMPLE OF A PARAGRAPH THAT DESCRIBES A PROCESS

Relatively simple but exacting techniques for reducing the size of circuits have made it possible to bring the computer into many homes and offices. Today a $25 computer chip does the work of many ENIACs (the first computer, which contained more than 18,000 vacuum tubes). These computer chips are produced by a process called photolithography. First, electronic circuits are drawn to specifications. Then these drawings are photographed and photographically reduced to a very small size. Next, through other procedures similar to ordinary photo-offset printing, these circuits are etched onto wafer-thin slices of crystalline germanium or silicon. Finally, when these chips are connected to a power source, the lines of the original drawing become tiny transistors and wires holding and conducting electricity. Imagine the lines of your handwriting conducting very tiny pulses of electricity, and imagine this writing reduced to a very small size and transferred to a sliver of stone. There you have it! Coming into the computer age, we have gone back to writing on stone tablets.

Process writing, because of its value in precise and specialized reporting, often involves relatively technical subjects. So the writer must be prepared to supply necessary definitions, synonyms, or paraphrases for difficult or technical terms.

EX 4-6   List the terms or phrases that the writer of the sample paragraph above should have further defined or paraphrased for an average audience.

_____

_____

_____

Here is another process paragraph, but this one is awkward in its sequence and transitions.

EXAMPLE OF A PARAGRAPH THAT DOES NOT DESCRIBE A PROCESS WELL

Falling asleep is a complex process, according to current scientific experiments using an electroencephalograph (EEG). For a few minutes, early light sleep produces an irregular brain wave or rhythm instead of the usual alpha wave on the EEG, during which time body temperature, breathing rate, blood pressure, and pulse also begin to decline. Brain waves occur with increased amplitude and frequency during the next half-hour. Temperature and blood pressure drop further during a transitional period. The EEG shows large, even delta waves to indicate full rest in deep sleep, with full relaxation. This process is repeated several times in the course of a night's rest.

EX 4-7   Revise and improve the preceding paragraph, in part by making the stages of the process clearer and easier to follow. Use a good dictionary to help you when you need to explain or define difficult or technical words. Write your revision on another sheet of paper.

EX 4-8   Here are some raw materials for narrating or describing a process. Choose from among these materials to compose your own successful process paragraph. Pay close attention to sequence and transitions, to technical terms, and to the clarity of the topic sentence. Try to make the paragraph interesting as well as accurate; in other words, do not reduce your subject to a monotonous recipe shorthand.

- *Fuel* or *fuelwood* is hardest to light, but biggest and longest burning.
- For safety, the ground around an open fire should be clear—scraped to plain dirt, gravel, clay, or rock.
- How to build a campfire.
- Light the *tinder*—dry grass, birch bark, weed-tops—with a match.
- *Tepee fire*, one of the easiest, most versatile campfires, is cone-shaped, with most flammable matter on the inside, fuel on the outside.
- Bring the marshmallows and the songs.
- The best fuel wood includes oak, hickory, and mesquite, but any substantial wood pieces will do.
- All combustibles should be dry or seasoned, not green.
- *Kindling* includes twigs and sticks of intermediate size, easier to ignite than fuel, harder to ignite than tinder.

EX 4-9   Cast yourself as a scientific observer and write a process paragraph describing some routine you have observed in the regular behavior of a teacher, roommate, or friend. For example, a professor preparing to lecture may repeat a series of gestures, movements, mannerisms, or activities that lend themselves to a process account. Write this paragraph on another sheet of paper.

D. DEVELOPING A PARAGRAPH THROUGH COMPARISON AND CONTRAST

Often the task of describing, explaining, or defining something is simplified by the use of comparison or contrast. Comparison usually helps a writer explain something relatively unfamiliar by means of something similar but relatively familiar. A writer might describe a rugby ball, for instance, by comparing it to a football. Contrast, however, is most helpful in separating or distinguishing something from other similar things with which it is often confused. A writer, for example, might distinguish Protestants from Catholics, Republicans from Democrats, snow skiing from water skiing by contrasting them ("snow skiing, unlike water skiing . . ."). Comparison or contrast can help you develop precision and vividness, but you must be selective. Since everything, in theory, is similar to and different from everything else, compare or contrast only when this strategy really does lend vividness, interest, or precision to your writing.

EX 4-10   Some of the following pairs are better suited to and more interesting as comparison; some better lend themselves to contrast. Identify which strategy better suits each pair by entering "contrast" or "comparison" in the blank. Be ready to justify your decisions.

1. _____ cricket and baseball

2. _____ country swing dancing and bebop

3. _____ ancient Olympic games and modern Olympics

4. _____ Russian manned spacecraft and U.S. manned spacecraft

5. _____ Cheyenne folklore and Anglo-American folklore

6. _____ mopeds and motorcycles

7. _____ Japanese samurai warrior and medieval knight

8. _____ ballet and modern dance

9. _____ medieval minstrels and modern folk singers

Where the average audience vaguely knows both terms, a contrast is helpful to sort out confusion and clear up the vagueness, as with ballet and modern dance. Where an average audience knows one term fairly well, but the second term—the term you really want to explain—hardly at all, then a comparison can be very helpful, as between the little-known samurai and the more familiar medieval knight.

A writer has successfully developed the following paragraph using the strategy of comparison.

EXAMPLE OF A PARAGRAPH OF COMPARISON

The famous Roman "circus," or chariot race, seems a strange form of amusement to us now, but in several respects the Roman circus—named after the *circle* or *circuit* of the track—resembles our modern professional sports. Like our horse racing, the circus took place around an oval track in a large, crowded, noisy stadium. And winning teams took away enormous prizes, comparable in size to today's top purses. But circuses were also *team* sports, like our pro football or basketball. As many as twelve chariots representing four different "factions" or teams—the Blues, the Greens, the Reds, and the Whites (we still use colors to name pro teams today!)—might vie for first place. Maybe you can imagine, in a twelve-chariot race, the mayhem that might be perpetrated, roller-derby fashion, in the name of teamwork. Ancient fans also loyally supported and wagered on their favorite faction with all the zeal of Dallas Cowboy or Green Bay Packer fans. Finally, chariot drivers, just like the Julius Ervings or George Bretts of today, earned enormous amounts of money and fame during their careers.

EX 4-11 Comparison and contrast depend on *important points* of similarity or difference. A successful writer of comparison or contrast specifies key similarities or differences. List five *points of comparison* between the ancient Roman circus and modern professional sports made by the writer of the sample paragraph above.

1. _____

2. _____

3. _____

4. _____

5. _____

Here is a descriptive paragraph that is unnecessarily flat and routine. As you read it, can you see how a comparison might better introduce the audience to the study of English?

EXAMPLE OF A PARAGRAPH THAT COULD BE BETTER DEVELOPED THROUGH COMPARISON

Studying English involves different learning tasks. A student learns many new technical terms for things in composition and grammar. Thus the student is able to distinguish, see, and study many things he or she may never before have noticed. A student is also expected to practice and improve careful procedures and techniques for producing polished or informative communication from the raw ingredients of ideas and experiences. So there are both theoretical and practical components to English coursework.

EX 4-12 Rework the preceding paragraph by introducing a comparison with a laboratory science class like chemistry. Try to let the comparison of an English class with a science class suggest ways you might expand and specify the topic further as you rewrite.

EX 4-13 Now write your own comparative description of some person, event, or thing. Find some topic you know better than most people and, in the interest of clarifying the less familiar for your audience by comparing it with the more familiar, find something with which you can compare your topic at several points. You might find a topic for your comparative paragraph among the following: going to a rock concert; preparing for a test, performance, or competition; practicing a sport or instrument; pursuing a hobby or passion.

E. EMPHASIZING POINTS OF DIFFERENCE

Contrast, as was mentioned before, can be used to distinguish something from other similar things with which it may be confused. The writer of the following successful paragraph of contrast tries to distinguish two similar things often vaguely confused. Notice how here the writer emphasizes key *points of difference*, where comparison emphasized key points of similarity.

EXAMPLE OF A PARAGRAPH OF CONTRAST

Now that the Republican Party seems to be gaining the upper hand in American politics, many people wonder just what differences they can expect after years of Democratic politics. Unlike the Democratic Party, which favors legislative and federal action where necessary to ensure social and economic justice, the Republican Party favors reduced government interference in and greater reliance on "free market" forces to satisfy social and economic needs. A freer market, Republicans say, will produce more real money, more jobs, and a better standard of living for the deserving. Republicans, differing from Democrats, advocate reduced government budgets and taxes and fewer public services. And unlike Democrats, who have allied their cause with the federal, Washington-based machinery built by President Franklin D. Roosevelt during the 1930s, the Republicans see state and local governments as more manageable and more responsive to their interests. Finally, in a larger sense, while Democrats push for community responsibility and a sense of belonging to a group, the Republicans seem to champion personal freedoms and a sense of individuality. Of course, most Americans, Democrat and Republican alike, favor *all* these aims, so perhaps those who seek a return to Thomas Jefferson and his "Democratic Republican" party really speak for the majority.

EX 4-14 List below four key *points of contrast* between Democrats and Republicans noted by the writer.

1. _____
2. _____
3. _____
4. _____

Here is an expository paragraph that has been developed in run-of-the-mill fashion. As you read it, can you see how a *contrast* might help pin down the special quality of its topic, "college study"?

**EXAMPLE OF A PARAGRAPH THAT COULD BE
BETTER DEVELOPED THROUGH CONTRAST**

College coursework is much harder than it looks. Actual classwork may involve only two or three hours a day. But much of this time is spent listening to complex lectures, taking notes furiously, and trying to comprehend dense material. To absorb class information effectively, a student must use notes to replay classes mentally after class. And teachers expect students to devote much out-of-class time to study, preparation, and independent research. Textbooks too are thick and complex, and they must quickly be consumed; required papers and tests are long and demanding. Furthermore, most of a college student's classmates regard themselves as superior in motivation, talents, and competitiveness. Add these facts together and you will see why college is much harder than it may appear at first.

EX 4-15 Rewrite and enliven the preceding paragraph by introducing a contrast with high school coursework. In other words, show how tough college coursework is by contrast with high school work. As with the comparison in EX 4-12, let this contrast suggest further ways you might expand and specify your point as you rewrite.

EX 4-16   Write your own contrast paragraph distinguishing for an average audience some similar things often vaguely confused. You might follow the above example and explore some other area of contrast—in leisure, living arrangements, sports, dating—between your life now and your life before you came to college. Or you might develop some other topic that strikes you as suitable for development by contrast. Use another sheet of paper to write this paragraph.

F. DEVELOPING A PARAGRAPH BY MEANS OF ANALOGY

Writing built around a surprising or poetical or imaginative comparison is customarily termed development by *analogy*. Here, as with comparison, a writer presents the less familiar or graspable in light of the more familiar, more vivid, or more accessible. For example, a writer may choose to explain the functioning of the lymphatic system, one of the human body's internal defense systems, by making an analogy between the lymphatic system and an army. Used wisely, development by analogy can be a powerful and entertaining way to describe or suggest the essence of a person, process, or thing.

EXAMPLE OF A PARAGRAPH DEVELOPED THROUGH ANALOGY

Psychologists tell us that much of our thought or mental process is unconscious; we are unaware of it. The unconscious side of the mind resembles those dragons and snakes of folklore and mythology. Thus our repressed or denied wishes occasionally flash out of darkness, in visionary dreams or in odd slips of the tongue, just like the surprised snake that whips quietly through the grass and then is gone back under the ground or into the denser foliage. And like a snake, such hints of our unconscious—what Freud called our *id*, or "it"—shows us both beauty and terror, like those marvelously decorated, ornamented, painted dragons of legend that, despite their cold beauty, brought plague and destruction. These two-sided images from the mind show us both the delightful beauty of fully satisfied desire and the destruction that would follow, like a dragon, the release of such power. Our feelings toward snakes in a way actually parallel our feelings toward the hidden part of ourselves.

EX 4-17   Here are some striking comparisons or analogies. In each case, list possible interesting correspondences between the two terms. Use your imagination. Do your writing on another sheet of paper.

1. A celebrity really is like a star.
2. Polishing writing is like applying makeup.
3. Football is like chess.
4. Roommates are more like pet cats than like pet dogs.

EX 4-18   Here are some topics. Find an analogy for each that you think you could use to develop an effective descriptive paragraph.

1. a science textbook (is like a) _____

2. an upperclassman or upperclasswoman _____

3. a white-collar criminal or embezzler _____

4. cruising Main Street _____

5. registration for the draft _____

EX 4-19 Choose one of the analogies from EX 4-17 or EX 4-18 and develop it into a paragraph. Analogy, like comparison, has a major and minor term; use the *minor term* (the item of comparison) primarily to highlight or focus on the *major term* (the topic of your paragraph).

G. PRESENTING AN INTERPRETATION BASED ON CAUSE AND EFFECT

A very important kind of college writing concerns the interpretation of a thing, a person, an event, a quotation, or a text. Often this strategy of development views a thing as an effect or result and then tries to explain that result in light of its probable causes. What made Winston Churchill so powerful a leader? Why has the United Nations proven so ineffective in preventing war and conflict? What has driven these pine grosbeaks so far off their usual migratory routes this year? What makes the sky blue?

Sometimes a process—a chain of causes and effects—may best account for such a thing as the color of the sky or changes in animal behavior. At other times, perhaps a list of likely causes and conditions is as close as you can come to an interpretive account, say, of Churchill's success or Neville Chamberlain's failure.

EXAMPLE OF A PARAGRAPH THAT DEVELOPS A CAUSAL INTERPRETATION OF AN EVENT

A number of factors brought about Custer's famous "Last Stand." For one, the battle came as a result of foul-ups in deployment, consolidation, and reinforcement of the huge army of which Custer's 7th Cavalry was a part. These foul-ups allowed Custer, an impetuous and politically ambitious individual, to seize personal initiative and prematurely engage the enemy. He apparently sought the instant celebrity that would come from a stunning, dramatic victory in the Indian wars. This hope seems to have led him greatly to underestimate the size of the Indian encampment he attacked. He also, perhaps foolishly, divided his 700-man force into three parts, thereby creating problems of battle communication and coordination that left his personal command to absorb the brunt of the Sioux and Cheyenne counterattack. Finally, his adversaries on this occasion proved exceptionally keen for battle. The Indian nations brought against Custer not only more troops with higher morale, but also fresher, better-armed fighters.

EX 4-20 List *five* causes or conditions that the writer cites as contributing to Custer's "Last Stand."

1. _____

2. _____

3. _____

4. _____

5. _____

Here is another, less successful interpretive paragraph. As you read it, notice how much clearer and more effective it would be if the writer focused simply on an enumeration or list of causes.

EXAMPLE OF A PARAGRAPH THAT DOES NOT EFFECTIVELY FOCUS ON CAUSES

Headaches afflict most people at some point or other in life. Scientists are not sure what causes headaches, although they have pinpointed a number of possible causes. The headache, after all, is usually a symptom, an indication of some underlying problem, and not itself the ultimate problem. Hormonal changes may cause headaches. Aspirin may not be able to help these. But it can help headaches brought about in some people by certain foods or chemicals in foods. Headaches may also occur when blood vessels in the brain expand and put pressure on sensitive nerves. Headaches may also be traced to sinus conditions or anemia or colds. Treatment of the headache then comes second to a more general cure of bed rest, extra fluids, and so on. Probably the most familiar headache comes from muscle tightness in the back, head, and neck. This tightness is in turn caused by exertion or worry or stress.

EX 4-21   On another sheet of paper, rewrite and simplify this paragraph by tying it to a clearer, more precise topic sentence. Focus on the *causes* of headache and eliminate half-hearted, irrelevant references to possible cures.

EX 4-22   On another sheet of paper, write your own paragraph of causal interpretation in answer to this question: What brought about the famous feud between the Hatfields and the McCoys (1863–1889)? Select your specifics from among facts given below. Some information may be irrelevant to the question.

- The Hatfields of West Virginia and the McCoys of Kentucky lived up in the same mountain valley but on opposite sides of a creek, in different states.
- During the Civil War, the Hatfields went Confederate; the McCoys fought for the Union.
- Many more McCoys than Hatfields died during the feud.
- Hatfields often defied the law.
- McCoys often complained to authorities and sought redress at law.
- Many trivial but inflammatory incidents occurred during the feud's early years: a dispute over a hog, jealousy over interfamily marriages and courtings.
- Moonshine whiskey often helped to reinforce passions.
- In the backwoods there was tremendous family pride and loyalty.
- Officers were unwilling or afraid to act in the dangerous mountain back country.
- Both families practiced mountain traditions of hunting, lawbreaking, and private justice.
- A number of violent incidents of increasing seriousness and killings triggered the full-scale feud.

H. PRESENTING INTERPRETATIONS OF TEXTS AND OF QUOTATIONS

A special but important kind of cause-effect writing focuses on the interpretation of texts or quotations. What features of a sentence, a saying, a story, a letter, a poem, or an essay account for its total effect? Readers or listeners often grasp such communications readily enough, in a vague way. But describing or analyzing precise content or intent often demands closer attention to the causes of an overall impression.

Here is a paragraph that takes a short quotation for its topic. The paragraph views the quotation as an effect or result and successfully interprets its intention or motivation as a cause.

EXAMPLE OF A PARAGRAPH INTERPRETING A QUOTATION

Plato, the famous Greek philosopher, wrote that "Wonder is the feeling of a philosopher, and philosophy begins in wonder." The first part of this quotation actually forms a tight denotative definition: "wonder" is a kind of human feeling, specifically the feeling that distinguishes the philosopher from other people. To the extent that you or I or Plato feels wonder, we are philosophers. The second part of the quotation suggests how thought—how questions of why, what, how—is born from this feeling, from the experience of surprise, amazement, awe, curiosity, all included in the word *wonder.* Philosophy thus springs from a human capacity for wonder and from a human desire for answers to basic questions. According to Plato's account, what a loss it is if everyone is not at least partly a philosopher!

Here is another interpretive paragraph in which the writer vaguely perceives the intention of a quotation, but fails to pay adequate attention to the quotation's specific content.

**EXAMPLE OF A PARAGRAPH THAT FAILS TO
EXPLORE THE SENSE OF A QUOTATION**

The founder of Islam, Muhammad, wrote that "The ink of the scholar is more sacred than the blood of the martyr." Such a statement is really surprising coming from a religious leader. You would expect him to praise the martyr for dying for his faith. Maybe Muhammad thought that it was better to live than to die.

EX 4-23   On another sheet of paper, rewrite the preceding paragraph. Try to account more precisely for the power of the quotation, as well as for the use of this particular phrasing. For instance, you might consider the contrast between *ink* and *blood.* Why might the founder of a major religion express more concern for scholars than for martyrs?

EX 4-24   Write your own paragraph interpreting the following quotation, attributed to Ben Joseph Akiba. Akiba was a great Jewish religious leader of the first century. He was burned at the stake along with the Torah, the sacred book of Judaism. He reportedly said, "The paper burns, but the words fly away." What did he mean? What is so powerful about this statement?

EX 4-25   Write a paragraph analyzing the most famous quotation of Calvin Coolidge, a Republican, the thirtieth President of the United States. He said, "The business of America is business." What did he mean? What is so powerful or memorable about this statement?

WORKSHOP

1. Narrate some personal experience that taught you practical knowledge the hard way, so that next time you knew how to do something better or were better able to perform some task or procedure. Take time to *describe* a beginning situation before you begin to *narrate* a rush of events. (Examples of such a narration include how not to light a pilot light, how not to study for a test, how not to make party punch, how not to bid a boyfriend or girlfriend goodbye.)

2. Narrate some serious encounter you have had with yourself, with nature, or with human nature—an encounter that surprised you with deeper truths about these subjects or that

taught you some wisdom. Describe a beginning situation before you begin to narrate significant moments of your encounter. Be selective and control your story's pace. Conclude your tale with a moral or statement of what you learned from your experience.

3. Write a paper for a general, average audience on some technical subject you know better than most people. Technical subjects can range from computers and physics to gardening, cooking, surfing, skiing, and baseball. Each of these areas involves special vocabulary and procedures; each is a mystery to many people, one that you may be able to help dispel. Find a good introductory topic or question for your audience: What are the keys to power hitting? What are the main differences between ballet and modern dance? As you develop your paper, be careful to define or paraphrase technical terms or phrases to help initiate your audience into the mysteries of these skills.

4. Find a paragraph or technical description in a textbook, lab manual, or cookbook and translate it into ordinary language for an average audience.

5. Narrative and process development organize a paragraph in a *time* sequence. But it is also possible to organize a descriptive paragraph spatially. Write a paragraph in which you describe the movements of someone you see right now. Relate the person's movements to fixed objects or structures. Help your reader to form a mental picture of the movements by using locational words and phrases—"along the south wall," "next to the drinking fountain," "across the open space at the front of the classroom"—to tell where this person goes.

6. Write a spatial description of your bedroom. Survey or inventory this space according to some logical progression. Be selective: describe only the most striking, important, or distinctive features of your room. Help your reader to form a mental picture of your room by using locational words and phrases to cue your survey.

7. Take one of your favorite poems or song lyrics and write a paragraph of interpretation explaining why you like it so well. What is so powerful or memorable about this poem or song lyric?

8. Write paragraphs commenting on one or all of the following slogans, sayings, or proverbs. Why are these sayings so powerful and so memorable?
   a. Haste makes waste.
   b. The meek shall inherit the earth.
   c. I never met a man I didn't like. (Will Rogers)
   d. Ask not what your country can do for you; ask what you can do for your country. (John F. Kennedy)
   e. Nice guys finish last. (attributed to Leo Durocher)
   f. Man is not material; he is spiritual. (Mary Baker Eddy)
   g. You're never too old to become younger. (Mae West)

Writing Sentences

Composing Simple and Compound Sentences

5

A. RECOGNIZING SENTENCES AND FRAGMENTS

The fundamental unit in verbal communication is the *sentence*. Individual words do have meaning, of course, but they communicate only when thoughtfully selected and arranged in sensible order—that is, when organized into sentences.

EX 5-1   Underline each item below that is a sentence.

        EXAMPLE: <u>Blue jays are intelligent birds.</u>

1. These sassy birds.
2. Bluejays learn quickly.
3. Birds at good these avoiding sassy are traps.
4. Avoiding traps.
5. These sassy birds are good at avoiding traps.
6. Faster than some cats and dogs.

A sentence is, by definition, the expression of a single complete thought. A group of words that does not express a complete thought is called a *fragment*.

EXAMPLE OF A SENTENCE
The Arctic Ocean is the northernmost body of water on earth.

EXAMPLES OF FRAGMENTS
The icy Barents Sea. [This does not tell what the Barents Sea *is* or *does*; it is not a complete thought.]

Looking to this icy region for future energy needs. [This does not tell *who* or *what* is looking.]

Because the land beneath the Beauford Sea may contain oil. [This is a half-thought. It states a cause, but does not state the effect that the writer has in mind.]

EX 5–2 Three of the numbered items below are sentences. Three are fragments. Underline the three sentences.

> EXAMPLE: <u>Many people dream of owning fancy cars.</u>

1. Sad news for new car buyers.
2. Daimler-Benz has discontinued production of the Mercedes 600.
3. The firm produced 2,677 of these autos between 1963 and 1981.
4. A favorite car of foreign oil tycoons and rock superstars.
5. Being faced with rising costs and decreasing demand.
6. Those with $75,000 to spend on a new car must now look elsewhere.

Why do well-schooled people unintentionally write fragments now and then? Some of their confusion may be explained by the fact that *spoken English* and *written English* do not parallel each other perfectly. Spoken sentences customarily leave out parts of thoughts that are understood by both the speaker and the listener. Formal written English, however, does not permit this.

Each of the sentences spoken in the conversation below would be a fragment if it appeared in a paragraph rather than as part of a conversation.

> *"Going somewhere?"* Toni asked.
> *"To the gym,"* Brad replied.
> *"With whom?"* Toni asked.
> *"Pete and Big Fred,"* he answered.

Think what words would be needed to make each of these comments into a complete sentence.

EX 5–3 Circle each item below that is *not* a sentence. On another sheet of paper, rewrite these fragments so that they become complete sentences.

> EXAMPLE: (Have listened to old blues recordings.) *Many rock singers have*
>
> *listened to old blues recordings.*

1. Today's rock musicians owe a large debt to the black Chicago blues musicians of the 1940s and 1950s.

2. Muddy Waters, the most popular of the Chicago blues singers.

3. Born on a farm near Clarksdale, Mississippi, on April 4, 1915.

4. Although his given name was McKinley Morganfield, he soon became known as Muddy Waters.

5. Because a muddy creek ran behind his family's small home.

6. He took up the harmonica at age thirteen.

7. Began learning guitar at seventeen.

8. Mississippi was then a hotbed of great blues performers.

9. Son House, Robert Johnson, Willie Brown, Tommy Johnson, and Charley Patton.

10. Muddy Waters learned from these masters.

11. A popular performer in the Clarksdale area when he was in his early twenties.

12. Still picking cotton, though, for less than 30 cents an hour.

13. He took a train north to Chicago in 1943.

14. In just a few years Muddy Waters became the most popular blues performer in Chicago.

15. The writer of numerous blues standards, such as "Rollin' and Tumblin'."

16. His band featured such fine musicians as harmonica player Little Walter Horton and pianist Otis Spann.

17. The Rolling Stones reportedly got their name from a line in one of Muddy Waters's songs.

18. Many rock groups have recorded his songs.

19. His vocal and guitar style imitated by thousands of rockers.

20. Muddy Waters still recording and touring in 1981, when he turned sixty-five.

EX 5–4   Find and underline the six fragments in the paragraph below. Then, on another sheet of paper, rewrite the paragraph, making sentences out of the fragments.

> Colored flags are used to give important signals to drivers during auto races. The green flag means "start" or "continue." The yellow flag tells drivers to slow down and hold position. The red flag, a signal to stop. When drivers see the black flag. They know they must pull into the pit area immediately. A blue flag with yellow stripes is used to tell slower drivers to pull over and allow the leaders to pass. The two favorite flags of most drivers. The white flag, which means "one lap to go." And the checkered flag. Which means "you have reached the finish."

B. RECOGNIZING COMPLETE SUBJECTS AND PREDICATES

Another way to distinguish sentences from fragments is by identifying *subject* and *predicate*. All written sentences have both a subject and a predicate.

Look at this sentence. Notice that it is divided into two parts.

The reptile trainer / patted the large iguana.

Which part of the sentence tells who did something? _____

Which part tells what happened? _____

The *complete subject* tells who or what the sentence is about. It usually consists of a naming word—a *noun* or a *pronoun*—and one or more modifiers. In some sentences, though, a single noun or pronoun is the complete subject.

EXAMPLES

Oxpeckers light upon the backs of African cattle.

These unusual birds search their hosts' hides for ticks.

The same ticks that torment cattle make tasty meals for oxpeckers.

The complete predicate usually includes all other words in the sentence. These words tell what the subject *does*, or they *explain* something about the subject. In sentences where the subject receives the action, the predicate tells what *is done* to the subject.

EXAMPLES
Other birds *follow African cattle, too.* [Here the complete predicate tells what the subject *does.*]

Swallows, cattle egrets, and carmine bee eaters *are cattle followers.* [Here the complete predicate *explains* something about the subject.]

Insects stirred up by the cattle's hooves *are devoured by bright-eyed birds.* [Here the complete predicate tells what *is done* to the subject.]

EX 5-5   The sentences below have been divided into complete subject and complete predicate. Write *CS* above each complete subject; write *CP* above each complete predicate.

                  CS   CP
        EXAMPLE: Julia Morgan / designed small homes and great public buildings.

1. "Buildings / should be unobtrusive elements on a landscape."

2. This sensible opinion / was espoused by Morgan throughout her career.

3. Morgan / earned an international reputation as an architect during the early twentieth century.

4. Her warm, inviting buildings of wood and rough-cut stone / were praised by many.

5. One of her most famous creations / violates her own credo of simplicity and harmony.

6. Julia Morgan / designed the showy, ornate Hearst Castle in San Simeon, California.

As you have noticed, the normal order of sentence elements is *subject / predicate.* The *verb* (either an action word or a form of *be*, such as *is* or *are*) is usually the first word in the predicate.

EX 5-6   Draw one line under the complete subject in each sentence below. Draw two lines under the complete predicate. (Note that in item 7, the first word in the predicate is not a verb.)

        EXAMPLE: Ball lightning is a terrifying phenomenon.

1. Ball lightning may occur during thunderstorms.
2. A globe of ball lightning looks bluish or reddish yellow.
3. Some globes are the size of grapes.
4. One was the size of a basketball.
5. A globe of ball lightning floats through the air like a soap bubble.
6. It can severely harm people and animals.
7. The sight of ball lightning usually terrifies onlookers.
8. Common objects are destroyed upon contact with ball lightning.

9. This strange fireball may suddenly disappear.

10. A loud bang may be heard at that moment.

11. Some scientists call ball lightning an imaginary phenomenon.

12. They do not believe in its existence.

13 Pyotr Kapitsa considers ball lightning a true phenomenon.

14. This Nobel Prize winner has investigated ball lightning.

15. Ball lightning is a light-emitting plasma, in Kapitsa's opinion.

16. Other eminent scientists hold different theories about ball lightning.

17. Physicist James Dale Barry has written a comprehensive book on the subject.

18. Future research may reveal the true nature of ball lightning.

You can improve your ability to describe action by thinking carefully about the subjects and predicates of your sentences. The subject should specify *who* or *what* was involved. The predicate should tell exactly what happened; it may also tell *how*, *when*, *where*, or *why* this happened.

EX 5–7   The following items need subjects to become complete sentences. Think of stores in your area as you fill the blanks. Try to provide enough information to enable someone reading the completed sentences to know which stores and people you are writing about.

> EXAMPLE: *The small green store on the corner of First and Locust streets* sells fresh-ground coffee.

1. _____
   sells athletic shoes.

2. _____
   offers film developing.

3. _____
   treats customers nicely.

4. _____
   has a good selection of video games.

5. _____
   sells groceries after 7 P.M.

6. _____
   seems unwilling to help customers

EX 5–8   The following items need predicates to become complete sentences. Think of a fast-food restaurant in your area. Fill the blanks with predicates that tell about actions. Try to provide enough information to enable someone reading the completed sentences to know what type of place you are writing about.

> EXAMPLE: The bright electric sign *towers over the shopping center*.

1. Some of the counter people _____

2. The elderly patrons _____

3. Young children _____

4. High school students on dates _____

5. The manager _____

6. People waiting for their orders _____

C. IDENTIFYING SIMPLE SUBJECTS AND PREDICATES

The *simple subject* is the noun or pronoun in the complete subject that tells what the sentence is talking about. The other words in the complete subject modify the simple subject.

EXAMPLES OF SIMPLE SUBJECTS
The steep steel *ladder* has become slippery.

The *woman* in blue overalls climbs slowly and carefully. [It is the *woman*, not the *overalls*, that is climbing.]

Passersby stare at this lonely figure. [In this sentence the simple subject and the complete subject are the same.]

The *cab* of the crane is still several feet above her. [The *cab* is being discussed here; the phrase *of the crane* is a modifier.]

Helen Hansen will soon be ready for the day's tasks. [In this sentence the two-word noun *Helen Hansen* is both the simple subject and the complete subject.]

The *simple predicate* in a sentence describing action is the word or phrase that tells what the subject did or what was done to the subject. It is the verb that goes with the subject. It usually appears at the beginning of the complete predicate, though occasionally a modifier will precede it.

EXAMPLES OF SIMPLE PREDICATES IN SENTENCES DESCRIBING ACTION
Hansen *grabs* her two-way radio.

She *must call* down to the signal person below. [*Must call* describes the action of the subject.]

The signal person *has been given* instructions by the foreman. [*Has been given* explains the action of the subject.]

The signal person quickly *flips* through the sheets of paper on her clipboard. [Here the modifier *quickly* precedes the simple predicate *flips*.]

The simple predicate in a sentence that *describes* or *defines* the subject is usually a form of the verb *be* or a phrase that ends with a form of *be*: *is, are, was, were, has been, have been, will be,* and so on.

EXAMPLES OF SIMPLE PREDICATES IN SENTENCES OF DEFINITION
Hansen's cab *is* high above the deck.

Yesterday *was* a rainy, blustery day.

The job *had been* on schedule until last Thursday. [*Been* is a form of *be*.]

Today *should be* a good day for making up time. [This verb phrase ends with *be*.]

EX 5-9 The sentences below have been divided into complete subject and complete predicate. Draw one line under the *simple subject* in each sentence. Draw two lines under the *simple predicate* (the verb).

EXAMPLE: <u>Laurie Anderson</u> / <u><u>surprises</u></u> people with her music.

1. She / uses tape machines in her performances.
2. This innovative performer / has sung duets with herself.
3. Some of these duets / feature a tape-delayed second vocal part.
4. Not many young composers / can blend strange sounds into listenable compositions.
5. Anderson / is known for her sharp sense of humor.
6. Radio stations with innovative programming / sometimes play Anderson's compositions.

EX 5-10 Draw one line under the simple subject in each sentence. Draw two lines under the simple predicate (the verb). (Remember that nouns following words like *in* and *of* cannot be simple subjects.)

EXAMPLE: A <u>native</u> of Hannibal, Missouri, <u><u>may be</u></u> America's greatest humorist.

1. Mark Twain wrote *The Adventures of Huckleberry Finn.*
2. Millions of Americans have learned about life on the Mississippi River from this book.
3. The town of Hannibal is no longer a small river town.
4. About 20,000 people live in Hannibal today.
5. Many of these people work in industrial plants in or near the town.
6. Tourism has been big business in Hannibal for some time, as well.
7. Small gift shops offer visitors mementos of Mark Twain country.
8. The town holds a unique celebration near the Mark Twain Boyhood Home each July.
9. The National Tom Sawyer Fence Painting Contest is held at the white board fence near Twain's home.
10. Young painters from all over the country can demonstrate their abilities with a whitewash brush.

EX 5-11 Imagine that you are writing a page for a time capsule. On another sheet of paper, write ten short sentences about notable things people have done during the last year. Draw one line under each complete subject. Draw two lines under each complete predicate.

EX 5-12 Now write ten short sentences about what certain friends of yours did during the past week. Draw one line under each simple subject. Draw two lines under each simple predicate. Use another sheet of paper for your writing.

D. WRITING COMPOUND SUBJECTS

Most of the sentences presented up to this point in this chapter have been *simple sentences*. That is, each has had *one* simple subject and *one* simple predicate, with no other subject–verb combinations. Many thoughts can best be expressed in simple sentences. It is often necessary, though, to add elements to the basic pattern of the simple sentence.

A sentence is said to have a *compound subject* if its subject includes two or more items joined by a conjunction, such as *and* or *or*.

EXAMPLES OF SENTENCES WITH COMPOUND SUBJECTS
<u>Santiago</u>, <u>Talcahuano</u>, *and* <u>Valparaiso</u> are cities in Chile. [This compound subject has three parts.]

<u>Fishmeal from ocean fish</u> *and* <u>copper from huge mines</u> are exported by Chilean firms. [*Fishmeal* and *copper* are two items that make up a compound subject.]

Neither <u>rain</u> *nor* <u>snow</u> falls for years on end on the Atacama Desert in Chile. [*Neither/nor* is a two-word conjunction.]

THIS SENTENCE DOES *NOT* HAVE A COMPOUND SUBJECT
The high Andes in eastern Chile are always covered with snow. [*Chile* is not an item in a compound subject. It is part of a phrase that modifies *Andes*.]

EX 5-13   Underline each sentence that has a compound subject.

> EXAMPLE: <u>Six-foot-long pencils and giant paper clips</u> are on sale at Pop/Eye Productions in New York City.

1. Phyllis Prinz and Robert Malkin are the owners of this unusual store.
2. Giant replicas of everyday objects are on sale.
3. Huge chocolate chip cookies and monstrous coat hangars catch the eyes of browsers.
4. The prices of the objects are large, too.
5. A six-foot paint brush and a super-sized screwdriver will cost a buyer about $1,000 apiece.
6. An unforgettable gift or a sure-fire conversation piece can be found for $100 or less.

EX 5-14   Eight of the following sentences have compound subjects. Underline each part of the compound subject in each sentence. Circle the conjunction that connects the parts.

> EXAMPLE: <u>Greeting cards</u> (and) <u>other tokens of friendship</u> were collected by
> many Americans during the first part of the twentieth century.

1. The colorful illustrations and the sentimental verses on the greeting cards appealed to many.

2. Young people and adults pasted these cards in albums.

3. The sarcastic verses on many of today's cards would be out of place in such a book.

4. Flowers and birds adorned a great many cards in former years.

5. Holidays and birthdays called for cards with special messages.

6. Valentine's Day, St. Patrick's Day, and even April Fool's Day were occasions for the exchange of cards.

7. Perhaps a grandparent, great-aunt, or great-uncle of yours put together an album of greeting cards.

8. You and your family might enjoy a look through the pages.

9. These little treasures from long ago reflect the social values of those times.

10. Thoughts and words from friends may indeed be worth preserving.

EX 5–15   Rewrite each sentence below as a sentence with a compound subject. Use your imagination as you supply the second part of each subject. Write your sentences on another sheet of paper.

> EXAMPLE: Kerosene lamps lit the parlors of American homes a century ago.
> *Kerosene lamps and gas lamps lit the parlors of American homes a century ago.*

1. Coal provided fuel for fireplaces.
2. Horse-drawn wagons carried goods from place to place.
3. Barges moved up and down America's great rivers.
4. Mules pulled plows on farms.
5. Electric streetcars carried people from place to place in cities.
6. New York had already become a great city by the early 1880s.

EX 5–16   Rewrite each pair of sentences below as a sentence with a compound subject. Use the conjunctions provided in parentheses. Write your sentences on another sheet of paper.

> EXAMPLE: Spies are a part of any war. Counterspies are a part of any war, too. (and)
> *Spies and counterspies are a part of any war.*

1. Australia fought against Japan in World War II. The United States fought against Japan, too. (and)
2. Foreign agents spied for the Japanese in Indonesia during the war. So did some Dutch residents of Indonesia. (and)
3. American troops in the area needed information about Japanese maneuvers. Australian forces also required this information. (and)
4. Banda MacLeod became a spy for the Allies. Banda's friend Abdul became a spy for the Allies, too. (and)
5. Banda's uncle believed Banda to be spying for Japan. The Japanese forces also believed Banda to be spying for Japan. (and)
6. Her uncle, who was himself a spy for the Japanese, did not suspect Banda MacLeod of being a double agent. Neither did the Japanese command in Indonesia. (neither/nor)

EX 5-17   Supply a compound subject to make each of the following items a complete sentence.

> EXAMPLE: *Cat howls and owl hoots* can be frightening noises at night.

1. _____ are two common sights in horror movies.

2. _____ often use their sharp teeth on foolish people in these films.

3. _____ hide in dark corners.

4. _____ make ideal settings for frightening scenes.

5. _____ are two well-known horror films.

6. _____ are featured creatures in several horror films.

7. _____ enjoy late-night horror films on TV.

8. _____ show classic horror films on Halloween night.

E. WRITING COMPOUND PREDICATES

A predicate may also be compound. A sentence is said to have a *compound predicate* when it contains two or more verbs that relate to the same subject and are joined by a conjunction.

> **EXAMPLES OF SENTENCES WITH COMPOUND PREDICATES**
> Babe Didrikson *ran* hurdles and *threw* the javelin. [*Ran* and *threw* are verbs that tell what Didrikson did.]
>
> She *won* two gold medals in the 1932 Olympics but *was* denied a medal in the high jump.
>
> **THIS SENTENCE DOES *NOT* HAVE A COMPOUND PREDICATE**
> Didrikson began to play golf in 1935. [The verb *play* does not relate directly to *Didrikson*. It is part of the phrase *to play golf in 1935*, which modifies the verb *began*. Note also that no conjunction is present here.]

EX 5-18   Underline each sentence that has a compound predicate.

> EXAMPLE: Armadillos move slow and think slower.

1. These small beasts sleep during the day and look for food at night.
2. Their armorlike covering protects them from most predators.
3. They root for grubs and insects and can quickly destroy a lawn.
4. Armadillos can be caught but cannot be trained.
5. Armadillo races are popular events in some parts of Texas.

6. Armadillos are not competitive runners like dogs or horses.

7. Handlers jump around and scream at the armadillos.

8. Sometimes a racing armadillo becomes confused, turns around, and runs in the wrong direction.

EX 5–19   Ten of the following sentences have compound predicates. Underline each part of the compound predicate in each sentence. Circle the conjunction that connects the parts.

EXAMPLE: The goddess Maia built a fire (and) heated some water.

1. She looked at her newborn son Hermes and smiled.

2. Hermes grew rapidly and was the size of a four-year-old in a few hours.

3. He left his cradle and walked out of the cave.

4. He was looking for adventure.

5. He saw a herd of magnificent cattle and thought of a clever scheme.

6. The cattle belonged to the god Apollo.

7. Hermes made shoes and placed them on the hooves of the cattle.

8. This mischievous youth led the herd away into a dark wood and tied them all to trees.

9. Apollo was not pleased by the mysterious disappearance of his cattle.

10. A satyr by the name of Silenus discovered the identity of the thief and reported it to Apollo.

11. Apollo flew down to earth and confronted Maia, Hermes' mother.

12. She yawned and denied the accusation.

13. Hermes was too young to steal cows, in her opinion.

14. Hermes later admitted his sin to Apollo and was granted forgiveness by the god because of his youthful charm and cleverness.

EX 5–20   Rewrite each sentence below as a sentence with a compound predicate. Use your imagination to supply the second part of each predicate. Write your sentences on another sheet of paper.

EXAMPLE: Hurricanes destroy houses.
Hurricanes destroy houses and uproot trees.

1. Tornadoes toss cars about.
2. Huge waves drown swimmers.
3. Hailstorms harm plants.
4. Earthquakes frighten people.
5. Floods destroy bridges.
6. Volcanic eruptions cover the land with ash.

EX 5–21   Rewrite each pair of sentences below as a single sentence with a compound predicate. Use the conjunction provided in parentheses. Write your sentences on another sheet of paper.

> EXAMPLE: Wilbert Heyman has reached the age of ninety-one. He has not retired. (but)
> *Wilbert Heyman has reached the age of ninety-one but has not retired.*

1. Heyman has been an inventor for more than half a century. He has received eighteen patents. (and)
2. Before World War II Heyman worked on chocolate beverages. He eventually developed one called Chocolate-Mello. (and)
3. This sterilized beverage tasted good. It did not spoil. (and)
4. During World War II the U.S. Army wanted coffee for its troops. They found ground coffee beans to be bulky and slow to prepare. (but)
5. Heyman had been working on an instant coffee. He heard of the army's interest in this product. (and)
6. The army's quartermaster tried Heyman's product. He found it quite tasty. (and)
7. Heyman manufactured several million pounds of instant coffee during the war. He was sent an official thank-you letter by the U.S. Army in 1946. (and)
8. Heyman has created coffee for millions. He never drinks it himself. (but)

EX 5–22   Write a compound predicate in each blank to make the following items complete sentences.

> EXAMPLE: Dentists *fill cavities and clean teeth.*

1. Receptionists _____
2. Carpenters _____
3. Delicatessen owners _____
4. Doctors _____
5. Fishing guides _____
6. College students _____

F. WRITING COMPOUND SENTENCES

Look at the following items.

a. Iceland is an island.
b. Italy is a peninsula.
c. Iceland is an island, and Italy is a peninsula.

What was done to the first two sentences to create the third sentence? _____

Underline the subject in the first part of sentence *c*; draw a circle around the predicate. Then underline the subject in the second part of sentence *c*, and circle the predicate.

A *compound sentence* has two or more subject–predicate combinations. The parts are joined by a coordinating conjunction—usually *and*, *but*, or *or*—or by a semicolon.

EXAMPLES OF COMPOUND SENTENCES

Red onions are zesty, but I prefer green onions on my chili.

Chili need not contain beans; champion chili makers often prepare all-meat chili.

THESE SENTENCES ARE *NOT* COMPOUND SENTENCES

Armadillo meat and rabbit meat make good chili. [This is a simple sentence with a compound subject.]

Chili with jalapeño peppers scorches the tongue and clears the nose. [This is a simple sentence with a compound predicate.]

EX 5–23   Underline each sentence that is a compound sentence.

> EXAMPLE: Many people have seen *Planet of the Apes*, but few know the origin of the story.

1. Pierre Boulle wrote the novel *Monkey Planet*, and its story line was made into a screenplay by Michael Wilson and Rod Serling.
2. In this science-fiction tale some astronauts become caught in a time warp.
3. They land on a mysterious planet; it is actually our planet Earth in a future time.
4. The people of Earth have become cruel beasts, and advanced apes are in control of the planet.
5. Many critics have called this movie "polished" and "thoughtful."
6. Some viewers have appreciated the philosophical message of the film, but many more have enjoyed the terrific ape makeup.

EX 5–24   Eleven of the following sentences are compound sentences. Underline each part of each compound sentence. Circle the conjunction or semicolon that connects the parts.

> EXAMPLE: The heart is a delicate organon, (but) it now can be operated upon safely.

1. Daniel Hale Williams was a bright child, but poverty forced him into hard work at an early age.

2. He served as a shoemaker's apprentice and worked aboard steamboats.

3. He joined his sister in Edgerton, Wisconsin, and she helped him establish a barbershop.

4. In time Williams entered a local academy; there he showed drive and intelligence.

5. Williams became fascinated by the skill of Dr. Henry Palmer; he apprenticed himself to Palmer in hopes of pursuing a medical career.

6. During his two years with Palmer, Williams read a great many medical text-books, performed simple medical tasks, and scrubbed the office each day.

7. Few doctors attended medical school then, but Williams enrolled in Chicago Medical College.

8. He graduated in 1883; soon afterward he opened an office in Chicago.

9. At that time no successful operation on the heart had ever been performed.

10. Operations on internal organs often resulted in death as a result of infection.

11. One day a man stumbled into a Chicago hospital. He had a knife wound in his heart.

12. Williams was called, and he rushed to the hospital.

13. The patient was losing blood fast; the wound had to be closed.

14. Williams opened up the patient's chest and sewed up the heart wound.

15. He used disinfectants and sterile instruments.

16. The bleeding was stopped, and no infection set in.

17. The patient recovered, and Williams became famous.

18. Williams had a long and distinguished medical career, but he is best known for his cool and careful work on that one wounded man.

EX 5–25   Rewrite each pair of sentences below as a compound sentence. Use the conjunctions provided in parentheses. Be sure to use a comma before the conjunction. Write your sentences on another sheet of paper.

> EXAMPLE: Most simple toys were developed long ago. The Frisbee is a modern creation. (but)
> *Most simple toys were developed long ago, but the Frisbee is a modern creation.*

1. The Frisbie Pie Company of Bridgeport, Connecticut, sold pies during the early 1900s. This company is not remembered for the quality of its pies. (but)
2. Somebody discovered the aerodynamic properties of Frisbie pie tins. Soon hundreds of New Englanders were flipping "Frisbies." (and)
3. A great number of World War II veterans went back to college in 1946. Many soon learned the joys of Frisbie flipping. (and)
4. Metal "Frisbies" were good. Plastic Frisbees are better. (but)
5. In 1948 Walter F. Morrison fashioned a crude flying saucer out of plastic. For the next ten years he produced small quantities of these. (and)
6. He entered into a licensing agreement with the Wham-O-Manufacturing Company in 1957. The product was not a big seller at first. (but)
7. The company's designers improved the shape of the Frisbee. Their marketing staff decided to sell Frisbees as athletic equipment instead of novelties. (and)
8. Wham-O has sold more than 100 million Frisbees worldwide so far. No signs of fading interest have yet appeared. (and)

Only closely related sentences should be combined into compound sentences. Use *and* to combine pairs of sentences that tell of one event following another.

> EXAMPLE: The noon whistle sounded, and the laborers picked up their lunch pails.

Use *and* to link sentences having parallel structure.

> EXAMPLE: Idaho produces potatoes, and Alabama produces yams.

Use *and* to link one statement or idea with another.

> EXAMPLE: It has been raining all day, and the thermometer has hovered around 5°C.

Use *but* to show opposition.

> EXAMPLES: She feels homesick today, but that will pass soon enough.
> The copy machine is working, but Enid will be using it for the next two hours or so.

EXAMPLE OF SENTENCES THAT SHOULD *NOT* BE JOINED BY *AND* TO FORM A COMPOUND SENTENCE
Tito scuffed the dirt around home plate. This would be his first time at bat against Torch Tolbert.

EX 5-26   Some of the pairs of sentences below can be combined into logical, informative compound sentences. Others are better left as separate sentences. Rewrite as compound sentences the pairs that should be combined. Use another sheet of paper for your writing.

> EXAMPLE: Chicago is the most important Great Lakes port. Its airport is the world's busiest.
> *Chicago is the most important Great Lakes port, and its airport is the world's busiest.*

1. Father Marquette and Louis Joliet stopped at the site of Chicago in 1673. No trading post was built there until more than a century after that visit.
2. Jean Baptiste Point du Sable established a trading post there. He was of French and African ancestry.
3. The Erie Canal was completed in 1825. Chicago soon benefited from the increased shipping activity in the Great Lakes region.
4. The railroads reached Chicago in the 1840s. This port city quickly became the rail hub of the Midwest.
5. A great fire almost completely destroyed Chicago in 1871. It may have been started by a kerosene lamp kicked over by a cow.
6. Chicago's energetic residents had the city back in working order in a few months. The process of expansion was delayed only slightly.

7. Not all of Chicago's history is glorious. It has earned a reputation as a tough, hard-working city.

8. In Italy, all roads lead to Rome. In the Midwest, all roads lead to Chicago.

G. CORRECTING RUN-ONS

Look at the sentence below.

Buddhism is a way of life Buddhists follow the teachings of Siddhartha Gautama.

What is wrong with the sentence as it is written? _____

_____

How could it be corrected? _____

_____

A *run-on* is a series of two or more simple sentences that are neither separated by end punctuation (period, comma, question mark, or exclamation mark) nor properly joined into a compound sentence.

EXAMPLE
Consolidated Everything declared a two-for-one stock split yesterday I do not own any of that stock.

CORRECTED BY CREATING TWO SENTENCES
Consolidated Everything declared a two-for-one stock split yesterday. I do not own any of that stock.

CORRECTED BY CREATING A COMPOUND SENTENCE
Consolidated Everything declared a two-for-one stock split yesterday, but I do not own any of that stock.

EX 5–27   Eight of the following items are run-ons. Place an end punctuation mark where the sentences should be broken apart. Make the first letter of the first word in the second sentence a capital letter.

> EXAMPLE: "If at first you don't succeed, try, try, again." $\overset{\text{T}}{t}$hat is usually good advice, but it doesn't guarantee success.

1. Many people write books few of these are ever published.

2. Many hopeful authors send a manuscript to a few publishers they generally quit after a few rejections.

3. Gilbert Young wrote *World Government Crusade* he thought it deserved to be published.

4. He began sending it to publishers in 1958 by 1980 he had been rejected by 109 publishers.

5. Mr. Young did more than just write books, though.

6. He once organized a public meeting in Bath, England, the meeting was held in support of his candidacy.

7. Mr. Young was running for Parliament he was running as a World Government candidate.

8. Only one person showed up at the meeting that person was Mr. Young himself.

9. Being a minority of one can be difficult and discouraging.

10. Being a minority of one doesn't automatically make a person wrong, however, as one great thinker remarked, all great social movements have begun with a minority of one.

EX 5–28   Choose four items from EX 5–27 that could be effectively written as compound sentences. Rewrite each as a compound sentence, using an appropriate conjunction. Be sure to use a comma before the conjunction. Write your sentences on another sheet of paper.

EX 5–29   Rewrite the following paragraph to eliminate run-ons. Use another sheet of paper to do this.

Grete Waitz begins her day with a predawn run. The air in Oslo, Norway, can be numbingly icy at 6 a.m. on a winter morning the cold just seems to energize this great distance runner. She covers mile after frozen mile at a blistering pace. She doesn't rest she doesn't slow down. The daylight hours will be spent at her paying job she must use these early hours to develop speed and strength. Few runners train under such severe conditions perhaps that is why few runners ever beat Grete Waitz.

H. IDENTIFYING KINDS OF SENTENCES

Look at the four sentences below.

a. Grass cannot grow without water.
b. Did you water the lawn last night?
c. What a tangled mess of crabgrass I see!
d. Bring me that trowel.

Which sentence states a fact? _____ This is a *declarative* sentence.

Which sentence asks a question? _____ This is an *interrogative* sentence.

Which sentence gives an order? _____ This is an *imperative* sentence.

Which sentence shows strong emotion? _____ This is an *exclamatory* sentence.

A *declarative sentence* states a fact; a period is used at the end of a declarative sentence. An *interrogative sentence* asks a question; a question mark is its end punctuation. An *exclamatory sentence* shows strong emotion. It ends with an exclamation mark. An *imperative sentence* makes a request or gives a command; it may end with a period or an exclamation mark. An imperative sentence has an understood subject, *you*. In other words, when you say, "Pass me the salt," you are really saying, "*You* pass me the salt."

EX 5–30   Identify each sentence below as *declarative, interrogative, imperative,* or *exclamatory*. Write *D* beside each declarative sentence, *INT* beside each interrogative sentence, *IMP* beside each imperative sentence, and *EX* beside each exclamatory sentence.

EXAMPLE: What a sight that wig is! __*EX*__

1. Huge wigs were fashionable in England during the late eighteenth century.
   _____

2. Put that wig upon my head, please. _____

3. Did some women wear wigs four feet high? _____

4. How sore their necks must have become! _____

5. Why did they dust the wigs with flour? _____

6. Look in an encyclopedia under "wigs." _____

7. Study these sketches of wigs. _____

8. This wig is decorated with stuffed birds. _____

9. Do you see the tiny ship atop that wig? _____

10. Wigmakers used lard to keep the wigs together. _____

11. Rodents and insects nested in these greasy creations. _____

12. Find the page with the sketch of the rat-resistant cap. _____

13. Why did the giant wigs lose popularity? _____

14. A hair powder tax was enacted in 1795. _____

15. This tax made it quite expensive to wear wigs regularly. _____

16. How glad many women must have been when those wigs went out of fashion!
    _____

EX 5–31   Add appropriate end punctuation to each sentence below. Place a period at the end of each declarative sentence. Place a question mark at the end of each interrogative sentence. Place an exclamation mark or a period at the end of each imperative sentence. Place an exclamation mark at the end of each exclamatory sentence.

EXAMPLE: What a disaster this is*!*

1. Did I leave my notebook in your dorm room
2. Look on your desk and on your bookshelf
3. Maybe I left it in the campus bookstore
4. What a zoo this place is
5. Has anyone turned in a blue notebook
6. Tell me again where the campus lost-and-found is
7. That's my notebook
8. What time is it now

9. I have only forty-five minutes to study for the exam
10. Ask me anything about the bonding properties of carbon

A sentence of one type can often be rewritten as a sentence of another type. For example, statements can be changed to questions or exclamations; questions can be changed to statements; imperative sentences can be rewritten as statements; and so on. Usually the word order and the end punctuation must be changed; occasionally one or more words must be added, dropped, or changed as well.

EXAMPLE OF A STATEMENT REWRITTEN AS A QUESTION
The first day of May is greeted by carols in Southampton, England.
Is the first day of May greeted by carols in Southampton, England?

EXAMPLES OF STATEMENTS REWRITTEN AS EXCLAMATIONS
The August bowls tournament in Southampton dates back to 1776.
The August bowls tournament in Southampton dates back to 1776!

Traditions can be glorious.
How glorious traditions can be!

EXAMPLE OF A QUESTION REWRITTEN AS A STATEMENT
Do the Knights of the Green supervise this tournament?
The Knights of the Green supervise this tournament.

EXAMPLE OF AN IMPERATIVE SENTENCE REWRITTEN AS A STATEMENT
Come with us to England this summer.
You must come with us to England this summer.

EX 5–32   Rewrite each question as a statement. Rewrite each statement as a question. Use another sheet of paper for your writing.

EXAMPLE: Lillian Wald was a member of a well-to-do family.
Was Lillian Wald a member of a well-to-do family?

1. She became interested in nursing.
2. Did she graduate from New York Hospital Training School for Nurses in 1891?
3. She saw the terrible living conditions on New York City's Lower East Side.
4. Didn't the city send workers to help the suffering residents?
5. More than a quarter of the people there slept five or more to a room.
6. Was tuberculosis a widespread illness?
7. Lillian Wald moved into this teeming slum.
8. Did she offer her services as a nurse to anyone in need?
9. Did she open Henry Street Settlement House as a health and educational facility?
10. Lillian Wald was an organizer of one of America's first nursing programs for children in public schools.

EX 5-33   Rewrite each sentence below as the type of sentence specified in parentheses. Use another sheet of paper for your writing.

> EXAMPLE: Murphy's Law strikes again. (exclamatory)
> *Murphy's Law strikes again!*

1. How hard it sometimes is to think positively. (interrogative)
2. If anything can go wrong, it will! (declarative)
3. Everything takes longer than you think. (interrogative)
4. Has someone written a book on Murphy's Law? (declarative)
5. Hand me the small red book by Arthur Block. (interrogative)
6. You should read the corollaries to Murphy's Law aloud. (imperative)
7. Left to themselves, do things go from bad to worse? (declarative)
8. That is only half of the sad truth. (exclamation)
9. Things also go from bad to worse when a person tries to keep them under control. (interrogative)
10. Would you buy me a copy of *The Power of Positive Thinking* by Norman Vincent Peale next time you go by the bookstore? (imperative)

You can add punch to the paragraphs you write by using your ability to change sentences into different types. A question or a quick exclamatory statement can break the monotony of a string of declarative statements. An imperative statement can force the reader to become more involved.

EX 5-34   Rewrite the paragraph below. Change one declarative sentence to a question and one to an exclamation, to add punch. You are welcome to make other changes as well. Use another sheet of paper for your writing.

> At least one highly artificial smell is more pleasing to many Americans than the smell of a rose or any other scent from nature. This smell, rich in more ways than one, is the aroma of a new car. No one has come up with a good descriptive word for this smell. It is a distinctive, reassuring smell. Now some chemists say they have synthesized the new-car aroma. People will spend money to spray that smell onto the interior of their old clunkers. It is cheaper than spending $8,000 for a new car.

I. REVIEWING SKILLS AND CONCEPTS

EX 5-35   Circle each item below that is not a complete sentence. On another sheet of paper, rewrite these items so that each becomes a complete sentence.

> EXAMPLE: (Lions excellent parents.)
> *Lions are excellent parents.*

1. Newborn cubs, many dangers in the wild.

2. One of every two cubs dies in the wild.

3. When the cubs join the pack at the age of ten weeks.

4. Protected from predators by adult lions.

5. Lionesses are affectionate toward all cubs.

6. Not just their own.

7. Male lions play a part in the upbringing, too.

8. Begin eating meat at about 6½ months.

9. Young lions playing at hunting and fighting with one another.

10. The parents share their kills with their hungry children.

EX 5–36   Underline the complete subject in each sentence. Circle the complete predicate.

EXAMPLE: The yellow vegetable on your plate is a sweet potato.

1. Sweet potatoes are high in vitamin A.

2. Many cooks serve sweet potatoes with ham.

3. The state of California is a major producer of sweet potatoes.

4. California growers harvest more than 700 million pounds a year.

5. John B. Avila planted California's first sweet potato fields in 1888.

6. He was a native of the Portuguese Azores.

7. The scientific name of the sweet potato is *Ipomoea batatas.*

8. The ancient Aztecs raised and ate sweet potatoes.

9. European explorers introduced this vegetable to Europe during the sixteenth century.

10. European immigrants such as Avila brought the sweet potato back across the ocean.

11. The yam is not of the same family as the sweet potato.

12. Sweet potato pie is the perfect dessert after a spicy dinner.

EX 5–37   Underline the simple subject in each sentence. Circle the simple predicate (the verb). Remember to mark auxiliary verbs, such as *may* and *are*, as part of the simple predicate.

EXAMPLE: Most American movies carry ratings nowadays.

1. A movie with a G rating is suitable for all audiences.

2. Other ratings indicate some material not suitable for young children.

3. The present system of ratings was established by the Motion Picture Association of America in 1968.

4. No law requires a rating for a film.

5. Most exhibitors will rent only rated films, however.

6. Movies are given ratings by the Classificaton and Rating Administration.

7. Its six full-time viewers are selected as people with tastes and values similar to those of most Americans.

8. These viewers watch movie after movie.

9. They give a rating to each film submitted.

10. A producer may appeal a seemingly unfair rating.

11. Producers sometimes make cuts in films for the sake of a less restricting rating.

12. A particular film may need a PG rating for maximum box office potential.

EX 5–38   After each sentence that has a compound subject, write *C. SUBJECT*. After each sentence that has a compound predicate, write *C. PREDICATE*. After each compound sentence, write *C. SENTENCE*.

> EXAMPLE: Neither Dizzy Dean nor Whitey Ford ever pitched a no-hitter in the majors. *C. SUBJECT*

1. Alva "Bobo" Holloman joined the St. Louis Browns in 1953 and quickly made a name for himself. _____

2. A large *N* and a large *G* were scratched on the diamond dirt by Holloman on his way to the mound each game during spring training. _____

3. *N* was his wife's first initial, and *G* was his son's first initial.

_____

4. Bobo was superstitious; he performed this ritual for luck. _____

5. The initials may not have had anything to do with it, but Bobo was very lucky on May 6, 1953. _____

6. Spring training and the early season had been disastrous for Bobo.

_____

7. The Browns were desperate, though, and Bobo was sent to the mound that day for his first big-league start. _____

8. Rain fell intermittently and interrupted the game several times.

_____

9. Several of the Philadelphia A's hit shots off Bobo, but the Brownie fielders turned them all into outs. _____

10. Left fielder Jim Dyck and shortstop Billy Hunter made spectacular plays on hard-hit balls. _____

11. Bobo himself belted a single and knocked in the Browns' first run.

_____

12. The Browns went into the ninth inning ahead by 6–0, and Bobo had not allowed a hit. _____

13. He began pitching too rapidly and walked the first two batters.

_____

14. Pitching coach Harry Brecheen talked to Bobo and calmed him down.

_____

15. The batter at the plate hit into a double play, but then Bobo walked the next batter. _____

16. Big Eddie Robinson socked Bobo's first pitch to him out of the park, but his drive was foul by a few feet. _____

17. Robinson then lifted a soft fly to Vic Wertz, and the small crowd went crazy. _____

18. Bobo Holloman had pitched a no-hitter and had become the first pitcher in history to do it in his first start! _____

19. Bobo never pitched effectively again, and he was back in the minors by the middle of July. _____

20. Bobo Holloman's moment of glory was brief, but his achievement ranks as one of the most memorable in the history of baseball. _____

EX 5-39   Rewrite the following paragraph to eliminate fragments and run-ons. Use another sheet of paper for your writing.

Salt water is harmful to most plants. Nevertheless, researchers are convinced that salt water can be used to produce large amounts of nutritious food. These researchers are working with *halophytes*. Which are plants that will tolerate salt water. Some halophytes are actually more nutritious than wheat, rice, or alfalfa they also can produce greater yields per acre. Palmer's grass is one promising salt-tolerant plant pickleweed is another. Someday eating the seeds of Palmer's grass like peanuts. Using pickleweed in salads. Obviously commercial salt-water farming is many years away, but it certainly is nothing to joke about much of the United States is chronically short of fresh water. May someday turn desert areas into productive farms.

EX 5-40   Rewrite each sentence below as the type specified in parentheses. Use another sheet of paper for your writing.

> EXAMPLE: Answer the telephone. (interrogative)
> *Will you answer the telephone?*

1. Is the caller offering newspaper subscriptions? (declarative)
2. Telephone salespeople call at the dinner hour. (interrogative)
3. You should hang up the telephone right now. (imperative)
4. Three months for the price of one is a bargain. (exclamatory)
5. Are you taking an international relations course this semester? (declarative)
6. The newspaper could be helpful. (exclamatory)
7. Will you explain the significance of recent events in East Africa? (imperative)
8. Save the sports section for me. (interrogative)

WORKSHOP

1. Find a full-page magazine ad that contains at least six lines of copy. Check the ad for fragments. Rewrite any fragments as complete sentences.

2. Write a paragraph about the work of one of the following people:
   - an auditor
   - a dentist
   - an auto mechanic
   - a file clerk

   Draw one line under the complete subject of each sentence you write. Draw two lines under the complete predicate.

3. Write a paragraph about a meat-eating animal. Draw one line under the simple subject of each sentence you write. Draw two lines under the simple predicate.

4. Find five statements in a textbook. Rewrite each as a question. Find five questions in the textbook. Rewrite each as a statement.

5. Listen to a radio news broadcast. As best you can, write the text of one news item in paragraph form. Add or change words to complete any statement you were not able to transcribe accurately. Punctuate the sentences properly. Be sure to avoid run-ons. Rewrite any fragments as complete sentences.

6. Find a paragraph you have written that could benefit from revision. This can be from any paper you have written this year. Rewrite the paragraph; as you do so, ask yourself these questions:
   - Are there any fragments?
   - Are there any run-ons?
   - Are there pairs of sentences that should be combined?
   - Would different kinds of sentences add punch?
   - Could a question or an exclamatory statement be added to sharpen focus?

Note that you will seldom if ever do all these things to a single paragraph. Nevertheless, trying the various possibilities is bound to lead you to a better way of saying what you have to say.

Working with Sentence Patterns

A. IDENTIFYING SENTENCE PATTERNS

Each English sentence follows one of a few basic patterns. To determine the pattern of a particular sentence, it is necessary to focus on the main elements of the sentence—the subject, the verb, and any items that complete the meaning of the verb. Modifying words should be disregarded.

The simplest sentence pattern is *subject–verb* (*S–V*). In this type of sentence, the verb does not transfer action to or from an object. It is complete in itself, though it may be modified by words telling *how, when, how much,* or *how often.* (Such a verb is called an *intransitive* verb.)

EXAMPLES OF S–V PATTERN

   S   V
Penguins swim.

   S   V
Crows caw loudly [*Loudly* tells *how* crows caw.]

      S   V
Mature eagles soar high above the clouds. [*Mature* modifies eagles; *high above the clouds* modifies *soar.*]

The first step in determining a sentence pattern, then, is to find the simple subject and the simple predicate (the verb).

EX 6-1   Write *S* above the simple subject in each sentence below. Write *V* above the verb in each sentence. Remember that some verbs may include one or more auxiliary verbs.

                    S   V
      EXAMPLE: Poppies can survive with little water.

1. Poppies bloom in spring.

2. Dandelions sprout in sidewalk cracks.

3. These hardy weeds grow wild almost everywhere.

4. Bees are buzzing in backyard gardens.

5. Moths are fluttering just above the grass.

6. Snails hide in the shade during the daytime.

7. Portable radios chatter.

8. Power lawn mowers have been roaring for hours.

9. Berries ripen in the summer heat.

10. Fall's cooler, shorter days will arrive soon.

EX 6-2   The sentences from EX 6-1 are reproduced below without their subjects. In each blank write a new subject that makes sense. Circle the simple subject.

EXAMPLE: (*Most thistles*) can survive with little water.

1. _____ bloom in spring.

2. _____ sprout in sidewalk cracks.

3. _____ grow wild almost everywhere.

4. _____ are buzzing in backyard gardens.

5. _____ are fluttering just above the grass.

6. _____ hide in the shade during the daytime.

7. _____ chatter.

8. _____ have been roaring for hours.

9. _____ ripen in the summer heat.

10. _____ will arrive soon.

EX 6-3   The sentences from EX 6-1 are reproduced below without their predicates. In each blank write a new predicate that makes sense. Circle the verb in each predicate you write. Try to preserve the S-V sentence pattern.

EXAMPLE: Poppies (*grow*) *alongside many Western highways.*

1. Poppies _____

2. Dandelions _____

3. These hardy weeds _____

4. Bees _____

5. Moths _____

6. Snails _____

7. Portable radios _____

8. Power lawnmowers _____

9. Berries _____

10. Fall's cooler, shorter days _____

B. FINDING DIRECT OBJECTS

Look at the sentence below.

Firecrackers wake sleeping children.

What word tells *whom* firecrackers wake? _____

One of the most common sentence patterns in English is *subject-verb-object (S-V-O)*. In this type of sentence, the verb transfers action from the subject to the object. This type of object is called a *direct object.* A verb that transfers action to a direct object is called a *transitive* verb.

EXAMPLES OF S-V-O PATTERN

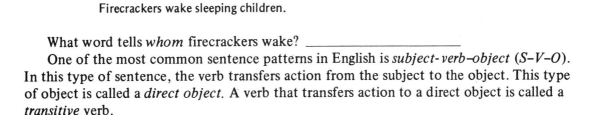

                      S   V   O
Georges Simenon wrote at least five hundred books.

             S   V   O
Many residents of Bermuda ride bicycles.

       S   V   O
Dentists in Japan pulled teeth with their fingers six hundred years ago.

THESE SENTENCES DO NOT HAVE THE S-V-O PATTERN

                              V
                       S
At least five hundred books were written by George Simenon. [The verb in this sentence transfers the action *to* the subject. There is no object in this sentence.]

                    V
       S
Bicycles are ridden by many residents of Bermuda. [Again, the verb transfers the action to the subject.]

EX 6–4   Write *S* above the simple subject in each sentence below. Write *V* above the verb in each sentence. Write *O* above the direct object in each sentence.

                        S   V   O
EXAMPLE: Josef Levi showed his watch to Benjamin Banneker.

1. Banneker had seen no devices of this type before.

2. Levi explained the workings of the watch to young Banneker.

3. The friendly gentleman gave the watch as a gift to the enthusiastic youth.

4. Banneker took the watch back to his family's farm.

5. He studied its internal movements.

6. Banneker drew plans for a clock of his own.

7. He carved each piece out of wood by hand.

8. Banneker's wooden clock kept perfect time for forty years.

EX 6-5 Rewrite each sentence below on another sheet of paper, replacing the direct object and its modifiers with another direct object that makes sense. You may add modifiers as well. Underline the direct object in each sentence you write.

> EXAMPLE: Specialty counters in supermarkets offer pickled octopus.
> *Specialty counters in supermarkets offer smoked oysters.*

1. Some shoppers carry pocket calculators.
2. Many supermarkets now sell generic products.
3. Penny-wise shoppers often buy these inexpensive products.
4. Most product labels today have on them a Universal Product Code marking.
5. This month's weather may affect next month's lettuce prices.
6. A good supermarket offers fresh produce.

C. FINDING INDIRECT OBJECTS

Look at the following sentence.

The photocopy gave the reporter the final clue.

Which word tells *what* the photocopy gave? _____

Which word tells *to whom* the clue was given? _____

A variation of the subject–verb–object pattern is *subject–verb–indirect object–direct object.* (*S–V–IO–O*). An *indirect object* is usually a word that answers the question *to whom* or *to what*.

EXAMPLES OF S-V-IO-O PATTERN

S   V   IO   O
A legislative aide had told the reporter a secret.

S   V   IO   O
However, the aide gave the newshawk no evidence.

A word that is part of a phrase beginning with *to* or *for* is *not* an indirect object. Any sentence with an indirect object can be rewritten as a sentence with this type of phrase instead of an indirect object.

EXAMPLES OF SENTENCES THAT DO NOT CONTAIN INDIRECT OBJECTS

S   V   O
A legislative aide had told a secret *to the reporter.* [*To the reporter* is a phrase modifying the verb *had told.*]

S   V   O
However, the aide gave no evidence *to the newshawk.* [*To the newshawk* is a phrase modifying the verb *gave.*]

EX 6–6 Write *S* above the simple subject in each sentence below. Write *V* above the verb in each sentence. Write *O* above the direct object in each sentence. Write *IO* above the indirect object in each sentence.

                                   S   V   IO   O

           EXAMPLE: Split fingernails give musicians problems.

1. Residents often give mail carriers presents during the holiday season.

    _____

2. Generous souls take shut-ins hot meals.

    _____

3. Family groups sing neighbors festive songs.

    _____

4. A covering of snow gives the hills a soft, magical look.

    _____

5. Calendar pictures show children sights of holiday seasons long past.

    _____

6. The constant repetition of holiday melodies gives some people headaches.

    _____

EX 6–7 Rewrite each sentence in EX 6–6, replacing the indirect object and its modifiers with other words that make sense. Write *S* above the simple subject of each sentence you write; write *V* above each verb, *IO* above each indirect object, and *O* above each direct object. Do this on another sheet of paper.

    EXAMPLE: Split fingernails give musicians problems.

                               S   V   IO   O
               Split fingernails give typists problems.

EX 6–8 Rewrite each of the sentences below to make a sentence with an indirect object. Use another sheet of paper for your writing.

    EXAMPLE: The exclamation of an astonished miner gave the name to the first gold mine in Creede, Colorado.
                    The exclamation of an astonished miner gave the first gold mine in Creede, Colorado, its name.

1. In 1889 Nicholas J. Creede and his partner gave a look to the rocks along Willow Creek.
2. Creede gave a hard tap with an iron tool to one likely-looking rock.
3. The color of the rock beneath gave quite a surprise to Creede.
4. Creede gave notice of the find to his partner with a shout of "Holy Moses!"
5. Developers of that vein of gold gave the name Holy Moses to the mine.
6. Wild doings and rich veins of gold brought quite a bit of publicity to this mountain boomtown in its day.

D. WORKING WITH LINKING VERBS AND SUBJECTIVE COMPLEMENTS

Look at the sentences below.

a. Jorge examined a topographical map.
b. The map was useless to him.
c. An atlas would be a more reliable source.

Which sentences include a verb that links the subject to a word that defines or describes

it? _____

Sentences that define or describe things usually follow the pattern *subject–linking verb–subjective complement (S–LV–SC)*. A *linking verb* is a verb that does not describe action; instead, it connects the subject with a word that defines or describes it. This word is called a *subjective complement.* In a sentence that defines something, the subjective complement is usually a *noun.* In a sentence that describes, the subjective complement is usually an *adjective* (a descriptive word).

EXAMPLES OF S–LV–SC PATTERN

S   LV   SC
Delaware is a small state. [*State* is a noun.]

S   LV   SC
Delaware appears relatively flat from the air. [*Flat* is an adjective that describes Delaware.]

S   LV   SC
Long ago the peach blossom became Delaware's state flower.

EX 6-9   Write *S* above the simple subject in each sentence below. Write *LV* above the verb in each sentence. Write *SC* above the subjective complement.

S   LV   SC
EXAMPLE: The sunbeam snake is an inhabitant of the Indo-Malaysian region.

1. Its skin is quite dark in color.

2. Chocolate brown is a common hue.

3. The skull of this Asian snake is broad.

4. Its lower jaw is flexible.

5. The sunbeam snake is a two-lunged snake.

6. A single lung is a characteristic of less primitive snakes.

7. The scales of this snake are smooth.

8. The advantage of smooth scales is a low degree of friction during burrowing.

9. Keratin is the smooth outer substance.

10. The dramatic appearance of this snake in sunlight is the result of the diffraction of light by tiny ridges on its back.

EX 6-10   Rewrite each sentence below on another sheet of paper, replacing the subjective complement and its modifiers with another subjective complement that makes sense. You may add modifiers as well. Underline the subjective complement in each sentence you write.

> EXAMPLE: Your power saw is dull.
> *Your power saw is a worthless _piece of junk_.*

1. These old boards beneath the porch are rotten.
2. High-quality lumber is quite expensive.
3. The carpenter seems competent.
4. The local building inspector is a most unpleasant person.
5. The cost of the new porch will be $5,000.
6. Those old, rickety stairs are very dangerous.

E. REVIEWING SIMPLE SENTENCE PATTERNS

EX 6-11   Identify the pattern of each sentence below as *S–V, S–V–O, S–V–IO–O,* or *S–LV–SC.*

> EXAMPLE: Tomorrow's cameras may not use film. _S–V–O_

1. These cameras will change light patterns into electronic impulses.

   _____

2. Tomorrow's roll of "film" may be a cassette of magnetic tape.

   _____

3. The photographer will insert the cassette into a viewer similar to a TV.

   _____

4. The TV will give the photographer a look at the pictures. _____

5. Good photographs will be printed electronically on paper. _____

6. The photographer can then erase the cassette. _____

7. Cassettes will be reusable. _____

8. Such cameras are only a dream right now. _____

9. Electronic filmless cameras could give inept photographers some welcome assistance. _____

10. The photographer can alter the electronic impulses of a picture with the push of a few buttons. _____

11. Washed-out areas will be darkened electronically. _____

12. Dark areas will become bright. _____

EX 6-12   Each item below needs a complement to become a complete sentence. Fill each blank with an appropriate complement (a direct object or a subjective complement). You may also add one or more modifiers. Circle each direct object you write. Underline each subjective complement.

> EXAMPLE: Our athletic facilities are *barely adequate for student needs*.

1. The director of athletics is _____

2. Varsity football players carry _____

3. Cheerleaders wear _____

4. The most popular intramural sport at this college is _____
_____

5. Quite a few students play _____

6. Most coaches at this school are _____

7. Rooters at basketball games wave _____

8. Exercise is _____

9. Volleyball games attract _____

10. The cost of a ticket to a varsity football game is _____
_____

EX 6-13   Write a paragraph about a type of computer video game. Explain what happens as a person plays the game. Include at least three sentences with the *S–V–O* pattern. Underline each S–V–O sentence you write. (If you are not familiar with any computer video games, you can write your paragraph about what modern electric kitchen appliances do.) Use another sheet of paper for your writing.

EX 6-14   Write a paragraph contrasting two precious metals or two types of cosmetics. Include at least three sentences with the *S–LV–SC* pattern. Underline each S–LV–SC sentence you write. You may want to do a little research before you begin writing. Use another sheet of paper for your writing.

F. WORKING WITH INVERTED SENTENCES

A writer may choose to emphasize a word or idea by rearranging a familiar sentence pattern. This reordering produces inverted sentences.
Look at these pairs of sentences.

> a. She kept the ring. She threw away the poem.
> b. The ring she kept. The poem she threw away.

In which pair of sentences is the subject–verb–object (S–V–O) pattern followed? _____

Which element comes first in each sentence in the other pair? _____

A writer wishing to emphasize the object in a simple sentence may use an object–subject–verb (O–S–V) pattern rather than the subject–verb–object (S–V–O) pattern.

Now look at these sentences.

> a. Fair was the city; foul was its air.
> b. The city was fair; its air was foul.

In which sentence is the subject–linking verb–subjective complement (S–LV–SC) pattern followed twice? _____

Which element comes first in each half of the other sentence? _____

A writer wishing to emphasize the subjective complement in a simple sentence may use a subjective complement–linking verb–subject (SC–LV–S) pattern rather than the subject–linking verb–subjective complement (S–LV–SC) pattern. The S–LV–SC pattern may also be changed to a subjective complement–subject–linking verb (SC–S–LV) pattern.

EXAMPLE OF SC–LV–S

SC LV   S
Mad was the moon on that awful night.

EXAMPLE OF SC–S–LV

                                          LV
SC   S   ⌢
How terrible the ensuing confrontations would be!

EX 6–15   Identify the pattern of each sentence below as S–V–O, O–S–V, S–LV–SC, SC–LV–S, or SC–S–LV. Note that inverted sentences are not always effective or desirable.

1. Barren were the rocky islands off the west coast of Alaska. _____

2. Empty of life the beaches had become. _____

3. Russian sailors had killed seals for their fur year after year. _____

4. The land was becoming valueless to the Russians. _____
5. Friendship with the United States the Russians valued at that time.

_____

6. Alaska the Russians offered to us at a small price. _____
7. Angry were many at the prospect of paying millions for a frozen wasteland.

_____

8. Steadfast William Seward was in his pursuit of the acquisition of this territory. _____

9. Fish and timber Alaska would surely yield in abundance. _____

10. Petroleum, gold, and coal the rugged terrain concealed. _____

11. The United States purchased Alaska for $7,250,000. _____
12. Seward history has certified as a wise and farsighted individual.

_____

EX 6-16   Rewrite each sentence below so that it follows the pattern indicated in parentheses. Do your writing on another sheet of paper.

> EXAMPLE: You are right! (SC–S–LV)
> *Right you are!*

1. The punishment will be swift. (SC–LV–S)
2. The judge has dismissed my case. (O–S–V)
3. The jury will decide your case tomorrow. (O–S–V)
4. Justice is swift in this county. (SC–LV–S)
5. You may be hesitant. (SC–S–LV)
6. The future that you face is bleak. (SC–LV–S)

As you have noticed, an inverted sentence can cause a reader to stop and reread its words. Its unusual structure thus draws attention to its message. Inverted sentences should be used sparingly; too many will tend to confuse the reader and will also make your writing sound unnatural.

G. WORKING WITH COMPOUND DIRECT OBJECTS, INDIRECT OBJECTS, AND SUBJECTIVE COMPLEMENTS

Look at the sentences below.

> a. Arnold Bly engraved prayers on rice grains and messages on strands of human hair.
> b. Visitors to the 1939 World's Fair watched Bly at work and admired his skill.
> c. Bly drew large crowds to his exhibitions.

Which sentence above has one action verb and one direct object? _____

Which sentence has two action verbs, each with a direct object? _____

Which sentence has one action verb with two direct objects? _____

An action verb may have two or more direct objects. A sentence with an action verb that has two or more direct objects linked by *and, but, or,* or *nor* is said to have a *compound direct object.*

> **EXAMPLE OF A COMPOUND DIRECT OBJECT**
> Visitors viewed the engraved rice *grains* and *hairs* through magnifying lenses.

EX 6-17   Underline the direct object or objects in each sentence below. Seven of the sentences have compound direct objects.

> EXAMPLE: Sylvester "Pat" Weaver formulated <u>*Your Show of Shows*</u> and <u>*The Tonight Show.*</u>

1. *Your Show of Shows* starred Sid Caesar and Imogene Coca.
2. The skits on *Your Show of Shows* featured verbal wit and outrageous horseplay.
3. Sid Caesar used facial contortions and foreign-sounding gibberish in many skits.
4. A film company made a feature film of ten of the funniest vignettes.

5. Unlike many humorous presentations, the best skits from *Your Show of Shows* lost neither relevance nor impact with the passage of time.
6. *The Tonight Show* has made friends and money for its network for more than twenty-five years.
7. Steve Allen hosted *The Tonight Show* for its first three years and was quite popular.
8. With Allen as host, the show blended music and comedy.
9. Jack Paar, a tart but humorous conversationalist, was the second host.
10. Johnny Carson boosted the show's ratings and advertising revenues to unprecedented levels during the 1970s.

EX 6-18   Rewrite each sentence below as a sentence with a compound direct object. Use your imagination to supply the second direct object in each sentence. Use another sheet of paper for your writing.

> EXAMPLE: The driving instructor clutched a crumpled paper cup.
> *The driving instructor clutched a crumpled paper cup and a rolled-up magazine.*

1. The driver adjusted the sun visor.
2. He saw a school bus behind him.
3. The instructor chewed her lip.
4. The inexperienced driver saw a service station ahead.
5. The car needed a quart of oil.
6. Cutting across two lanes of traffic, the driver barely missed a small sedan.

The verb in a sentence may have two or more indirect objects. This structure is called a *compound indirect object.*

EXAMPLE OF A COMPOUND INDIRECT OBJECT
Loren gave *Bill, Ralph,* and *Tony* copies of last month's phone bill.

THIS VERSION OF THE SENTENCE HAS NO INDIRECT OBJECT
Loren gave copies of last month's phone bill to Bill, Ralph, and Tony.

EX 6-19   Underline the indirect object or objects in each sentence below. Four of the sentences have compound indirect objects.

> EXAMPLE: Bill gave <u>Loren</u> and <u>Jack</u> an I.O.U. for $28.87.

1. Bill usually gave his father and his sister in Miami a call on Monday evening.
2. Ralph told his girlfriend and his former tennis partner jokes over the phone twice or three times a week.
3. The phone company gave Loren and his roommates ten days to pay.
4. None of them had cash or liquid assets at the moment.
5. Finally Tony sold his tape deck and his motorcycle helmet.
6. He sent the phone company, the landlord, and the electric company personal checks.

EX 6–20   Rewrite each of the sentences below so it becomes a sentence with a compound indirect object. Use another sheet of paper for your writing.

> EXAMPLE: Astro-Apoplexy Amusement Park gives passes to its "Monday Madness" to students and senior citizens.
> *Astro-Apoplexy Amusement Park gives students and senior citizens passes to its "Monday Madness."*

1. The Slam 'n' Spin gives a real workout to riders' necks and backs.
2. Sheer Heart Attack, a roller coaster, gives some anxious moments to riders and spectators.
3. The publicity director of the amusement park gives charts and graphs of operational safety to reporters and insurance investigators.
4. Unfortunately, one of the park's rides has just given some business to several doctors and lawyers.

A linking verb may be followed by two or more subjective complements. This structure is termed a *compound subjective complement.*

EXAMPLES OF COMPOUND SUBJECTIVE COMPLEMENT
Winston Churchill was an eloquent, persuasive *orator* and a polished *writer.* [compound subjective complement—two nouns]

His books, unlike those of many other politicians, are *readable* and *informative.* [compound subjective complement—two adjectives]

EX 6–21   Underline the subjective complement or complements in each sentence below. Seven of the sentences have compound subjective complements.

> EXAMPLE: Rooms in many Western-style hotels in Japan are <u>comfortable</u> but quite <u>expensive</u>.

1. Rooms in traditional Japanese hotels are simple but not inexpensive.
2. A new type of Japanese inn is efficient in its use of space and competitive in its rate structure.
3. The rooms are small locking capsules with bunks inside.
4. Each seven-foot by three-foot by three-and-one-half-foot capsule is clean and comfortable.
5. With a color TV, a radio, a telephone, a bedside lamp, and a reading stand in the capsule, the traveler will be neither lonely nor bored.
6. The capsule doors resemble double rows of washing machines.
7. The cost of a night in a capsule inn is one-third the cost of a room in a traditional Japanese hotel and one-eighth the cost of a room in a Western-style hotel.
8. These capsule inns are almost full every night and also quite popular with their guests.
9. This type of hotel may never become popular in Western nations.
10. Two sensations likely to be felt by Westerners in such accommodations are claustrophobia and a lack of privacy.

EX 6-22   Make each item below into a complete sentence by writing a compound subjective complement in the blank. Include modifying words and phrases that make the sentences more informative. You may have to refresh your knowledge of the American Revolution in order to complete all items properly.

>   EXAMPLES: Abigail Adams was *sharp-eyed and courageous.*
>
>   Thomas Jefferson was *the author of the Declaration of Independence and the third President of the United States.*

1. Benjamin Franklin was _____

_____

2. Many of the Minutemen were _____

_____

3. King George III of England was _____

_____

4. Two of the colonists' demands were _____

_____

5. Two items carried by most American soldiers were _____

_____

6. George Washington was _____

_____

As you have seen, complements may be compounded. As a rule, though, a compound structure should include only one *kind* of complement. Another way of saying this is that if more than one complement is used, the complements should be *parallel.*

EXAMPLES OF PARALLEL COMPOUND COMPLEMENTS
Butterflyfish are active and quite hardy. [compound subjective complement—two adjectives]

In captivity, the copper-banded, long-nosed butterflyfish will eat daphnia, brine shrimp, and dry fish food. [compound direct object]

EXAMPLE OF A SENTENCE CONTAINING NONPARALLEL STRUCTURES
The pantherfish is a dark-spotted fish and gray. [compound subjective complement—one noun and one adjective]

POSSIBLE REVISIONS
The pantherfish is a dark-spotted gray fish.
OR   The pantherfish is gray with dark spots.

EXAMPLE OF A SENTENCE CONTAINING NONPARALLEL STRUCTURES
Many fish eat algae and every few hours. [compound with one direct object and one modifying phrase]

POSSIBLE REVISIONS
Many fish eat algae every few hours.
OR   Many fish eat algae, feeding every few hours.

EX 6-23 The sentences below have compound predicates that are not parallel structures. Rewrite each either as two sentences or as a single sentence with no parallelism problem. Use another sheet of paper for your writing.

> EXAMPLE: My aquarium is a large Plexiglas tank and in the living room.
> *My aquarium is a large Plexiglas tank. It is in the living room.*

1. Tropical fish are rather delicate organisms and beautiful.
2. Siamese fightingfish attack others of their species and aggressively.
3. Some of the color varieties of Siamese fightingfish are indigo, crimson, claret, and available from quality pet stores.
4. In nature Siamese fightingfish fight each other but usually harmlessly.
5. A fight in a tank can cause serious injuries or even one fish to die.
6. The wild species is a native of muddy ponds and brown in color.

H. WORKING WITH VERBS IN ACTIVE VOICE AND PASSIVE VOICE

Most sentences with the subject–verb–object (S–V–O) pattern can be rewritten so that the direct object becomes the subject and receives the action of the verb.
Look at the following sentences.

> a. Herschel bought a rude bumper sticker.
> b. A rude bumper sticker was bought by Herschel.

Which sentence follows the S–V–O pattern? _____

In which sentence does the subject receive the action? _____

What phrase in this sentence tells whom the bumper sticker was bought by? _____

_____

A verb that directs action *from* the subject is said to be in the *active* voice. This designation is often simplified to *active verb*. A verb that directs action *to* the subject is said to be in the *passive* voice. This description is often simplified to *passive verb*.

EXAMPLES OF VERBS IN THE ACTIVE VOICE
Mrs. Robey *feeds* her begonias twice a day.

The Yuens *have been attending* the annual flower show since 1969.

Someone *has stolen* the prize-winning orchid!

EXAMPLES OF VERBS IN THE PASSIVE VOICE
Mrs. Robey's begonias *are fed* by her twice a day. [The subject, *begonias*, receives the action of the verb.]

The annual flower show *has been attended* by the Yuens since 1969. [The subject, *show*, receives the action of the verb.]

The prize-winning orchid *has been stolen*! [The subject, *orchid*, receives the action of the verb. The phrase *by someone* has been dropped here, since it gives no meaningful information.]

EX 6–24   Write *ACTIVE* after each sentence that has a verb in the active voice. Write *PASSIVE* after each sentence that has a verb in the passive voice.

> EXAMPLE: Mary McCarthy, orphaned at age six, was raised by grandparents.
>
> _____*PASSIVE*_____

1. The child was treated harshly by the grandparents. _____

2. McCarthy earned good marks in school and at Vassar College. _____

3. She then wrote reviews of plays for the *Partisan Review.* _____

4. McCarthy was encouraged by her husband, Edmund Wilson, to try writing fiction. _____

5. The *Southern Review* published her first story in 1939. _____

6. Venice and Florence were depicted by this author in impressive travel books.

_____

7. Critics favored McCarthy's nonfiction over her fiction. _____

8. *The Group* chronicled the lives of seven Vassar students over several decades.

_____

9. *The Group* was made into a sophisticated movie by director Sidney Lumet.

_____

10. McCarthy's writings on the Vietnam War were scorned by many critics but praised by others for the sensitivity they showed. _____

EX 6–25   Rewrite each sentence in EX 6–24. Change each verb in the active voice to the passive voice. Change each verb in the passive voice to the active voice. You may have to add, delete, or change other words as you do this. Be especially careful of where you place modifying words and phrases. Use another sheet of paper for your writing.

> EXAMPLE: *Grandparents raised Mary McCarthy, orphaned at age six.*

EX 6–26   Compare the sentences in EX 6–24 with the sentences you wrote in EX 6–25. Place an asterisk (*) next to the version of each sentence that sounds better to you.

In general, sentences with verbs in the active voice communicate ideas faster and more forcefully. These sentences carry the reader from event to event and from thought to thought. An article or an essay with a greater number of passive verbs, in contrast, may cause the reader to slow down and perhaps lose interest. Use passive-voice verbs only when necessary.

EXAMPLE OF WISE USE OF PASSIVE VOICE
Each block of stone on that pyramid was lifted by hundreds of workers. [This pattern emphasizes the enormity of the task.]

AN UNWISE USE OF PASSIVE VOICE
Thirty-seven points were scored by Ralph Sampson in yesterday's game.

REWRITTEN IN ACTIVE VOICE
Ralph Sampson scored thirty-seven points in yesterday's game.

EX 6-27   Rewrite the paragraph below. Change at least four sentences with passive-voice verbs into sentences with active-voice verbs. Use another sheet for your writing.

> An unusual name was chosen by Betty and Bernie Hannaford for their café in Hines, Oregon. It was named The Worst Food in Oregon by them. Most restaurant owners claim they offer excellent food and fast, friendly service. Not the Hannafords. A reporter was told by Betty Hannaford, "It's the worst food you ever ate." Her husband then said, "No, the service is even worse than the food." So why, if the Hannafords claim to run such a terrible restaurant, is the place usually packed? The fact is that these extravagant claims are not lived up to by the Hannafords. Quite good food at fair prices is served by the Hannafords, and top-quality service is given by them, too. Open for more than ten years, The Worst Food in Oregon has earned itself a good reputation. Of course, some new diners are undoubtedly made uncomfortable by such signs as "Come in and sit with the flies." Surely they realize, though, that any restaurant with bad food and flies would not be likely to joke about them publicly.

I.   REVIEWING SKILLS AND CONCEPTS

EX 6-28   Write ten sentences about a building on campus. You may want to explain what the building looks like and how it is used. Write your sentences on the lines below. Follow the sentence pattern indicated for each sentence.

> EXAMPLE: S–V–IO–O   *The revolving doors at the entrance to the school library give students real problems.*

1. S–V–O _____
2. S–V–O _____
3. S–V–O _____
4. S–V–IO–O _____
5. S–V _____
6. S–LV–SC _____
7. S–LV–SC _____
8. S–LV–SC _____
9. SC–V–S _____
10. O–S–V _____

EX 6-29   Underline each direct object in the sentences below. Draw a box around each indirect object. Circle each subjective complement. Note that some sentences have compound complements.

> EXAMPLE: An investment banker is the (person) in the middle of a new securities offering.

1. XYZ Corporation offers new stock.

2. Several investment bankers form a pool.

3. They buy the entire new issue of stock from XYZ Corporation.

4. Large amounts of money are necessary for such purchases.

5. The investment bankers then form a syndicate.

6. They sell individuals and institutions the stock.

7. An investment banker may also help people or institutions in the disposal of large blocks of securities.

8. The investment banker offers the stocks or bonds to other buyers.

9. The American Exchange and the New York Stock Exchange are two arenas for the trading of securities.

10. Another name for an investment broker is an underwriter.

EX 6-30   Rewrite each sentence that has a verb in the passive voice so its verb is in the active voice Make other changes as necessary. Do nothing to the sentences with verbs already in the active voice. Use another sheet of paper for your writing.

> EXAMPLE: The Sears Tower was climbed by Daniel Goodwin in early 1981.
> *Daniel Goodwin climbed the Sears tower in early 1981.*

1. The tower had been climbed by no one before Goodwin.
2. Suction cups and metal clips were used in the climb by the twenty-five-year-old acrobat.
3. A red and blue Spiderman costume was worn by Goodwin for the occasion.
4. He was cheered by dozens of onlookers.
5. Goodwin battled forty-mile-an-hour winds during the seven-and-a-half-hour climb.
6. Climbing hooks were stuck by Goodwin into grooves used by window washers.
7. The hooks were used by Goodwin as steps.
8. After inserting a hook above his head, Goodwin would remove the hook beneath his lower foot.
9. Goodwin was handcuffed by Chicago police at the conclusion of his stunt.
10. According to Goodwin, climbs of this sort should not be attempted by everyone.

WORKSHOP

1. Write a paragraph describing your most stylish outfit. Underline each sentence that follows the S-LV-SC pattern. Be sure that some sentences in the paragraph follow other patterns.

2. Write a paragraph about a faculty member who stands out on campus. Describe this person by describing his or her actions. Underline each sentence that follows the S-V-O pattern. Be sure that some sentences in the paragraph follow other patterns.

3. Write five sentences about a birthday party you attended recently or about a holiday celebration during which gifts were exchanged. Write one sentence with a *compound subject*, one sentence with a *compound predicate*, one sentence with a *compound direct object*, one sentence with a *compound subjective complement*, and one *compound sentence*. Label each.

4. Write a paragraph describing the action in a TV program or a movie you saw recently. Write several sentences with verbs in passive voice. Then rewrite the paragraph, changing sentences with verbs in passive voice to sentences with verbs in active voice. Indicate which paragraph sounds better.

5. Look at the first sentence in each article on the front page of a daily newspaper. Count how many first sentences have verbs in *active voice* and how many have verbs in *passive voice.*

6. Find a paragraph you have written that could benefit from revision. This can be from any paper you have written this year. Rewrite the paragraph; as you do so, ask yourself these questions:
   • Does this paragraph show variety in its sentence patterns?
   • Could the paragraph be tightened by rewriting a particular pair of sentences with compound elements?
   • Should some sentences with verbs in passive voice be rewritten as sentences with verbs in active voice?

   Note that you will seldom make all these kinds of corrections in a single paragraph. Nevertheless, trying out a number of possibilities is bound to lead you to a better way of saying what you have to say.

Using Phrases
to Expand Sentences

7

A. WRITING NOUN PHRASES

A *phrase* is a group of words that work together to carry out a single sentence function. A phrase, in other words, operates as if it were a single part of speech, such as a noun or a verb.

EXAMPLES OF PHRASES PERFORMING THE SAME FUNCTIONS AS SINGLE WORDS
a. *Bottles* contained correction fluid.
b. *Several small bottles* contained correction fluid. [Here a phrase replaces a single word as the subject.]
c. The *swift* train roared through the small town of Golden, B.C.
d. The train, *moving at top speed*, roared through the small town of Golden, B.C. [In sentence *d* a phrase modifies the noun *train*; in sentence *c* a single word modifies *train*.]

The phrase in sentence *b* is a *noun phrase*. A noun phrase contains a noun and one or more modifiers; the modifers normally precede the noun. A sentence can be expanded by adding modifiers to a noun to create a noun phrase.

EXAMPLES OF NOUN PHRASES
A tattered red T-shirt hung on the clothesline.

Its owner was a *foul-tempered, ill-mannered drifter* from somewhere up north.

EX 7-1 Underline each noun phrase in the following sentences.

EXAMPLE: <u>Plush buses</u> carry <u>professional musicians</u> from concert to concert.

1. Outlandish paintings often adorn the buses.
2. A bus may contain attractive wooden furniture.
3. Custom-built bunk beds allow passengers to sleep comfortably.
4. A ten-week national tour can be an exhausting, draining experience.
5. A normally calm, level-headed musician can come apart at the seams under the pressure.
6. Crowded airports, overbooked hotels, and unavailable rental cars are sources of irritation.

7. A custom-outfitted bus eliminates many travel hassles.
8. The weekly tab for it may exceed $3,000.
9. Big-name groups can easily afford that.
10. Lesser-known but equally capable groups often drive beat-up station wagons from town to town.

EX 7–2   Write an appropriate noun phrase in each blank below. Use the noun in parentheses below the blank in the noun phrase you write.

EXAMPLE: *Overripe produce* is sold at bargain prices in many markets.
(produce)

1. _____ can be cooked up into a delicious
(tomatoes)   sauce.

2. _____ are better than yellow ones for
(bananas)   making banana bread.

3. _____ can be mashed, seasoned, and
(avocados)   served as guacamole.

4. _____ make flavorful jam.
(peaches)

5. _____ are fine for applesauce.
(apples)

6. _____ take advantage of these bargains.
(shoppers)

7. _____ is not fit for human consumption,
(produce)   however.

8. _____ should be thrown away rather than
(oranges)   eaten.

9. _____ force people to try to stretch each
(prices)   dollar.

10. Even so, _____ is wasted in many homes.
(food)

Some pairs of short sentences can be combined through the creation of noun phrases.

EXAMPLE
According to myth, Dido founded the city of Carthage. It was a mighty and splendid city.

Combined version: According to myth, Dido found the mighty and splendid city of Carthage.

EX 7–3   The following paragraph contains too many short, uninformative sentences. On another sheet of paper, rewrite this paragraph, combining pairs of short sentences into single sentences with noun phrases.

China is a producer of numerous mineral products. In fact, it happens to be a significant world producer. This nation is huge and geographically diverse. It has deposits of most minerals and metals. It boasts deposits of several scarce and useful metals. These deposits are the world's largest! The metal known as tungsten or wolfram is one of these. It is very hard and silver-white. Light bulbs contain tungsten filaments. Virtually all of them do. Tungsten alloys withstand very high temperatures without losing hardness or strength. Antimony is another metal that China has in abundance. It is also scarce and useful. This metal is brittle, nonconductive, and easily powdered. This metal is used in alloys and compounds. Bearings, storage batteries, and matches contain antimony. Some mining projects are underway in China at present, but the mineral wealth of that nation remains largely untapped.

B. WRITING APPOSITIVES

An *appositive* is a word or phrase that follows another term and explains it. Appositives are frequently used to identify people or to define words.

EXAMPLES OF APPOSITIVES
Harets ben Billizet, *a sixth-century Arabian poet,* always wore seven veils on his face in public. [This appositive phrase follows the noun *Harets ben Billizet* and explains who this person was.]

Your cousin *Emil* should wear at least that many veils and a Lone Ranger eye mask as well. [The appositive *Emil* follows the noun *cousin* and explains which cousin is being discussed.]

Serena brought to the dock a foldboat, *a small canoe that can be collapsed.* [This appositive phrase defines *foldboat.*]

EX 7–4   Underline the appositive phrases in the following sentences.

> EXAMPLE: The great nineteenth-century painter <u>Camille Pissarro</u> was born in the Virgin Islands in 1830.

1. Pissarro, a young man with no taste for the comforts of bourgeois life, refused to go into the family business.
2. He arrived in Paris, the center of the art world, in 1855.
3. He already had an awareness of his true calling, painting.
4. Pissarro painted *Coconut Palms by the Sea, St. Thomas,* a painting still admired today, in 1856.
5. The landscape *The Banks of the Marne in Winter* was exhibited in 1866.
6. The great French writer Émile Zola praised the painting highly.
7. By that time Pissarro was already an acquaintance of Monet, Manet, Cezanne, and Renoir, all great, innovative painters.
8. The label Impressionism has been given to the soft-focus paintings of these masters.
9. The paintings of Monet, shimmering configurations of dots, embody the characteristics of this school of painting.
10. Pissarro, an individualist in artistic and political thought, used a technique of building up the surface of his paintings that differed considerably from techniques used by other Impressionists.

Some sentences can be made clearer through the addition of appositive phrases. Also, pairs of sentences can sometimes be effectively combined through the use of appositive phrases. In most situations an appositive phrase should be set off from the rest of a sentence by commas.

EXAMPLE OF TWO SENTENCES COMBINED INTO ONE
WITH AN APPOSITIVE PHRASE
Fred Allen was a great radio comedian. He wrote 90 percent of the material used on his show.

Combined version: Fred Allen, a great radio comedian, wrote 90 percent of the material used on his show.

EX 7-5   Rewrite each pair of sentences below as a single sentence with an appositive phrase. Use another sheet of paper for your writing.

> EXAMPLE: The pygmy hippopotamus is a native of West Africa. It is now considered an endangered species by many wildlife experts.
> *The pygmy hippopotamus, a native of West Africa, is now considered an endangered species by many wildlife experts.*

1. Hippopotamuses are herbivores. Herbivores are plant-eating creatures.
2. *Hippopotamus amphibius* is the familiar big hippopotamus. *Hippopotamus amphibius* is still relatively common in the wilder regions of West Africa.
3. *Choreopsis liberiensis* is its small relative. This animal has become rare even in the most remote forest areas.
4. The pygmy hippopotamus is a nocturnal animal. It spends less time in water than does its larger relative.
5. The pygmy hippo is hunted by inhabitants of the dense forests. It is a tasty source of protein.
6. People desperately in need of protein cannot be faulted for killing and eating wild animals in their traditional homeland. Protein is a dietary substance necessary for health.
7. The extinction of the pygmy hippopotamus in the wild may be fast approaching. This is an unfathomable tragedy.
8. The pygmy hippopotamus is a shy animal in the wild. Fortunately, it breeds regularly in captivity if conditions are right.

C. IDENTIFYING VERB PHRASES

The simple predicate in a sentence may consist of a single-word verb or of a *verb phrase—* a main verb plus one or more auxiliary verbs.

EXAMPLE OF A SINGLE-WORD VERB
Joseph Dunninger *exposed* dozens of spiritualists as frauds.

EXAMPLE OF A VERB PHRASE
Dunninger *would explain* the mechanics of the spiritualists' illusions to the audience.

The following verbs may be used as auxiliaries:

am, is, are, was, were
be, being, been
do, does, did
has, have, had
shall, will, should, would
may, might, must, can, could

Some auxiliaries—such as *has, have,* and *had*—are used to signify the time at which something happened or existed. Others, such as *may* and *might*, are used to express the possibility of an action or state of being. (The uses of particular auxiliaries is the focus of section H of Chapter 12.)

NOTE: The word *not* is a modifier, not an auxiliary verb; it should not be considered a part of any verb phrase.

EX 7-6   Underline each verb phrase in the following sentences.

> EXAMPLE: Scientists at the University of California, Berkeley, <u>are designing</u> a marvelous new telescope.

1. The new device will be a ten-meter telescope of revolutionary design.
2. The famous telescope atop Mount Palomar, an instrument with a primary mirror approximately five meters in circumference, has been the largest optical telescope for many years.
3. Technical problems have prevented the construction of larger instruments.
4. A new type of mirror has been designed by UC astrophysicists.
5. This revolutionary reflecting surface will be an array of six-sided mirrors.
6. Each will be controlled by sophisticated sensors and alignment mechanisms.
7. The mirrors can be adjusted to tolerances of millionths of an inch.
8. This new telescope should be completed by 1990.
9. It may be installed in a building at the top of Hawaii's Mauna Kea, a mountain on an island in the middle of the ocean.
10. Air pollution and artificial light will not pose problems to researchers there.

EX 7-7   Write an appropriate verb phrase in each blank. Be sure to consider any words in the sentence that give time information as you select an auxiliary verb or verbs.

> EXAMPLE: The contract *must be signed* by five o'clock tomorrow.

1. My lawyer _____ later today.

2. I _____ her several times about this matter.

3. She _____ not _____ the contract yet.

4. She _____ law in this city for seven years.

5. She _____ already _____ a reputation as an expert in contract law.

6. A poorly written contract _____ tremendous headaches.

7. She _____ a number of constructive suggestions.

8. The other party in this business deal _____ not _____

_____ a lawyer.

9. He _____ for trouble.

10. Two hundred dollars spent on lawyers' fees at the contract-writing stage of a

deal _____ a person thousands of dollars in
subsequent costs and fees.

D. WRITING PREPOSITIONAL PHRASES

Look at the following sentences.

    a. Eliza and Mary Chulkhurst of Biddenden, Kent, England, were Siamese twins.
    b. In their will the twins made a generous bequest.
    c. All income from land left by the Chulkhursts would be used for food for the poor.

Which phrase in sentence *a* modifies *Eliza and Mary Chulkhurst*? Note that this phrase

modifies a pair of *nouns*. _____

Now find the phrase in sentence *b* that tells *where* about the verb *made*. _____

_____

Finally, find the two phrases in sentence *c* that modify the verb phrase *would be used*.

_____

All the phrases you have identified are *prepositional phrases*. Prepositional phrases most
frequently function as modifying elements. A prepositional phrase consists of a *preposition*—
a word that shows relationship—and its *object*—normally a noun or pronoun. The prepositional phrase may also contain one or more words that modify the object of the preposition.

EXAMPLES OF PREPOSITIONAL PHRASES
The four new sales representatives attended a meeting *in Tulsa*. [This prepositional phrase
consists of the preposition *in* and its object, the noun *Tulsa*.]

The meeting began *with a lavish banquet*. [This prepositional phrase consists of the preposition *with*; its object, the noun *banquet*; and two words—*a* and *lavish*—that modify *banquet*.]

Here is a list of some commonly used prepositions. Note that some prepositions consist
of more than one word.

in	down	from	since	between	in spite of
as	off	in	through	along	as well as
by	for	like	till	behind	out of
at	of	on	to	outside	in accordance with

Prepositional phrases do not contain subject–verb combinations.

**EXAMPLE OF A SENTENCE WITH A PREPOSITIONAL PHRASE
BEGINNING WITH *TILL***
We play soccer *till dusk*.

THIS SENTENCE DOES NOT CONTAIN A PREPOSITIONAL PHRASE
We play soccer till the sun sets. [*Till the sun sets* contains the subject–verb combination *sun/sets*; it is therefore a *clause* rather than a prepositional phrase. Clauses are discussed in the next chapter.]

Prepositional phrases can be used to modify nouns and pronouns. As you probably know, single words that modify nouns or pronouns are called *adjectives*. Prepositional phrases that modify nouns or pronouns are thus called *adjectival prepositional phrases*.

**EXAMPLE OF A SENTENCE WITH ONE PREPOSITIONAL PHRASE MODIFYING
A PRONOUN AND ANOTHER MODIFYING A NOUN**
One *of the saddest Sunday sights* is a pro football player *with a newly damaged knee*. [Each italicized phrase is an *adjectival* prepositional phrase.]

EX 7–8 Each of the following sentences contains a prepositional phrase that modifies a noun or a pronoun. Underline each of these phrases. Draw an arrow from the phrase to the word it modifies.

EXAMPLE: The power of the wind can be harnessed.

1. The use of wind power is not a new breakthrough.

2. At least forty generations of farmers have used windmills.

3. Farmers in thirteenth-century Holland apparently used windmills.

4. The fictional sixteenth-century hero Dox Quixote de la Mancha assaulted several of these long-armed machines.

5. Sails of canvas sometimes adorn the long arms.

6. Some traditional windmills had arms with light wooden panels.

7. The newest generation of windmills does not resemble the elegant traditional European varieties.

8. A tall pole with two rotating arms is quite an efficient configuration.

9. "Wind farms" with many windmills are now being constructed in windy passes.

10. Many of the new electricity-generating windmills produce a loud, low-pitched humming noise.

11. Communities near wind farms may find the noise maddening.

12. Engineers must solve this problem of excessive low-frequency noise.

Prepositional phrases can also be used to modify verbs. Single words that modify verbs are called *adverbs*, so prepositional phrases that modify verbs are call *adverbial prepositional phrases*. Adverbial prepositional phrases usually tell *how, when, where,* or *how much* about a a verb.

EXAMPLES OF SENTENCES WITH PREPOSITIONAL PHRASES MODIFYING VERBS
That report was thoroughly censored *before its release.* [This prepositional phrase modifies the verb *was censored* and answers the question *when.*]

The agency released the report *without comment.* [This prepositional phrase modifies the verb *released* and answers the question *how.*]

EX 7–9   Each of the following sentences contains one or more prepositional phrases that tell *when, where, how,* or *how much* about a verb. Underline each of these phrases. Draw an arrow to the verb modified by the phrase.

EXAMPLE: Flagpole sitting became a fad during the 1920s.

1. A flagpole sitter climbed a flagpole with much fanfare.

2. The sitter affixed a small platform to the pole's top.

3. The sitter remained there for days.

4. The hardiest flagpole sitters performed feats in winter.

5. A few of these performers remained aloft during blizzards.

6. Why did this strange practice attract so much attention during those years?

7. "Shipwreck" Kelly was recognized as America's premier flagpole sitter.

8. Kelly spent 1,177 consecutive hours atop an Atlantic City flagpole.

9. He did this in 1930.

10. Two holes had been drilled in the flagpole shaft.

11. Kelly slept with his thumbs in these holes.

12. Any movement during sleep would cause pain.

13. Without this safety procedure Kelly might have fallen from his perch during sleep.

14. Kelly spent 20,613 hours atop flagpoles during his career.

15. His record should remain safe for a good long time.

EX 7–10   Write an appropriate prepositional phrase to complete the following sentences.

EXAMPLE: Rents in college towns may be lower *during the summer.*

1. A basement apartment can be cold and damp _____.

2. Students _____ seldom end up in luxurious accommodations.

3. Some rent a room _____.

4. Keeping a kitchen clean is not always easy _____.

5. A perpetual mess _____ can create a health hazard.

6. Apartments do not stay clean _____.

7. A vacuum cleaner _____ doesn't do much good.

8. Threats _____ are remarkably effective in motivating lazy roommates.

9. A scheduled party usually forces each roommate to push a broom or mop _____, too.

10. Unfortunately, the apartment winds up looking filthier than ever _____
_____.

The placement of prepositional phrases is extremely important. As a general rule an adjectival prepositional phrase should follow immediately the noun or pronoun it modifies. An adverbial phrase should be placed close enough to the word or words it modifies so that no confusion arises.

EXAMPLE OF PROPER PLACEMENT OF AN ADJECTIVAL PREPOSITIONAL PHRASE
This porcelain factory produces statuettes *with delicate birds* for shipment to the Far East.

PLACEMENT THAT CAUSES CONFUSION
This porcelain factory produces statuettes for shipment to the Far East *with delicate birds*.
[This placement leaves the reader in doubt as to whether the statuettes *feature* birds or are shipped *along with* birds that are separate pieces.]

EXAMPLE OF PROPER PLACEMENT OF AN ADVERBIAL PREPOSITIONAL PHRASE
The horse ran *with new vigor* past its master out into the open field.

PLACEMENT THAT MAY CAUSE CONFUSION
The horse ran past its master *with new vigor* out into the open field. [The reader will probably decide that *with new vigor* describes how the horse ran rather than how the master was feeling. Nevertheless, the placement of the phrase does not make the meaning clear.]

EX 7–11   Rewrite each of the following sentences, inserting the prepositional phrase in parentheses in the proper place. Use another sheet of paper for your writing.

EXAMPLE: The people of India honor the memory with a celebration on his birthday, October 2. (of Mohandas Gandhi)
The people of India honor the memory of Mohandas Gandhi with a celebration on his birthday, October 2.

1. Several holidays of special interest to Americans occur each month. (of particular ethnic backgrounds)
2. An important holiday is National Foundation Day, October 3. (for Koreans)
3. Americans of Norwegian descent hold a celebration in honor of explorer Leif Ericson on the Sunday closest to October 9 each year. (at Jensen Beach, Florida)
4. General Casimir Pulaski led American forces. (during the Revolutionary War)
5. October 11 has become Pulaski Day, an official holiday. (in Indiana)

6. The first Columbus Day celebration was held. (on October 12, 1792)
7. Thanksgiving Day is October 13. (in Canada)
8. Many Americans celebrate Greek National Day on October 28. (of Greek descent)
9. October 29 is an important day, for that is the national holiday known as Republic Day. (in Turkey)
10. There are ethnic aspects, too. (to Halloween)
11. The modern symbol apparently came to us from Ireland. (of Halloween)
12. The jack-o'-lantern carries the name of a legendary Irish fellow with no generosity. (in his heart)
13. Jack was not welcomed by the guardian of the gates of heaven. (upon his death)
14. Jack had played tricks on the Devil, and he was not welcome in hell, either. (during his life)
15. Jack was condemned to walk aimlessly until Judgment Day. (upon the earth)
16. He carries a lantern to light his way. (in his hand)
17. Our jack-o'-lanterns grin at passersby. (with an eerie light)
18. Youngsters hollow out turnips and place candles inside them. (in Switzerland)

EX 7-12 Rewrite six of the sentences you wrote in EX 7-11; in each sentence move one prepositional phrase to a new position. Be sure the revision does not affect the meaning of the sentence. Use another sheet of paper for your writing.

EX 7-13 Each sentence below has a misplaced prepositional phrase. Rewrite each so that the phrase appears in the proper place. Use another sheet of paper for your writing.

> EXAMPLE: The mouth is a highly developed organ of the octopus.
> *The mouth of the octopus is a highly developed organ.*

1. To a human, the bite of an octopus can be deadly.
2. On September 18, 1954, two people handled a small blue octopus on a spear-fishing outing.
3. Over his shoulder one of the fishermen allowed the octopus to slide.
4. It briefly with its beak attached itself to the skin of the young man.
5. The small creature then dropped and propelled itself away into the water.
6. Soon in his throat the young man felt a dryness, as well as some nausea.
7. The wound from the octopus bite was bleeding on his back.
8. He vomited and became unable to walk, and his friend at top speed drove him to the hospital.
9. He received excellent medical treatment, but he died two hours after being bitten at the hospital.
10. The poison gland behind the neck is located in the flabby, bulbous body of the octopus.

EX 7-14   Use each prepositional phrase below in an original sentence. Identify whether you use the phrase as an *adjectival prepositional phrase* or as an *adverbial prepositional phrase*. Use another sheet of paper for your writing.

> EXAMPLE: in a blue windbreaker *A person in a blue windbreaker tossed a*
> *Frisbee into a hornet's nest. (adjectival prepositional phrase)*

1. at the picnic table
2. with mayonnaise
3. in the sky
4. up a large tree
5. into the potato salad
6. until sunset

E. WRITING INFINITIVE PHRASES

Look at the sentences below. The italicized words in each sentence are verbs.

> a. My friend *wants* to *try* windsurfing.
> b. The instructor *has told* her to *learn* the principles of sailing first.

Which verb in sentence *a* would change its form if the subject were *friends* rather than *friend*? _____ What word precedes the other verb in sentence *a*? _____ Which verb or verb phrase in sentence *b* would be in different form if the subject of the sentence were *instructors* rather than *instructor*? _____ What word precedes the other verb? _____

An *infinitive phrase* is a phrase that begins with *to* and a verb or verb phrase. It may also include one or more complements as well as modifiers. Infinitive phrases may function as nouns or as modifiers. The verb in an infinitive phrase does not directly tell anything about any subject; it does not change form to show agreement.

EXAMPLES OF INFINITIVE PHRASES
Charles Dickens' novels are not difficult *to understand* [This infinitive phrase contains just *to* and the verb *understand*. It modifies *difficult*.]

Hobie wants *to read Oliver Twist*. [This infinitive phrase contains *to*, the verb *read*, and the direct object *Oliver Twist*. The entire phrase functions as a noun—the direct object of *wants* in the sentence.]

Hunger drives poor Oliver *to ask Mr. Bumble, the workhouse boss, for more oatmeal*. [This long infinitive phrase includes both an appositive phrase, *the workhouse boss*, and a prepositional phrase, *for more oatmeal*. The entire infinitive phrase modifies the verb *drives*.]

To read Oliver Twist is *to glimpse the pathos of poor children's lives in Dickens' day*. [The first infinitive phrase functions as a noun and is the subject of the sentence. The second infinitive phrase functions as a noun and is the subjective complement.]

SENTENCE THAT DOES NOT CONTAIN AN INFINITIVE PHRASE
These books will be lent to the first person who shows a valid library card. [Here *to* is a preposition and *person* is its object. The verb *shows* relates to the pronoun *who*; it would change form if the sentence read *These books will be lent to the first people who show valid library cards.*]

EX 7–15   Underline the infinitive phrase in each sentence below.

> EXAMPLE: Competitors in power-lifting meets must be able <u>to lift great weights</u>.

1. A power lifter must perform well in all three events to be successful.
2. One exercise, the squat, is performed to demonstrate leg strength.
3. To begin the exercise, the lifter takes the weighted bar from a rack onto the shoulders.
4. The lifter must be able to do a deep knee bend.
5. To rise to the standing position with 300 pounds on your back is not easy.
6. The bench press is performed to demonstrate arm and shoulder strength.
7. Two spotters are required to help the lifter.
8. The lifter lies on a bench with feet on the floor to increase stability.
9. The spotters lift the bar to the contestant's waiting hands; the contestant tries to extend both arms fully.
10. To return the heavy bar to the chest requires strength and concentration.
11. After the lift the spotters must be ready to take the bar away.
12. The dead lift gives competitors the chance to show thigh, hip, and lower-back strength.
13. The lifter bends down to grasp the bar on the floor.
14. To stand up with 400 pounds in hand is a tremendous achievement.
15. The winner of a power-lifting competition is the person able to lift the greatest total weight in the three events.
16. A few lifters in the super heavyweight class have been able to lift more than 2,300 pounds in the three events!

EX 7–16   In the sentences below, circle each infinitive phrase that is used as a noun. Underline each infinitive phrase that is used as a modifier; draw an arrow to the word it modifies.

> EXAMPLES: Only a fool tries (to fish in Mono Lake.)
> Visitors come <u>to enjoy the scenery</u>.

1. Hundreds of thousands of seagulls come to lay eggs.
2. Some insect species are able to live in the salty water.
3. Desert sun causes water to evaporate.
4. Evaporation causes the proportion of minerals in the water to increase.
5. Many writers have tried to describe Mono Lake's tufa towers.
6. To some, these appear to be goblin castles.
7. To imagine the towers as creatures from underground worlds is not difficult.
8. Fresh water from springs under the lake bottom reacts with minerals in Mono Lake's water to produce particles.
9. A long period of time was required for the carbonate deposits to form the largest of the castles.
10. Mono Lake, east of Yosemite National Park, is a sight to see.

Many people concerned with style in English prose feel that no words should come between *to* and the verb in an infinitive phrase. Therefore, it is a good idea to eliminate such *split infinitives* from your writing.

EXAMPLE OF SPLIT INFINITIVE
The clerk began to carefully arrange the tomatoes. [*Carefully* comes between *to* and the verb *arrange.*]

REVISION TO ELIMINATE THE SPLIT INFINITIVE
The clerk began carefully to arrange the tomatoes.

EX 7-17   On another sheet of paper, rewrite each sentence below to correct the split infinitive.

> EXAMPLE: People have begun to enthusiastically talk about a new musical comedy.
> *People have begun to talk enthusiastically about a new musical comedy.*

1. Andrew Lloyd Webber decided to somehow create a musical comedy around T. S. Eliot's poems from *Old Possum's Book of Practical Cats.*
2. As he demonstrated in *Evita* and *Jesus Christ Superstar*, Lloyd Webber is one who is able to cleverly present ideas in song.
3. He began to closely work with Trevor Nunn, artistic director of the Royal Shakespeare Company.
4. The show began to uniquely develop a character when choreographer Gillian Lynne became involved.
5. Designer John Napier helped the audience to magically enter the world of cats by fashioning a stage set made of oversized pieces of junk.
6. Dancers must employ jumpiness as well as grace to convincingly portray cats.
7. Lloyd Webber gives the audience at least one hit tune—"Memory"—to happily hum on the way out of the theater.
8. Perhaps you will have the opportunity to someday enjoy the musical comedy *Cats.*

EX 7-18   Complete each sentence by writing an infinitive phrase in the blank. Use your imagination.

> EXAMPLE: The rat in this cage apparently wants *to attract some attention.*

1. Soon I will begin _____.

2. Last summer I wanted _____.

3. _____ is usually not a good idea.

4. I wish someone would give me the chance _____.

5. One of my greatest dreams is _____.

6. Every college student has _____.

F. WRITING PARTICIPIAL PHRASES

Look at the following sentences.

> a. I was running for my life.
> b. The figure running after me looked like a desperate person.

In which sentence is *running* part of a verb phrase that relates to the subject? _____

In which sentence is *running* the first word in a modifying phrase? _____

Verbs ending in *-ing, -en,* and *-ed* are called *participle* forms. These forms can be used as modifiers; when they are used as modifiers, they are called *participles.* Often these words introduce modifying phrases called *participial phrases.*

EXAMPLES OF PARTICIPLES AS SINGLE-WORD MODIFIERS
The *broken* dish could not be mended. [The participle *broken* is a form of the verb *break*; it modifies the noun *dish.*]

Wailing sirens affirmed the seriousness of the situation. [The participle *wailing* is a form of the verb *wail*; it modifies the noun *sirens.*]

EXAMPLES OF PARTICIPIAL PHRASES
The grocery, *devastated by the earthquake,* was not open for business. [The participle *devastated* introduces the phrase; the prepositional phrase *by the earthquake* modifies *devastated.* The entire participial phrase modifies the noun *grocery.*]

A helicopter *carrying supplies to a village in a remote canyon* crashed and burned. [The participle *carrying* introduces the phrase; *supplies* is the direct object of *carrying,* and the two prepositional phrases modify *carrying.* The entire participial phrase modifies *helicopter.*]

SENTENCE THAT DOES NOT CONTAIN A PARTICIPIAL PHRASE
Mr. Sanchez is bringing food to the refugees in the gymnasium. [The participial form *bringing* is part of the verb phrase *is bringing.*]

EX 7-19   Underline the participial phrase or phrases in each of the following sentences. Draw an arrow from each phrase to the word it modifies.

> EXAMPLE: The glass slippers worn by Cinderella are a recent embellishment to the story.

1. This tale, loved by so many generations of children, may have its origins in China.

2. Stories bearing similarities to our *Cinderella* may have evolved in several locales.

3. The tale of Cinderella originally may have been a myth personifying forces of nature.

4. Cinderella, representing dawn, was subjugated by her sisters, representing darkness.

5. The prince, shining forth as the sun, rescues fair Cinderella from the forces of darkness.

6. Slippers fashioned of precious metal are key elements in many old versions of this tale.

7. Some versions tell of magic slippers festooned with jewels.

8. Early versions written in French mention *pantoufles en vair*, slippers of white squirrel fur.

9. The version created by Charles Perrault in the late seventeenth century contains a mistranslation of the archaic word *vair*.

10. Perrault, believing *vair* to be an old spelling of *verre*—the word for glass—put Cinderella in a most uncomfortable pair of slippers.

As you may have noticed, a participial phrase may be set off from the rest of a sentence by commas. Look at the sentences below.

a. The oldest person wearing a Royals cap won the prize.
b. The oldest person, wearing a Royals cap, won the prize.

In which sentence is age the only criterion for winning the prize? _____ In which sentence is the identity of the winner determined by what he or she was wearing, as well as by age? _____

Commas are used to set off participial phrases that give nonessential information. These phrases are called *nonrestrictive* participial phrases because they do not really restrict or pin down the identity of the thing they describe. Sentence *b*, above, contains a *nonrestrictive* participial phrase.

If the identity of something named by a noun or pronoun will not be clear to readers if the participial phrase is not included, the participial phrase must *not* be set off by commas. This type of phrase is called a *restrictive* participial phrase, because it *restricts* the identity of what it describes. Sentence *a*, above, contains a *restrictive* participial phrase.

It is not always easy to decide whether a phrase should be considered restrictive or nonrestrictive. In general, you should consider a phrase restrictive and omit commas *only if* you use the phrase to differentiate one thing from others of its kind by the characteristic specified by the participial phrase. If, however, you are just including an interesting descriptive point, the phrase should be considered nonrestrictive; use commas to set it off from the rest of the sentence.

**EXAMPLE OF A PARTICIPIAL PHRASE BETTER HANDLED
AS A RESTRICTIVE PHRASE**
Several kings were present; the king *holding the golden sword* proposed an alliance. [The participial phrase *holding the golden sword* is needed to inform readers which of the kings was speaking. It is therefore a *restrictive* participial phrase and should *not* be set off with commas.]

**EXAMPLE OF A PARTICIPIAL PHRASE BETTER HANDLED
AS A NONRESTRICTIVE PHRASE**
Several ambassadors were present; the king, *holding the golden sword*, proposed an alliance. [The participial phrase *holding the golden sword* is not needed here, since there is only one king present. It therefore is a *nonrestrictive* participial phrase and *should* be set off with commas.]

Participial phrases that come before the subject of the sentence must be set off from the rest of the sentence by commas.

EXAMPLE
Waving his fists wildly, the green-robed ambassador rejected the king's proposal.

EX 7-20 Six of the following sentences contain participial phrases that make better sense as nonrestrictive phrases. Add commas to these sentences to set off these phrases. Also, set off with commas any introductory participial phrases.

EXAMPLE: The Aleutian Islands, extending south and west from the Alaska mainland, are cold, foggy, and barren.

1. A woman joining a wild goose chase there might be considered crazy by some.
2. Elaine Rhode seeking information for a film script came by boat to Buldir Island.
3. Buldir lying between Kiska and Near Island is a nesting ground for Aleutian geese.
4. The Aleutian goose related to the common Canadian species has disappeared from other Aleutian islands.
5. Sailors seeking to establish fur farms released Arctic foxes on almost all other islands in the Aleutian chain during the early 1900s.
6. The Aleutian geese being unable to protect themselves or their young from the foxes quickly disappeared from those islands.
7. In 1974 the U.S. Fish and Wildlife Service having become aware of the geese on Buldir Island established a study program there.
8. In 1975 Elaine Rhode joined the wildlife biologists studying the geese in their natural habitat.
9. Proving herself equal to the demands of the project Ms. Rhode became a respected member of the team.
10. Elaine Rhode's film called *Chain of Life—the Aleutian Islands* earned the Conservation Film of the Year award from the Outdoor Writers' Association of America.

EX 7-21 Write an appropriate participial phrase in each blank to complete the following sentences. Insert commas where needed.

EXAMPLE: A cook *kneading bread dough* should not be interrupted.

1. A driver _____ should not be distracted.

2. A student _____ wants quiet.

3. Young children _____ do not understand the concept of silence.

4. Libraries _____ attract many serious students.

5. They also attract people _____.

6. "Silence is golden" is a phrase _____.

7. People _____ should consider the job of fire lookout.

8. Fire lookouts spend the summer _____.

9. These people _____ endure and perhaps enjoy long stretches of solitude.

10. Some people, though, work better _____ than sitting in a silent room miles from the nearest settlement.

EX 7-22   Combine each of the following pairs of sentences into a single sentence with a participial phrase. Insert commas where needed. Use another sheet of paper for your writing.

> EXAMPLE: Sturdy automobiles were made available to Americans during the first decade of the twentieth century. These vehicles offered swift, independent transportation.
> *Sturdy automobiles offering swift, independent transportation were made available to Americans during the first decade of the twentieth century.*

1. Cars were offered during those years. They were relatively expensive.
2. Many people chose not to buy an auto then. These people were earning good salaries.
3. Cars traveled the streets of eastern cities. These vehicles were ridiculed as being expensive toys.
4. Autos carry people from place to place. They need roadways with level, even surfaces.
5. Roads linked American cities at the turn of the century. Most were hardly deserving of the designation "road."
6. Problems were inevitable for motorists. These motorists were seeking to travel through the countryside by car.
7. Arthur J. Eddy had taken a long auto trip. He published *Two Thousand Miles on an Automobile* in 1902.
8. His tires were easily punctured by road hazards. They required repair or replacement every few hundred miles at least.
9. Signs forbade travel by horseless carriage. These were posted at the entrances to many villages.
10. Some villages posted signs. These signs limited autos to a speed of ten miles an hour.
11. Eddy drove a car capable of averaging thirty miles an hour. He seldom cruised as fast as twenty miles an hour.
12. Many of today's cars have little clearance between the roadway and the undercarriage. They would undoubtedly have done even worse on those roads than did the horeseless carriages of yesteryear.

A participial phrase must be placed close enough to the word it modifies to prevent confusion. A participial phrase that is placed so that it appears to modify a word other than the one it actually modifies is called a *misplaced* participial phrase.

EXAMPLE OF A SENTENCE WITH A MISPLACED PARTICIPIAL PHRASE
The Baby Ruth candy bar was named after Ruth Cleveland, the first daughter of a President *born in the White House.* [The sentence seems to talk about the daughter of a *President* who was born in the White House, but it is actually talking about a President's *daughter* born in the White House.]

CORRECTED VERSION
The Baby Ruth candy bar was named after Ruth Cleveland, the first daughter *born to a President and his wife in the White House.*

A participial phrase must clearly modify a word or words in the sentence in which it appears. A participial phrase that does not clearly modify any word is termed a *dangling* participial phrase.

EXAMPLE OF A SENTENCE WITH A DANGLING PARTICIPIAL PHRASE
Feeling very tired, the hike ended none too soon. [This participial phrase modifies neither *hike* nor any other word in the sentence.]

CORRECTED VERSION
Feeling very tired, the scouts said that the hike had ended none too soon. [The participial phrase here modifies *scouts.*]

Misplaced participial phrases and dangling participial phrases are common errors. Watch for these errors when you edit and proofread your written work. Be sure to correct any you spot.

EX 7-23   Each sentence below has a dangling or misplaced participial phrase in it. Rewrite the sentences so that all participial phrases are properly placed and clearly modify one or more words. Use another sheet of paper for your writing.

> EXAMPLE: Checking the mail, a brown envelope caught Penny's eye.
> *Penny, checking the mail, had a brown envelope catch her eye.*

1. Reading the huge green letters on the front, it was probably a piece of junk mail.
2. Having nothing better to do, the blurb about a free trip around the word was scanned by Penny.
3. Becoming more curious, the envelope was opened by Penny.
4. A new magazine was looking for subscribers featuring international vacation ideas.
5. One person would win a free trip around the world returning the postpaid reply card.
6. Having nothing to lose, Penny's card went into the mail.
7. Penny forgot about the contest becoming busy with summer clothes.
8. Seeing the mail carrier at the door with a registered letter, Penny's heart stopped.
9. Penny ripped open the envelope holding her breath.
10. Learning that she had won second prize, there was a feeling of disappointment.
11. The three-year free subscription was a big let-down awarded to her.
12. Realizing how desperately she wanted to travel, a serious plan of action was designed that very night.

EX 7-24   On another sheet of paper, rewrite the paragraph below. Correct sentences with dangling or misplaced participial phrases.

The secretary bird attacks poisonous snakes showing no fear at all. Feeding primarily on lizards and snakes, its quick reflexes allow it to attack reptiles without being bitten by them. When a secretary bird spots a venomous snake, it attacks it, crawling on the ground. Related to American hawks, its wings are useful as shields. Jumping out of reach of the deadly fangs, the snake is attacked by the secretary bird's tough, powerful claws. The snake is tossed into the air several times by the bird, exhausted from the battle. Finally the bird delivers a killing blow to the stunned reptile. Having worked hard for its meal, the snake is then devoured.

G. IDENTIFYING GERUNDS

Look at the following sentences.

> a. The woman *soaring high above the canyon* is my sister.
> b. *Soaring high above the canyon* is an unforgettable experience.

In which sentence does the phrase *soaring high above the canyon* modify a noun? _____
In which of the two sentences does the phrase *soaring high above the canyon* function as the subject? _____

A verb form that functions as a noun is called a *gerund.* A *gerund phrase* is comprised of a gerund and the words that relate to or modify it. Most gerunds end in *-ing.*

EXAMPLES OF GERUNDS
Passing is foolish on this country road. [The gerund *passing* is a form of the verb *pass.* Here *passing* functions as the subject of the sentence.]

The law prohibits *tailgating.* [The gerund *tailgating* is a form of the verb *tailgate.* Here *tailgating* functions as the direct object of the verb *prohibits.*]

EXAMPLES OF GERUND PHRASES
Claiming illness on the day after a three-day weekend is not a good idea. [*Claiming* is the gerund; *illness* is the direct object of *claiming*; the two prepositional phrases modify *claiming.* The entire gerund phrase functions as the subject of the sentence.]

The office manager dislikes *hearing lame excuses.* [*Hearing* is the gerund; *excuses* is its direct object; *lame* modifies *excuses.* The entire gerund phrase functions as a direct object.]

EX 7–25   Underline the gerund phrase in each of the following sentences.

> EXAMPLE: Reading James Thurber's preface to *The Thurber Carnival* is a
>   good introduction to his work.

1. Making people laugh is not a difficult task.
2. Mixing wit and wisdom takes considerable skill.
3. Not everyone enjoys reading satire.
4. James Thurber had a talent for creating humor in a variety of veins.
5. His fables encourage thinking about human foibles.
6. Tweaking self-important people was a favorite pastime of Thurber's.
7. Millions of readers have enjoyed meeting Thurber's character Walter Mitty.
8. Dreaming of himself in heroic situations is this meek fellow's vice.
9. Readers also enjoy seeing Thurber's thoughts in the form of line cartoons.
10. Reading Thurber's description of his childhood in his preface to *The Thurber Carnival* will give you an idea of how he saw the world.

EX 7-26   Use each phrase below as a gerund phrase in an original sentence. Write your sentences on another sheet of paper.

EXAMPLE: picking blackberries *Another hour of picking blackberries will reduce my hands to hamburger.*

1. remembering a nine-digit code
2. standing in line at the post office
3. licking fifty stamps
4. opening a manila envelope
5. wrapping a parcel for overseas delivery
6. receiving a letter from an old friend

H. WRITING SENTENCES WITH PARALLEL PHRASES

When similar ideas are being expressed in a sentence, the forms expressing the ideas should be the same, if at all possible. Look at the following sentences.

a. Counselors at the Ralph Lunchwagon Athletic Training Camp teach hurdling, pole vaulting, and to throw the javelin.
b. Counselors at the Ralph Lunchwagon Athletic Training Camp teach hurdling, pole vaulting, and javelin throwing.

Which sentence uses similar forms to express similar ideas? _____
When similar structures are used to express ideas linked together in a sentence, the structures are said to be *parallel*.

EXAMPLES OF PARALLEL STRUCTURE
Some campers come *to develop athletic skills* and *to build confidence.* [Two infinitive phrases are linked by *and.*]

Brochures *outlining camp activities* and *listing fees* are available in sporting goods stores throughout the city. [Two participial phrases are linked by *and.*]

Climbing a mountain beats *climbing a junkpile.* [This sentence compares two activities; gerund phrases are used to name the activities.]

SENTENCES MADE AWKWARD BY NONPARALLEL CONSTRUCTIONS
Some campers come *to develop athletic skills* and *building confidence.* [An infinitive phrase and a participial phrase are linked by *and*; these structures are not parallel, and the participial phrase does not seem to express the writer's intended meaning.]

Brochures *to outline camp activities* and *listing fees* are available in sporting goods stores throughout the city. [An infinitive phrase and a participial phrase are linked.]

To climb a mountain beats *climbing a junkpile.* [The activities compared are stated in an infinitive phrase and a gerund phrase rather than in two parallel phrases.]

EX 7-27   Rewrite each sentence below so that ideas linked within the sentence are expressed in parallel phrases. Use another sheet of paper for your writing.

> EXAMPLE: Gas stations that require self-service but offering lower prices are becoming more prevalent.
> *Gas stations requiring self-service but offering lower prices are becoming more prevalent.*

1. Proper car care involves more than to fill the tank and wash the windshield.
2. To take proper care of your car means filling it with the proper grade of gasoline.
3. Motorists pulling up to any empty stall and to stick whichever hose is not in use into the tank are asking for trouble.
4. A motorist should know how to read an oil dipstick and checking air pressure in the tires.
5. Underinflated tires can cause a car to handle poorly and using more gasoline.
6. Driving a car with too little engine oil is to play with fire.
7. Which makes better sense, to spend $2 for a quart of oil or spending $1,000 for a new engine?
8. A fan belt cracked by cold, softened by heat, or having been weakened by years of use can cause the worst sort of engine problems.
9. Auto manufacturers recommend inspecting fan belts and to check radiator hoses periodically.
10. Neither being in a hurry nor without enough money to pay for oil or minor repairs is a valid excuse for failing to check the condition of your vehicle.

EX 7-28   Complete the following sentences by writing parallel infinitive, participle, or gerund structures in the blanks. Use your imagination.

> EXAMPLE: Two things I detest are cleaning the oven and *fixing the sink trap*.

1. Even the worst apartment can be made livable by painting the walls and

_____.

2. Furniture having a few nicks or _____

_____ can be purchased at garage sales.

3. It's not difficult to reupholster a sofa or _____.

4. Admittedly, spending a day at the beach is more fun than _____

_____.

5. Renting a rug shampooer, buying a $2.49 bottle of rug shampoo, and

_____ is not much of a chore.

6. If you are able to read these sentences, you should be able _____

_____.

EX 7-29   On another sheet of paper, rewrite the following paragraph; correct nonparallel expressions.

In 1894, many Americans felt that to go on strike was declaring war on management. But when company management moved to cut wages and firing union representatives in that year, the employees of the Pullman Palace Car Company in Chicago felt they had no choice: on May 11, 1894, they went on strike. The workers, planning strategy and to seek support, talked with officials of their union, the American Railway Union. Support was forthcoming from the ARU; on June 26 its president, Eugene V. Debs, called for a boycott of all trains pulling Pullman railroad cars. Fifty thousand railroad workers heeded Debs's call, and soon trains were no longer moving out of Chicago. Railroad owners asked the courts to declare the strike illegal and forcing the workers to handle trains with Pullman cars; they did obtain an injunction on July 2, but it did not cause the union members to back down and beginning to handle trains again. Then, on July 4, President Grover Cleveland sent troops to Chicago enforcing the ruling and to force union members back to work. Riots, violence, and to shed blood resulted; nevertheless, the troops succeeded in forcing the workers back on the job and so to break the strike. Four union leaders, including Debs, spent time in jail for ignoring the injunction and encourage the workers to continue the boycott.

I. REVIEWING CHAPTER CONCEPTS

EX 7-30   Write *NP* above each underlined phrase that is a noun phrase. Write *VP* above each underlined phrase that is a verb phrase. Write *PP* above each underlined phrase that is a prepositional phrase.

　　　　　　　　　　　　　　　　　　　　　　　PP
　　　　EXAMPLE: *Children of a Lesser God* began <u>as a college workshop production</u>.

1. Playwright Mark Medoff <u>had won</u> prizes <u>for previous plays</u>.

2. <u>The innovative play</u> deals with a relationship <u>between a hearing speech instructor</u> and a deaf student.

3. Medoff revised the play <u>after the workshop production</u>.

4. <u>This gifted writer</u> enlarged the part <u>of the deaf student</u>.

5. She <u>would use</u> only sign language to communicate.

6. <u>With the deaf student's expanded part</u>, the play became <u>a love story</u>.

7. The deaf actress Phyllis Frelich helped Medoff develop the part <u>of the student</u>.

8. *Children of a Lesser God* <u>has played</u>/to enthusiastic audiences.

9. <u>Some dialogue</u>/in the play/is presented in sign language only.

10. The expressiveness <u>of sign language</u>/is demonstrated to audience members during the course of the play.

EX 7–31 Write appositive phrases to complete the following sentences. Add commas where needed. You may want to consult an encyclopedia or dictionary before you begin writing.

> EXAMPLE: Ecuador, *a South American nation*, is a major producer of cocoa.

1. Costa Rica _____ produces fine coffee beans.

2. Manganese _____ is mined in Costa Rica.

3. The mines of Costa Rica also yield gold _____ .

4. A considerable number of workers from Jamaica _____ _____ emigrated to Costa Rica during the nineteenth century.

5. Some of these workers do not speak Spanish _____ _____ .

6. They continue to speak English _____ _____ even though several generations of their families have resided in Costa Rica.

EX 7–32 Four of the following sentences contain misplaced prepositional phrases. Rewrite these sentences so that each prepositional phrase appears near the word or words it modifies. Use another sheet of paper for your writing.

> EXAMPLE: Spiders of many sorts are in the Spider Museum on display in Richmond, Virginia.
> *Spiders of many sorts are on display in the Spider Museum in Richmond, Virginia.*

1. With an interest in trapdoor spiders, anyone will find the museum fascinating.
2. Visitors to the museum watch live black widow spiders behind glass.
3. Live tarantulas in the museum are also on display.
4. Photographs of spider life instruct visitors on the walls of the museum.
5. Systems of biological classification separate spiders, with eight legs, from insects, with six legs.
6. Spiders actually are fascinating creatures; they help to keep populations of insect pests in check, like flies.

EX 7–33 Circle each gerund phrase in the sentences that follow. Draw one line under each participial phrase. Draw two lines under each infinitive phrase.

> EXAMPLE: Superconductivity appears to have promise as an energy-saving technology.

1. Some materials, cooled to –460°F, exhibit the property of superconductivity.

2. These materials become ideal for transmitting electrical energy.

3. An ordinary metal conducting electricity at normal temperatures wastes electricity.

4. Some of the electrons making up the electrical current collide with some particles of conducting material.

5. Electrons colliding with these particles produce unusable heat.

6. At temperatures approaching absolute zero, almost no collisions occur between particles.

7. A superconductive material is thus able to carry a great deal of power.

8. Researchers are now using helium to cool materials to very low temperatures.

9. To make profitable use of the energy-saving properties of superconductivity may soon be possible.

10. Industries using huge, power-hungry motors are very interested in using superconductive materials for power transmission.

EX 7-34 Write three sentences using the phrase *eating peanuts in the back seat of a Rolls-Royce.* In the first sentence use the phrase as a gerund. In the second, use it as a participle. In the third, add a subject and a helping verb, so that *eating* becomes part of a verb phrase. Write your sentences on another sheet of paper.

EX 7-35 Some of the sentences below have dangling participial phrases; some have misplaced participial phrases; some have split infinitives; and some have nonparallel structures. Rewrite each sentence so that it communicates clearly and contains no errors. Do your writing on another sheet of paper.

> EXAMPLE: Preparing for the history examination, the night hours crept by.
> *Preparing for the history examination, the student was barely conscious of the night hours creeping by.*

1. Studying the history of Montenegro is to encounter a rugged and steadfast people.
2. Located on a high plateau across the Adriatic Sea from Italy, outsiders for centuries have tried to dominate this tiny nation but have always failed.
3. The fierce soldiers of the Ottoman Empire tried to repeatedly dominate the Montenegrins but never succeeded.
4. Rifles captured from the Turkish invaders and to have been made into fence posts can be seen in the capital of Montenegro.
5. The student hopes to someday visit that capital, Cetinje.
6. Starting at the Gulf of Kotor and to career up the spiral road is the most picturesque and instructive way to enter Montenegro.
7. Featuring fifteen loops, tourists frequently hold their breath on the road.
8. Montenegro, attracting ambassadors to Cetinje from Russia, England, France, and other nations, flourished as an independent kingdom for a period of forty years.
9. Becoming part of Yugoslavia in 1919, the brief period of independence passed.
10. Written by Franz Lehar, the pomposity and quaintness of the imperial era in Montenegro is kept alive in *The Merry Widow*, a delightful operetta.

WORKSHOP

. Describe the precise location of an object in your place of residence. Do this in a series of sentences containing prepositional phrases. Underline each adverbial prepositional phrase you write.

2. Write sentences with appositive phrases about the character and behavior of four of the people listed below.

W. C. Fields   Bruce Lee
Charles de Gaulle   Janet Guthrie
Ringo Starr   David Smith
Eva Perón   Mary Shelley

3. Make a list of five book and movie titles that begin with infinitive phrases.

4. Watch an animal, a fish, a bird, or an insect for an hour or so. Write a paragraph describing the actions of this creature. Use at least three participial phrases in your description; underline each participial phrase you use.

5. Write a paragraph about the New Year's resolutions you have kept and the ones you have not kept. Underline each gerund phrase you write in the paragraph.

6. Find a paragraph you have written that could benefit from revision. This can be from any paper you have written this year. Rewrite the paragraph; as you do so, ask yourself these questions:
   - Are the prepositional phrases in this paragraph properly placed?
   - Should one or more nouns be explained by appositive phrases?
   - Is the paragraph free of split infinitives?
   - Are expressions that express similar ideas parallel in structure?
   - Are nonrestrictive participial phrases set off with commas?
   - Are the participial phrases in this paragraph properly placed?

Note that you will seldom make all these kinds of corrections in a single paragraph. Nevertheless, trying out a number of possibilities is bound to lead you to a better, clearer way of saying what you have to say.

Using Clauses to Expand Sentences

8

A. RECOGNIZING INDEPENDENT AND DEPENDENT CLAUSES

A *clause* is a group of words having a subject and a predicate.

EXAMPLES OF CLAUSES
Marengo was the name of Napoleon's horse. [*Marengo* is the subject of the clause; *was* is the verb.]

when Napoleon rode Marengo [*Napoleon* is the subject of the clause; *rode* is the verb.]
which was Napoleon's final battle [*which* is the subject of the clause; *was* is the verb.]

THESE ARE NOT CLAUSES
saluted by his troops [This is a participial phrase; it has no subject.]

the most valorous soldiers in his army [Here a prepositional phrase follows a noun phrase. There is no verb.]

EX 8–1   Underline each item below that is a clause.

EXAMPLE: <u>when Rocky Marciano retired</u>

1. he was undefeated as a professional boxer
2. the heavyweight champion of the world
3. winning all forty-nine of his professional bouts
4. because he defended his title six times
5. although his skills had not deteriorated
6. he chose retirement at an early age
7. he had met all challengers
8. the tragic death of Rocky Marciano
9. killed in a plane crash the day before his forty-sixth birthday
10. who will be remembered as one of boxing's greatest champions

Look at the clauses below.

a. although a greyhound can overtake a jackrabbit
b. ordinary dogs cannot outrun a jackrabbit

130

Which clause could stand as an independent sentence if its first word was capitalized and a period was added at its end? _____ Which clause would be a fragment if its first word was capitalized and a period was added at its end? _____

A clause that can stand alone as an independent sentence is called an *independent* clause. A clause that would produce a fragment if left to stand alone is called a *dependent clause.*

EXAMPLES OF INDEPENDENT CLAUSES
Romantic films please some viewers. [*Films* is the simple subject; *please* is the verb.]

Although *Maytime* may seem rather corny to us today, *moviegoers loved it in 1937.* [*Moviegoers* is the simple subject; *loved* is the verb. The other clause in this sentence is a dependent clause.]

Nelson Eddy played a handsome baritone in this film, and *Jeanette MacDonald portrayed a lovely prima donna.* [This is a compound sentence—a sentence with two independent clauses joined by *and.* The subject of the first independent clause is *Nelson Eddy*; the verb is *played. Jeanette MacDonald* is the subject of the second independent clause; *portrayed* is the verb.]

EXAMPLES OF DEPENDENT CLAUSES
Whoever wrote the script must have had a heart of sugar. [*Whoever* is the subject of the dependent clause; *wrote* is the verb. Note that this dependent clause is the subject of this sentence.]

Because they sang beautifully separately and together, Eddy and MacDonald co-starred in a number of romantic films. [*They* is the subject of this dependent clause; *sang* is the verb. The word *because* introduces the dependent clause. The other part of this sentence is an independent clause.]

MacDonald, *who was known as "the Iron Butterfly,"* was the subject of a biography by Robert Parish. [*Who* is the subject of the dependent clause; *was* is the verb. Note that the rest of the sentence consists of an independent clause.]

EX 8-2 Underline the items below that are independent clauses; add capital letters and end punctuation to these so that they become sentences. Circle the items that are dependent clauses.

EXAMPLES: if a blindfolded person can consistently differentiate between different-colored pieces of identical material

H
He or she may possess dermal vision.

1. eyeless vision is a phenomenon

2. that has been studied by several researchers

3. people with dermal vision apparently can "see" colors and other visual phenomena with their fingers

4. because Rosa Kuleshova could correctly name colors of papers when blindfolded

5. she was studied at length by Soviet scientists

6. although her abilities at first seemed real

7. she was eventually exposed as a cheat

8. a Bulgarian researcher completed an experiment in 1964

9. that may indicate the existence of dermal vision

10. he worked with sixty children

11. who had been blind from birth

12. the researcher reported to the world

13. that the children could identify colors by touch

14. some scientists deny the existence of dermal vision

15. others believe

16. that heat absorption is the explanation for this phenomenon

17. dark colors absorb more heat

18. than light colors do

EX 8-3   Combine each dependent clause in EX 8-2 with an independent clause from EX 8-2. Write the new sentences on a separate sheet of paper. Place commas where you think they are needed. Underline the dependent clause in each sentence you write.

> EXAMPLE: *If a blindfolded person can consistently differentiate between different-colored pieces of identical material*, he or she may possess dermal vision.

B. IDENTIFYING COMPLEX SENTENCES

Look at the following sentences.

> a. President Calvin Coolidge kept two canaries as pets.
> b. One was named Nip, and the other was named Tuck.
> c. Although Coolidge was generally considered a stern individual, he obviously was not without a sense of humor.

Which sentence has a single subject–verb relationship? _____ Because this sentence is made up of a single independent clause, it is a *simple sentence.*

Which sentence is made up of two independent clauses, each with a subject–verb relationship, joined by a coordinating conjunction? _____ This is a *compound sentence.*

Which sentence is made up of one independent clause and one dependent clause? _____ A sentence that includes at least one dependent clause is termed a *complex sentence.*

> **EXAMPLES OF COMPLEX SENTENCES**
> *When the conversation turns to love of dogs,* you must mention the name of Francis Henry Egerton. [*When* introduces the italicized dependent clause.]
>
> He is the fellow *who dressed his dogs in fine leather boots.* [*Who* introduces the italicized dependent clause.]
>
> *That Egerton dined nightly with a dozen favored dogs* is a historical fact. [The italicized dependent clause functions as the sentence subject.]

THESE ARE NOT COMPLEX SENTENCES

Butlers were on hand *to tie napkins around the dogs' necks.* [The italicized word group is an infinitive phrase, not a dependent clause. The sentence is a simple sentence.]

Dogs *eating their food sloppily* were dismissed from the table by the fussy Egerton. [The italicized word group is a participial phrase; the sentence is a simple sentence.]

EX 8–4   Write *S* after each simple sentence. Write *CD* after each compound sentence. Write *CX* after each complex sentence.

> EXAMPLE: The United States Coast Guard is the agency that searches for shipwreck victims. <u>*CX*</u>

1. The Coast Guard also handles rescues of people who bail out of airplanes over water. _____

2. Coast Guard personnel may soon use pigeons as assistants. _____

3. Pigeons have sharp eyes, and they can be trained. _____

4. A three-year test of pigeon spotters has been completed. _____

5. Five pigeons were placed inside a clear chamber in a helicopter that was used in open-sea search-and-rescue operations. _____

6. When one of these trained birds spotted anything orange, red, or yellow, it would peck an electrical switch. _____

7. These are standard colors for emergency gear. _____

8. The electrical switch would signal the pilot that a person in distress was in sight. _____

9. The pigeons were quite effective in spotting floating targets. _____

10. The birds spotted targets 90 percent of the time on the first pass; the humans did so only 38 percent of the time. _____

11. Trained pigeons should soon be saving lives. _____

12. Because this project is unusual, to say the least, it will certainly be given close scrutiny by officials and by reporters alike. _____

EX 8–5   The following paragraph contains several short sentences that should be written as dependent clauses in complex sentences. Rewrite the paragraph, incorporating the short sentences into other sentences. Underline the dependent clause or clauses in each complex sentence you write. Do your writing on another sheet of paper.

Did you know this fact? The common flashlight began as an electric flowerpot. The inventor of this useful device was a Russian immigrant, Akiba Horowitz. He came to New York in 1890 and promptly changed his name to Conrad Hubert. He opened a small restaurant. Soon afterward he met Joshua Lionel Cowan. Cowan was the maker of Lionel toy trains. Hubert saw an opportunity for bettering himself. He left his restaurant and became a sales representative for Cowan's company. Cowan developed an electric flowerpot. It featured an artificial plant with tiny bulbs. They lit up. Hubert bought all rights and licenses to the product. The canny salesperson realized something. People would not buy a novelty like the electric flowerpot in quantity. They would buy a handy portable light. He improved the batteries. These supplied power to the lights. He then perfected a design. It featured two batteries in a cylinder with a light at the end. He submitted designs. Hubert received patents on his invention. He then organized the Ever Ready Company. It is still a major producer of flashlights and batteries today.

C. WRITING ADJECTIVE CLAUSES

In Chapter 7 you saw that phrases can function as adjectives by modifying nouns. Clauses can also function as adjectives. Look at the sentences below.

    a. Shih Huang-Ti was a *mighty* ruler.
    b. Shih Huang-Ti was a ruler *of ancient China.*
    c. Shih Huang-Ti was the ruler *who ordered the public burning of virtually all books in China.*

In which sentence does a clause modify the noun *ruler*? _____
A clause that modifies a noun is called an *adjectival dependent clause*, or an *adjective clause* for short. Adjective clauses introduced by the relative pronouns *who, which, that,* or *whose* are also called *relative clauses.*

> ### EXAMPLES OF ADJECTIVAL DEPENDENT CLAUSES
> Peter Sellers, *who became one of the greatest visual comedians of the twentieth century*, rose to prominence as a voice on a radio comedy show. [The italicized adjective clause modifies the noun *Peter Sellers.* The relative pronoun *who* begins the clause and is its subject; *became* is the verb that relates to *who.*]
>
> The program *that Sellers appeared on* was called *The Goon Show.* [The italicized adjective clause modifies the noun *program.* The relative pronoun *that* begins the clause, but it is not the subject of the clause: *Sellers* is the subject, and *appeared* is the verb.]
>
> The scripts *Spike Milligan wrote for this program* are truly loony. [The italicized adjective clause modifies the noun *scripts.* Note that the relative pronoun here is not stated; it is understood: either *that* or *which* could have been used as the first word in the adjective clause.]

EX 8–6   The adjective clause in each of the following sentences is italicized. Circle the relative pronoun. Draw a box around the subject of the clause, if it is not the relative pronoun. Draw two lines under the verb in the adjective clause. Draw an arrow from the clause to the word it modifies. (Be careful. In two of the sentences the relative pronoun is not stated.)

    EXAMPLE: John Stuart Mill, (whose) philosophical writings *have inspired many*, was a child genius.

1. Friends *who visited the Mill household* were amazed.

2. Little John, *who was only three years old*, was reading Greek classics.

3. These classics, *which were not translations*, expressed complex ideas.

4. His father, *who sat across the table from young John*, explained difficult words.

5. By the age of eight John had read many Greek works *that few scholars had attempted.*

6. Mill, *whose opportunities for play were almost nonexistent*, then began studying Latin.

7. He was also given another task by his father, *who was a stern taskmaster.*

8. He would teach his sister the lessons *his father considered important.*

9. The education *Mill received* certainly contributed to his development into a brilliant philosopher.

10. Nevertheless, the rigorous program *that he was forced to undergo during his early years* left Mill with bitter feelings toward his father.

EX 8-7   Underline the adjective clause in each sentence below. Draw an arrow from each clause to the word it modifies.

> EXAMPLE: The police officer who gave me this ticket is no friend of mine.

1. The ticket, which carries a $20 fine, is for parking in my own driveway.

2. A car which is obstructing a sidewalk may deserve a ticket.

3. The sidewalk that passes in front of our house is broad.

4. A person who was traveling along the sidewalk in a wheelchair would not have had his or her progress impeded.

5. My car would not have obstructed a person who was pushing a stolen grocery cart.

6. The fact that my car was not blocking the sidewalk obviously did not impress the police officer.

7. In a city that is ravaged by violent crime, this is what one officer spends time doing.

8. Motorists fly through the stop signs that decorate the corner below us.

9. This situation, which someday will result in someone's injury or death, is not of interest to the local ticket writer.

10. The respect that our many competent, courageous law-enforcement officers earn and deserve is undermined by the actions of the unprincipled few.

Adjectival dependent clauses, like participial phrases, are either *restrictive* or *nonrestrictive*. *Restrictive* adjective clauses are essential to the identity of the noun they describe. They are *not* set off by commas. *Nonrestrictive* clauses give information about a noun that is not necessary to establish its identity. Nonrestrictive clauses *are* set off by commas.

EXAMPLE OF A RESTRICTIVE ADJECTIVE CLAUSE
The thin woman *who sells soft pretzels outside the student union* was featured on the news last night. [The writer has used the restrictive clause to tell the reader exactly who is being talked about. The sentence structure suggests that the reason the woman was featured was her activity as a pretzel seller.]

EXAMPLE OF A NONRESTRICTIVE ADJECTIVE CLAUSE
The thin woman, *who sells soft pretzels outside the student union*, was featured on the news last night. [The writer provides incidental information in the nonrestrictive clause. By punctuating the sentence in this way, the writer indicates an assumption that the reader does not need the information in parentheses to know who is being talked about.]

EX 8-8   In the paragraph below, insert commas to set off the adjective clauses that seem to make better sense as nonrestrictive clauses.

The person who had been killed was an eminent Londoner named Ronald Adair. The crime which was committed in strange circumstances came to the attention of Sherlock Holmes who had long since established a reputation as a stalwart investigator. The account of the crime that was presented to the public did not tell the whole story. Perhaps the prosecutor who seemed then to have a solid case felt no need to make public facts that seemed unimportant. Those who are familiar with Holmes's methods must already sense his part in eventually piecing together the odd clues to form a clear picture of a crime that was not as it first seemed. Dr. John H. Watson who then served as Holmes's assistant recounts, ten years after the original murder, the specifics of the Adair case in a story that carries the title "The Adventure of the Empty House." This story which was the first of the group collectively called "The Return of Sherlock Holmes" appeared in the *Strand* magazine in October 1903. Its author whom millions consider the greatest writer of detective fiction was Sir Arthur Conan Doyle.

When writing relative clauses, it is important to use appropriate relative pronouns. In general, current standards of usage call for *who* or *whom* to be used to refer to people, *that* to be used to refer to animals and things in *restrictive* adjective clauses, and *which* to be used to refer to animals and things in nonrestrictive clauses. *Whose* may be used to refer to any person or thing.

EXAMPLES OF THE APPROPRIATE USE OF RELATIVE PRONOUNS
Samuel S. Laws was the person *who invented the stock ticker.* [*Who* refers to a person, *Samuel S. Laws.*]

The stock ticker is a device *that in former days transmitted share value data directly to brokers.* [*That* refers to a thing, *device.* This adjective clause is a restrictive clause.]

Data from the New York Stock Exchange, *which is the largest stock trading arena in America,* now reach most brokers via computer hookups. [*Which* refers to a thing, *the New York Stock Exchange.* This adjective clause is a nonrestrictive clause.]

Laws, *whose invention was a boon to the financial community of yesteryear*, was a scholar as well as an inventor. [*Whose* refers here to a person, *Laws.*]

A machine *whose function aids the wealthy and powerful* seldom remains a secret long. [*Whose* refers here to a thing, *machine.*]

That can be used to refer to people as well as to things, and *which* can be used in restrictive clauses. Nevertheless, the preferred style is to use *who* for people and *that* in restrictive clauses.

There are two exceptions to the foregoing guidelines: (1) Use *which*, not *that*, in prepositional phrases in restrictive adjective clauses. (2) In a sentence with several restrictive adjective clauses referring to things, it is a good idea to replace at least one *that* with a *which*.

EXAMPLE OF THE USE OF *WHICH* **FOR A PREPOSITION
IN A RESTRICTIVE CLAUSE**
The job *for which I applied* paid $5.63 an hour.

EXAMPLE OF ALTERNATION OF *THAT* **AND** *WHICH* **IN A SENTENCE
WITH SEVERAL RESTRICTIVE CLAUSES**
The note *that* had been posted on the bulletin board *which* I happened to see on my way into the building *that* housed the firm's offices told of another, more interesting job opening.

EX 8-9   Fill each blank with the appropriate pronoun: *who, which, that,* or *whose.*

> EXAMPLE: The Allied soldiers *who* invaded Sicily in September 1943 found the going extremely rough.

1. The terrain, _____ was rugged and hilly, was ideal for defensive warfare.

2. The German troops, _____ were led by General Albert Kessel-ring, resisted each forward thrust.

3. The cold, winter rains, _____ made the unpaved roads

   _____ connected villages soft and muddy continued week after week.

4. The snow _____ fell added to the difficulty and discomfort.

5. The Allies, _____ leaders were then planning the landing at Normandy, suffered heavy casualties.

6. General George Patton, _____ was one of the Allies' finest tacticians, pushed his troops hard.

7. The June day on _____ the Allies reached Rome was a day of rejoicing.

8. The continent of Europe, _____ had been almost entirely under Axis control since late 1940, was slowly but surely being liberated.

EX 8-10   Rewrite each pair of sentences below into a single sentence with an adjective clause. Set off with commas each adjective clause that makes better sense as a nonrestrictive clause. Use another sheet of paper for your writing.

> EXAMPLE: Bert Bell went on to win high praise while serving as the Commissioner of the National Football League. He was a flop as a professional football coach.
> *Bert Bell, who went on to win high praise while serving as the Commissioner of the National Football League, was a flop as a professional football coach.*

1. Bell was then the co-owner of the Pittsburgh Steelers. Bell took over the reins of the team in 1941.
2. Bell inherited a team. The team had won only five games during the previous three years.
3. Bell apparently believed in positive thinking. He issued confident statements during the early days of the Steelers' 1941 training camp.

4. The fans read Bell's comments. They expected a winner.
5. Bell had brought in some new players. They were supposed to help the team.
6. One newcomer was Arthur Jarrett, a 230-pound tackle. He had come to the Steelers from Hawaii.
7. The Steelers needed many things. One of these was a kicker.
8. According to Bell, Jarrett was the one. He would solve the Steelers' kicking problem.
9. Jarrett, however, kicked barefoot. This was quite a surprise to Bell.
10. Jarrett kicked fairly well barefooted. He could not learn to kick well wearing shoes.
11. He also lacked strength. This made him useless as a lineman.
12. This player was back in Hawaii before the start of the regular season. He had been so highly touted by Bell.
13. Jarrett returned to his former job. It was assistant hangman at a Hawaiian penal colony.
14. The team had been held in high regard by Bell. It lost its first two games.
15. Bell felt he himself was not a good coach. He stepped down in favor of Aldo Donelli.
16. The record went into the books for the 1941 Pittsburgh Steelers. It showed one win, nine losses, and one tie.

EX 8–11   Write an appropriate adjective clause in each blank. Add commas to set off each adjective clause that makes better sense as a nonrestrictive clause.

> EXAMPLE: The sun shining through the window is making Alicia, *who must finish her research paper today*, very restless.

1. The grassy park _____
_____ looks so inviting.

2. A person _____
_____ cannot afford to think thoughts of this kind.

3. The report _____
_____ is almost finished.

4. Alicia _____
does not want to let last-day laziness spoil her effort.

5. A weather forecast _____
_____ makes her frown.

6. Today's sunny weather _____
_____ may not last till tomorrow.

Look at the following sentences.

    a. The handbag from the local department store that has seven pockets is already coming apart.

    b. The handbag that has seven pockets, which I bought at the local department store, is already coming apart.

    c. The handbag that has seven pockets from the local department store is already coming apart.

Which sentence clearly states the writer's idea? _____

A restrictive clause must follow as closely as possible the noun or pronoun it modifies. When several phrases or restrictive clauses modify the same noun, it may be necessary to make one phrase or restrictive clause a nonrestrictive clause or to place one of the modifying structures in a second sentence.

EXAMPLE OF A SENTENCE IN WHICH MODIFYING STRUCTURES CAUSE CONFUSION

The medicine for the dog with worms that must be mixed with dry dog food must be delivered to the Dickinsons by four o'clock. [This seems to say that the worms are what must be mixed into the dog food.]

REWRITTEN VERSIONS

The medicine for the dog with worms, which must be mixed with dry dog food, must be delivered to the Dickinsons by four o'clock. [The restrictive clause is changed to a nonrestrictive clause.]

This is the medicine that must be mixed with dry dog food; it is for the dog with worms, and it must be delivered to the Dickinsons by four o'clock. [This revision emphases the identity of the medicine as the one *that must be mixed with dry dog food*, an emphasis that is not present in the first revision.]

EX 8-12   Revise each of the following sentences to eliminate confusions of reference. Some sentences can be corrected simply by making a restrictive clause nonrestrictive or by moving the restrictive clause nearer to the noun it modifies. Other sentences will need to be thoroughly restructured. Write your sentences on another sheet of paper.

    EXAMPLE: A document in a museum that has been exposed to the atmosphere eventually becomes yellowed and brittle.
        A document that has been exposed to the atmosphere while being kept in a museum eventually becomes yellowed and brittle.

1. A document that has been exposed to weather that crumbles into powder is lost to future generations.
2. A new protector of newsprint that prevents yellowing has been discovered.
3. The formula for the solution that is now in general use around the country that protects newsprint is quite simple.
4. Drop one tablet of milk of magnesia into a quart of club soda of any brand that has not gone flat.
5. The solution then must be chilled in a refrigerator for a day that maintains an internal temperature of approximately 6°C.

6. Pour the chilled solution into a large flat pan and soak the document or newspaper for several hours that you wish to preserve.
7. Give the document a few pats with a fluffy towel before placing it on a surface that will not be marred by moisture that is free of oil and dust.
8. A document such as a family tree that has been soaked and dried properly may remain in good condition for three centuries.
9. The soaking process must be repeated every fifty years, which was described earlier.
10. Ordinary newspapers usually crumble within one hundred years, which have no protection from the effects of atmospheric elements.

EX 8–13   The following paragraph contains too many repeated phrases and short, uninformative sentences. It also contains sentences with misplaced adjective clauses. Rewrite the paragraph, creating complex sentences with properly placed adjective clauses. Use another sheet of paper for your writing.

Tiddlywinks is a game. Most Americans do not take it seriously. Yet it is a game played seriously throughout the world that requires great skill and concentration. Dedicated winkers say the game requires intelligence and coordination. The object of the game is to put all your winks into the pot, a 1 7/8″ plastic cup, which almost everyone knows. However, most non-winkers are not familiar with strategies used in serious competitions that do not involve shooting for the cup. A skilled winker may *squope*, or *freeze*, an opponent's wink by popping his or her wink on top of it. The winker may do this when he or she sees an opponent's wink in good position. The wise winker also engages in *boondocking*, a defensive strategy. It involves sending an opponent's winks far from the cup. A third strategy is *nurdling* that is used by defense-minded winkers. This means popping an opponent's wink so close to the cup that it cannot be potted easily. Does a game have a place on your table that allows for such crafty moves? You may find tiddlywinks seriously addictive. But do not feel that you have become an adept player the first time that you pot ten winks in a row. One champion who gave an exhibition from the Massachusetts Institute of Technology scored 996 pots in 1,000 attempts. The four shots must have been tough ones that the champion missed!

D. WRITING ADVERBIAL CLAUSES

Look at the following sentences.

a. The roof does not leak yet. We had better call a roofer soon.
b. Although the roof does not leak yet, we had better call a roofer soon.

How does sentence *b* make clear the relationship between the thoughts stated in its two

clauses? _____

_____

An *adverbial clause* (sometimes called an *adverb clause*) usually tells something about the action or state of being expressed by the verb in an independent clause. It commonly answers the question *when, where, why, how,* or *how much.* Adverbial clauses are introduced by *subordinating conjunctions.* A subordinating conjunction makes clear the relationship between the thought in the dependent clause and the thought in the independent clause. Here is a list of some common subordinating conjunctions.

when	although	because	if
since	whenever	where	unless
as	after	before	until
so that	whether	while	though

That can also be used as a subordinating conjunction.

An adverbial clause that comes at the beginning of a sentence is called an *introductory* adverbial clause. An introductory adverbial clause should be separated from the rest of the sentence by a comma.

EXAMPLES OF SENTENCES CONTAINING ADVERBIAL CLAUSES

I did not attend the party *because I was not invited.* [This adverbial clause answers the question *why*; the subordinating conjunction is *because.*]

When I first learned of the party, I felt hurt. [This adverbial clause answers the question *when*; the subordinating conjunction is *when*. Because this clause is an introductory adverbial clause, it is set off from the rest of the sentence with a comma.]

THESE SENTENCES DO NOT CONTAIN ADVERBIAL CLAUSES

When are you arriving? [Here *when* is an adverb that modifies the verb *are arriving*. It does not introduce a dependent clause.]

I have been feeling sorry for myself since Tuesday. [*Since* is a preposition rather than a subordinating conjunction in this sentence. No verb appears after it.]

EX 8-14 The adverbial clause in each of the following sentences is italicized. Underline the subordinating conjunction. Circle the simple subject of the adverbial clause. Put a box around its verb.

EXAMPLE: *When* (Susan Stavers) [served] *the recuperating sailor a bowl of tapioca pudding*, she probably expected a compliment.

1. Ms. Stavers, the proprietor of a convalescent home, asked the young man *whether he liked the pudding.*

2. *Because he was none too tactful*, the sailor said no.

3. *After she regained her composure*, Ms. Stavers asked the young man to be specific with his complaint.

4. He was complaining *because the pudding was too lumpy.*

5. Those were days *when tapioca was sold in large flakes.*

6. *After he delivered his complaint*, the sailor gave Ms. Stavers some good advice.

7. "Grind the tapioca in your coffee grinder *before you cook it.*"

8. *When Ms. Stavers served her guests pudding made with fine-ground tapioca*, they complimented her highly.

9. *Once she realized the excellence of fine-ground tapioca*, Ms. Stavers began grinding it, bagging it, and selling it.

10. *Because tapioca now is imported in flour form rather than in flakes*, Ms. Stavers' process is no longer used in the preparation of tapioca for desserts.

EX 8-15   Underline the adverbial clause in each sentence below.

EXAMPLE: Although Roald Dahl's parents were Norwegian, Dahl was born in Wales.

1. After he spent time as a member of an exploring expedition on the island of Newfoundland, Dahl went to work for an oil company in London.
2. While he was on an assignment in East Africa, World War II broke out.
3. Although he was badly wounded early in the war, he later flew as a fighter pilot.
4. Because he was an intelligent person and an experienced pilot, Dahl was sent by the British government to Washington, D.C., as an assistant air attaché.
5. Since he had time on his hands, Dahl wrote a series of short stories about flying.
6. Because these stories were clever and dealt with a timely theme, they were published in magazines and later as a book.
7. He also had success when he sent a script called *The Gremlins* to Walt Disney.
8. Although Disney did not make a film from the script, he did publish it in adapted form as a children's book.
9. Dahl is now well-known as a children's writer because his *Charlie and the Chocolate Factory* became the very popular movie *Willy Wonka and the Chocolate Factory*.
10. You may find Dahl's short stories entertaining, unless you are bothered by stories dealing with bizarre occurrences.

EX 8-16   Fill each blank with an appropriate subordinating conjunction.

EXAMPLE: *If* you are a squeamish person, you would not have wanted to see Giovanni Bartolomeo Bosco perform.

1. _____ Bosco cut the heads off a black pigeon and a white pigeon, the audience gasped.

2. _____ he completed this gruesome task, Bosco placed the black pigeon's head into a box with the white pigeon's body.

3. The audience murmured _____ he did this.

4. The white pigeon's head was then placed _____ the black pigeon's body lay.

5. _____ the audience was horrified, they were also curious.

6. _____ the entire audience stared intently, Bosco opened the containers.

7. _____ two live pigeons with mismatched heads appeared, the audience went crazy.

8. _____ he was the greatest conjurer of his day, Bosco could amaze any audience, no matter how sophisticated.

EX 8-17 Rewrite each pair of sentences below as a single sentence with an adverbial clause. Set off with commas each introductory adverbial clause. Do your writing on another sheet of paper.

> EXAMPLE: Margaret Mead studied under the noted anthropologist Ruth Benedict. She chose anthropology as her own profession.
> *After Margaret Mead studied under the noted anthropologist Ruth Benedict, she chose anthropology as her own profession.*

1. Mead wished to study a society still following traditional ways. She traveled to Samoa.
2. She must have found much about life on the island of Tau interesting. Mead concentrated her studies on one aspect of the culture.
3. Children pass into adulthood. In most societies ceremonies are held to mark the event.
4. Mead noted the customs and beliefs of the Tau islanders concerning this rite of passage. She wrote the book *Coming of Age in Samoa.*
5. She had her next opportunity to do field work. She traveled to the Admiralty Islands.
6. She completed her field work. She published *Growing Up in New Guinea.*
7. She continued her interest in the rites of passage from childhood. Mead broadened her focus in the studies she undertook during the 1930s.
8. In her writings Mead frequently compared the cultural values of two or more peoples. Readers could clearly see similarities and differences.
9. Mead's works were generally considered to be important scholarly works. They became popular with the general public as well.
10. You take an anthropology course. You will undoubtedly come across references to one or more of Mead's books.

EX 8-18 Write an appropriate adverbial clause in each blank. Add commas to set off each introductory adverbial clause you write.

> EXAMPLE: You should dial phone numbers carefully *so that you do not get wrong numbers*.

1. You should wear shoes _____.

2. You should wash your hands _____.

3. _____ you should see a doctor immediately.

4. _____ you should follow the instructions on the label.

5. _____ many people do not brush their teeth regularly.

6. _____ they wish they had taken better care of their teeth.

EX 8-19   The following paragraph contains too many short, improperly related sentences. Rewrite the paragraph, creating complex sentences with properly punctuated adverbial clauses. Use another sheet of paper for your writing.

John Fairfax completed a solo journey across the Atlantic in 1969. He swore he would never pick up an oar again. He had succeeded in rowing across the broadest part of that mighty ocean. He looked back on the journey as a brutal, senseless, self-inflicted punishment rather than a triumph. Yet on April 26, 1971, Fairfax had oars in hand again—this time with a companion, Sylvia Cook. The pair would row across the Pacific, from San Francisco to Australia. That is, if weather and fatigue did not interfere. The first effort by Cook and Fairfax to row out of San Francisco Bay ended in failure. Twenty-mile-an-hour headwinds prevented progress. But the wind quieted late that night. The two friends began rowing in earnest. With the help of the outgoing tide they cleared the Golden Gate and began a journey that would take them almost one year to complete. You may be interested in reading about this unique adventure. You should locate a copy of Fairfax and Cook's book, *Oars Across the Pacific.*

E. WRITING NOUN CLAUSES

Clauses can function as nouns. Look at the following sentences.

    a. A thick pork chop is *what I want for dinner.*
    b. *What I can afford* is another matter entirely.
    c. I will eat *whatever is inside this plastic container.*
    d. The smell of *whatever I am cooking* is not particularly pleasant.

Which of the italicized noun clauses is the subject of a sentence? _____ Which is a

direct object? _____ Which is a subjective complement? _____ Which is the object of a

preposition? _____

A noun clause most frequently begins with *that, what, whatever, whoever, whomever, wherever,* or *whenever.* It can perform any sentence function performed by a noun.

> **EXAMPLES OF SENTENCES WITH NOUN CLAUSES**
> *Whoever selected this watch* has no sense of style. [This noun clause functions as the sentence subject.]
>
> Please return it to *wherever it came from.* [This noun clause is the object of the preposition *to.*]
>
> I know *that you meant well.* [This noun clause functions as the direct object of the verb *know.*]
>
> My main objection to the watch is *that it does not play a catchy melody every hour on the hour.* [This noun clause is a subjective complement. See Chapter 6, section D.]

EX 8–20   The noun clause in each of the following sentences is italicized. Circle the simple subject of the noun clause. Draw a box around the verb in the clause.

> EXAMPLE: (*Whomever*) you [*pushed*] *aside on the bus this morning* will not soon forget your face.

1. I will sign up for *whichever section meets on Friday mornings.*

2. *Whoever signs up for a Saturday section* must have a terribly tough schedule.

3. Please give my sympathy to *whoever is in that section.*

4. I do *whatever I want* on Saturday.

5. You may think *that studies are not important to me.*

6. Actually I do *whatever is required* in order to achieve success.

7. I have found *that six days of study a week are enough.*

8. *What I have finally learned to do* is work during work time and play during playtime.

EX 8–21   Underline the noun clause in each sentence below.

> EXAMPLE: What happened to Darryl Stingley will be remembered by pro football fans for a long, long time.

1. Stingley, a wide receiver for the Boston Patriots, gave problems to whoever tried to cover him.
2. Third-and-long was when Stingley was most valuable.
3. That the Oakland Raiders' secondary has a reputation for rugged play is a matter of public record.
4. Raider defenders punish whoever grabs a pass over the middle.
5. Jack Tatum's hard but clean hit caused what athletes fear most to happen to Stingley.
6. That Stingley would never walk again became apparent soon after that fateful game.
7. That football is a violent game troubles few fans.
8. Nevertheless, many fans wonder what can be done to prevent crippling injuries such as the one sustained by Darryl Stingley.

EX 8–22   Write an appropriate noun clause in each blank.

> EXAMPLE: I take *whatever books I want* from the library.

1. Please give this magazine back to _____

   _____.

2. At its annual book sale the library sells _____

   _____.

3. _____

   is the time to visit the library.

4. _____
   can safely be assumed.

5. The sign near the main library desk says _____
   _____ .

6. _____
   may borrow phonograph records from the library's collection.

EX 8-23   Rewrite the following sentences as sentences with noun clauses. Use another sheet of paper for your writing.

> EXAMPLE: You need some time to think this through.
> *What you need is some time to think this through.*

1. You will decide something that will shape your future.
2. You know about your choices.
3. You must work hard to become an expert in the field that you choose.
4. You will decide something, and that will be fine with me.
5. You must decide soon; that is something you already realize.
6. You are going to do something; when you decide, let me know.

F. WRITING CLAUSES THAT STATE COMPARISONS

Comparative statements include or imply a dependent clause. Look at the following sentences.

> a. Brown sugar is no better for you *than white sugar.*
> b. Brown sugar is no better for you *than white sugar is for you.*

Notice that the italicized portion of sentence *a* is a shortened version of the italicized dependent clause in sentence *b*. Actually, the complete comparative statement would be even longer: *Brown sugar is no better for you than white sugar is good for you.*

EX 8-24   Rewrite each of the following comparative statements so that the entire thought in the dependent clause is stated. Use another sheet of paper for your writing.

> EXAMPLE: Whole roasts last longer than other cuts of beef.
> *Whole roasts last longer than other cuts of beef last.*

1. Whole chickens last longer than individual parts.
2. Fish spoils more quickly than meat.
3. Dark hamburger meat is no less healthy than red hamburger meat.
4. Smell is a better indicator of freshness than sight.
5. Bread mold is far more dangerous than mold on cheese.
6. Whole wheat flour has a shorter shelf life than white flour.

EX 8-25 Rewrite each of the following comparative statements so that the thought in the subordinate clause is condensed into the fewest words that communicate the comparison clearly. Use another sheet of paper for your writing.

> EXAMPLE: Rancid corn meal tastes less pleasant than fresh corn meal tastes.
> *Rancid corn meal tastes less pleasant than fresh corn meal.*

1. Rancid corn meal is in most instances no less healthful than fresh corn meal is healthful.
2. Canned meats last longer than canned vegetables last.
3. Plastic film is a much better wrapping for ham than foil is for ham.
4. Liquid oils stored in a cool place age slower than liquid oils stored at room temperature age.
5. Root vegetables last longer than leafy vegetables last.
6. People who take time to learn how to store foods properly enjoy safer and better-tasting meals than those who do not pay attention to these things enjoy.

A comparative statement must compare items that can logically be compared. Comparisons not properly stated may cause confusion.

EXAMPLES OF COMPARISONS NOT PROPERLY STATED
The gardener was pleased to learn that his potatoes were bigger than his neighbor. [This statement appears to compare the size of the potatoes with the size of the neighbor.]

CORRECTED VERSION
The gardener was pleased to learn that his potatoes were bigger than his neighbor's.

Cheetahs are faster than all four-legged animals. [The cheetah is itself a four-legged animal; this sentence seems to compare the cheetah with itself as well as with other four-legged animals.]

CORRECTED VERSION
Cheetahs are faster than all other four-legged animals.

The flavor of Uncle Multinational's Chocolate Microchip Ice Cream is superior to Omnicorp's "Simple 'n' Artificial" Fudge Crunch Ice Cream. [This construction appears to compare *flavor* with *ice cream.*]

CORRECTED VERSION
The flavor of Uncle Multinational's Chocolate Microchip Ice Cream is superior to the flavor of [*or* to that of] Omnicorp's "Simple 'n' Artificial" Fudge Crunch Ice Cream.

EX 8-26   Seven of the following ten sentences include improperly stated comparisons. Rewrite each of these sentences so that comparisons are correctly stated. Indicate the sentences in which the comparisons are already correctly stated by writing "Correct" after each sentence number. Use another sheet of paper for your writing.

> EXAMPLE: The arguments for razing the school building took longer than converting it into a community center.
> *The arguments for razing the school building took longer than the arguments for converting it into a community center.*

1. Mount Logan, the highest mountain in Canada, is higher than Europe.
2. Poland's tallest TV service tower is taller than the Soviet Union.
3. The number of floors in the John Hancock Building in Chicago is greater than the Standard Oil Company of Indiana's building in Chicago.
4. Nevertheless, the Standard Oil building is taller.
5. Alaska is bigger than every state in the Union.
6. The guitar is more popular than any musical instrument.
7. The chemical makeup of honey makes it easier for the human kidney to handle than any other sugar.
8. The absorbency of Blue Whale Paper Towels is greater than Special Occasion Paper Towels.
9. Shoppers say that the checkout lines at Outside Super are usually shorter than Food Suburb.
10. These old rugs are sturdier than those new ones.

G. REVISING SENTENCES THAT HAVE UNNECESSARY CLAUSES

Look at the following sentences.

> a. It is a fact that paper towels were first marketed in 1907.
> b. Paper towels were first marketed in 1907.

Which sentence is a complex sentence? _____ What is the difference in meaning, if any, between the two sentences? _____

Many complex sentences that begin with relatively meaningless statements such as "It is important to remember that," "The truth is that," and "It is a fact that" are better written as simple sentences. Simple sentences communicate quicker and are less likely to confuse.

EXAMPLE OF A SENTENCE WITH AN UNNECESSARY CLAUSE
It is only right that dogs should be kept leashed on city streets.

REVISED
Dogs should be kept leashed on city streets.

EX 8-27   Rewrite each of the following sentences as a simple sentence by eliminating any unnecessary clauses. Use another sheet of paper for your writing.

> EXAMPLE: There is a strange car that has been in Mrs. Chow's driveway.
> *A strange car has been in Mrs. Chow's driveway.*

1. There is no one who is at home at the Chows' house today.
2. It is a fact that the Chows have left town for the weekend.
3. It is obvious to me that I must keep an eye on that car.
4. It is no secret that the Chows have been very kind to me.
5. There is a hammering sound that is coming from the Chows' back porch.
6. The thing that I should do is call the police.

H. SELECTING APPROPRIATE STRUCTURES FOR EXPRESSING IDEAS

Most ideas can be stated in a variety of ways. A writer must be able not only to produce a variety of linguistic structures but also to choose from among the possible structures the one that is brief, clear, and appropriate.

Look at the following sentences.

> a. A paperback novel *without its final ten pages* is a candidate for the trash can.
> b. A paperback novel *that no longer has its final ten pages* is a candidate for the trash can.
> c. A paperback novel *missing its final ten pages* is a candidate for the trash can.

What type of structure appears in italics in sentence *a*? _____

What type of structure appears in italics in sentence *b*? _____

What type of structure appears in italics in sentence *c*? _____

Which sentence—*a, b,* or *c*—seems most effective? _____ Why? _____

Note that *a, b,* and *c* all appear to be brief, clear, and appropriate in structure. A writer might choose one over the others because it sounds smoother (*c*), because it hints at past events (*b*), because it subtly emphasizes the magnitude of the deficiency (*a*), or because it sounds best within a particular paragraph.

Now look at three additional versions of the same sentence.

> d. This paperback novel is a candidate for the trash can because it is missing its ten final pages.
> e. This paperback novel is missing its final ten pages; therefore, it is a candidate for the trash can.
> f. This paperback novel is missing its final ten pages. It is a candidate for the trash bin.

Which item is a complex sentence? _____ Which is a compound sentence? _____

Which is made up of two simple sentences? _____ Which item—*d, e,* or *f*—seems most

effective? _____ Why? _____

Once again, all three versions are adequate. The least fancy approach here is probably *d*. It is a simple explanatory statement. Sentence *e* is more formal in tone than the other versions and may in fact be too high-toned for the idea it conveys. No transition links the two sentences in item *f*; yet this version may be the most effective of all, since it allows the reader to infer the rather obvious relationship between the two statements.

Several other legitimate variations could be constructed without changing the basic vocabulary:

> g. Is this paperback novel missing its final ten pages? Then it is a candidate for the trash bin.
> h. This paperback novel, a candidate for the trash bin, is missing its final ten pages.
> i. This paperback novel is missing its final ten pages and is a candidate for the trash bin.

The brevity and clarity of a sentence can sometimes be assessed when it is not in context. The appropriateness of a sentence, though, cannot be determined without careful consideration of the context in which it appears.

EX 8-28   Write three alternate versions of each item below. Use as much of the original vocabulary as possible. Strive for clarity in what you write. Use another sheet of paper for your writing.

> EXAMPLE: The terrible winter of 1886–87 killed thousands of range animals and made paupers out of Montanans with large herds of cattle.
> a. *The terrible winter of 1886–87 killed thousands of range animals and made paupers out of Montanans who had large herds of cattle.*
> b. *The terrible winter of 1886–87 killed thousands of range animals, making paupers out of Montanans with large herds of cattle.*
> c. *The terrible winter of 1886–87 made paupers out of Montanans with large herds of cattle. It killed thousands of range animals.*

> 1. Ranching came to Montana in 1866; a cattle owner named Nelson Story drove a thousand longhorn cattle north from Texas in that year.
> 2. The Battle of the Little Bighorn took place in 1876. It is also known as "Custer's Last Stand." The Cheyennes and Sioux killed General George Custer and more than two hundred of his soldiers.
> 3. Chief Joseph and his Nez Percé warriors were captured in 1877. They were captured near the Canadian border. This event marked the end of significant Indian resistance in Montana.

EX 8-29   Rewrite each group of sentences as a single sentence. Use the method specified in parentheses. Use another sheet of paper for your writing.

> EXAMPLE: Halifax is the capital of the province of Nova Scotia. It is the premier city of Atlantic Canada. (appositive phrase)
> *Halifax, the capital of the province of Nova Scotia, is the premier city of Atlantic Canada.*

> 1. The city was founded in 1749 as a British settlement. It was later home to United Empire loyalists. (participial phrase)
> 2. Halifax was called Chebucto by the Indians. It was primarily a military garrison. (nonrestrictive adjective clause)
> 3. Halifax's deep-water harbor is excellent. This has been the city's greatest asset for centuries. (adjectival prepositional phrase)
> 4. The harbor is large, deep, and well-protected. Ships of all sizes are able to use it. (adverbial clause)

5. The Royal Canadian Navy has its headquarters in Halifax. It is one of three branches of the Canadian Armed Forces. (appositive phrase)
6. The tragedy that occurred in Halifax is now known as the "Halifax Explosion." December 5, 1917, was the date. (adjectival prepositional phrase)
7. The Norwegian freighter *Imo* and the French munitions ship *Mont Blanc* collided in Halifax harbor. The latter caught fire. (adverbial clause)
8. The *Mont Blanc* and its volatile cargo exploded. The explosion killed 2,000 people and destroyed much of the city. (compound participial phrase)
9. A monument has been erected in Halifax. It commemorates Canadian soldiers who died at sea in wartime and have no grave but the ocean. (infinitive phrase)
10. Life is linked to the sea in Halifax. So is death. (compound subject)

EX 8-30   Rewrite the following paragraph. Combine groups of sentences that contain closely related ideas. Choose structures that make clear the relationships between ideas. Use another sheet of paper for your writing.

The chemist must be able to handle distilled water easily. A supply of distilled water must always be present. A chemist keeps a wash bottle handy. It is filled with distilled water. A wash bottle may be constructed from a 250 ml flask. A two-holed stopper is also used. It fits the flask. Several lengths of glass tubing are also needed. The chemist consults an article. The article explains how to make the wash bottle. The chemist cuts the pieces of tubing to size. The chemist uses a Bunsen burner. The chemist heats and bends several pieces of the glass tubing. The bends are made according to specifications. The specifications are given in the explanatory article. The pieces of tubing are finished. Two of these are inserted into the stopper. The rest are placed in a safe, convenient location. The wash bottle is now ready to be used.

I. REVIEWING CHAPTER CONCEPTS

EX 8-31   Underline the dependent clause in each of the following sentences. In the blank following the sentence, write whether the clause is an *adjective clause*, an *adverbial clause*, or a *noun clause*.

> EXAMPLE: That the honeybee is a valuable friend of humanity cannot be disputed. *noun clause*

1. Anything that threatens the well-being of the honeybee threatens the food supply of the human race. _____
2. Because honeybees pollinate fruits and vegetables, they aid in food production. _____
3. Honey, which only bees can produce, is a nutritive and delicious substance.
   _____
4. A mite that preys on bees is causing concern throughout the world.
   _____
5. This mite, which once lived only in Asia, is now found in Europe, Africa, and South America. _____

6. What particularly frightens scientists is their lack of a weapon against these mites. _____

7. If no weapon is found, the mite may in time become prevalent throughout the world. _____

8. Although major honey-producing nations such as the United States and Mexico have so far been spared, great damage has been caused by the mite elsewhere. _____

9. Since the mites first arrived in Italy, many colonies of bees have been wiped out. _____

10. Scientists have learned that the mites affect the health of a hive in several ways. _____

11. Once the adult female mites invade a hive, they lay their eggs in the brood cells of a honeycomb. _____

12. The eggs hatch, and the young that emerge become adults within eight days. _____

13. They eat the bee pupa and the food that has been provided for it. _____

14. If the mites do too much damage, the young bee dies before emerging. _____

15. The adult bees that do emerge from mite-infested cells usually have mites attached to them. _____

16. What the mites do to the bees during their development often causes malformations. _____

17. These bees, which cannot perform necessary chores, are driven from the hive by healthy bees. _____

18. What the deaths and evictions cause is an underpopulated hive. _____

19. A hive that does not have a large, healthy population is at the mercy of other predators. _____

20. Will researchers find an anti-mite weapon before these creatures move onto the North American continent? _____

EX 8-32   Rewrite each pair of sentences as a single complex sentence. Underline each relative pronoun you write. Set off nonrestrictive clauses with commas. Use another sheet of paper for your writing.

EXAMPLE: P. T. Barnum was a promoter. He knew how to part a fool and his money.
P. T. Barnum was a promoter who knew how to part a fool and his money.

1. A person once said, "There's a sucker born every minute." Barnum was that person.

2. Barnum made more than $2 million by exhibiting amazing people and exotic animals. He became America's most famous impresario.
3. Many of the exhibits were not exactly as they were advertised to be. Barnum presented these.
4. He sneered at people. These people paid good money for the briefest moment of visual fascination.
5. Yet Barnum was an investor. He apparently could not tell a legitimate deal from a fraudulent one.
6. Several companies turned out to be shells fabricated by swindlers. Barnum invested in these.
7. Barnum took joy in fleecing the public. He himself was fleeced several times.
8. The Jerome Clock Company became insolvent in 1855. Barnum had just invested half a million dollars in that company.
9. Barnum's savings had been wiped out. He was forced to declare bankruptcy.
10. Barnum suffered deep depression soon after going bankrupt. The depression did not last, and Barnum went on to recoup his fortune in the business he knew best.

EX 8–33   Underline the adjective clause in the sentences that follow. Add commas to set off clauses that make better sense as nonrestrictive clauses.

> EXAMPLE: Advertisers on old-time radio programs wanted listeners to identify them with the entertainers <u>whom they sponsored</u>.

1. Jack Benny who was a very popular comedian became the voice of Jell-O.
2. Chase and Sanborn which produced ground coffee for home brewing was represented by ventriloquist Edgar Bergen and his dummy Charlie McCarthy.
3. Tom Mix who fought bad guys on the wild Western plains was sponsored by Ralston, a manufacturer of grain products.
4. A comedian who still makes Americans laugh, Bob Hope, was once a spokesperson for Pepsodent toothpaste.
5. Shows that are sponsored by a single company are a rarity on TV today.
6. There are very few currently popular stars who sign contracts to promote particular products in televised ads.
7. Most of the entertainers who appear on behalf of particular firms are not hot box-office properties anymore.
8. There are, however, some big-name entertainers who do promote products on the tube.
9. Sponsors who seek known personalities usually want big names.
10. But these sponsors who must be careful of tarnishing their public image shun controversial individuals.

EX 8–34   On another sheet of paper, write four complex sentences about what you do on a typical Saturday morning. Use one of the following subordinate conjunctions in each sentence: *if, unless, when, after, because, although.*

EX 8–35   Rewrite each of the following sentences as a comparative statement. Add items that create meaningful comparisons. Use another sheet of paper for your writing.

> EXAMPLE: Denali is a tall mountain.
> *Denali is a taller mountain than Pike's Peak.*

1. The Sears Tower is a tall building.
2. The eruption of Mount St. Helens in 1980 was devastating.
3. Arsenic is a toxic element.
4. Lead is a heavy metal.
5. A chimpanzee is a dangerous animal.
6. Strawberries grown in a home garden taste sweet.
7. A person who learns something through experience remembers that lesson a long time.
8. Dogs with short legs are good rodent catchers.

EX 8–36   The following paragraph contains numerous errors, including fragments punctuated as sentences, repetitive sentences that should be combined, and misplaced phrases. Rewrite the paragraph to eliminate these errors. Use another sheet of paper for your writing.

The accumulated evidence of the past two decades indicates something beyond any doubt. Our nation faces a serious problem. The problem has to do with the reading abilities of our young people. Moreover, the situation has grown worse, not better. That is what has happened during the last few years. Educators and parents have given their best efforts. They have tried to combat the problem. So have members of boards of education. Statistics cannot console us. No matter how they are interpreted. The message of the evidence is what I am going to say next. This country faces a twofold reading problem of major proportions. On the one hand, a number of children are unable to read effectively either for information. Or for pleasure. This number is increasing. Many children on the other hand have learned to read. But they do not read. This second group of nonreading readers does not even enter into the statistics. These statistics tell us we have a reading problem. Yet the end result is an increasing population of adults which spend their lives unable or unwilling to read.

EX 8–37   The following announcement contains numerous errors, including fragments punctuated as sentences, poorly stated comparisons, and nonparallel constructions. Rewrite the announcement to eliminate these errors. Use another sheet of paper for your writing.

To our customers: Trying to serve a pleasing dessert, several recipes have been tested by the staff here at A-OK Food Services, serving a Banana Yummee Cake to you today. A banana cake as good if not better than your grandmother or neighborhood baker. A blend of ingredients including bananas, whole wheat flour, brown sugar, buttermilk, and allspice that was developed by our baking staff. Plus more bananas frosted with a whole wheat and butter mixture on top. We would like to after you have tasted this hear how you like it. We would like to especially know if you think the texture of this cake is lighter or heavier than other cakes you enjoy. Please return your reactions to the waiter or waitress inside the red envelope. We thank you for your honest comments and to welcome any other suggestions you may have.

WORKSHOP

1. Write a paragraph explaining the plot of a movie, play, or TV drama you saw recently. Include at least four sentences with adjective clauses; underline each of these clauses.

2. Write a paragraph discussing a major decision you have just made or one you will soon have to make. Include at least four sentences with adverbial clauses; underline each of these clauses.

3. Write a paragraph in which you recount a conversation you overheard this week; do this by using indirect quotations (*He said that he would be busy* . . ., *She said that he was avoiding* . . .). Underline each noun phrase you write.

4. Search one of your other textbooks for a sentence that includes so many clauses that it is difficult to read and understand. Rewrite this sentence as two or more shorter sentences; be careful to make your revision clearer and more direct than the original.

5. Find five comparative statements in advertisements, editorials, or sports columns. Rewrite each, substituting another item for the item used for the purpose of comparison. Be sure your comparisons are properly stated, even if the original comparisons were not.

6. Find a paragraph you have written that could benefit from revision. This can be from any paper you have written this year. Rewrite the paragraph; as you do so, ask yourself these questions:
   - Are the adjective clauses in this paragraph properly placed?
   - Is the correct relative pronoun used in each adjective clause?
   - Are nonrestrictive adjective clauses set off with commas?
   - Are subordinating conjunctions used properly to show relations between ideas?
   - Are introductory adverbial clauses set off with commas?
   - Are comparisons properly stated?
   Note that you will seldom make all these kinds of corrections in a single paragraph. Nevertheless, trying out a number of possibilities is bound to lead you to a better way of saying what you want to say.

Punctuating Sentences

9

Punctuation reflects in writing the nuances, pitches, catches, and pauses of the spoken voice, and so punctuation helps to convey precise meanings. This chapter surveys and offers practice in the major conventions of English punctuation.

A. PUNCTUATING THE END OF A SENTENCE AND ABBREVIATIONS

Use a *period* to mark a full stop or conclusion to a statement or assertion.

EXAMPLE
The Indian elephant is much easier to train than its African cousin.

Also use a period to mark many, but not all, abbreviated words and initials.

EXAMPLE
Ship this elephant to Dr. Pickford A. Anselm, D.V.M., Univ. of Minnesota, 1610 Lake St., Minneapolis, Minn.

Other abbreviations marked by periods include: Mr., Mrs., A.D., B.C., A.M., P.M., Jr., Ph.D., Rev., M.D., e.g. [means "for example"], i.e. [means "that is"], etc. [means "and so forth"]. Some familiar initials do not take periods: NATO, GOP, FHA, HEW, FBI. Many of these denote governmental agencies.

Use a *question mark* to mark the end of a question.

EXAMPLE
What does Anselm want with an African elephant?

Use an *exclamation point* to mark the end of an exclamation—that is, of a loud, emphatic, or surprised statement or command.

EXAMPLE
"An elephant!" roared Dr. Pickford Anselm. "I never ordered an elephant!"

EX 9-1   Correctly punctuate the following sentences and pairs of sentences with periods, question marks, and exclamation points.

> EXAMPLE: Where would you like us to put this elephant, Dr. Anselm?

1. Since at least 350 B C elephants have been used as draft animals
2. Hannibal led an army supported by elephants over the Alps in 218 B C
3. Who was Hannibal
4. Hannibal, Mo , is named after the famous general of Carthage, a city in No Africa that wrestled Rome for supremacy of the ancient world
5. What else is Hannibal famous for
6. Do you mean Hannibal, Mo or Hannibal the general
7. Which Hannibal is famous as the boyhood home of Mark Twain, the celebrated writer
8. The city is, of course Twain lived there as Sam Clemens till 1857
9. Do you know where that name came from Riverboat men, when they measured a depth of two fathoms, hollered to the boat pilot, "Mark twain"
10. As a riverboat pilot, Sam Clemens often heard them call to him, "Mark twain"

Note: In formal writing the names of states are usually written out rather than abbreviated when they appear in sentences.

B. PUNCTUATING WITH COMMAS

The *comma* is the most versatile punctuation mark in English, the most challenging to learn, but also the most useful.

Use commas to separate three or more items in a list or series.

EXAMPLES
Town founders in America drew place names from ancient history, geography, and mythology.

These names came mostly from Greek, Jewish, and Roman traditions.

Use a comma, when necessary, to mark a pause between an opening word, phrase, or clause and the main clause of a sentence.

EXAMPLES
Listen, I have more to say about place names. [word]

Of course, many current American place names stem from American Indian languages and traditions. [phrase]

Even though settlers cleared the lands of native peoples, they let stand many of the old names. [adverbial clause]

EX 9-2   Correctly punctuate the following sentences with commas.

>EXAMPLE: Yes, many cities and towns in the state of Washington have Indian names.

1. For instance Seattle is named after a chief of the Suquamish nation.
2. Though Minnesota was settled by Scandinavians Indian place names far outnumber Swedish Norwegian and Finnish place names.
3. Michigan Dakota Wisconsin Iowa and Nebraska all also derive their names from Indian languages.
4. Of course not all the Great Lakes have Indian names.
5. No Superior is not an Indian name.
6. According to the dictionary Ontario's name comes from a Huron word meaning "great lake."
7. Furthermore many common names of North American birds fish mammals and plants stem from Indian words.
8. In fact Indian languages usually discriminate between American species much more carefully than ordinary English does.
9. Because we often wrongly measure degree of culture by technology we do not always give native American cultures credit for their complex, well-organized ways of life.
10. While biologists have learned a few things from Indian lore social scientists studying Indian lore have learned a great deal about human language thought and culture.

Use pairs of commas to frame words, phrases, or clauses that interrupt the main clause of a sentence.

EXAMPLES

American Indian plant and animal lore, of course, makes up only one side of our many-sided heritage.

Immigrant Americans who forged their own pioneer or slave culture have, as you may realize, bequeathed us a very rich folklore.

Perhaps your grandmother, when you have complained of growing pains, has offered you some peculiar folk remedies.

EX 9-3   Correctly punctuate with pairs of commas the obvious interrupting words, phrases, and clauses in the following sentences.

>EXAMPLE: These twigs, you realize, have curative properties.

1. Putting a drop of buttermilk in the ear for example is supposed to cure earache.
2. Kissing the nose of a mule they say helps to relieve symptoms of catarrh.
3. For a common cold however drinking hot camomile tea is enough to bring relief.
4. Why would anyone I wonder believe that flapping your right arm three times would relieve indigestion?
5. Pick the tooth with a splinter preferably a splinter from a tree struck by lightning in order to cure a toothache.

6. Some people believe strange to say that a horse blowing in one's mouth will cure tonsillitis.
7. An alternate cure if you can call it a cure prescribes a dirty sock tied around the neck of the tonsillitis sufferer.
8. Some cures such as the cure for sideache involve passing the hurt to some other person, animal, or thing.
9. One cures sideache for instance by spitting under a rock and thereby transferring the pain to the rock.
10. The rock because it cannot in turn spit the hurt away must be stuck with a sideache forever.

When punctuating interruptions, be sure to use commas to set off *nonrestrictive* clauses and appositives. (See Chapter 7, pp. 119–20, and Chapter 8, pp. 135–38, to review these.) These interruptions can be trickier than the more obvious interruptions that you have just been practicing.

EX 9–4   Correctly punctuate the following sentences with commas, carefully distinguishing the *nonrestrictive* elements that should be set off with commas from the *restrictive* clauses and phrases that should not be set off with commas.

> EXAMPLE: "Hänsel and Gretel," a story collected by the Brothers Grimm, terrifies some young children.

1. Folklore which comprises the traditions or lore of a people or folk has existed since the first folk on earth.
2. But the folklore that is the scholarly study of unwritten popular tradition is really less than two hundred years old.
3. This study flowered during the cultural period called Romanticism an intellectual movement that advocated sentimental views of nature, folk culture, and history in the late eighteenth and early nineteenth centuries.
4. The work of Jakob and Wilhelm Grimm the famous Brothers Grimm illustrates the increasing respectability of folklore.
5. Jakob Grimm who formulated Grimm's Law which described an important principle of language evolution was a highly respected philologist.
6. Together with his brother Wilhelm Jakob also collected and published German folktales in a very popular book *Grimm's Fairy Tales.*
7. Romanticism helped to make folktales which formerly were enjoyed mostly by the young, illiterate, or uneducated a pleasant entertainment even for the highly educated.
8. A wider respect for all folklore which really includes all folk customs, crafts, and ways followed the increase in popularity of folktales.
9. Romanticism a brief but important movement in art and thought is gone now, but the two folklores march on.
10. You already participate in one folklore the unwritten culture of your folk and perhaps a school class will enable you to participate in the other folklore the scholarly study of traditional beliefs, practices, and stories.

Use commas between parallel adjectives not joined by *and*. If two adjacent adjectives might be joined by *and*, they are parallel and need the comma. If joining the adjectives with *and* sounds awkward, no comma is needed.

EXAMPLES

Creative, innovative genius cannot always successfully buck the system. [*Creative and innovative genius* would be an acceptable phrase, so a comma is needed between the two adjectives.]

Let me tell you about a bright young actor who learned this truth the hard way. [*Bright and young actor* sounds stilted, so in this case no comma is needed.]

EX 9–5   Correctly punctuate with commas the following sentences, paying special attention to commas between adjectives.

EXAMPLE: A tough, uncompromising film is hard to ignore or bury.

1. One of America's fine ambitious daring young artists won and lost a career on one superb blacklisted movie.
2. Orson Welles based the screenplay of *Citizen Kane* on the life of William Randolph Hearst, first son of one of America's richest most powerful most uncompromising families.
3. Hearst had fashioned a powerful obedient chain of newspapers and had also acquired large influential holdings in magazines, motion pictures, and radio.
4. Hearst also became famous for advocating flagrant distorting yellow journalism and for supporting extreme rigid nationalistic political views.
5. He opposed the international cooperative aims of the League of Nations; he campaigned for prompt total cash repayment of World War I debts; and he advocated legal action against American radical internationalist minorities.
6. Welles portrayed the cold distant high-minded newspaper baron Charles Kane in an impressive biting, but sympathetic manner.
7. Still, Hearst's media empire took the film as an act of impiety toward their righteous godlike employer.
8. The Hearst empire controlled enough of entertaining advertising publicizing Hollywood society to disgrace Orson Welles, despite his courageous highly praised now popular film.
9. For thirty years after *Citizen Kane*, a busy exiled Welles pursued a lower-key career in Europe while his films received ever louder more favorable applause.
10. Welles's daring irreverent rebellious film proved both his curse and his blessing.

Use a comma before the coordinating conjunction—*and, but, or, so, for, yet, nor*—that separates independent clauses in a compound sentence.

EXAMPLE

Generally, magic is a skill or a kind of knowledge, and mystery is a very special lack of knowledge.

If the two clauses are imperative statements, you may omit the comma.

EXAMPLE

Step forward and give your full name.

Use a comma, where necessary, to punctuate a word, phrase, or clause that concludes a sentence.

EXAMPLE
Don't let education erase your sense of wonder, if you can help it.

EX 9-6 Correctly punctuate the following sentences with commas, paying particular attention to the comma conventions just mentioned.

EXAMPLE: I am not superstitious, but I keep my eyes open for clues to the future.

1. Many people practice magic even today but it is a kind of magic we prefer to call superstition.
2. Many superstitious people try to affect the environment with signs or tokens hoping to bring about some desired change.
3. Turn a dead snake belly-side up and you will make it rain for example.
4. Sometimes an occurrence threatens bad luck and the magician must act to counter the threat.
5. Spilling salt always brings bad luck unless you counteract the spill by tossing the salt over your shoulder.
6. Not all superstitions involve magic since prediction of the future does not really aim to alter events.
7. Some people see a ring around the moon so they superstitiously predict a rain.
8. Others see early migrations of birds and predict a long winter but this sort of observation may be scientific rather than superstitious because birds retreat south before an advancing early winter to the north.
9. Superstition, like science, depends on cause–effect relationships but unlike science, superstition often links causes and effects superficially connecting an event to something accidentally present at it.
10. A wise Navajo was once asked to predict the severity of the coming winter and he predicted hard months ahead based on the signs and tokens.
11. The winter would be severe said the Navajo wise man squinting off into the sun because he had observed the white man piling up unusually large amounts of firewood a sure harbinger of hard winters.

Use commas to punctuate dates.

EXAMPLE
Thomas Jefferson died on July 4, 1826, on the fiftieth anniversary of the American independence he had helped to forge.

Use commas to punctuate place references.

EXAMPLE
Thomas Jefferson is buried at Monticello, Virginia, the famous estate he built near Charlottesville, Virginia.

Use commas, where necessary, to punctuate quotations. Place these commas before quotation marks [" "], as in the following example.

EXAMPLE
"That's one small step for man," said Neil Armstrong when he first set foot on the moon, "one giant leap for mankind."

Note that when the end of a quotation and the end of the sentence coincide, a period replaces the comma. This period still precedes the quotation mark.

EX 9-7   Correctly punctuate with commas the following sentences.

EXAMPLE: America's first train robbery took place on May 5, 1865, at North Bend, Ohio.

1. On May 24 1844 Samuel F. B. Morse relayed the first telegraph message from Washington D.C. to Baltimore Maryland. It asked "What hath God wrought?"
2. Marie Antoinette was guillotined in Paris France on October 16 1793 during the aftermath of the French Revolution. Stepping on the foot of her executioner, she reportedly said "Pardon, sir, I did not mean to do it" and marched quietly to her death.
3. On October 21 1805 Admiral Horatio Nelson defeated the combined French and Spanish fleets off Cape Trafalgar Spain. Nelson was one of only 1,500 people that the British lost in this enormous sea battle, and he reportedly said while dying "Thank God, I have done my duty."
4. At his laboratory in Menlo Park New Jersey Thomas Edison made and replayed the world's first phonograph recording. "Mary had a little lamb" Edison sang "its fleece was white as snow."
5. Shortly after his July 20 1969 moon walk, Neil Armstrong confessed that he had really meant to say "There's one small step for *a* man."

Though commas often mark pauses in writing, you do not mark punctuation everywhere that you pause to draw breath or to add up meaning. Avoiding unnecessary commas is often as important as supplying needed commas.

Do not set a solitary comma between subject and verb.

EXAMPLE
[Incorrect] What Armstrong had meant to say, was "*a* man."
[Corrected] What Armstrong had meant to say was "*a* man."

However, you may insert a word, phrase, or clause marked off by a *pair* of commas between the subject and verb.

EXAMPLE
What Armstrong had meant to say, he later confessed, was "*a* man."

Avoid using commas between words, phrases, or dependent clauses joined by coordinating conjunctions *and* or *or*.

EXAMPLE
[Incorrect] Armstrong, and fellow moonwalker Buzz Aldrin flew to the moon, and then flew back to earth again.
[Corrected] Armstrong and fellow moonwalker Buzz Aldrin flew to the moon and then flew back to earth again.

Note: Bend these rules only to prevent misreading or serious confusion on your reader's part.

EX 9-8   Comma punctuation in the following sentences is erratic. Circle unnecessary commas, and add commas where necessary.

EXAMPLE: If infection is to be avoided, surgery must be performed in an environment free from germs.

1. Two scientists Louis Pasteur and Joseph Lister working separately in different countries helped medical personnel to control bacteria, that threatened human health.
2. Pasteur the French chemist, sought to reduce, or eliminate the number of bacteria spoiling such foods as milk, wine, and beer.
3. Most other scientists who were skeptical of Pasteur's theories thought, that the spoiling came from a simple, chemical reaction.
4. Before coming upon the heating method soon to be known as pasteurization Pasteur tried various chemical additives.
5. Pasteur generously publicized his new method, and gladly forfeited all the royalties, and fees, that he might have collected, from his patents.
6. Lister, for his part was a surgeon in Scotland in the days, when surgery was extremely risky, and extremely painful and uncertain, even when successful.
7. In August 1865, a year after Pasteur's important revolutionary discoveries, Lister followed the theories of the successful, French chemist in treating a young boy, who had suffered a compound fracture of the leg.
8. The thought that the boy's wound might swell, or become poisoned, or develop gangrene, bothered Lister.
9. So, before setting, and splinting the leg, Lister applied carbolic acid, which had been used as a general disinfectant in waste disposal, to the wound, as an antiseptic.
10. Much to Lister's delight, and the boy's relief, the wound healed quickly, and entirely without infection.

EX 9-9   The following sentences lack any comma punctuation. Read and study each sentence carefully, and then write in commas where necessary according to the rules you have practiced.

EXAMPLE: Discoveries of scientists sometimes find their way into novels, short stories, and plays.

1. H. G. Wells and Jules Verne two literary sons of nineteenth-century science are often compared as forerunners of modern science fiction but Wells scholars scholars agree far surpasses Verne in quality.

2. Jules Verne a French writer plotted many of his books on absurd cartoon-like implausible premises such as a spaceship shot from a cannon.
3. The British Wells in contrast based his more learned scientific philosophical tales on a better sense of both technology and human nature.
4. Though both writers make enjoyable reading Verne more closely resembles the science-fiction comic book and Wells more closely resembles today's science-fiction novel at its best.
5. Wells was born into a modest lower-middle class British family and could reasonably have expected at best the career of an ordinary merchant.
6. But his ambition intelligence and articulateness helped him to raise his sights higher.
7. The famous nineteenth-century biologist T. H. Huxley influenced Wells who studied with Huxley at the Normal School of Science to which Wells had won a scholarship.
8. Forging his first career there Wells decided to become a biologist.
9. Even after he later became a journalist and fiction writer Wells continued to write biology textbooks and he also wrote *The Outline of History* which quickly became a classic history text.
10. Wells's real talent however was science fiction a genre in which he wrote such successful books as *The Time Machine The Invisible Man* and *The War of the Worlds*.

EX 9–10   Read and study carefully each of the following sentences. Then circle unnecessary commas, and write in necessary but omitted commas.

> EXAMPLE: Soldiers, as you know, are required(,) to be obedient.

1. Hiroo Onoda a member of World War II Japan's Fourteenth Army fought on for nearly thirty years after Japan's surrender on August 14 1945.
2. Onoda who became the last Japanese to surrender, fought his stubborn conscientious war on Lubang a small Philippine island.
3. Exactly obeying his orders Onoda firmly refused to surrender, or to believe the war was over.
4. And true to his orders he refused the expedient of suicide even though this can be an honorable act for a Japanese warrior.
5. Although he began his personal resistance with three other comrades only Onoda was alive to surrender on March 9 1974.
6. For nearly thirty years Lieutenant Onoda and his men, had lived off the rain forest, and off island farmers whom Onoda's raiders plagued with shootings fires and thefts.
7. Onoda and his last two comrades Shimada and Kozuka lived on bananas coconuts, and other food, stolen from farmers and they also relied on forest plants for clothing fibers palm oil and palm-leaf paper.
8. Friends, relatives and fellow citizens of Japan as a matter of fact made dozens of attempts over the years to persuade Onoda that the war was over, and that he could honorably surrender.
9. Onoda suspected every appeal however and feared, that his enemies sought to trap him.
10. Finally Onoda's old unit commander Major Yoshima Taniguchi came from Japan to deliver new orders which were the only orders Onoda had vowed to acknowledge and Onoda upon hearing them promptly surrendered.

C. USING THE SEMICOLON

Use a semicolon to separate independent clauses that are more closely connected than a period or other full stop suggests.

EXAMPLE
Italy in the Middle Ages was not really a country; each of its many cities was a state unto itself.

Note: Do not use a comma to separate closely related independent clauses, or you will make the error called "comma splice" or "comma fault."

EXAMPLE
[Incorrect] Florence was not just a city, it was a powerful sovereign state.
[Corrected] Florence was not just a city; it was a powerful sovereign state.

EX 9-11 Use semicolons to improve and correct the following sentences. Some of these sentences have periods where semicolons might better reflect the close connection between two independent clauses. Other sentences mistakenly use a comma to "splice" two independent clauses together.

EXAMPLE: Some people think all classics are dry. Many, though, are full of drama.
Some people think all classics are dry; many, though, are full of drama.

1. Exiled from his home, Dante Alighieri was famous for his wanderings through fourteenth-century Italy. He was more famous, however, for an imaginary journey he took.
2. As a young man Dante wanted to be a patriot, his ambition carried him to the office of prior, one of the highest positions in the city of Florence.
3. In medieval Italy, party politics was dangerous. Rival factions slandered, executed, and assassinated one another.
4. Dante was caught on the losing side of a political conflict, his party was forced from office.
5. Many of his comrades were arrested on false charges. Dante, however, was away at Rome on an embassy during the final confrontation between factions.
6. Dante was forced out of his active role in civil life, instead, he devoted his efforts and ambitions to writing.
7. Dante's greatest work is the *Divine Comedy*. In it, he journeys through hell, purgatory, and heaven.
8. To some of Dante's contemporaries, his reported journey was foolish superstition. However, many Christians of the fourteenth century believed that the afterlife really was divided by God into these three parts.
9. Unrepentant sinners suffered forever in hell. Saved and repentant sinners purified their souls in purgatory. Once purified, the saved rejoiced in heaven.
10. In his writing Dante created the justice that he did not experience on earth, many of his enemies end up in his hell, and many of his friends, allies, and mentors end up in his heaven.

D. USING THE DASH

Use a pair of dashes to set off a word, phrase, or clause that emphatically interrupts a sentence. This usage is similar to the use of commas to set off interrupting elements, except that dashes usually mark stronger pauses than commas.

EXAMPLE
Queen Cleopatra of Egypt—no matter whether you consult fact or legend—ranks as one of the most intriguing historical figures of all time

For clarity, use a pair of dashes to set off an interrupting phrase or clause that contains commas.

EXAMPLE
Antony and Cleopatra—supreme rulers of Greece, Asia, and Egypt—fought with Augustus Caesar for control of all the world.

Use a dash to isolate dramatic introductory phrases or series.

EXAMPLES
Pompey, Lepidus, Antony—all these famous Roman leaders fell before the power and skill of Augustus.

Success in war and in politics—that is what the Romans prized.

Use a dash to set off climactic or concluding words, phrases, or clauses.

EXAMPLES
The Romans valued one thing above all else—success in war and politics.

The wars with Cleopatra produced in Romans both courage and fear—especially the fear that Rome might be ruled by a woman.

EX 9–12   Use dashes to complete the punctuation of the following sentences. Each sentence needs at least one dash added where there currently is no punctuation.

EXAMPLE: Wealth and power—how many have fallen seeking these!

1. Queen Cleopatra of Egypt ranks as one of the most interesting, most powerful women of all time even allowing for the exaggerations of story tellers and moviemakers.
2. Julius Caesar, Pompey the Great, Mark Antony, Octavian all these great lords to some extent came under her spell.
3. Cleopatra was born historians tell us in Alexandria, Egypt, in 69 B.C.
4. She was a Ptolemy a member of a dynasty founded in Alexandria some 300 years earlier by the Macedonian conqueror Alexander the Great.
5. As a Greek ruler of Egyptian wealth wealth the Romans regularly fought over Cleopatra held a powerful, but very vulnerable position.
6. She used her personality her personal, sexual, and intellectual charm to win back status and prestige that Roman generals had roughly taken from Egypt.
7. Astronomy, philosophy, history, literature, languages as a youth at the cultural center of Alexandria, she had studied them all.

8. And as a clever young princess at the Ptolemaic court a nest of plotting, flattery, influence peddling, and ambition she quickly learned tough political skills.

9. Ancient Romans feared the mighty Mark Antony's subjection to the charms of Egyptian Cleopatra probably because it went against their beliefs about both male supremacy and Roman domination.

10. Plutarch's *Lives of Noble Greeks and Romans* a huge, fascinating collection of ancient biographies contains in its life of Mark Antony an interesting version of Cleopatra's story.

EX 9-13 Rewrite the following sentences, using dashes and some of the sentence patterns you have just practiced to produce more interesting, more mature, or more dynamic sentences. Add relevant detail where necessary. Use another sheet of paper for your writing.

> EXAMPLE: It is hard to read books nowadays with all the worl 's distractions.
> *All the world's distractions—television, music, movies—make it hard to read books nowadays—even good, wise, gripping books.*

1. Still, there are some books and magazine that really appeal to me.
2. There are a few things about such writing that really interest me.
3. "Dull" is the only word to describe textbooks, however.
4. To have my mind worked and stretched, not to be swept away into some fantasyland, is the main reason that I am paying to go to school, however.
5. I can find my entertainment in other places besides school.

The rules you have just studied show you a similarity between the semicolon and the period and a similarity between the dash and the comma. The semicolon often functions as a weaker, less emphatic stop than the period. The dash serves as a stronger, more emphatic comma. As you ponder whether to use dash or comma, period or semicolon, remember not to cross the double line in the following diagram.

semicolon [;]	comma [,]
or	or
period [.]	dash [—]

EX 9-14 Where possible, replace periods in the following sentences with semicolons, and replace commas with dashes.

> EXAMPLE: Andrew Jackson̷–"Old Hickory̷"–was a commanding figure.

1. Andrew Jackson was our first popularly elected President. Thanks to a recent easing of voter requirements, nearly twice as many men voted in 1828 as had ever voted before.

2. In the eyes of his critics, Jackson brought only a few questionable talents to the White House, a habit of dueling, a penchant for gambling, and a knack for fighting.

3. Jackson won a popular reputation as an extremely successful Indian fighter. However, even his Indian-fighting fellow Tennesseean Davy Crockett opposed Jackson's rough treatment of Indians.

4. Seminoles, Creeks, Cherokees, Chickasaws, Sauks, all these nations lost legal rights under Jackson. Sad to say, his hatred of Indians seems greatly to have helped Jackson win the love of white citizens.
5. Jackson's stubbornness often made him a poor politician. Nevertheless, historians credit it with helping to prevent rebellion, specifically with helping to prevent a rebellious South Carolina from starting the Civil War thirty years early.
6. Jackson's raw, tough, sinewy, uncompromising manner and appearance gave him a very famous nickname, "Old Hickory."
7. In 1791 Jackson unwittingly married an already married woman. Though a divorce and remarriage soon remedied this scandal, Jackson was to defend his wife's honor in numerous duels throughout his life.
8. Jackson not only massacred Indians. He also supervised a crushing defeat of the British at the Battle of New Orleans, even though the battle occurred after the United States and England had signed a peace treaty.
9. But Jackson, historians tell us, cannot be blamed for this brilliant postwar victory. News of peace had not yet reached America from London by the day of the battle.
10. Jackson is, it seems to me, a familiar kind of American hero. On the one hand, he symbolizes the common, democratic spirit. On the other hand, he too often showed, according to historians, his bad temper, his intolerance, and his ambition, qualities that do not really promote democratic harmony, though they might promote personal success.

E. USING THE COLON

Use the colon, like the dash, to set off climactic concluding words, phrases, or clauses in sentences. For setting off a climactic or concluding sentence element, the colon is slightly more formal than the dash.

EXAMPLE
Jackson's raw, tough, sinewy, uncompromising manner and appearance gave him a very famous nickname: "Old Hickory."

Use a colon to introduce a list, series, or sometimes a quotation.

EXAMPLE
Dante's *Divine Comedy* consists of three parts: hell, purgatory, and heaven.

Use a colon to introduce and a semicolon to mark a series or list with long parts or components.

EXAMPLE
Each part of Dante's journey involved a very different experience: first, he trudged down the murky pit of hell; then he laboriously climbed the bright mountain of purgatory; finally, he flew through the crystalline spheres of heaven to an ultimate vision of God.

EX 9-15   Use colons and semicolons to complete the punctuation of the following sentences. Each sentence needs at least one colon or semicolon added where there currently is no punctuation.

> EXAMPLE: Plato knew the value of education: "The direction in which education starts a man will determine his future life."

1. Many philosophers lived before Plato Thales, Heraclitus, Parmenides, even Socrates.
2. Still, history has granted Plato the grandest title of all "Father of Philosophy."
3. Most of Plato's writings, however, feature the same situation Socrates talking to his fellow citizens of Athens, Greece, about truth.
4. Plato's obvious indebtedness to Socrates may require us to invent a new title for Socrates "Father of the Father of Philosophy."
5. Greeks of ancient Athens easily recognized Socrates by his appearance he was bald, bearded, and snub-nosed he wore an old, grubby cloak and he always went barefoot.
6. He believed that there were things far more important than material possessions the well-being of one's soul, for instance.
7. Socrates was also famous for always claiming to be ignorant I am wise, he would say, only because I know that I know nothing.
8. Most other people lacked this self-knowledge they were ignorant, but did not know or would not admit it.
9. Socrates also practiced courage philosophical courage rather than warrior's courage.
10. The men of Athens—no doubt annoyed by Socrates' constant questioning and criticism—gave him the ultimate chance to prove his philosophical courage they killed him for his convictions in 399 B.C.

F. PUNCTUATING WITH QUOTATION MARKS

Use quotation marks to enclose word-for-word quotations. Do not use quotation marks for paraphrases or indirect quotations.

EXAMPLE
"What hath God wrought?" asked Samuel F. B. Morse in code over the telegraph.

End punctuation goes *inside* the quotation marks, unless the question or exclamation comes from the sentence enclosing the quotation.

EXAMPLE
Why did Armstrong say "one small step for man"?

In dialogue, each quotation from a speaker usually begins a new paragraph.

> **EXAMPLE**
> "Knock! knock!" she said.
> "Who's there?" he asked.
> "Cantaloupe," she said.
> "Cantaloupe who?" he asked.
> "Can't elope tonight," she answered. "Dad's got the car."

Use single quotation marks within double quotation marks to mark a quotation within a quotation.

> **EXAMPLE**
> "Plato is wrongly called the 'Father of Philosophy'," announced the philosophy professor on the first day of class.

Use quotation marks to enclose a word or phrase used in a special sense—a slang sense, for instance, or a technical sense.

> **EXAMPLE**
> Jody was reluctant to "redline" or "over-rev" her car's engine.

Information on using quotation marks around titles of works such as poems appears in Section G of this chapter.

EX 9-16   Correctly punctuate with quotation marks the following sentences. Be sure you place quotation marks in proper relation to other marks of punctuation such as commas and periods.

> EXAMPLE: Folklorists give the name proverb to a wide variety of popular slogans or sayings, such as "A stitch in time saves nine."

1. A rolling stone, the old hobo said, gathers no moss.
2. Ian Fleming's titles *Live and Let Die* and *You Only Live Twice* are based on the proverbs Live and let live and You only live once.
3. The editor remarked, It's not always easy to tell a proverb from a cliché.
4. Perhaps a cliché, he added, is a proverb that misfires.
5. However, he continued, clichés like viable alternative or in terms of lack the homely color of lower than a snake's belly or red as a beet.
6. Effective formal writing, the book states, avoids both proverbs and clichés.
7. In proverbs and clichés, said the professor, the language uses the writer. In real essays, the writer uses the language.
8. What did he just say? whispered one student to another in the back of the room.
9. Silence in the back! roared the lecturer.
10. Sorry, sir, responded the student, but it wasn't me talking; it was the language.
11. That's I, not me, corrected the professor. Apology accepted.

G. USING MISCELLANEOUS PUNCTUATION

Use quotation marks when referring to the titles of magazine articles, titles of short stories or essays, chapter titles, titles of poems and songs, and names of radio or television programs.

Use underlining to indicate italics when referring to titles or names of books, plays, movies, magazines, ships, and other substantial titled human works.

> **EXAMPLE**
> My favorite Melville story is "Bartleby, the Scrivener," published in The Collected Works of Herman Melville.

Use underlining to mark foreign words or phrases in your writing.

> **EXAMPLE**
> Correct spelling is an obsession with my boss, a real idée fixe.

Use ellipses (. . .) to mark any material you have purposely omitted in quoting some person or source. (*Note:* In omitting material for the sake of brevity or clarity, you cannot in fairness alter the basic meaning or intent of the original statement.)

> **EXAMPLE**
> Stepping onto the surface of the moon, Neil Armstrong exclaimed, "That's . . . one giant step for mankind." [By writing "That's . . . one giant . . .," someone could alter Armstrong's meaning entirely to suggest that the astronaut had seen a huge moon man.]

Use parentheses () to enclose additions to a sentence that make too great an interruption to be contained by dashes.

> **EXAMPLE**
> There are many special cases of punctuation that cannot easily be handled in a short survey (for fuller reference, consult a complete handbook or style manual), but few writers ever need these special cases.

EX 9-17 Punctuate the following sentences with appropriate punctuation marks drawn from all your work in this chapter. In the parentheses in each sentence, place a correct mark of punctuation; if no punctuation is needed, leave the parentheses empty. *Hint:* The double parentheses in sentence 7 frame a quotation, at each end of which you need two marks of punctuation.

> EXAMPLE: The Nobel Prize (,) perhaps the most coveted award of all (,) was an inventor's gift to humanity.

1. Alfred B. Nobel ( ) a Swedish chemist and inventor ( ) established annual prizes in physics ( ) chemistry ( ) medicine ( ) literature ( ) and the promotion of peace ( )
2. Proving a wizard at profitable inventions ( ) Nobel patented a mixture of gunpowder and nitroglycerin in 1863 ( ) in 1866 ( ) he patented dynamite ( )
3. In addition to dynamite ( ) Nobel registered numerous other patents ( ) for instance ( ) on synthetic rubber ( ) on blasting gelatin ( ) and on smokeless powder ( )

4. Why did Nobel establish these prizes ( ) He did it ( ) some say ( ) to atone for a life spent ( ) inventing weapons ( )

5. Others say ( ) however ( ) that Nobel ( ) a reclusive ( ) exiled bachelor ( ) did not want his relatives to inherit his estate ( )

6. The Nobel Prizes are financed by Nobel's fortune ( ) which every year produces interest income ( ) interest to be divided among the prizewinners ( )

7. According to Nobel's will ( ) a winner is one who has ( ) ( ) contributed most materially to the benefit of mankind during the immediately preceding year ( ) ( )

8. The Royal Academy of Science ( ) Sweden's honorary society of scientists ( ) chooses winners of physics and chemistry awards ( ) the staff of the Caroline Institute ( ) a Swedish medical center ( ) chooses the recipient of the prize for medicine ( )

9. However ( ) a committee ( ) of five Norwegians chooses the winner of the Peace Prize ( ) apparently because Norway ( ) in Nobel's eyes ( ) was politically more impartial ( )

10. At the spectacular award ceremonies in Stockholm ( ) each winner receives a threefold prize ( ) first ( ) a gold medal ( ) second ( ) a magnificent diploma ( ) and third ( ) a check for a large sum of money ( ) sometimes as much as $145 ( ) 000 ( )

H. REVIEWING CHAPTER CONCEPTS

EX 9–18   The following sentences contain none of their needed punctuation marks. Fill in appropriate, correct punctuation marks, drawing on all that you have studied and practiced in this chapter.

1. The bluegrass band plays while the mandolin player sings Farewell, first lady of the air

2. Who was Amelia Earhart first lady of the air

3. She was many things medical student nurse's aide truck driver social worker but above all she was an airplane pilot

4. Although she was along only as a passenger on June 17 1928 she was the first woman to cross the Atlantic Ocean by air

5. In May 1932 she piloted her own plane solo across the Atlantic thereby duplicating Charles Lindbergh's flight of 1927

6. Thereafter Earhart collected numerous other flight records the women's trans-American nonstop speed record the first solo flight from Hawaii to California the first solo flight from Los Angeles to Mexico City the first solo flight from Mexico City to New Jersey.

7. However Earhart's dream was a flight around the world and she embarked on this dream on June 1 1937

8. Speaking about her plan to fly the equator the longest toughest route around the earth Earhart said Women must try to do things as men have tried When they fail their failure must be a challenge to others

9. Flying a long-range twin-engined Lockheed Electra 10-E Earhart and Frederick Noonan her navigator planned an easterly route Oakland to Miami to Puerto Rico Brazil Africa Pakistan Burma Singapore Australia New Guinea Howland Island Hawaii and Oakland

10. Some time after 8 45 a m on July 3 1937 Earhart lost her bearings in cloudy weather near Howland Island and disappeared seemingly without a trace even though she was within radio range of the Coast Guard cutter Itasca
11. However rumors of her survival her capture as a spy by the Japanese and her subsequent life persist and deepen the legend of Amelia Earhart
12. Two books can tell you more about this amazing woman and about her mysterious disappearance and legacy Fred Goerner's The Search for Amelia Earhart and Joe Klaas's Amelia Earhart Lives

WORKSHOP

1. Recall some exceptionally memorable conversation or verbal exhange you have heard, from real life if possible, or, if not, from television, movies, or radio. Select the sort of conversation people often report to one another verbally. Transcribe this conversation or exchange, effectively using punctuation and quotation marks. Each time the speaker changes, remember to begin a new paragraph.

2. Write an imaginary conversation or dialogue between you and some other person who interests you: perhaps imagine taking with (a) someone you do not know well but would like to talk with, (b) some figure in authority with whom you would like a meeting of minds, (c) some famous living person you admire or dislike, or (d) some historical personage. Transcribe this conversation or dialogue, effectively using punctuation and quotation marks. Each time the speaker changes, remember to begin a new paragraph.

3. List all the conversational clichés you can think of in five minutes. Then write a short dialogue between two people in which you use all those clichés. Again, punctuate accurately, using apostrophes and quotation marks to capture this conversation.

4. Freewrite a paragraph in which you address some absent listener, perhaps some person like those mentioned in item 2. In this freewriting, try to copy your speech patterns, rhythms, and habits as closely as you can, preserving phrases, words, interruptions, repetitions, and so on. Then try to punctuate this colloquial, freewritten paragraph, using your fresh knowledge of punctuation, so that a reader can both understand what you are saying and appreciate the music and vitality of your written voice.

5. Write five meaningful sentences, preferably on the same subject, that use the principle of climax—the buildup to a key term or phrase at the conclusion or climax of a sentence. Try to use colons or dashes to set off the climactic elements of your sentences.

6. Find a paragraph you have written that could benefit from revision. This can be from any paper or exercise you have completed this year. Review the paragraph; ask yourself these questions:
   - Have you correctly punctuated this paragraph with periods, question marks, and exclamation points?
   - If you have punctuated correctly, have you also punctuated *effectively*? That is, have you let your insecurity about correct punctuation cramp your style and restrict your options?
   - Have you used dashes, semicolons, or colons where you might have to produce more interesting, more mature, more dynamic sentences?

• Have you used quotation marks accurately?

Revise and rewrite this paragraph. If you can, use either a dash or a semicolon in every sentence to experiment with a more involved, more mature style. Often this will mean splicing in more detail and descriptiveness, but usually these additions, if not silly or trivial, will improve and strengthen your writing. Remember the value of semicolons, in particular, for splicing an afterthought onto a sentence. And remember the value of a pair of dashes for splicing further detail, definition, or qualification into the middle of a sentence.

Choosing Words

Working with Nouns

A. IDENTIFYING NOUNS

A *noun* is a word that names a person, place, thing, or idea.

EXAMPLES OF NOUNS
garden   field   rake   freedom   Isamu Noguchi   Armenia   United Nations

Most nouns change form to indicate number (singular or plural). Nouns often occur after the articles *a, an,* or *the.* A noun typically functions as the subject of a verb, the object of a verb, the object of a preposition, or the subjective complement. A noun may also modify another noun.

EXAMPLES
Humphrey Bogart was the *actor* who played the *part* of *Roy Earle* in the *movie High Sierra.* [*Humphrey Bogart, Roy Earle,* and *High Sierra* are two-word nouns. Note that *High Sierra* is an appositive that explains *movie.*]

Several other *actors,* including *George Raft* and *James Cagney,* turned down the lead *role* in this *1941 movie.* [Here *actors,* the plural form of *actor,* is used; *1941* is a noun that modifies the noun *movie.*]

EX 10-1   Underline each noun in the following sentences.

> EXAMPLE: <u>Richard Rodgers</u> wrote <u>tunes</u> that have entertained <u>America</u> throughout the twentieth <u>century</u>.

1. Richard Rodgers was raised with the sound of music in his ears.
2. His father, a physician, would sing songs from popular operettas.
3. His mother, an amateur pianist, was the accompanist.
4. Rodgers taught himself to play piano when he was four; he learned to play by ear.
5. His aunt gave the talented child lessons, but he resisted formal study.
6. Scales, exercises, and written music had no appeal for Rodgers.
7. He preferred the challenge of composition to the discipline of skill development.

177

8. Rodgers also became fond of theatrical productions at an early age.
9. He became a lover of American musical comedies, particularly those created by Jerome Kern.
10. By the age of fifteen Rodgers was writing music for theatrical productions.
11. Dozens of melodies composed by Rodgers, such as "With a Song in My Heart" and "You Took Advantage of Me," remain favorites of sophisticated audiences.
12. *Oklahoma!* and *The Sound of Music* are produced anew annually, to the delight of millions.

A word that is a noun in one sentence may be used as a different part of speech in another sentence.

EXAMPLE

The *call* was for Mrs. Biondi. [*Call* is used as a noun in this sentence.]
Wesley and Wanda *call* each other several times a day. [*Call* is used as a verb in this sentence.]

EX 10-2   Write six sentences about public transportation. Use each word provided as a noun.

EXAMPLE: train   *The diesel commuter train is an energy-efficient means of transporting large numbers of people to and from a business district or an industrial park.*

1. commute _____

_____

2. fare _____

_____

3. demand _____

_____

4. fuel _____

_____

5. plan _____

_____

6. ride _____

_____

B. WRITING PROPER AND COMMON NOUNS

Proper nouns name particular persons, places, and things. Proper nouns begin with capital letters. In a proper noun that is made up of several words, the first word and all important words are capitalized.

EXAMPLES OF PROPER NOUNS
Thomas Gutierrez Alea   *The Death of a Bureaucrat*   La Pena Cultural Center   Cuba
Europe   Rome   Mount Etna   Atlantic Ocean

THIS PHRASE DOES NOT CONTAIN A PROPER NOUN
the Egyptian pyramids [*Egyptian* is an adjective.]

All nouns that are not proper nouns are common nouns. A common noun is not capitalized unless it begins a sentence.

EXAMPLES OF COMMON NOUNS
chance   coast   pilgrim   shirt   love [Note that many words that can be used as common nouns can also function as other parts of speech.]

EXAMPLES OF WORDS THAT ARE NOT NOUNS
many   those   several   none   always   that

EX 10-3   Underline each proper noun in the following sentences. Circle each common noun.

EXAMPLE: <u>Maxine Hong Kingston</u> is a perceptive and poetic (writer).

1. Her first book will never be published, according to Ms. Kingston.

2. She wrote this volume "to find out plot and character and the shape of a novel" soon after she and her family moved from Berkeley, California, to Hawaii.

3. The writer composed sections in various moods and states of mind.

4. She studied the results to gain an understanding of how these factors influenced her prose.

5. *The Woman Warrior* is a commentary on the experiences of Chinese-American women in America.

6. The book is a personal and partially autobiographical work: Stockton, California, where Kingston grew up, is the locale for part of the story.

7. Maxine Hong Kingston won high praise for this unconventional volume.

8. The National Book Critics Circle named *The Woman Warrior* the best non-fiction work of 1976.

9. *China Men*, a subsequent volume focusing on experiences of Chinese men in the United States, became a best seller and won critical acclaim.

10. Not all Americans of Chinese ancestry feel that the portrayals in *The Woman Warrior* and *China Men* are accurate, but many have had high praise for them.

EX 10–4   In the following sentences, underline each word that should be capitalized.

EXAMPLE: One of the <u>wild</u> <u>west's</u> wildest tales is told in *a shameless hussy*
<u>who made good and bad</u>, a book by <u>john burke</u>.

1. This historical work by burke is about baby doe tabor.
2. Born poor in oshkosh, wisconsin, baby doe craved wealth and success.
3. Her first husband was harvey doe, a member of the richest family in oshkosh.
4. harvey and his bride set out for the mining camps of colorado; the family hoped that young mr. doe would make their mining properties profitable again.
5. Poor harvey doe was not cut out for life in the rocky mountains, but baby doe dressed in miner's clothes and dug into the family's holding with a pickaxe.
6. Having divorced the luckless harvey, baby doe soon became involved with horace tabor.
7. tabor, the owner of the matchless mine, was one of the richest people in the western united states in those days.
8. president chester a. arthur joined the well-to-do of denver at the wedding of horace and baby doe.
9. The tabors spent more than twelve million dollars on themselves during their ten years of marriage, and horace tabor died penniless.
10. For baby doe tabor, the final forty years of life were grim; she held onto the matchless mine, almost worthless because of the drop in value of silver, but she never escaped poverty.
11. She was found dead in her mountain cabin on march 7, 1935; she had frozen to death.
12. In all the wild mining towns of colorado—central city, leadville, cripple creek, victor, fairplay, creede—no other character achieved the notoriety that baby doe tabor did.

Many proper nouns are difficult to spell because they are not of English origin. The only way to be sure that a proper noun is spelled correctly is to look in a geographical encyclopedia, atlas, textbook, almanac, encyclopedia, or other appropriate reference book. Of course, it is not easy to find the entry for a word you do not know how to spell, but guessing at spellings of proper nouns almost guarantees spelling errors.

EX 10–5   Circle each proper noun that is misspelled. Rewrite each of these, with correct spelling, on a separate sheet of paper.

1. Kebnekasie	8. Côte d'Ore	15. Culbertson County, Texas
2. Franklin D. Roosevelt	9. C. S. Lewis	16. Ole Rölvaag
3. Emma Lazuras	10. Sierra Lione	17. Lake Teshepkuk
4. Lebenon	11. Talcott Parson	18. Jerez de la Frontera
5. Osceola	12. Murmansk	19. Emanuel Kant
6. William Falkner	13. Robert E. Perry	20. Mauretania
7. Toowoomba	14. Tagalic	21. Antartica

C. WRITING PLURAL FORMS OF NOUNS

The great majority of nouns form plurals by adding *s* or *es* at the end. Most nouns with singular forms ending in *s, sh, ch, x,* or *z* have a plural form that ends in *es.*

EXAMPLES OF NOUNS ADDING *S* TO FORM THE PLURAL
car—cars   boot—boots
chime—chimes   syllogism—syllogisms

EXAMPLES OF NOUNS ADDING *ES* TO FORM THE PLURAL
box—boxes   excess—excesses
witch—witches   dish—dishes

Several small groups of nouns form plurals in different ways. These irregular plurals of nouns are listed along with the singular form in virtually all dictionaries; if you are unsure of the correct plural form of a noun, check your dictionary. If no plural form is listed, you can assume that *s* or *es* is added to the singular form according to the rule stated above.

Nouns that end in a consonant and *y* change the *y* to *i* and add *es* to form their plurals.

EXAMPLES
fly—flies   eternity—eternities
army—armies   robbery—robberies

THESE NOUNS DO *NOT* CHANGE *Y* TO *I* AND ADD *ES*
chimney—chimneys   valley—valleys
[These nouns end in a *vowel* and *y* rather than a *consonant* and *y*.]

Some nouns that end in *f* or *fe* form the plural by changing the *f* to *v* and adding *es* (if the singular form ends with *f*) or *s* (if the singular form ends with *fe*).

EXAMPLES
knife—knives   wolf—wolves
life—lives   shelf—shelves

Most nouns that end in *o* simply add *s* to form the plural. Many of these words are musical terms. A few nouns ending in *o* add *es* to form the plural; *potato* (*potatoes*) and *tomato* (*tomatoes*) are among this group.

EXAMPLES OF NOUNS ENDING IN *O* THAT ADD *S* TO FORM THE PLURAL
piano—pianos   radio—radios
solo—solos   contralto—contraltos

Some nouns change form in other ways to indicate the plural. A few nouns have the same form for singular and plural.

EXAMPLES OF NOUNS THAT CHANGE FORM TO INDICATE THE PLURAL
mouse—mice   woman—women
child—children goose—geese

EXAMPLES OF NOUNS THAT HAVE THE SAME FORM FOR SINGULAR AND PLURAL
deer—deer   moose—moose
fish—fish   sheep—sheep

Compound nouns form their plurals by the addition of the plural ending to the second word of the compound. Nouns that are phrases form the plural by adding the correct ending to the main noun in the phrase.

EXAMPLES OF PLURALS OF COMPOUND NOUNS
second baseman—second base*men*
peace officer—peace officer*s*
stepsister—stepsister*s*

EXAMPLES OF NOUNS THAT ARE PHRASES
father-in-law—father*s*-in-law
babe-in-arms—babe*s*-in-arms
officer of arms—officer*s* of arms

Proper nouns that are last names of people add *s* or *es* to form the plural; *es* is added to pluralize last names ending in *s, sh, ch, x,* or *z.*

EXAMPLES OF PLURALS OF PROPER NOUNS
Lucas—the Lucases [NOT the Lucas's]
Rose—the Roses [NOT the Rose's]
Jones—the Joneses [NOT the Jones']
Donnelly—the Donnellys [NOT the Donnellies]
Musselman—the Musselmans [NOT the Musselmen]

Today most style books suggest that plurals of letters and numbers be indicated by adding *s*. When writing letters as letters or numbers as numbers, remember to underline them.

EXAMPLES
9—9s (*Your 9s look like zeros.*)   A—As (*Rita got straight As last term.*)
Δ—Δs   ch—chs   100—100s   B+—B+s

EX 10-6   On another sheet of paper, write the plural form of each noun listed. Check each irregular plural in your dictionary.

EXAMPLE: lane *lanes*

1. mouse	18. alley	35. bus
2. deer	19. sentry	36. autoclave
3. shelf	20. potato	37. pass
4. ox	21. alto	38. chimney
5. ax	22. contralto	39. tyranny
6. hutch	23. maestro	40. oath of office
7. punch	24. tomato	41. woman
8. paintbrush	25. sheikh	42. sheep
9. fox	26. editor-in-chief	43. larceny
10. wolf	27. basketball	44. stereo
11. child	28. half hitch	45. calabash
12. snowman	29. half-life	46. matrix
13. Reese	30. cheese	47. octopus
14. Smith	31. colloquy	48. mongoose
15. pulley	32. survey	49. colluvium
16. bat	33. Chapman	50. spoonful
17. ally	34. Kislingbury	

EX 10-7 On another sheet of paper, rewrite the following sentences, making the italicized nouns plural. Change any other words that must be changed for the sentence to be correctly written.

> EXAMPLE: In ancient Rome the *goose* was raised for the table.
> *In ancient Rome geese were raised for the table.*

1. The *mouse* is a small *rodent* with a hairless *tail.*
2. The *deer* is a *ruminant* possessing great quickness.
3. A *butterfly* has knobs at the ends of the antennae; the antennae of a *moth* are characteristically feathery at the ends.
4. The *thrush* is noted for beautiful *song.*
5. An *ox* is far more placid than a *bull.*
6. The *aardwolf* is a *relative* of the *hyena.*
7. The *whale shark* is the largest *fish* on earth.
8. The *gecko* is found in many a warm *region*; this *lizard* can run upside down across a *ceiling.*

EX 10-8 For each sentence below, write *five* plural nouns that would make sense when used to fill the blank. Do your writing on another sheet of paper.

> EXAMPLE: _____ add flavor and vitamins to soups.
> *Carrots, Tomatoes, Beans, Potatoes, Turnips*

1. Cooks often serve _____ along with roast beef.
2. A sink full of dirty _____ means at least an hour of hard work for someone.
3. _____ are familiar nighttime sounds in our area.
4. Researchers study the effects of drugs on _____ before they test them on human beings.
5. Today's great actresses often play _____ in feature films.
6. As a group, _____ are underpaid and should receive greater financial compensation for the work they do.

D. WRITING POSSESSIVE FORMS OF NOUNS

A possessive form indicates ownership or some other close relationship.

> **EXAMPLES**
> Joan's hat ⟶ the hat that belongs to Joan
> sharks' characteristics ⟶ the characteristics that all sharks have in common

An apostrophe (') and an *s* are added to a singular noun to create the possessive form.

> **EXAMPLES**
> the plan*'s* shortcomings
> the ewe*'s* bleating
> truth*'s* bitter taste
> the bus*'s* graffiti-covered sides
> Michele Ross*'s* cousin
> Russ*'s* twin brother

An apostrophe (') is added to a plural noun ending in *s* to create the possessive form. An apostrophe (') and an *s* are added to a plural noun that does not end in *s* to create the possessive form.

EXAMPLES
the plans' shortcomings [more than one plan]
the ewes' bleating [more than one ewe]
the buses' grafitti-covered sides [more than one bus]
the Rosses' cousins [more than one member of the Ross family]
the twin sisters' younger brother [the brother of both sisters]
the children's toys [*Children* is a plural noun that does not end in *s*, so *'s* must be added.]
the sheep's pens [*Sheep* here is a plural noun that does not end in *s*, so *'s* must be added.]

EX 10-9   Write the singular possessive, plural, and plural possessive forms of each singular noun listed below.

Singular	Singular Possessive	Plural	Plural Possessive
EXAMPLE: wolf	*wolf's*	*wolves*	*wolves'*
1. card			
2. batch			
3. class			
4. entry			
5. life			
6. mouse			
7. woman			
8. Fast Eddie			
9. Minnesota Fats			
10. Commissioner Smith			
11. Walter Horton			
12. novella			
13. auditorium			
14. musk ox			
15. irony			

Prepositional phrases and participial phrases indicating ownership or other close relationship can often be rewritten as possessive expressions.

EXAMPLE
the tracks of the wolves ⟶ *the wolves' tracks*
the final item on the questionnaire ⟶ *the questionnaire's final item*
the hat belonging to Joan ⟶ *Joan's hat*

EX 10–10   Rewrite the following sentences so that the italicized expressions become possessive expressions. Do your writing on another sheet of paper.

> EXAMPLE: The jump shot possessed by *Oscar Robertson* may have been the finest in pro basketball history.
> *Oscar Robertson's jump shot may have been the finest in pro basketball history.*

1. *The physical abilities of a basketball player* can carry him or her only so far.
2. *The seriousness and dedication of an athlete* make him or her a champion.
3. *The roster of the Cincinnati Royals* mostly listed players of limited ability during the 1960s.
4. *The acknowledged star of the team* was Robertson.
5. It is to *the credit of Robertson* that he remained a team player throughout those years and never complained about *the shortcomings of his teammates.*
6. In *the first year completed by Robertson* as a pro, he finished third in the league in scoring and first in assists.
7. Nevertheless, *the record of the Royals* was the worst in *the Western Division of the NBA.*
8. *The contribution of rookie Jerry Lucas* during the 1963–64 season lifted the Royals to their best record in years, 55–25, but *the might of the Boston Celtics* was too much for Robertson, Lucas, and company to overcome.
9. *The ten seasons played by Oscar Robertson* at Cincinnati never brought him the satisfaction of being a member of a championship team.
10. Traded to the Milwaukee Bucks in 1970, Robertson teamed with Kareem Abdul-Jabbar, then known as Lew Alcindor, to power one of *the youngest teams in the league* to the championship.

EX 10–11   On another sheet of paper, rewrite each of the following sentences. Change each singular possessive noun to a plural possessive noun. Change each plural possessive noun to a singular possessive noun. Change other words as necessary. Circle each plural possessive noun you write.

> EXAMPLE: The cars' headlights illuminated the fir's scraggly branches.
> *The car's headlights illuminated the (firs') scraggly branches.*

1. The map's markings showed this to be an improved dirt road.
2. My passengers' aching bones said otherwise.
3. The creeks' loud gurgling could occasionally be heard.
4. The welcome sight of the cabin's signposts was still miles away.
5. The last of the thermoses' hot coffee was distributed.
6. The telephone wire's presence along the road was the only indication that we were not on a forgotten road to nowhere.

When a noun precedes a gerund or gerund phrase that describes an action done by the noun, the possessive form of the noun is used.

EXAMPLES

Pippi's coughing was driving everyone crazy. [NOT *Pippi coughing*]

Her *collie's howling at the moon* was also quite irritating. [NOT *collie howling at the moon*]

The two pet *rats' nibbling of peanuts and scratching on their cage's metal floor* sent chills up and down the guests' spines. [NOT *rats nibbling . . . and scratching . . .*]

When a noun is used as the object of the preposition *of* in a phrase that shows possession, the possessive form must be used.

EXAMPLE

That new coat *of Ed's* is ugly beyond belief. [NOT *of Ed*]

THIS CONSTRUCTION DOES NOT CALL FOR THE POSSESSIVE FORM

The picture *of Ed* in the yearbook is a little fuzzy. [This sentence talks about a picture taken *of* Ed. If it was talking about a picture taken *by* Ed, it would read *The picture of Ed's in the yearbook is a little fuzzy.*]

EX 10-12   In each blank write the correct form of the noun in parentheses. Be sure to use the possessive form before each gerund. Also, be sure to use the possessive form after *of* in a phrase showing possession. Note that not all sentences require a possessive form.

> EXAMPLE: A *baby's* screaming is normally louder than an alarm clock's ringing. (baby)

1. A _____ hammering may produce sound exceeding 100 decibels. (jackhammer)

2. A _____ thoughtless honking of a horn while a gas-station attendant is checking the oil can cause damage to the attendant's hearing. (motorist)

3. A _____ roaring produces a level of sound that can be extremely destructive to attendants' hearing. (jet engine)

4. Those earplugs of _____ help protect his ears during band practice. (Julio)

5. The _____ wearing a white coat is an otolaryngologist. (person)

6. She is studying the destructive effect of loud _____ on people's hearing. (noise)

7. That power mower of _____ produces 108 decibels of sound, according to the doctor's metering device. (Holly)

8. _____ turning the TV volume to the maximum is a destructive habit. (Pat)

EX 10-13   Rewrite the following paragraph, correcting misspelled plural forms and writing possessive expressions properly. Do your writing on another sheet of paper.

> Brad Gjermundson was hailed as one of the rodeo worlds brightest young stars in 1981. Gjermundson winning $50,000 during the first half of the year placed him far ahead of other competitor's in his specialty, bronc busting. This rodeo cowboys' success was not the result of luck or overnight blossoming: Brad and his brotherses learned rodeo skilles from their father at an early age, in the little town of Marshall, North Dakota, and worked year after year to improve. To capitalize on his expertise, Brad, like other men and woman on the pro rodeo circuit, must travel from rodeo to rodeo throughout the season. A typical week of Brad might begin in Denver, Colorado; end in Nampa, Idaho; and include midweek rides in Salt Lake City, Utah; Cheyenne, Wyoming; and Salinas, California. Brad Gjermundsons' driving hundreds of miles each day with muscle's still aching from the previous day's bronc-riding event sets him apart from other sport's star athletes who jet from competition to competition in first-class comfort. The life of the rodeo rider has always been a tough one; Brad Gjermundson is no exception.

E. WORKING WITH GENERAL AND SPECIFIC NOUNS

Scholars in most disciplines have developed systems of classification for the phenomena they study. In these systems of classification, some nouns are used for all items in large groupings; these nouns can be considered to be *general* nouns. *Bird* is an example of a general noun; the word *bird* is applied to creatures which have some key characteristics in common—*all birds lay eggs*; *all birds have wings*—but which have many more characteristics that differ greatly among members. Other nouns are more specific, but still serve to name all members of a separate group; for example, *raptor* is a noun used for all birds of prey. Still other nouns are used for subgroups; thus, *day raptor* separates swift hunters from owls, the stealthy hunters of the night. *Falcon* is a still more specific noun that is used for one type of day raptor. The most precise nouns—or, often, noun phrases—are used for particular organisms: the *hobby* is a small European falcon; the *sparrow hawk* is a small American falcon. Writers must always be aware of the level of specificity of nouns they use when discussing phenomena in a particular discipline.

Even when writing on general topics, writers must keep in mind the level of specificity of the nouns they use. As a rule, a writer should use the noun that applies most specifically to the situation being discussed.

EXAMPLE OF A STATEMENT WEAKENED BY THE USE OF GENERAL NOUNS
The *worker* set down her *tool* and reached for some *food*.

STATEMENT REVISED TO GIVE MORE SPECIFIC INFORMATION
The *cabinetmaker* set down her *plane* and reached for some *roasted sunflower seeds.*

In contrast, a writer will occasionally err by choosing a noun that is too specific to convey the breadth of a thought.

STATEMENT MADE TOO NARROW BY THE USE OF A NOUN THAT IS TOO SPECIFIC
Every *voter* in this city has a right to be heard on the issue of aerial spraying of insecticides. [This statement ignores the rights of children, resident aliens, visitors, and other nonvoters.]

STATEMENT REVISED TO BECOME MORE INCLUSIVE
Every human being in this city has a right to be heard on the issue of aerial spraying of pesticides.

EX 10-14   Circle the noun or noun phrase that is the most *general* in each group. Underline the noun or noun phrase that is the most *specific.*

EXAMPLE: fish   (creature)   mackerel   <u>skipjack</u>

1. cantaloupe	fruit	food	melon
2. furniture	bench	item	piano bench
3. leader	governor	politician	citizen
4. institution	college	school	university
5. healer	surgeon	medic	doctor
6. watch	timepiece	wristwatch	device
7. blue whale	creature	whale	mammal
8. communicator	humorist	writer	creative writer
9. ball	object	sphere	volleyball
10. competitive game	tournament	chess match	competition

EX 10-15   Complete each sentence by writing in the blank a general noun that includes the italicized specific nouns.

EXAMPLE: A *gun*, a *knife*, and a *baseball* bat are all <u>*weapons.*</u>

1. A *knife*, a *fork*, and a *spoon* are _____ .

2. A *jar*, a *coffin*, and a *matchbox* are _____ .

3. A *carpenter*, a *joiner*, and a *cabinet maker* are all _____ .

4. _____ include *fortune tellers*, *astrologers*, and *psychic healers.*

5. *Swedes*, *Danes*, and *Norwegians* are _____ .

6. *Termites*, *rats*, and *cockroaches* are _____ .

EX 10-16   Underline the more appropriate word of the pairs of words given in parentheses. Select specific nouns to complete statements about particular things. Select general nouns to complete summary statements.

A particularly clear illustration of the selling power of a great idea is provided by Mark Twain in *The Adventures of Tom Sawyer.* Twain's young (character, hero) finds himself one (Saturday, day) facing the prospect of having to spend a long, hot (day, afternoon) whitewashing his aunt's (fence, enclosure). He decides to try to convince someone else to do the (work, activity) and he tries two rather ordinary (offers, ideas) toward this end: "I'll trade you my (responsibility, job) for yours"; "I'll pay you to do it." These yield no positive results. But then he comes up with a new (thought, concept): "Does a (boy, human being) get a chance to whitewash a fence every day?" The concept has (pluses, possibilities). It presents (whitewashing, work) as an unusual recreational activity. And the idea proves effective. Suddenly everyone who passes ends up whitewashing part of the fence. Deft execution of the (effort, campaign) makes this happen: the great (thought, idea) is presented in the right way at opportune moments. So this idea yields substantial (rewards, gains). Not only does (the boy, Tom Sawyer) get to sit and watch his (friends, acquaintances) do the work he was assigned, but he also receives (payments, things)—twelve (marbles, objects), part of a jew's harp, and so on. It should be noted that he spent no more time or effort on his "Does a boy get a chance to whitewash" (deal, campaign) than he would have spent pursuing one of his other, more commonplace (approaches, ways); yet his reward is easily ten times greater. Tom Sawyer thus learns at a young age that it doesn't necessarily pay to advertise; but it pays to advertise shrewdly.

Choosing nouns involves more than selecting for specificity. As was explained in Chapter 3, many groups of nouns with similar literal meanings (*denotations*) have emotional shadings (*connotations*) that imply quite different things.

EXAMPLES
An *animal* approached the campfire.
A *beast* approached the campfire.
[*Animal* and *beast* both mean "nonhuman creature"; *beast*, though, implies one that is cruel or dangerous.]

The *eccentricity* of the delicatessen owner could not be denied.
The *peculiarity* of the delicatessen owner could not be denied.
The *abnormality* of the delicatessen owner could not be denied.
[*Eccentricity* implies oddness with a certain charm. *Peculiarity* implies oddness bordering on the unpleasant. *Abnormality* implies oddness that is obvious and disturbing.]

The study of the connotations of words is called *general semantics*. Sensitivity toward the connotations of words is a requirement for success in any communications field. A good dictionary and a college thesaurus or dictionary of synonyms can help a writer to choose nouns with appropriate connotations.

EX 10-17 Rewrite each of the following advertising headlines so that its nouns have more appropriate connotations. Do your writing on another sheet of paper.

EXAMPLE: The smell of Sauce Continentale's rare weeds fills your kitchen!
The aroma of Sauce Continentale's rare herbs fills your kitchen!

1. The rumble of the LR-38's engine says force!
2. At Silver Zeus Health Spa, our hired hands can help you firm up your gut in one short week!
3. Curs can't resist Maximeal!
4. Choose the elegant Somerset GT—experience luxurious isolation.
5. Italy's most elegant designer assemblage for men is now on display at Hedley's.
6. When it comes to payoffs, Breadwinners' Bank delivers!
7. Experience a new mode of existence in a natural encompassment.
8. The new Skysea Villa hostelry has created instant hysteria on the archipelago.

F. RECOGNIZING CONCRETE AND ABSTRACT NOUNS

Look at the italicized words in the following sentence.

> The Puritans boarded clumsy *ships* and braved the treacherous *waters* of the *Atlantic Ocean* in search of a land where they could practice their *religion* without *fear* of *persecution*.

Which italicized nouns name objects, places, or living beings? _____

_____

Which name ideas or concepts? _____

Concrete nouns are nouns that name tangible, observable things—people, places, objects. *Abstract nouns* are nouns that name ideas or concepts. A writer normally defines concrete nouns only when there is a good chance that their literal meanings are unfamiliar to readers of average education. But a writer who uses abstract nouns must often specify what he or she means by these terms, since the concepts named by these nouns generally encompass a great many principles. What constitutes *religion* has been argued about for millennia by philosophers, politicians, anthropologists, jurists, clerics, and millions of ordinary people; one nation's idea of *justice* may differ greatly from a neighboring nation's idea of justice; what one person labels *progress* may be *despoilment* to another; and who is to say where the boundary lies between *love* and *possessiveness*? Because of the breadth and complexity of concepts named by abstract nouns, writers must use supporting or defining statements to help readers see what is meant by these terms as they are being used.

EX 10–18 Circle the seven italicized nouns below that seem to be better classified as *concrete* nouns, and underline the seven nouns that seem to be better classified as *abstract* nouns. Note that these are not mutually exclusive categories; many nouns—*pain*, for instance—may represent something either concrete or abstract, depending on the context in which they are used.

> The factor used in this *study* to determine responsiveness to the *ethics* of the ethnic community rather than to the *rules* of society at large was attendance at organized animal fights. *Society* maintains that animal *fights* are instances of *cruelty* rather than *sport*, and imposes severe *penalties*—negative publicity, *fines*, *imprisonment*—not only on those who organize the fights but also on those who participate only as *spectators*. Twenty-nine percent of *residents* returning *surveys* indicated that they had attended an animal fight within the past *year*. While our study group does not provide a random sample, it does show a difference of opinion about animal fighting between the ethnic community and society at large.

EX 10–19 On a separate sheet of paper, write a sentence or two defining one of the concrete nouns you circled in EX 10–18.

EX 10–20 On a separate sheet of paper, write a paragraph of definition for one of the abstract nouns you underlined in EX 10–18. Try to use concrete nouns—and concrete illustrations—to explain the meaning of this abstract noun.

G. EXAMINING WORD ORIGINS

The meanings of some nouns can best be understood—and most easily remembered—through an examination of their origins. *Coo* is believed to have originated as an attempt to imitate the sound made by a dove. *Flare* was created by combining *flame* with *glare*. *Ravine* was a French word for a swollen mountain stream, but in English it has come to mean a deep gorge or a notch in the mountains—land formations *produced* by swollen streams.

Collegiate and international dictionaries give helpful information on word origins. More extensive information can be found in books on word origins.

EX 10-21   Practice using your dictionary as a source of information on word origins by looking up the following nouns and writing in sentence form the information given about the origin of each. Do your writing on another sheet of paper.

1. smog
2. hummock
3. skunk
4. boonies
5. Ping-Pong
6. cab

H. PRACTICING CORRECT USAGE OF PROBLEM NOUNS

A small group of easily confused word pairs accounts for the majority of word-usage errors made by writers. One section in each of the chapters in Part III—that is, Chapter 10-13—focuses on several confusing pairs.

Advice/advise. Advice is a noun meaning a recommendation for action. *Advise* is a verb that means "to give a recommendation for action."

EX 10-22   Write *advice* or *advise* in each blank.

EXAMPLE: This pamphlet will *advise* you of your options.

1. Some people will not take _____ from a friend.

2. I _____ you to take a foreign-language course this summer.

3. These astrology books _____ me to work hard, save money, and buy more astrology books.

4. Much of the _____ given by Benjamin Franklin in *Poor Richard's Almanack* is worthwhile today.

5. When I want your _____ , I will ask for it.

6. Those who _____ hastily do a disservice to themselves as well as to their friends.

Affect/effect. Affect is usually used as a verb, pronounced *af-FECT* and meaning "to influence." As a noun, *affect* is pronounced *AF-fect* and has a single specific meaning: the psychological response resulting from experiencing an emotion. *Effect* is usually used as a noun meaning "the result." As a verb, *effect* is pronounced *ee-FECT*; it means "to cause" or "to bring about."

EX 10–23   Write *affect* or *effect* in each blank.

> EXAMPLE: You should not let current business conditions *affect* your state
> of mind.

1. The immediate _____ of the ban on food vendors was the reduction of litter on the campus.

2. Hunger can _____ a student's ability to concentrate.

3. Resolutions adopted by the student government occasionally have an

   _____ on what campus rules and regulations are adopted.

4. The ban's _____ on the amount of income earned by vendors was at first devastating.

5. In time, though, the students' desire for snacks had an _____ on where they spent their free time.

6. The presence of vendor carts will almost certainly _____ the way foot traffic moves through the downtown area.

Allusion/illusion. An *allusion* is an indirect reference to something. An *illusion* is a false sensation or belief.

EX 10-24   Write *allusion* or *illusion* in each blank.

> EXAMPLE: The newcomer made an *allusion* to a scene in Shakespeare's
> *Macbeth.*

1. The newcomer's conservative appearance helped create an _____ of respectability.

2. His new friend missed the _____ to possible danger in what the newcomer said.

3. The _____ of tranquility was shattered when three toughs burst through the door.

4. The leader's _____ to an oil-drilling scam caused the newcomer to wince.

5. He made an _____ to friends who would not look kindly on harm done to him.

6. The mirrors behind the three thugs created a most unpleasant optical

   _____ .

Capital/capitol. Capital, when used as a noun, usually means (1) a supply of goods or money or the net worth of a business; (2) a capital letter; or (3) the city that serves as the seat of government. The noun *capitol* is used *only* to refer to *buildings* in which state or federal legislators meet.

EX 10–25   Write *capital* or *capitol* in each blank.

> EXAMPLE: A guard stood beside the northwest entrance to the *capitol*.

1. Olympia is the _____ of the state of Washington.

2. Students are taken on tours of the _____ by uniformed guides.

3. The first letter of the first word in a title must be a _____ .

4. The representative stood with her constituents on the steps of the

   _____ .

5. Auto traffic in the _____ is worst on Tuesdays, Wednesdays, and Thursdays.

6. A wholesale firm without sufficient _____ does not remain in business for long.

Compliment/complement. A *compliment* is a flattering comment. A *complement* is something that completes or goes well with something else.

EX 10–26   Write *complement* or *compliment* in each blank.

> EXAMPLE: Yogurt is a fine *complement* to curry.

1. Please repeat my _____ to the chef.

2. A noun that follows a linking verb and defines the subject is a subjective

   _____ .

3. A _____ is due you on your excellent taste in books.

4. Tonight we have a full _____ of kitchen helpers.

5. This angle is the _____ of that angle.

6. I do not extend a _____ merely to ingratiate myself to the host!

Council/counsel. A *council* is a group of people who meet to discuss matters and give advice. *Counsel*, when used as a noun, means "advice" or refers to a lawyer representing someone in a legal matter. *Counsel* is frequently used as a verb; it means "to advise."

EX 10–27   Write *council* or *counsel* in each blank.

> EXAMPLE: Fifty students sought seats on the chancellor's student affairs *council*.

1. Rosa Hernandez served as _____ for the defense.

2. She has always given wise _____ to students who have sought her help.

3. The growers' _____ planned to take legal action against states instituting a quarantine.

4. Newly elected members of the _____ will be seated first.

5. A faculty member may be willing to _____ you about choosing a graduate school.

6. A _____ that is made up of ideologues is unlikely to recommend equitable actions.

Datum/data. Datum is a *singular* noun meaning "an item of factual information." *Data* is the *plural* form of *datum.*

EX 10-28   Write *datum* or *data* in each blank.

EXAMPLE: These *data* must be checked.

1. The _____ on iceberg movements have been misplaced.

2. You are missing at least one _____ in your appendix on glaciers.

3. Has the institute released _____ on last week's tsunami yet?

4. One _____ you may have overlooked is here on page 1253.

Principal/principle. A *principal* is a person in charge of something or a leading performer. A *principle* is a fundamental law, idea, or component.

EX 10-29   Write *principal* or *principle* in each blank.

EXAMPLE: The *principle* of self-determination holds that residents of an area have a right to choose the area's future political status.

1. We spoke with one _____ of the ballet company.

2. A _____ of sound defense in football is pursuit.

3. The _____ of the high school presented several awards.

4. I will soon become a _____ in this consulting office.

5. Which _____ does this experiment demonstrate?

6. The _____ of nonintervention will be debated vigorously in Congress today.

EX 10-30   Underline the correct word of each pair given in parentheses.

EXAMPLE: The (principal, principle) of the local grammar school spoke at a conference on elementary education.

1. The full (compliment, complement) of professors from the education department attended the conference.

2. The (principal, principle) had some (advise, advice) for students contemplating a teaching career.

3. "I (advise, advice) you to choose another field unless you truly enjoy working with young people," she said.

4. (Data, Datum) concerning local pupils' mathematical skills were presented by a consultant.

5. The data indicated that the (principals, principles) of addition and subtraction were grasped by most second graders in the local district.

6. Several members of a statewide (counsel, council) of social studies teachers attended the conference.
7. One member offered to (counsel, council) informally any students having an interest in teaching social studies.
8. A visiting speaker paid the organizers of the conference a nice (compliment, complement).
9. She made several (illusions, allusions) to the chaotic nature of last year's conference.
10. That conference had been held in a downtown hotel near the (capitol, capital).
11. "What we teachers do in the classroom can (effect, affect) the course of history," said one young speaker.
12. His bombastic speech had little noticeable (effect, affect) on the audience.

I. REVIEWING CHAPTER CONCEPTS

EX 10-31   Underline each proper noun in the following sentences. Circle each common noun.

EXAMPLE: The year 1876 saw celebrations throughout the United States.

1. The Centennial Exposition, commemorating the one hundredth anniversary of the Declaration of Independence, was held in Philadelphia.
2. Luxury travel by rail had become a reality; the handsomely appointed cars produced by George Pullman and his workers were on display at the fair.
3. Two promoters, Henry C. Jarrett and Harry Palmer, came up with an idea for a singular journey.
4. At that time the trip from New York to San Francisco by rail took about seven days.
5. Jarrett and Palmer wanted to prove that passengers could be whisked from the East Coast to the West Coast in half that time
6. Their train, the Transcontinental Express, would include the most elegant and comfortable car that Pullman made.
7. The publisher of the New York *Herald*, James Gordon Bennett, footed half the cost of the special excursion in return for the exclusive right to print news about the trip in his paper.
8. Passengers included officers of the British Army and actors on their way to California to perform the play *Henry V*, by William Shakespeare.

9. The train pulled out of New York at 1:00 A.M. on Thursday, June 1, and chugged into the depot on Madison Street in Chicago twenty-one hours later.

10. As the train roared across the Great Plains in the dark of night, the passengers who were awake saw the glow of bonfires built by local residents wanting to show their admiration for what was being attempted.

11. The engineer pushed the Transcontinental Express to the dizzying speed of sixty miles an hour as it thundered westward across Nebraska.

12. The train was ahead of schedule by more than three hours when it pulled into Cheyenne, Wyoming, so the engineer halted the train for five minutes; the residents of Cheyenne gave the train and its passengers the most raucous welcome imaginable.

13. Henry Jarrett was handed a telegram in Cheyenne; its message was that a flash flood had destroyed a section of track near Ogden, Utah.

14. Fast work by local laborers got the track repaired by the time the Transcontinental Express came into sight.

15. The promoters had promised that lunch on Sunday would be served in San Francisco; the promise was kept, for the passengers of the Transcontinental Express reached San Francisco at 9:30 A.M. on that day.

16. Dee Brown, who also wrote *Bury My Heart at Wounded Knee*, has written a fine popular history of railroads in America; the title of this book is *Hear That Lonesome Whistle Blow*.

EX 10–32   Cross out each letter that should be a capital letter. Write the capital letter above.

>   T   O
> EXAMPLE: ~~t~~oronto, ~~O~~ntario

1. paule viguier of toulouse, france

2. elbe river

3. samuel gompers

4. kealakekua bay

5. *the deltoid pumpkin seed*, by john McPhee

6. dorothy scarborough

7. *the beast from twenty thousand fathoms* (movie)

8. a fifty-cent piece

9. lucretia coffin mott

10. this university

EX 10-33 Write the correct forms of the nouns in the blanks.

	Singular	*Plural*		*Singular*	*Plural*
EXAMPLE:	arrow	*arrows*		*watch*	watches
1.	entry	_____	16.	salve	_____
2.	hobo	_____	17.	_____	potatoes
3.	_____	milliliters	18.	_____	slashes
4.	shelf	_____	19.	mouse	_____
5.	_____	belfries	20.	gulf	_____
6.	_____	eaves	21.	conservatory	_____
7.	soprano	_____	22.	_____	fathers-in-law
8.	sister-in-law	_____	23.	violoncello	_____
9.	_____	knives	24.	_____	waxes
10.	Mary	_____	25.	wife	_____
11.	tomato	_____	26.	library	_____
12.	touch	_____	27.	ox	_____
13.	_____	maestros	28.	_____	half-lives
14.	osprey	_____	29.	_____	moose
15.	_____	laboratories	30.	_____	kiwis

EX 10-34 Rewrite each sentence so that the italicized phrase becomes a possessive expression. Do your writing on another sheet of paper.

> EXAMPLE: Books *by Edward Gorey* contain some chilling surprises.
> *Edward Gorey's books contain some chilling surprises.*

1. Many of the characters *in the* stories are meek-looking children.
2. The acts *of some of the adults* toward children are not exactly gentle.
3. In other stories, the worst fears *of youngsters* come true.
4. The artwork *in the books* is rather formal, claustrophobic, yet charming.
5. One of the simple sentences *written by Edward Gorey* can convey an overwhelming sense of horror.
6. Readers who dislike dark thoughts and mordant humor are advised to avoid the works *of this author-artist.*

EX 10-35 Write the singular possessive, plural, and plural possessive forms of each singular noun listed below.

	Singular	*Singular Possessive*	*Plural*	*Plural Possessive*
EXAMPLE:	sky	sky's	skies	skies'
1.	quartet	_____	_____	_____
2.	nuthatch	_____	_____	_____

Singular	Singular Possessive	Plural	Plural Possessive
3. Lucy	_____	_____	_____
4. fruitfly	_____	_____	_____
5. Jackson	_____	_____	_____
6. correspondent	_____	_____	_____
7. yo-yo	_____	_____	_____
8. brother-in-law	_____	_____	_____
9. knife	_____	_____	_____
10. goose	_____	_____	_____
11. Briton	_____	_____	_____
12. survey	_____	_____	_____
13. slide	_____	_____	_____
14. Cass	_____	_____	_____
15. pass	_____	_____	_____

EX 10–36 Write a sentence about the most recent class meeting of each course you are taking at present. Underline each concrete noun you write. Circle each abstract noun you write. Do your writing on another sheet of paper.

EX 10–37 On a separate sheet of paper, write four sentences about your last day in high school. In each sentence use one of the nouns listed below.

principal	advice	council	affect
principle	advise	counsel	effect
complement	data	allusion	capital
compliment	datum	illusion	capitol

EX 10–38 Underline the correct word of each pair in parentheses.

> EXAMPLE: (Datum, <u>Data</u>) were collected from weather stations throughout the state.

1. Inside the (capital, capitol) the debate raged.
2. Lawmakers argued over the probable (affect, effect) of building the canal.
3. "Those who (advice, advise) us to abandon this plan are selfish and short-sighted!" thundered one representative.
4. "We must remember from whom this (council, counsel) is coming," said his opponent.
5. "A member of a (council, counsel) of builders and developers has a vested interest in a yes vote!" she continued.
6. Supporters of both sides of the issue staged outdoor rallies and held press conferences at various locations in the (capital, capitol).

7. Mimeographed sheets presenting (datum, data) in support of the canal ended up in the same litter receptacles as sheets espousing (principals, principles) of conservation and growth limitation.
8. TV news reporters did their best to create the (allusion, illusion) that the nuances of the struggle could be accurately conveyed to viewers in less than a minute.
9. One lobbyist gave a rival lobbyist a grudging (compliment, complement).
10. "I think that last (datum, data) you passed to Representative Haack had a significant (affect, effect) on the way she voted."

WORKSHOP

1. Joel Shapiro, a former classmate of one of the authors, once made the observation that "if one of something is good, two are much better." Test the logic of Shapiro's dictum by writing singular and plural nouns to create ten sentences that follow this pattern: *One* _____ *is good; two* _____ *are much better.* Then write a sentence or two explaining why you think the statement is or is not valid.

2. Write a paragraph about great treasures mentioned in fictional or historic literature. Include at least four possessive forms of nouns in the paragraph.

3. Fill the blanks on this noun tree; begin by writing a general noun, such as *recreation* or *landform,* in the left-hand blank. Write nouns that are increasingly specific as you move toward the right.

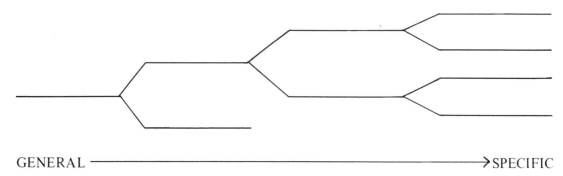

GENERAL ⟶ SPECIFIC

4. Write a paragraph of definition for one of the following concrete nouns.
   quasar   rotifer   helium
   samovar   hatchet   square

5. Write a paragraph of definition for one of the following abstract nouns.
   sanity   chance   communication
   humor   art   risk

6. Find a paragraph you have written that could benefit from revision. This can be from any paper you have written this year. Rewrite the paragraph. As you do so, ask yourself these questions:
   • Do all proper nouns begin with capital letters?
   • Do all common nouns begin with lower-case letters?
   • Are all plural nouns written correctly?
   • Are possessive forms of nouns used where required?

- Are singular possessive and plural possessive nouns used and written correctly?
- Could increased clarity be achieved by substituting specific nouns for some general nouns?
- Are the remaining general nouns properly inclusive?
- Have abstract nouns been clarified or defined so that readers know the sense in which each is used?
- Are the following words used correctly?

principal	advice	council	affect
principle	advise	counsel	effect
complement	data	allusion	capital
compliment	datum	illusion	capitol

Note that you will seldom make all these kinds of corrections in a single paragraph. Nevertheless, trying out a number of possibilities is bound to lead you to a better way of saying what you want to say.

Working with Pronouns

A. IDENTIFYING PRONOUNS

Pronouns are words that can be substituted for nouns and their modifiers.

EXAMPLES
Competitors in Masters events are over forty years of age.
They are over forty years of age. [*They* is a pronoun that has been substituted for *competitors in Masters events.*]

Jim Lem is a Masters powerlifter.
He is a Masters powerlifter. [*He* is a pronoun that has been substituted for the noun *Jim Lem.*]

Setting twelve records in one weekend is quite an accomplishment.
That is quite an accomplishment. [*That* is a pronoun that has been substituted for the gerund phrase *setting twelve records in one weekend.*]

EX 11–1 The pronouns in the following sentences have been italicized. On the blank following each sentence write the noun that the pronoun stands for. Note that a pronoun may refer to a noun mentioned in a previous sentence.

EXAMPLE: Tasha Tudor has illustrated several dozen children's books; *she* is one of America's most popular book artists. *Tasha Tudor*

1. Tasha Tudor's drawings reflect *her* fondness for the nineteenth century.

   _____

2. *They* do not contain the bright, dense colors of this mechanized era.

   _____

3. The pastels and creamy beiges of a more romantic time are employed by *her.*

   _____

4. Mrs. Tudor's farmhouse, *which* is in a pine clearing in rural Vermont, does not have running water. _____

5. Because of this, Mrs. Tudor must carry *it* in buckets from the barn into the house. _____

6. A person *who* spins yarn and makes candles and butter keeps in touch with America's pioneer heritage. _____

EX 11-2   Underline each pronoun in the following sentences.

EXAMPLE: <u>What</u> would <u>you</u> do in this situation?

1. Thirty residents on the east side of Cumberland Court in Foster City, California, have had no mail delivered to them for a year.
2. They must travel two miles to a post office to pick up their mail.
3. The mail carrier walks down Cumberland Court six times a week, but he delivers mail only to residents who live on the west side of Cumberland Court.
4. What is the problem, you may ask.
5. The houses on the east side of Cumberland Court are relatively new; they were completed after 1978.
6. A federal law that was enacted in 1978 requires houses in new developments to erect curbside mailboxes.
7. If a resident in a new development does not have a curbside mailbox, he or she receives no mail deliveries.
8. What has prevented residents of homes on the east side of Cumberland Court from erecting curbside mailboxes?
9. A Foster City ordinance prohibits these.
10. Although virtually everyone in city government and in the Postal Service acknowledges the ridiculousness of the situation, no one has moved to fix it.
11. What would you do if you lived on the east side of Cumberland Court?
12. I myself would have consulted a lawyer long ago.

B. IDENTIFYING PERSONAL PRONOUNS

I, me, you, we, us, he, him, she, her, they, them, and *it* are called personal pronouns. Each can be substituted for particular persons or things.

EXAMPLE
André Gide wrote *Strait Is the Gate.*
He wrote *Strait Is the Gate.* [The personal pronoun *he* has been substituted for *André Gide.*]

I and *me* are *first-person singular* pronouns. They refer to the speaker or the writer. *We* and *us* are *first-person plural* pronouns. They normally refer to a group of two or more people that includes the speaker or the writer. *You* is a second-person pronoun; it may be singular or plural. *You* refers to the person or persons being addressed. *He* and *him* are *third-person singular* pronouns used to refer to males. *She* and *her* are *third-person singular* pronouns used to refer to females. *It* is a *third-person singular* pronoun used to refer to animals, places, objects, and concepts. *They* and *them* are *third-person plural* pronouns.

TYPES OF PERSONAL PRONOUNS

	Singular	Plural
First Person	I, me	we, us
Second Person	you	you
Third Person	he, him / she, her / it	they, them

EX 11-3   Underline each personal pronoun in the following sentences.

> EXAMPLE: Before <u>he</u> was a bandleader, Desi Arnaz was a birdcage cleaner.

1. We sometimes forget that many famous people once worked at ordinary jobs.
2. Before Paul Gauguin decided to become a painter, he worked as a stockbroker.
3. Former Israeli Prime Minister Golda Meir was a schoolteacher before she entered the political arena.
4. People credit her with having had a good sense of humor.
5. It seems to me that a schoolteacher without a sense of humor does not last long.
6. Dean Martin and Bob Hope wear tuxedos when they work nowadays.
7. Did you know that Martin was once a steelworker or that Hope was once a boxer?
8. Knowing the previous occupation of an entertainer may make you regard him or her with greater admiration.

In writing, a personal pronoun normally refers back to a noun or phrase used earlier in the sentence or in a previous sentence. The word or phrase to which a pronoun refers is called its *antecedent*.

> EXAMPLE: Though Alissa, the main character in *Strait Is the Gate*, seems at first without depth, *she* is ultimately seen as a deep and complex individual. [*Alissa* is the antecedent of *she*.]

EX 11-4   The personal pronouns in the following sentences are italicized. Draw an arrow from each pronoun to its antecedent. Remember that an antecedent may appear in a sentence that precedes the one in which the pronoun appears.

> EXAMPLE: Freddie Laker decided that *he* could revolutionize international travel.

1. *He* set out to provide travelers with cheap flights between Great Britain and the United States.

2. *They* welcomed fares that were half what other airlines charged.

3. Freddie Laker grew up poor; *he* learned the value of a penny early.

4. His mother raised *him* in humble surroundings.

5. *She* ran a junkyard, and her son helped her.

6. At the age of sixteen *he* began working in an aircraft factory thirty miles from London.

7. Freddie Laker was one of the youths who swept *it* and brought tea to the workers.

8. The determined youth learned about aircraft of various kinds, and soon he was ferrying *them* into war zones.

9. Profits from buying and selling spare aircraft parts helped put *him* in the aircraft business in 1948.

10. Laker proved to be a brilliant manager; *he* built British United Airways into Britain's largest independent airline.

11. Laker started Laker Airways on April Fool's Day, 1966; *it* was a no-frills operation from the beginning.

12. Thousands have appreciated what Laker Airways has offered *them*: safe, fast transportation at a budget price.

A personal pronoun that is the subject of a sentence or a clause is in the *subjective* case. A personal pronoun that is the direct object of a verb, the indirect object of a verb, or the object of a preposition is in the *objective* case.

EXAMPLES

I never wear jogging shoes to work. [*I* is the subject of the sentence; it is in the *subjective* case.]

Leather shoes suit *me* fine. [*Me* is the direct object of the verb *suit*; it is in the *objective* case.]

When *I* run, I wear athletic shoes. [*I* is the subject of the dependent clause introduced by *when*; it is in the *subjective* case.]

Are you making fun of *me*? [*Me* is the object of the preposition *of*; it is in the *objective* case.]

You and *it* do not have distinct subject and object forms; all other personal pronouns do.

SUBJECT AND OBJECT FORMS
OF PERSONAL PRONOUNS

	Singular		Plural	
	Subject	Object	Subject	Object
First Person	I	me	we	us
Second Person	you	you	you	you
Third Person	he, she, it	him, her, it	they	them

EX 11-5 In the following sentences, circle each personal pronoun that is a subject form; underline each personal pronoun that is an object form.

EXAMPLE: (We) saw her sink to a kneeling position.

1. My friend wondered aloud whether he should offer her some help.

2. Then we saw the woman's face become pale and grayish.

3. She was lying against the wall and gasping for breath.

4. He rushed over to her; she could barely speak.

5. He called to us to telephone for an ambulance.

6. As I ran to a public telephone, I checked to see if I had the right coins with me.

7. The dispatcher for the ambulance company said they would have paramedics there within five minutes.

8. As we had guessed, the woman had suffered a heart attack.

9. The woman whispered that she felt weak and sick.

10. The paramedics roared around the corner, stopped the ambulance, and carried a stretcher with them as they hurried over to where the woman was resting.

11. "Will she be all right?" someone asked.

12. "I never thought this would happen to me," said the woman as the paramedics eased her into the back of the ambulance.

EX 11-6 Underline the correct case form of the pronoun in parentheses.

EXAMPLE: (We, Us) are told by some that there is no second; there is only first, followed by all others.

1. (I, Me) would not be ashamed to be the second person in history to do some great thing.
2. Few of (we, us) know the name Millie Gade Corson.
3. Some old-timers may remember (she, her) as the second woman to swim the English Channel.
4. Because (she, her) made her heroic crossing a month after Gertrude Ederle made hers, Corson missed her chance at a measure of immortality.
5. If (I, me) could conquer such a treacherous stretch of water, the fact that someone else had done it before (I, me) would not bother (I, me).
6. When Sir Edmund Hillary became the first person to climb Mount Everest, (he, him) became one of the heroes of the twentieth century.
7. Standing beside (he, him) on the top of the world was Tenzing Norkay, a Sherpa guide.
8. Ernest Reiss and Fritz Luchsinger reached the top of Everest three years after Hillary and Norkay; though (they, them) did not become famous as a result of their conquest, (they, them) had the satisfaction of having achieved what most people had considered impossible just a few years before.

Personal pronouns that are part of compound expressions appear in the same case that they would if they were used alone.

EXAMPLES
She rode her bicycle from Golden to Denver.
Alf and *she* rode their bicycles from Golden to Denver. [*She* is part of a compound subject; the *subjective* case is required.]

The ride tired *her*.
The ride tired Alf and *her*. [*Her* is part of a compound direct object; the *objective* case is required.]

Although *she* enjoyed the ride, she will not repeat it soon.
Although Alf and *she* enjoyed the ride, they will not repeat it soon. [*She* is part of the compound subject of the dependent clause; the *subjective* case is required.]

Pass the jar of peanut butter down to *her*.
Pass the jar of peanut butter down to Alf and *her*. [*Her* is part of the compound object of the preposition *to*; the *objective* case is required.]

EX 11-7   Complete each of the following sentences by writing in the blank a pronoun to stand for the word or phrase beneath the blank.

EXAMPLE: Christopher Columbus and   *they*   landed on   *it*
                                             his crew   the island of
            _____ on November 19, 1493.
            Puerto Rico

1. San Juan Bautista was the name given _____ by _____
                                            the island   Columbus.

2. When Ponce de León landed on the island, _____ reportedly said,
                                                Ponce de León

   "Que puerto rico!"

3. How the island happened to be called Puerto Rico rather than San Juan

   Bautista remains a mystery to _____ and _____
                                  scholars   you, me, and others without

   _____ .
   special knowledge on this subject

4. Before _____ arrived, the island was called
            Columbus and Ponce de León

   Boriquen by _____ .
                 its Indian residents

5. The name used by _____ still survives, though *Borinquen* is the spelling
                      the Indians

   now used by _____ .
                residents

6. When _____ and _____ attend a public event today, _____ may sing
         a boy   a girl   the boy and girl
   "La Borinqueña," the anthem of Puerto Rico.

7. Although _____ did not send expeditions to attempt
              Queen Elizabeth I of England

    to colonize _____, _____
                      Puerto Rico and the other Caribbean islands Queen Elizabeth
    made her country's presence known in the area.

8. _____ sent Sir Francis Drake and _____ to
    This powerful monarch   Sir Richard Hawkins

    the West Indies to prey upon _____.
                                        Spanish treasure ships

9. Drake and _____ did not disappoint her.
            Hawkins

10. Swift ships commanded by _____ and other privateers captured
                                  Drake and Hawkins
    and looted many of the slow Spanish galleons.

EX 11-8   On another sheet of paper, rewrite the following paragraph. Use personal pronouns to replace nouns and phrases that are used repetitively.

Bob Elliott and Ray Goulding have been entertaining America with wit and satire for more
than thirty years. Bob and Ray first came to prominence as radio comedians in the late 1940s;
television audiences met Bob and Ray during the 1950s. Bob and Ray have published several
books of humorous sketches; these are as much fun to read as to hear or see performed. Kurt
Vonnegut, Jr., the noted author, numbers himself among the millions of Bob and Ray fans;
Kurt Vonnegut, Jr., wrote the introduction to *Write If You Get Work: The Best of Bob and
Ray*. In this introduction Vonnegut discusses a broadcast done by Bob and Ray in about
1965, a broadcast during which Vonnegut talked to Elliott and Goulding about writing
comedy sketches for their program. Vonnegut recalls a bit from the broadcast in which the
two comedians were selling advertising space on the Bob and Ray Satellite. The Bob and Ray
Satellite was going to be orbited at an altitude of twenty-eight feet, so the advertisements on
the Bob and Ray Satellite would be easily visible to the people below. Vonnegut also mentions that Bob and Ray offered listeners sweaters from the Bob and Ray Overstocked Surplus
Warehouse. The Bob and Ray Overstocked Surplus Warehouse was filled with sweaters carrying the monogram *O*. Bob and Ray told listeners that if any of the listeners did not have a
name that began with *O*, Bob and Ray would help the listener get the name legally changed.
As Vonnegut concludes his introduction, Vonnegut mentions a belief that underlies the
humor of Bob and Ray: "Man is not evil. He is simply too hilariously stupid to survive."
Vonnegut says that Vonnegut, too, believes this to be true.

The subjective case of personal pronouns should be used after forms of the verb *be* in
written work.

EXAMPLES

It is *I*. [NOT It is *me*.]

The final speaker was *she*.

Was it *he* who fell asleep during the speeches?

EX 11-9   Write personal pronouns to complete the following statements.

> EXAMPLE: Was it *they* who asked to borrow my windsurfer?
>
> 1. It is _____ who have the strength to handle that craft easily on a windy day.
>
> 2. The one with the greatest knowledge of sailing was _____ .
>
> 3. Is that _____ on the poster?
>
> 4. If one of them damages my windsurfer, it will be _____ or _____ who will be responsible.
>
> 5. Yes, it is one of _____ who will be responsible.
>
> 6. A voice asked for Donna Delgado, and I said, "This is _____ ."

Clauses that complete statements of comparison are called *elliptical clauses*; these were introduced in Chapter 8. A pronoun that is the subject of an elliptical clause must be a *subject* pronoun form. A pronoun that is a direct or indirect object or an object of a preposition in an elliptical clause must be an *object* form.

EXAMPLES

Harvey ran faster than *I*. [The complete comparative statement is *Harvey ran faster than I ran fast*; *I* is the subject of the elliptical clause.]

They gave Harvey a nicer trophy than me. [The complete comparative statement is *They gave Harvey a nicer trophy than they gave me*; *me* is the direct object of the verb *gave*.]

EX 11-10   Write personal pronouns to complete the following sentences. Remember that the pronoun which is the subject of an elliptical clause must be a subject form.

> EXAMPLE: No linebacker in the league is fiercer than *he*.
>
> 1. I would be happier wrestling with a bear than with _____ .
>
> 2. Most other backs are quicker than _____ .
>
> 3. Nevertheless, he has been in the league longer than most of _____ .
>
> 4. The backs know that no one hits harder than _____ .
> 5. Would that younger, less aggressive linebacker be more effective on pass coverage than _____ ?
>
> 6. The defense responds to the old pro more energetically than to _____ .
>
> 7. The fans like the old pro better than _____ .
>
> 8. He may be a bit slower than _____ , but he makes up for his lack of speed in many ways.

When *I, me, we,* or *us* is used as part of a compound structure, it should appear as the final element in the compound structure.

EXAMPLES

The black labrador retriever growled at *Edie and me*. [NOT at *me and Edie*.]

The chemists, the laboratory assistants, and we are on strike. [NOT *We, the chemists, and the laboratory assistants*.]

EX 11-11 Write four sentences about events you have attended with other people. Use the pronouns given in parentheses in compound structures.

1. (I) _____

2. (me) _____

3. (we) _____

4. (us) _____

A personal pronoun may precede a noun or phrase that specifies its identity. If the pronoun functions as the sentence subject, the subject form must be used. If it functions as an object, the object form is required.

EXAMPLES

We gymnasts have reserved the field house. [*We* is the sentence subject; it is in the subjective case.]

No one cares about *us* badminton players. [*Us* is the object of the preposition *about*; it is in the objective case.]

A subjective-case personal pronoun must never be used immediately after a noun that is its antecedent and is the subject of a sentence.

EXAMPLE OF INCORRECT USAGE
John he comes to practice early on Tuesdays.

CORRECTED VERSION
John comes to practice early on Tuesdays.

EX 11-12 Six of the following sentences contain usage errors. On another sheet of paper, rewrite these six sentences to correct the errors. Do not rewrite the sentences that are correct as written.

> EXAMPLE: Elzie Crisler Segar he gave we Americans a host of piquant cartoon characters.
> *Elzie Crisler Segar gave us Americans a host of piquant cartoon characters.*

1. Segar he started a new comic strip shortly after World War I.
2. This strip it was called "Thimble Theater."
3. It focused on the doings of the Oyl family.
4. Olive Oyl she was the leading female character in the strip.
5. We "Thimble Theater" fans know the names of her father, her mother, and her brother.
6. Olive's father he was Cole Oyl, her mother she was Nana Oyl, and her brother he was Castor Oyl.
7. A few years later a funny-looking sailor was introduced to we readers.
8. We landlubbers could not get enough of Popeye the Sailor.
9. You the reader may have seen a recent film based on the "Thimble Theater" comic strips.
10. Robin Williams he played Popeye, and Shelley Duvall she had the role of Olive Oyl.

EX 11-13 On another sheet of paper, rewrite the following paragraph. Correct all errors in personal-pronoun usage.

> I and Kate understand how desperate you are. Kate she is probably more afraid of what might happen if you don't get out than you are. But you must be aware of what this does to her and I. As I said, she and me have been working out of duty, out of necessity, and working is not the word for it. We attendants at this station are the enemy as far as the people who live around here are concerned. I actually have taken every conceivable insult, physical and mental, and had to ride with them in order to stay alive. People at our station have been slugged, threatened with knives and lead pipes and chains, and shot at. It was me whom a car tried to run down two weeks ago. Us employees have closed the station three times because of riot conditions. It's been no more pleasant for Kate than for I. She has worked for so many hours at a time that she was too sore to sleep. We have both had chest colds and earaches since the second week of summer, but I and her have continued to work so us two could get away to somewhere healthy and sane for a week or two. If we do send you the money, either me or she or both of us will have to work right up to the day school starts. So you see this is difficult for her and I.

Some writers have problems with consistency of voice in compositions; that is, they do not stay with one group of pronouns when speaking to the reader.

EXAMPLE OF INCONSISTENT VOICE
"When we laugh, the whole world laughs with us; but when you cry, you cry alone." If one keeps this old saying in mind, one will have a good chance of getting along with his or her roommates. Family members, for whatever reasons, put up with me through extended periods of surliness or self-pity. We cannot expect the same of roommates, though; humoring grouches is not part of the rental agreement.

PARAGRAPH REWRITTEN TO ACHIEVE CONSISTENCY OF VOICE
"When you laugh, the whole world laughs with you; but when you cry, you cry alone." If you keep this old saying in mind, you will have a good chance of getting along with your roommates. Family members, for whatever reasons, put up with you through extended periods of surliness or self-pity. You cannot expect the same of roommates, though; humoring grouches is not part of the rental agreement.

EX 11-14 On another sheet of paper, write a paragraph expressing a point of view on one of the following matters. Choose an appropriate voice and stay with it; select your pronouns carefully. Be sure you have an audience in mind before you begin writing.

> keeping a dog while living in an apartment
> becoming a volunteer blood donor
> keeping up with national and international news
> watching soap operas
> sharing lecture notes with friends
> telling the truth
> choosing a career on the basis of probable financial reward

C. WRITING POSSESSIVE PRONOUNS

Each personal pronoun can change form to show possession or close relationship. Look at the following sentences.

> a. You took your marine biology book with you yesterday.
> b. This one is mine, and I need it tonight because our section has a quiz scheduled for tomorrow.
> c. Biff might not need his book tonight.

What possessive pronoun appears in sentence *a*? _____ What would the form of this pronoun be if it stood alone rather than preceding a noun? _____

What possessive pronouns appear in sentence *b*? _____ Which does not precede a noun? _____ What would the form of this pronoun be if it did precede a noun? _____

What possessive pronoun appears in sentence *c*? What would the form of this pronoun be if it did not precede a noun? _____

The following chart is an expansion of the chart shown earlier in the unit; it now includes the possessive forms of personal pronouns.

SUBJECT, OBJECT, AND POSSESSIVE FORMS OF PERSONAL PRONOUNS

	Singular			Plural		
	Subject	Object	Possessive	Subject	Object	Possessive
First Person	I	me	my, mine	we	us	our, ours
Second Person	you	you	your, yours	you	you	your, yours
Third Person	he, she, it	him, her, it	his; her, hers; its	they	them	their, theirs

Possessive pronouns take the place of possessive expressions that include nouns. *My, your, her, our,* and *their* are forms used before nouns or words that function as nouns. *Mine, yours, hers, ours,* and *theirs* cannot precede nouns; they are used by themselves. *His* and *its* may be used before nouns as well as by themselves; the use of *its* by itself, though, is extremely rare.

EXAMPLES
The time *achieved by Jan Oehm* in the 1981 San Francisco "Bay-to-Breakers" run was the fastest ever for a woman runner.

Her time in the 1981 San Francisco "Bay-to-Breakers" run was the fastest ever for a woman runner. [*Her* is a third-person singular feminine possessive form; it precedes the noun *time.*]

The presence of *several world-class athletes* did not faze this UC–Berkeley distance runner.

Their presence did not faze this UC–Berkeley distance runner. [*Their* is a third-person plural possessive form; it precedes the noun *presence.*]

Oehm's stamina was greater than *the stamina possessed by the more famous athletes.*

Oehm's stamina was greater than *theirs.* [*Theirs* is a third-person plural possessive form; it stands by itself and functions as a noun.]

Cindy Schmandt is a teammate *of Oehm's.*

Cindy Schmandt is a teammate of *hers.* [*Hers* is a third-person singular feminine possessive form; it stands by itself and functions as a noun. Note the use of the possessive form after *of.*]

EX 11–15   In the following sentences, underline the possessive pronouns that precede nouns; circle the possessive pronouns that stand by themselves.

EXAMPLE: (Mine) is the blue leather jacket with the chrome buttons.

1. My clothes came from a next-to-new store.

2. Where did you buy yours?

3. I always tell my friends how frugal I am.

4. Their expenses are counted in dollars; mine are counted in cents.

5. Her pocket comb cost more than my jeans.

6. Our expenditures for food are minimal.

7. That lawn of yours is a living salad bowl.

8. With your permission I will gather edible greens from it for our salad tonight.

9. By the way, may I borrow your new ski equipment this weekend?

10. Why should I let my penchant for economizing get in the way of a good time?

Look at the following sentences.

a. My buying an electric typewriter was a big mistake.
b. Me buying an electric typewriter was a big mistake.
c. I buying an electric typewriter was a big mistake.

Which sentence is correct? _____ What kind of phrase is *buying an electric typewriter*?

You have seen that the possessives *my, your, his, her, its, our,* and *their* are used before nouns as modifiers. These forms are also used before gerunds and gerund phrases as modifiers; this usage follows logic, since gerunds and gerund phrases function as nouns.

**EXAMPLES OF POSSESSIVE PRONOUNS USED WITH
GERUNDS AND GERUND PHRASES**
Your shoveling has impressed me. [*Shoveling* is a gerund.]

Now I know that *our* finishing this job by 5:00 is a possibility. [*Finishing this job by 5:00* is a gerund phrase.]

EX 11-16   Underline the correct pronoun form of each pair given in parentheses.

>   EXAMPLE: Those jokes of (your, <u>yours</u>) are awful.
>
>   1. I didn't know (your, yours) sister was fond of chinchilla coats.
>
>   2. (Your, You) crossing a chinchilla with a gorilla sounds like quite an accomplishment.
>
>   3. Will (me, my) asking you to get to the point interfere with (you, your) telling of the joke?
>
>   4. I'm sure that the coat (you, your) made for (her, hers) was lovely.
>
>   5. Why were (it, its) sleeves too long?
>
>   6. It isn't (my, mine) fault that you don't know how to tell a joke.
>
>   7. What happened to that guitar of (you, yours)?
>
>   8. I didn't realize that it belonged to (you, your) sisters.
>
>   9. (Them, Their) selling the guitar must have come as a blow to (you, yours).
>
>   10. Now that that guitar of (their, theirs) is gone, I'll bet they just pick on you.

EX 11-17   Rewrite each of the following sentences so that a possessive pronoun is used to replace the italicized expression. Do your writing on a separate sheet of paper.

>   EXAMPLE: Ouray was one of the leaders *of the Ute Indians.*
>   *Ouray was one of their leaders.*
>
>   1. The ability *of Ouray* to speak Spanish and English made him an especially important individual.
>   2. Settlers were encroaching on the lands *of the Indians* during the mid-1800s.
>   3. Ouray used the wisdom and linguistic abilities *of Ouray* to keep southwestern Colorado peaceful.
>   4. Admiration *felt by settlers* for Ouray resulted in an honor being accorded him.
>   5. A town *of the settlers'* was given his name.
>   6. Many of the summers *of my aunt's life* have been spent in Ouray, Colorado.

Personal pronouns that do not have clear antecedents can confuse readers. A personal pronoun is assumed to refer to the noun most recently used that could logically be its antecedent. Problems arise when a pronoun refers not to the noun most recently used but to a prior one, when a pronoun refers to a noun that last appeared several sentences back, or when a pronoun has no logical antecedent at all.

EXAMPLES OF PRONOUNS WITH UNCLEAR ANTECEDENTS
Her father was frantic when he learned that it had carried Europa away; he sent them to look for her and told the brothers not to come back until their sister had been found. Cadmus did not follow his orders directly but went instead to consult with the god Apollo as to her whereabouts. His response, though, was bewildering to him; how could he ignore her plight as well as his edict and go off instead to found a city of his own?

CORRECTED VERSION
When Europa's father learned that a bull had carried his daughter away, he was frantic. He sent his sons to look for Europa and told them not to come back until they had found their

sister. Cadmus, one of Europa's brothers, did not follow his father's orders directly but went instead to consult with the god Apollo as to his sister's whereabouts. Apollo's response, though, was bewildering to Cadmus; how could he, Cadmus, ignore his sister's plight as well as his father's edict and go off instead to found a city of his own?

EX 11–18 Rewrite the following paragraph so that a reader can easily tell the antecedent of each pronoun. Do your writing on a separate sheet of paper.

The Wild Tchoupitoulas, the Neville Brothers Band, Earl King, James Booker, and the New Orleans All-Stars brought a large, spicy helping of New Orleans music to the 1977 Monterey Jazz Festival. Their unusual name comes from a street in its French Quarter. True to its burlesque spirit, they dressed in garish feathered costumes and sang Mardi Gras Indian chants celebrating the raucous, occasionally violent goings-on of the weeks before Mardi Gras. The Neville Brothers helped to provide solid instrumental support for the Big Chief and his tribe. They also performed a number of Louisiana-inflected rhythm-and-blues numbers, including Aaron Neville's hit, "Tell It Like It Is." Guitarist King and keyboardist Booker also showed off their talents as songwriters and instrumentalists during the New Orleans set. His song "Come On (Let the Good Times Roll")" never fails to generate excitement; Jimi Hendrix once used it as a showcase for his guitar skills. Booker's instrumental number "Gonzo" proved popular with them as well. Its finale, bringing all the Crescent City performers onstage at once as the New Orleans All-Stars was, in the words of the Big Chief, a "wild, wild creation." It may not have pleased some jazz purists, but they roared their approval right up until the last day-glo pink Indian feather vanished from the stage.

D. USING COMPOUND PERSONAL PRONOUNS

Compound personal pronouns are words formed by adding the suffix *self* or *selves* to personal pronouns. *Myself, yourself, himself, herself,* and *itself* are the singular forms; *ourselves, yourselves,* and *themselves* are the plural forms.

Compound personal pronouns may be used *intensively* or *reflexively*. Look at the following sentence.

> a. I *myself* did not want to go.
> b. I promised *myself* that this would never happen again.

In which sentence is a compound personal pronoun used to *intensify* the identity of a noun or pronoun? _____ In which sentence does a compound personal pronoun stand for the subject and function as an object or a subjective complement? _____ A compound personal pronoun that is used to indicate that the subject is the receiver of his or her own action is said to be a *reflexive* pronoun; any compound pronoun that is not used intensively is a reflexive pronoun.

EX 11-19 Underline the compound personal pronoun in each of the following sentences. On the line after each sentence write whether the pronoun you underlined is used an an *intensive* pronoun or as a *reflexive* pronoun.

> EXAMPLE: Chuck Mangione has fashioned a solid career for <u>himself</u> as a jazz performer and a recording artist. *reflexive*

1. Musicians frequently find themselves being asked whether they came from a musical family. _____

2. Mangione himself came from a family that loved music. _____

3. His parents were not musicians themselves, but they raised their children in a musical atmosphere. _____

4. Mr. Mangione says that he himself played the cash register, in order to pay for his children's college educations. _____

5. Mr. Mangione did take his children to jazz clubs in Rochester, New York, where they enjoyed themselves. _____

6. Afterward he would often invite the musicians back to the Mangione house to help themselves to a big meal and then jam a bit. _____

7. As a result young Chuck found himself trading licks with jazz greats such as Julian "Cannonball" Adderly. _____

8. I myself cannot think of a finer way to run a household. _____

Several variant forms of compound personal pronouns are occasionally heard in conversation. These include *meself, youself, youselves, hisself, theirselves,* and *theyselves.* These forms should never be used in written work; they are considered incorrect when used in formal speech or writing.

EX 11-20 Underline the correct pronoun form of each pair given in parentheses.

> EXAMPLE: Don't fool (youself, <u>yourself</u>) about taxes.

1. I had to give (meself, myself) a good talking-to the other day.
2. What happens to you when you find (yourself, youself) in a stereo store with cash in your pocket?
3. Some people can force (theirselves, themselves) to walk out without spending a penny.
4. I found (meself, myself) starting to buy things I didn't really need with cash I didn't really have to spend.
5. The salesperson lost (himself, hisself) a sale when he said something about taxes driving up the cost of things.
6. He is probably kicking (hisself, himself) for having made that comment; it reminded me that April 15 is only three weeks away, and I will need every bit of money I have to pay my taxes.

E. WORKING WITH DEMONSTRATIVE PRONOUNS

This, that, these, and *those* are the four *demonstrative pronouns.* They are used to point out persons and things. Look at the following sentences.

    a. *The tires over there* are recaps.
    b. *The tire I am touching* is on sale.
    c. *The tire you are pointing to* looks to me to be defective.
    d. *The tires here in front of us* are overpriced.

With which demonstrative pronoun would you replace the italicized phrase in sentence *a*?

_____ in sentence *b*? _____ in sentence *c*? _____ _ _ _ __

in sentence *d*? _____

Use *this* and *these* to refer to things close at hand and to events that are occurring at present. Use *that* and *those* to refer to things far away and to events that have already happened.

EXAMPLES OF DEMONSTRATIVE PRONOUNS
These are mine; *those* are yours.
This is our finest hour!

THESE ARE NOT DEMONSTRATIVE PRONOUNS
These socks are mine; *those* towels are yours. [Here *these* is a demonstrative adjective modifying *socks*; *those* is a demonstrative adjective modifying *towels*.]

EX 11–21   Underline the demonstrative pronouns in the following sentences.

    EXAMPLE: <u>These</u> are being sucked dry by aphids.

    1. This is a spray made from garlic juice and water.
    2 First I will spray these.
    3. I will spray those if I have any of this mixture left over.
    4. That is not a plant pest; it is a flea.
    5. Are these things red spider mites?
    6. Will you help me hang these from the ceiling?

Demonstrative pronouns are used frequently in conversation; the speaker's gestures often help the listener understand to what these pronouns refer. In writing, however, the use of demonstrative pronouns can cause confusion if the writer does not make clear what words or ideas they stand for.

EXAMPLE OF A PARAGRAPH WITH A CONFUSING DEMONSTRATIVE PRONOUN
Ulysses S. Grant was a military officer who had no fondness for war. He disliked army routine even more than he disliked fighting. During the Mexican War he had established a reputation as a capable military leader, but he was a terrible peacetime soldier; he had been forced to resign from the army because he could not control his drinking. He had disgraced himself—and the army—one too many times. Moreover, Grant had failed in all his business ventures after leaving the army. This made him an unlikely candidate for a responsible position of command in the Union Army. [It is unclear what *this* refers to.]

FINAL SENTENCE REWRITTEN FOR CLARITY
His attitudes, vices, and failures made Grant an unlikely candidate for a responsible position of command in the Union Army.

EX 11-22   Think of a retail store or restaurant you are familiar with. On another sheet of paper, write a paragraph directed to the owner in which you explain how the physical layout of the store or restaurant could be improved. Use at least two demonstrative pronouns in the paragraph. Make sure that the pronouns' antecedents can easily be deduced by the reader.

F. WRITING INTERROGATIVE AND RELATIVE PRONOUNS

When the pronouns *who, whom, whose, which,* and *what* are used in questions, they are called *interrogative pronouns.*

EXAMPLES OF INTERROGATIVE PRONOUNS
Who are you?
For *whom* is this message intended?
Whose are these?
Which are the jeans that are guaranteed against shrinkage?
What are you trying to do?

THESE ARE NOT INTERROGATIVE PRONOUNS
I wonder *who* she is. [Here *who* is a relative pronoun; note that *who* would be an interrogative pronoun if this sentence were stated as a question—*Who is she?*]

Whose scarf is this? [Here *whose* is a possessive pronoun modifying *scarf.*]
Which hanger do you want? [Here *which* functions as an adjective modifying *hanger.*]

Who, whom, whose, which, and *what* can also be used as *relative* pronouns. As you saw in Chapter 8, relative pronouns are used in adjective clauses and noun clauses. Other words used as relative pronouns are *that, whoever, whomever, whatever,* and *whichever.*

EXAMPLES OF RELATIVE PRONOUNS
Charles Goodyear was the chemist *who* discovered how to vulcanize rubber. [*Who* is the subject of an adjective clause.]

Rubber was a natural substance *that* was not very useful. [*That* is the subject of an adjective clause.]

Vulcanizing, *which* involves adding sulfur to hot rubber, made the rubber stable throughout a range of temperatures. [*Which* is the subject of a nonrestrictive adjective clause.]

Goodyear, *whose* discovery would make the age of the automobile possible, had previously been jailed for debt. [*Whose* here functions as a relative possessive pronoun.]

EX 11-23 Underline the interrogative pronouns in the following sentences. Circle the relative pronouns.

> EXAMPLE: "Professor of the Year" is an award (that) is given annually to a college faculty member.

1. Who gives this award?

2. The award, which carries a $5,000 cash prize, is given by the Council for Advancement and Support of Education.

3. Who received the 1981 award?

4. Mary Eleanor Clark, who teaches at San Diego State University, was the 1981 recipient of the award.

5. What does she teach?

6. Clark is a professor of biological sciences who specializes in animal physiology.

7. Students who have used the textbook *Contemporary Biology* know of Professor Clark's ability to convey difficult concepts clearly and simply.

8. Professor Clark, whose teaching responsibilities run from freshman biology classes to graduate seminars, has not let the demands of research and committee work interfere with the quality of her teaching.

9. What has she asked students to do with that egg yolk in the dish?

10. Is that really just salt that is being shaken onto the yolk?

11. What will happen when the dish containing the heavily salted egg yolk is turned upside down?

12. The salt that has been added has made the egg yolk rock-hard.

13. The egg yolk stays in the dish that has been turned upside down.

14. The protein that was in the egg yolk has been denatured and has had its properties of solubility changed.

Who is a *subjective* pronoun form, and *whom* is the corresponding *objective* form. Use *who* as the subject of a sentence or a clause, or as a subjective complement. Use *whom* as a direct object, an indirect object, or the object of a preposition.

EXAMPLES

Who will come? [*Who* is the subject of the sentence.]

She is the architect *who* designed the student union building. [*Who* is the subject of the dependent clause *who designed the student union building.*]

Whom do you represent? [*Whom* is the direct object of the verb phrase *do represent.* When the word order is changed to *you do represent whom,* the correctness of *whom* becomes a bit easier to see.]

Are you the person to *whom* I spoke on the telephone? [*Whom* is the object of the preposition *to.*]

It is very important to remember that the form of a pronoun that is part of a dependent clause is determined by its function *within the clause.*

EXAMPLES

Who shall I say is calling? [*Who* is the subject of a dependent clause. When the word order is changed to *I shall say who is calling,* the correctness of *who* becomes easier to see.]

Whom do you wish to speak to? [*Whom* is the object of the preposition *to.* When the word order is changed to *you do wish to speak to whom,* the correctness of *whom* becomes apparent.]

EX 11-24   Underline the correct pronoun form of each pair given in parentheses.

EXAMPLE: For (who, <u>whom</u>) was the insult intended?

1. (Who, Whom) called while I was at the movie?
2. I don't know (who, whom) that is.
3. To (who, whom) is that package addressed?
4. (Who, Whom) should I thank for this?
5. Everyone (who, whom) forgot my birthday should be ashamed.
6. The neighbor (who, whom) I asked to join us for dinner next Thursday will not be able to come.
7. Is there anyone else (who, whom) you would like to invite?
8. (Who, Whom) is calling at this hour?
9. (Who, Whom) is ringing the doorbell?
10. I am a person (who, whom) is seldom surprised.
11. (Who, Whom) would not be caught off guard by a midnight surprise birthday party?
12. The people (who, whom) have showed up are true friends.
13. Is there anyone (who, whom) I would honor by staying up to attend a party at such a ridiculous hour?
14. The people (who, whom) you invited are good sports indeed.
15. Is Sal the one (who, whom) brought the homemade pasta?
16. (Who, Whom) did you say brought the twin cheesecakes?
17. Anyone (who, whom) comes to a midnight party deserves a second dinner.
18. The neighbors are the ones (who, whom) this party is surprising the most.
19. I think I know (who, whom) will call first to complain about the noise.
20. (Who, Whom) haven't I danced with?

In interrogative sentences *who* and *whom* are used in questions about people, *what* is used in general questions about animals and things, and *which* is used in questions about groups of animals or things (*which one of those?*).

EXAMPLES
Whom did Prince Charles marry?
Who married Prince Charles?
What were Charles and Diana given by Nancy Reagan?
Which of these chafing dishes will they keep?

EX 11-25   On another sheet of paper, write a question using *who, whom, which,* or *what* to go with each of the following answers.

> EXAMPLE: Massachusetts is the New England state with the largest population.
> *Which is the New England state with the largest population?*

1. The Connecticut River makes the Connecticut Valley a rich farming area.
2. Leif Ericsson is said to have landed on the Massachusetts coast in about A.D. 1000.
3. The Massachusetts coast was explored by John Smith in 1614.
4. Provincetown was the island where the Pilgrims first landed.
5. The Pilgrims' Mayflower Compact became the basis for American democracy.
6. Berkshire County is the westernmost county in Massachusetts.

In relative clauses, as has been mentioned before, *who* and *whom* are used to refer to people; *that* may be used to refer to people or things but may not be used to begin a non-restrictive clause; and *which* is used to refer to things.

EXAMPLES
Are they the people *who* greeted you at the door?

Is this the dog *that* bit you?

That incident, *which* I would prefer to forget, was mentioned in a gossip column in today's newspaper.

What should not be used at the beginning of a relative (adjective) clause.

EXAMPLES OF INCORRECT USE OF *WHAT*
Those are the bluejays *what* keep eating my strawberries.
Was she the exterminator *what* you went to see?

CORRECTED VERSIONS
Those are the bluejays *that* keep eating my strawberries.
Was she the exterminator *whom* you went to see?

EXAMPLE OF CORRECT USE OF *WHAT*
You can't always get *what* you want. [Here *what* begins a noun clause.]

EX 11-26   Underline the correct pronoun form of each pair given in parentheses.

> EXAMPLE: The first gold rush stories (what, <u>that</u>) Bret Harte wrote were immensely popular when they were first published.

1. The characters (that, what) Harte introduced to his readers were colorful and untamed.
2. Harte's stories, (that, which) tended to follow a few predictable patterns, wore out their welcome with the public after a while.
3. The readers (who, which) had once believed his every word began to suspect that life in the gold country was not exactly as Harte described it.
4. Harte did not personally observe much of (what, which) he wrote about.
5. Most of the critics (who, which) have evaluated Harte's writings have found them lacking in depth.

6. Nevertheless, Harte must be given credit for writing stories (what, that) provided Americans with their first images of (what, that) life was like in the California mining camps.
7. Harte was also a better storyteller than many writers (which, who) have received critical acclaim.
8. Any writer (which, who) creates character types (what, that) become literary stereotypes should not be dismissed as utterly inconsequential.
9. The canny, chivalrous gambler and the foul-mouthed, reckless stagecoach driver are two of the character types (that, what) Harte created and dozens of other writers later utilized in stories of the Old West.
10. The schoolteacher (which, whom) Harte described in "The Idyl of Red Gulch" became the model for hundreds of frontier schoolteachers in movies, books, and TV programs.

G. USING INDEFINITE PRONOUNS

Indefinite pronouns refer to persons or things not definitely enumerated or identified. The following words are often used as indefinite pronouns: *all, another, any, anybody, anyone, both, each, either, everybody, everyone, few, many, more, most, much, neither, no one, none, one, other, several, some, somebody, someone.*

EXAMPLES
Many seemed disappointed; a *few*, however, cheered wildly.
Everybody who pays for a ticket is entitled to express an opinion.
No one walked out during the performance.

EX 11-27　Underline the indefinite pronouns in the following sentences.

EXAMPLE: No one had been informed of the hikers' plans.

1. Surely someone would realize that they had been gone too long.
2. Both of the hikers had been injured in the rock slide.
3. Neither had brought a safety flare.
4. Several planes passed overhead, but none seemed to be searching the area.
5. Anybody hiking the trail would see the rock slide or spot the hikers' fire.
6. The injured hikers looked at each other; they knew their only hope was to attract attention by building a large, smoky fire.

A common error in pronoun usage is the use of *their* following *anybody, anyone, everybody, everyone, no one, somebody,* or *someone.* These pronouns are considered to be *singular* in number, so a possessive pronoun that refers to one of them must also be singular.

EXAMPLES
Everyone on the Raiders wore *his* Super Bowl ring proudly. [NOT . . . *wore their Super Bowl rings proudly.*]

Did anyone forget to bring a facsimile of *his or her* birth certificate? [NOT . . . *of their birth certificate.*]

EX 11-28   Underline the correct form of each pair given in parentheses.

> EXAMPLE: Someone left (<u>her</u>, their) purse on a lunchroom table.

1. Everyone pass (their, his or her) paper forward.
2. Someone on the women's gymnastics team injured (her, their) back this afternoon.
3. Has anyone been back to (his or her, their) dorm room yet?
4. No one in the fraternity has received (their, his) grades yet.
5. Everybody seems to have (his or her, their) reading lamp on late tonight.
6. Somebody with a sense of humor has dressed (himself, themselves) up as a clown and is handing out cookies shaped like *A*s to everyone on the campus.

EX 11-29   On another sheet of paper, rewrite the following paragraph. Correct all errors in pronoun usage.

Why would anyone choose to spend their summer vacation getting up at dawn each day and walking up and down the beach holding a machine? The answer, as I have now learned, is to find treasure. Some which walk the beaches with metal detectors actually refer to theirselves as treasure hunters, but others simply call theyselves scavengers. One beach walker who I talked to had just found hisself a treasure of no little value: a diamond engagement ring, that had the initials L.V.K. on it. He explained that, rather than keeping this treasure, he would try to find the person to whom the ring belonged by placing an ad in the local newspaper offering to return it. The beach walker he said that he did this with any item what obviously had sentimental value for a particular person. Nonpersonal findings, such as coins, however, were his to keep, he felt. This friendly scavenger let me use one of his metal detectors for a few minutes, and I surprised meself by finding a fifty-cent piece what had the date 1917 on it. This coin, that is worth about ten dollars, is mine first treasure find, but it will not be mine last: the treasure hunter who I talked to offered to sell me one of his three metal detectors. The price? A 1917 fifty-cent piece. What did I choose? I chose the one who had found the fifty-cent piece, of course. Anyone whom seeks treasure can't afford to turn their back on the forces of good fortune.

H. PRACTICING CORRECT USAGE OF PROBLEM PRONOUNS

Its is the possessive form of *it*. *It's* is a contraction of *it* and *is*.

EX 11-30   Write *its* or *it's* in each blank.

> EXAMPLE: The hatchetfish uses <u>*its*</u> pectoral fins as wings.

1. _____ capable of briefly leaving the water in flight.

2. _____ method of flight is different from that of flying fish.

3. The flying fish glides rather than flies; it uses _____ powerful tail to gain enough momentum to leave the water.

4. The hatchetfish is small and light; _____ fin movements actually lift it into the air.

5. _____ not a wise choice for a home aquarium.

6. Perhaps when more is known about _____ habits and nutritional needs, the hatchetfish will have a better chance for long life in a closed environment.

Their is the possessive form of *they*. *They're* is a contraction of *they* and *are*. *There* is used to indicate location; it is also used as an introductory word.

EX 11–31   Write *their, they're,* or *there* in each blank.

EXAMPLE: I don't buy cassettes *there* anymore

1. _____ cassettes are not well made.

2. _____ inexpensive, but _____ fidelity is poor.

3. The employees are helpful and friendly _____ .

4. Some of _____ audio products are excellent.

5. These miniature speakers sound great; _____ only $49.99 each.

6. The speaker towers over _____ , on the other hand, are unbalanced and overpriced.

Whose is the possessive form of *who*. *Who's* is a contraction of *who* and *is*.

EX 11–32   Write *whose* or *who's* in each blank.

EXAMPLE: *Who's* ringing the doorbell?

1. Our neighbor wants to know _____ parked in her driveway.

2. I don't know _____ grey '57 Chevy that is.

3. Maybe it belongs to someone _____ at the party around the corner.

4. Here comes the person _____ car it is.

5. _____ going to tell him not to park there again?

6. Now _____ truck is blocking our driveway?

Your is the possessive form of *you*. *You're* is a contraction of *you* and *are*.

EX 11–33   Write *your* or *you're* in each blank.

EXAMPLE: Would you write down *your* telephone number for me?

1. _____ the first student I've met here who uses business cards.

2. I see that _____ a furniture refinisher and reupholsterer.

3. Do you spend all of _____ free time doing that?

4. _____ rates seem very reasonable.

5. Are you sure _____ charging enough for _____ time?

6. I can see from these pieces that _____ work is excellent.

The easiest way to avoid mistakes writing these pronoun forms is to commit this rule to memory: *Never use an apostrophe when writing the possessive form of a personal pronoun or of who.* There are no exceptions to the rule, so it is not difficult to apply.

I. REVIEWING CHAPTER CONCEPTS

EX 11-34   Underline each pronoun in the following sentences. Write *PERS* above each *personal* pronoun. Write *POSS* above each *possessive* pronoun. Write *C.PERS* above each *compound personal* pronoun. Write *DEM* above each *demonstrative* pronoun. Write *REL* above each *relative* pronoun. Write *INTER* above each *interrogative* pronoun. Write *INDEF* above each *indefinite* pronoun.

PERS   POSS
EXAMPLE: Can you keep all those abbreviations in your head?

1. I bet this will take me an hour to do.

2. Who can remember seven types of pronouns and seven abbreviations?

3. Whoever wrote this has a lot of gall.

4. Can someone explain to me the difference between a relative pronoun and

   an interrogative pronoun?

5. Which is used only in questions?

6. Interrogative pronouns, which are only used in questions, almost always

   occur at the beginning of a sentence.

7. I am surprising myself by how much I remember.

8. No one remembers all that he or she reads.

9. This is not that difficult, in my opinion.

10. Why is this book trying to put words in my mouth?

EX 11-35 Underline the correct form of each pair given in parentheses.

     EXAMPLE: Will someone lend (<u>me</u>, I) a comb?

1. Some of (we, us) will have the opportunity to work as extras in a movie being filmed here by a Hollywood crew.
2. I wonder what kinds of people (they, them) are looking for?
3. (Me, My) being first in line will force (they, them) to notice (I, me).
4. (You, Your) red hair may help (you, your) be noticed.
5. My roommate shaved off (his, him) beard because (he, him) thought (they, them) would want clean-cut students in this film.
6. His girlfriend is wearing a punk costume, since (she, her) is sure (they, them) want colorful character types.
7. All this excitement has interrupted (me, my) studying for the history final.
8. (Jack, Jack he) is a drama major.
9. If (he, him) wins a part in the film, (he, him) will add a nice credit to (he's, his) portfolio.
10. (We students, Us students) like the idea of being paid, too; a little extra money never hurts.

EX 11-36 Underline the correct item of each pair given in parentheses.

     EXAMPLE: The person (who, <u>whom</u>) I must talk to about auto insurance is
                 out of the office now.

1. I (myself, meself) have a good driving record.
2. Auto insurance, (which, that) is quite expensive nowadays, must be carried by all car owners in this state.
3. With (who, whom) do you have your auto insurance listed?
4. When my sister was in an accident, her insurance company did very little for (her, herself).
5. She gave the insurance company the name of two people (which, who) witnessed the accident.
6. No one in the insurance company was willing to take (his or her, their) time to follow up on the information supplied.
7. When the insurance company raised my sister's rate even though it was not (she, her) who was at fault in the accident, she contacted someone at the state insurance commission.
8. The person at the commission said that he (himself, hisself) could do nothing until my sister obtained signed statements from witnesses and provided these to the insurance company.
9. My sister found the addresses of the people (who, whom) had witnessed the accident.
10. She sent copies of their statements to the insurance company, the police, and the person to (who, whom) she had spoken at the insurance commission.
11. (What, Which) did the insurance company do then?
12. (What, Which) of the statments convinced them (what, that) my sister was not at fault?
13. At first the person (who, whom) was handling my sister's file at the insurance company said that the company would not lower my sister's rate.

14. When my sister told the company representative that she had sent copies of all documents to the state insurance commission, however, the representative said she would see (what, which) could be done.
15. Was it (she, her) who called my sister later that day to tell (she, her) that her premium would be lowered?
16. A rebate for the additional amount (that, what) my sister had paid was sent to (her, herself) about a month later.

EX 11-37   Rewrite the following paragraph so that the antecedent of each pronoun is obvious. You may need to consult an encyclopedia or history book to make sure your rewritten paragraph is historically accurate. Do your writing on a separate sheet of paper.

The tragic duel between Alexander Hamilton and Aaron Burr put an end to a brilliant, though far from blameless, career. He had first risen to prominence more than three decades earlier as a writer of anti-British pamphlets. During the War for Independence he came to George Washington's notice while serving as a captain of artillery. He became his secretary and aide-de-camp and earned high marks for his intelligence and seriousness. This was not enough for him, though, and in 1781 he left his staff and served as a field commander, leading them to victory at Yorktown. After peace was established, he was chosen as a member of the Continental Congress. Throughout the 1780s he worked to convince them that we needed a strong central government. At his suggestion they called for a constitutional convention to be held in Philadelphia in 1787. Although this was not entirely satisfactory to him, he worked hard to get it ratified. He and James Madison emerged as perhaps the most influential voices on the nature of the new government; Washington chose him as his Secretary of the Treasury. This required self-confidence and financial acuity, two traits which he certainly possessed; thanks to his efforts, we were put on sound economic footing by the end of his term as President. A shrewd politician he certainly was, but a diplomat he was not; he made enemies easily and never learned to turn the other cheek. His unwillingness to try to mollify Burr, whose political career he had effectively thwarted, ultimately cost him his life. He stands as a major figure in American history despite his faults; without his championing of a strong, fiscally responsible central government, it might never have become a powerful and unified nation.

EX 11-38   Underline the correct item of the forms given in parentheses.

EXAMPLE: (They're, Their, There) jerseys are ragged and torn.

1. (You're, Your) going to kill them.
2. (They're, Their, There) not very tall, and they don't look quick either.
3. (It's, Its) going to be a cakewalk.
4. Better test the scoreboard; (it's, its) going to get quite a workout today.
5. Has that dorm really sent (it's, its) best five people to play?
6. (You're, Your) center should go for at least thirty points.
7. (Who's, Whose) supposed to be covering the little guy with the beard?
8. (Who's, Whose) fault was that turnover?
9. If you don't hit the offensive boards harder, (they're, their, there) fast break will kill you.
10. Why wasn't someone (they're, their, there) to give weak-side help?
11. (It's, Its) almost halftime, and (your, you're) center still hasn't scored.
12. I hope (you, you're) a good second-half team.

WORKSHOP

1. Write a paragraph about a deed done by a famous person, such as the crossing of the Delaware River by George Washington during the Revolutionary War. Substitute pronouns for as many nouns and noun phrases as you can. Pass the paragraph to a classmate; see if this person can guess what event is being described.

2. As you scan articles, advertisements, handouts, announcements, and personal communications, keep your eyes open for misuses of *its/it's; there/their/they're; whose/who's;* and *your/you're.* See how long it takes you to find an example of misuse of one word in each group.

3. Make up five relative clauses about historical figures or things. Here are two examples: *who defeated Napoleon at Waterloo* and *which Vivien Leigh wore in Gone with the Wind.* Exchange the clauses with a classmate. Write five complete, informative sentences that include the relative clauses written by your classmate.

4. Rewrite each relative clause you wrote in activity 3 as a question beginning with an interrogative pronoun. For example, *who defeated Napoleon at Waterloo* would be rewritten to read *Who defeated Napoleon at Waterloo?*; *which Vivien Leigh wore in Gone with the Wind* would be rewritten as *What did Vivien Leigh wear in Gone with the Wind?*

5. Find and copy down advertisement headlines, movie titles, or book titles that contain each of the following: a personal pronoun, a possessive pronoun, a compound personal pronoun, a demonstrative pronoun, an indefinite pronoun, an interrogative pronoun, and a relative pronoun. Write a sentence or two about each title or headline explaining why the pronoun is used. (Why does a fast-food restaurant spend millions to say "*You—you're the one*"? What does the word *it* stand for in the beer slogan "It's the Water"?)

6. Find a paragraph you have written that could benefit from revision. This can be from any paper you have written this year. Rewrite the paragraph. As you do so, ask yourself these questions:
   • Are subject and object forms of pronouns used properly?
   • Are the possessive forms of personal pronouns and the possessive form of *who* written correctly, without apostrophes?
   • Can the antecedent of each pronoun be easily determined?
   • Are *which* and *what* used properly in interrogative sentences?
   • Are the relative pronouns *who* and *whom* used only to refer to people and the relative pronoun *which* used only to refer to things?
   • Are singular, not plural, possessive pronouns used in possessive expressions relating to singular indefinite pronouns such as *everybody, no one,* and *anybody*?

   By using these questions to make sure a composition is free from errors in pronoun usage, you give your writing a better chance of making a positive impression on those who read it.

Working with Verbs

12

A. IDENTIFYING VERBS

A *verb* specifies action or acts as a link between a subject and words that define or describe that subject.

EXAMPLES

Ivan the Terrible *was* a cruel, impulsive ruler. [*Was* links the subject and a defining noun phrase.]

He *killed* his own son. [*Killed* specifies an action.]

Ethelred the Unready, King of England, *earned* no respect from his subjects. [*Earned* specifies an action.]

He and his troops *were* unprepared for the Danish invasion of England. [*Were* links the subject and a descriptive phrase.]

EX 12-1   Underline the verbs that specify action in the following sentences. Three of the sentences do not have action verbs.

EXAMPLE: Alexander Graham Bell <u>invented</u> the telephone in 1876.

1. Bell developed the first commercial telephone that same year.
2. It was a boxlike device.
3. Bell designed the device with a single opening.
4. The opening was both transmitter and receiver.
5. The user shifted the device between the mouth and the ear.
6. The device went into service for the first time in 1877.
7. A banker leased a pair of telephones from Bell.
8. The banker attached them to a wire between his Boston office and his home in Somerville, Massachusetts.
9. The telephone is an indispensable item of equipment for most businesses nowadays.
10. An office temporarily without telephone service finds itself out of contact with customers and suppliers alike.

228

EX 12-2 Write an action verb to complete each of the following sentences.

EXAMPLE: Mockingbirds *imitate* the songs of other birds.

1. Bats _____ insects at night.

2. Goats _____ highly digestible milk.

3. No snakes _____ in Ireland.

4. An elephant's trunk _____ 40,000 muscles.

5. Alligators seldom _____ people unless they feel threatened.

6. An elephant _____ water over itself with its trunk while bathing.

Verbs that specify action are said to be used *transitively* if they transfer action from the subject to a direct object. For convenience, such verbs are called *transitive* verbs.

EXAMPLES OF TRANSITIVE VERBS

Members of the Junag Tribe in India *construct* raised *huts.* [The verb *construct* transfers action from the subject *members* to the direct object, *huts.*]

Their goats *occupy* the *huts.* [The verb *occupy* transfers action from the subject *goats* to the direct object, *huts.*]

Verbs that specify action are said to be used *intransitively* if they do *not* transfer action to a direct object. These verbs are often referred to as *intransitive* verbs.

EXAMPLES OF INTRANSITIVE VERBS

The members of the tribe *sleep* outside on the ground. [No object receives the action of the verb *sleep.*]

The goats certainly *live* comfortably. [No object receives the action of the verb *live.*]

EX 12-3 Underline the verb in each sentence. Circle each direct object that appears. Write *T* after each sentence that has a transitive verb. Write *I* after each sentence that has an intransitive verb.

EXAMPLE: Hiram Fong's parents immigrated to Hawaii from Kwangtung Province in China. *I*

1. They came to the lush islands in 1872. _____

2. As indentured servants they worked on sugar plantations on the island of Oahu. _____

3. Together they received twelve dollars a month as pay. _____

4. The Fongs raised eleven children. _____

5. Hiram paid for his own Harvard Law School education. _____

6. He returned to Hawaii with a law degree and ten cents. _____

7. Fong made wise investments in real estate. _____

8. The people of Hawaii elected Hiram Fong as one of their first two United States senators. _____

Many verbs can be used either transitively or intransitively. A few verbs can only be used intransitively, however.

EXAMPLE OF A VERB THAT CAN ONLY BE USED INTRANSITIVELY
Simone *agrees* with that argument. [NOT Simone agrees that argument.]

EX 12-4   Circle each sentence in which a verb is used incorrectly as a transitive verb. Rewrite each sentence you circle so that the sentence contains an intransitive verb. Use another sheet of paper for your writing.

EXAMPLE: (We died all the dandelions in our lawn.)
We killed all the dandelions in our lawn.

1. Sara foolishly itches the poison oak rash on her arm.

2. The direct sunlight rises the temperature minute by minute.

3. I sat the hedge clippers right here a few minutes ago.

4. The gentleman next door crooks his finger at me.

5. We chuckle his jokes out of politeness.

6. He subscribes the same magazines we do.

A verb that acts as a link between a subject and words that define or describe the subject is called a *linking verb*. Linking verbs usually are forms of *be*. Some other verbs that are used as linking verbs are *seem, appear, look, remain,* and *turn.*

EXAMPLES OF LINKING VERBS
William Henry Harrison *was* the choice of 52.9 percent of the voters in the presidential election of 1840. [*Was* links the subject with the subjective complement *choice.*]

He *became* ill soon after the election. [*Became* links the subject with the descriptive adjective *ill.*]

The campaign *seemed* too much for the elderly warrior's health. [*Seemed* links the subject with the descriptive phrases.]

EX 12-5   Write linking verbs to complete the following sentences.

EXAMPLE: Catherine the Great of Russia _was_ an insomniac.

1. Nights _____ endless to those who cannot sleep.

2. Insomniacs often _____ restless soon after retiring.

3. The thought of another sleepless night _____ too much to bear.

4. Some who do not sleep well _____ pale.

5. Counting sheep _____ a practice often suggested to those who cannot sleep.

6. A relaxed state of mind _____ a requirement for restful sleep.

Frequently the main verb in a sentence is preceded by one or more auxiliary verbs. A phrase made up of a main verb and one or more auxiliary verb is called a *verb phrase*. (See Chapter 7, pages 108–10, to review verb phrases.)

EXAMPLES OF VERB PHRASES

Some Greek villages *are abandoned* for as long as six months each year. [*Are* is the auxiliary verb here.]

Sheep *must have* grass to eat throughout the summer. [*Must* is the auxiliary verb here. Note that *to eat* is not a verb phrase; it is an infinitive phrase.]

EX 12-6   Underline the verb phrases in the following sentences.

EXAMPLE: Orpheus had become a marvelous musician.

1. He could make surpassingly beautiful music with his lyre.
2. Orpheus had tamed wild animals with his music.
3. Rocks and trees would move to follow him.
4. Some modern musicians have acquired unusual musical powers, too.
5. They can drive animals wild with their music.
6. Their music has caused people to move rocks and trees.
7. Walls and soundproof buildings have been constructed with these materials.
8. Orpheus was able to use his music to charm the rulers of Hades.
9. Some people have mentioned Hades as an appropriate place for a performance by some contemporary musicians.
10. These musicians, like Orpheus, have woken the dead, according to some people.

EX 12-7   Write one or more auxiliary verbs to complete the following sentences. (For a list of auxiliary verbs, see page 109.)

EXAMPLE: I have obtained a ticket and *will* attend tomorrow's performance.

1. Not long ago Sir John Falstaff _____ poaching near Windsor.

2. Bardolph, Pistol, and Nym, three scoundrels, _____ assisting him.

3. Honest citizens of the area _____ outraged by these actions.

4. These citizens _____ prepared a protest.

5. They _____ soon accost Falstaff at a social gathering.

6. They have done so; the host _____ not want a noisy, unseemly confrontation at his party.

7. The good citizens have put aside their hostile feelings and _____ enjoying hot venison pie.

8. Meanwhile Falstaff _____ becoming well acquainted with two wealthy attractive ladies.

9. _____ either of these women succumb to the rogue's charms?

10. You _____ find out what happens by reading *The Merry Wives of Windsor*, by William Shakespeare.

Verbs specifying actions can be classified as being in the *active* or the *passive* voice. *Active* verbs tell what the subject does; *passive* verbs tell what is done to the subject. (To review active and passive voice, see Chapter 6, pages 100–02.)

EXAMPLE OF A SENTENCE WITH A VERB IN THE ACTIVE VOICE
King Darius led a Persian force of 100,000 onto the Greek mainland.

SENTENCE REWRITTEN SO THAT ITS VERB IS IN THE PASSIVE VOICE
A Persian force of 100,000 was led onto the Greek mainland by King Darius.

EX 12-8   Rewrite each sentence with a verb in the active voice as a sentence with the verb in the passive voice. Rewrite each sentence with a verb in the passive voice as a sentence with the verb in the active voice. (In the complex sentences you may change either the sentence verb or the verb in the dependent clause.) Do your writing on another sheet of paper.

> EXAMPLE: Jelly Roll Morton was taught a great deal by Tony Jackson.
> *Tony Jackson taught Jelly Roll Morton a great deal.*

1. Audiences knew Jackson as "The World's Greatest Single-Handed Entertainer."
2. Patrons of cafés on the South Side of Chicago were amazed by Jackson's piano technique.
3. All sorts of music from blues to opera were played and sung by Jackson.
4. Someone told Morton that Jackson would be entering the 1904 ragtime contest in St. Louis.
5. The contest was not entered by Morton because of this.
6. Later Morton did beat Jackson in a ragtime contest.
7. The decision was not applauded by Morton.
8. He felt that he had been outperformed by Jackson.
9. Jelly Roll Morton is considered by many to be the greatest of the early jazz pianists.
10. Not many of today's jazz fans know the name of the pianist whom Morton considered his superior.

EX 12-9   Decide which version of each sentence in EX 12–8 communicates more clearly—the original or your rewrite. When you have done this, count how many of the preferred versions have predicates with verbs in the active voice and how many have predicates with verbs in the passive voice. (To review predicates, see Chapter 5, pages 65–69.)

ACTIVE VOICE _____   PASSIVE VOICE _____

B. STUDYING PRINCIPAL PARTS OF VERBS

Every verb has three *principal parts*: its *present* form, its *past* form, and its *past participle* form. The majority of verbs in English add *-ed* to the present form to create both the past form and the past participle form. These verbs are called *regular* verbs.

EXAMPLES OF REGULAR VERBS

Present	*Past*	*Past Participle*
ask	asked	asked
plant	planted	planted
trap	trapped	trapped
scrape	scraped	scraped

[Note that regular verbs ending in a short vowel and a consonant, like *trap*, double the consonant before adding *ed*. Note also that regular verbs ending with a long vowel, a consonant, and a silent *e*, like *scrape*, simply add *d*.]

A number of frequently used verbs form their past and past participle forms in other ways. These verbs are called *irregular* verbs.

EXAMPLES OF IRREGULAR VERBS

Present	*Past*	*Past Participle*
run	ran	run
freeze	froze	frozen
go	went	gone

Although some groups of irregular verbs follow consistent patterns of change, others do not. English speakers and writers must memorize the forms of each irregular verb individually. If you are in doubt as to the correct past or past participle form of a verb, look in a dictionary. Dictionaries customarily give the past and past participle forms of all irregular verbs.

The *present* form of a verb is used alone and with auxiliary verbs such as *do*. The *past* form is only used alone—never with auxiliary verbs. The *past participle* form must be used with auxiliary verbs (such as *have*) when it is used as a verb. It can be used as a modifier (a participle) without a helping verb.

EXAMPLES

I *run* before dinner each day. [*Run* is the present form.]

Do you *run* for fun? [Here the present form *run* is used with the auxiliary verb *do*.]

I *have run* farther than that several times. [Here the past participle form *run* is used with the auxiliary verb *have*.]

EX 12-10 Write the correct past and past participle forms of each verb in the appropriate blanks. Circle the present form of each irregular verb.

	Present	*Past*	*Past Participle*
EXAMPLE:	(take)	*took*	(have) *taken*
1.	bake	_____	(have) _____
2.	make	_____	(have) _____
3.	fly	_____	(have) _____
4.	try	_____	(have) _____
5.	rise	_____	(have) _____
6.	advise	_____	(have) _____
7.	beat	_____	(have) _____

Present	*Past*	*Past Participle*
8. seat	_____	(have) _____
9. meet	_____	(have) _____
10. become	_____	(have) _____
11. begin	_____	(have) _____
12. bite	_____	(have) _____
13. fight	_____	(have) _____
14. light	_____	(have) _____
15. bleed	_____	(have) _____
16. blow	_____	(have) _____
17. flow	_____	(have) _____
18. sow	_____	(have) _____
19. sew	_____	(have) _____
20. come	_____	(have) _____
21. creep	_____	(have) _____
22. deal	_____	(have) _____
23. do	_____	(have) _____
24. eat	_____	(have) _____
25. fall	_____	(have) _____
26. stall	_____	(have) _____
27. feed	_____	(have) _____
28. lead	_____	(have) _____
29. read	_____	(have) _____
30. give	_____	(have) _____
31. have	_____	(have) _____
32. hit	_____	(have) _____
33. fold	_____	(have) _____
34. hold	_____	(have) _____
35. keep	_____	(have) _____
36. know	_____	(have) _____
37. throw	_____	(have) _____
38. show	_____	(have) _____
39. tow	_____	(have) _____
40. pay	_____	(have) _____

Present	*Past*	*Past Participle*
41. play	_____	(have) _____
42. stay	_____	(have) _____
43. rid	_____	(have) _____
44. ride	_____	(have) _____
45. swim	_____	(have) _____

EX 12-11   Fill each blank with the correct principal part of the verb given in parentheses.

> EXAMPLE: Jacques Cartier *sought* a western route to Asia. (seek)

1. During his first westward journey he _____ the land now known as Labrador. (see)

2. He had never _____ such a cold, desolate region. (see)

3. He _____ that it seemed to be "the land God gave to Cain." (write)

4. If you have _____ the fourth chapter of the Book of Genesis, you will understand the allusion. (read)

5. Cartier _____ time to explore the Gulf of St. Lawrence. (take)

6. He did not _____ the river's mouth on that expedition. (find)

7. Cartier's second voyage to North America was _____ in 1535. (begun)

8. Soon he had _____ the St. Lawrence River and had begun to explore it. (find)

9. He and his crew _____ the winter near the present site of Quebec City. (spend)

10. The next spring Cartier _____ the name *Montreal* ("Mount Royal") to the great hill behind a small village on an island in the St. Lawrence. (give)

11. That small village has _____ into one of the world's most colorful cities. (grow)

12. Montreal has _____ a center for finance, manufacturing, commerce, and the arts. (become)

EX 12-12   Rewrite the following paragraph, changing incorrect verb forms. Do your writing on another sheet of paper.

The Jim Smiths of America have make quite a name for themselves—and more than seven hundred of them have joined a society celebrating that name. For the past dozen years the Jim Smiths of America have holded an annual convention. Boiling Springs, Pennsylvania, hosted the 1981 convention of the Jim Smith Society; seventy people, each having the name of Jim Smith, come to the event. As you might guess, no one at this convention weared a nametag. The scorekeeper at the convention softball game has no trouble with players' names; all forty-five participants gone by the name of Jim Smith. One family actually had three official conventioneers: Mrs. Jimmie D. Smith was joined by her husband James L. Smith and her son James L. Smith, Jr. A highlight of the convention was a variation of Bingo called

"Jimgo"; Jim Smith winned every round played. The founder of the Jim Smith Society felt that the convention was a huge success. He remarked that he had not heared a single angry word during the convention. Anyone who has been gave that most common of common names may attend upcoming Jim Smith festivals and swap "Now tell me your *real* name" stories. The rest of us can only watch from a distance and speculate upon what it would be like to go through life as good old Jim Smith.

C. WORKING WITH VERB TENSES

Look at the following sentences.

> a. Now we *rise* for the seventh-inning stretch.
> b. Before the game began we *rose* for the playing of our national anthem.
> c. We *will rise* at the end of the game to applaud Carl Yastrzemski, who is retiring.

Which sentence contains an italicized verb that specifies an action occurring in *past* time?

_____ Which contains an italicized verb that specifies an action occurring at *present*? _____

_____ Which contains an italicized verb that specifies a *future* action? _____

Simple past and present tenses are indicated in English by single-word verbs. Future tense is indicated by the auxiliary *will* plus the present form of a verb.

EXAMPLES
The crowd *cheers* the pinch hitter. [present tense]

They *cheered* Evans's sixth-inning home run. [past tense]

These Red Sox fans soon *will cheer* themselves hoarse. [future tense]

EX 12-13   Underline the verb or verb phrase in each sentence. Identify each as indicating *past*, *present*, or *future* tense.

> EXAMPLE: Next week I will read *The Legends and Myths of Hawaii*, by his Hawaiian Majesty King David Kalakaua. *future*

1. King David Kalakaua lived from 1836 to 1890. _____

2. Histories of the Hawaiian Islands speak favorably of his rule. _____

3. The king took a great interest in the traditional legends of the Hawaiian

   people. _____

4. Because of Kalakaua's efforts the legends will remain a part of the heritage

   of future generations of Hawaiians. _____

5. Kalakaua wrote forcefully and gracefully. _____

6. His retellings of the legends are entertaining as well as authentic.

   _____

7. European residents of the islands opposed Kalakaua's work. _____

8. They saw it as preservation and glorification of a pagan religion.

   _____

9. Most present-day scholars feel differently. _____

10. Terence Barrow reminds us of the importance of preserving elements of

traditional culture. _____

11. "The dignity of a people rests largely in respect for their culture. . . ."

_____

12. When reading *The Legends and Myths of Hawaii*, you will encounter such

heroic divinities as Pele, goddess of the volcanoes. _____

EX 12-14 In each blank write the appropriate form of the verb given in parentheses.

> EXAMPLE: "Now you *laugh* at my predictions," said the disheveled
> necromancer. (laugh)

1. "Tomorrow you _____ for your skepticism and stubbornness," he wheezed. (pay)

2. "Today the birds _____ in a clear blue sky." (soar)

3. "Once, long ago, locusts _____ the air, a million times more plentiful than your graceful birds." (fill)

4. "That day of decimation _____ again soon." (come)

5. "In that ancient time the rain clouds _____ misers." (become)

6. "After years of sparse rain the soil _____ to powder." (turn)

7. "Hot winds _____ its fine dry grains into the distant sky." (send)

8. "Yes, you too _____ your green valleys," he muttered. (lose)

9. "Then you _____ my warnings." (remember)

10. Limousines and sporty sedans _____ past the lone figure on their way to the evening's pleasures. (whiz)

Look at the following sentences.

> a. The professor *has assigned* a term paper.
> b. Her students *had* not *expected* such an assignment this late in the quarter.
> c. By next Thursday Hugo *will have completed* research for his paper.

Which sentence contains an italicized verb that specifies action completed in the recent past? _____ Which contains an italicized verb that specifies action completed previous to the action in sentence *a*? _____ Which contains an italicized verb specifying action that will have been completed by a certain time in the future? _____

The perfect tenses in English are created using forms of the auxiliary verb *have* plus the past participle forms of verbs. The *present perfect* tense is used to specify action that has recently been completed; it is formed by placing *has* or *have* before the past participle form of a verb. The *past perfect* tense is used to specify action that was completed by a certain time or time period in the past; it is formed by placing *had* before the past participle form of a verb. The *future perfect* tense is used to specify action that will have been completed by a certain time or time period in the future; it is formed by placing *will have* before the past participle form of a verb.

EXAMPLES

Henny Youngman *has unreeled* more lines than have all the fishers in Lake Michigan. [present perfect]

Some of his jokes *had grown* whiskers long before your parents were born. [past perfect]

By the time you leave Las Vegas, you *will have heard* at least fifty jokes stolen from Henny. [future perfect]

EX 12-15 Underline the verb phrase in each sentence. Identify each as indicating *past perfect, present perfect,* or *future perfect* tense.

EXAMPLE: These film students have seen *Dragonslayer* four times. *present perfect*

1. Their professor has assigned a class project. _____
2. The professor had selected only students with craft and construction skills.

   _____

3. One student had worked as a carpenter. _____
4. She has shown the other students how to use power tools safely.

   _____

5. Another student had been a production assistant in a special-effects production company. _____
6. By the end of the semester he will have shared with his classmates a great

   deal of his knowledge. _____
7. The students have carefully observed the dragon footage in *Dragonslayer*.

   _____

8. By this weekend they will have completed sketches for their own replicas of

   the dragon's various forms. _____
9. A local film production company has donated 35 mm film and two cameras.

   _____

10. The students had not known about this generous donation until the day

    before yesterday. _____

EX 12-16 In each blank write the appropriate perfect tense form of the verb given in parentheses.

EXAMPLE: The ornithologists and the photographers *have constructed* a blind high in that lauan tree. (construct)

1. An eagle _____ its nest in a nearby tree many weeks ago. (build)

2. A female _____ a single egg in the nest before the
   ornithologists spotted the nest. (lay)

3. Now the egg _____ . (hatch)

4. By Sunday the observers _____ their first opportunity to
   observe the chick from the blind. (have)

5. The chick's mother _____ a close eye on the doings in
   the tree near her baby. (keep)

6. None of the researchers _____ before last week exactly
   how these eagles of the Philippine Islands catch tree-dwelling creatures.
   (realized)

7. A young eagle _____ just _____ them
   a demonstration. (give)

8. It _____ something and had stuck its head into that hole
   high in the dead tree. (sensed)

9. After a while it pulled its head out and reached into the hole with a strong

   claw; it _____ since _____ the young owl it pulled
   from the hole. (devour)

10. By the time the researchers return to Manila, the lab _____

    _____ their photographs of this sequence of events. (develop)

EX 12-17   The following paragraph is written as if the events it describes are happening
right now. Rewrite it so that the events are described as having happened in the
past. Do your writing on another sheet of paper.

> Burdell Hutchers finds himself halfway through one of those "America is in danger of
> becoming a nation of _____" editorials without being able to fill in the blank.
> He closes the magazine and tells himself it is the occupational disease: he has caught himself
> reading with a copy editor's eye, paying attention to pronoun cases and referents while
> sloughing off the message. He laughs a little to himself. "Most people have the problem of not
> being able to concentrate, but we copy editors have the problem of overconcentration."
> Burdell has lost track of time once again, but he knows it is late; the lesson pages he has been
> working on are perfectly dreadful, the noxious output of his firm's newly acquired West Coast
> subsidiary. He squares the manuscript pages and prepares to leave; he tells himself that 8:30
> is late enough for anyone to stay on a Friday night. He whisks the eraser crumbs into the beige
> plastic wastebasket with a draftsman's desk brush. As he leaves the building, he bids the
> janitor good night.

EX 12-18   On another sheet of paper, write a paragraph predicting what will have happened
to you by January 1 of next year.

EX 12-19   On another sheet of paper, write a paragraph predicting what will happen to you
next year.

Progressive tense forms of verbs are used to specify continuing action. Progressive tense forms are created by placing a form of the verb *be* before the *present participle* form (usually the present form + *ing*) of a verb.

EXAMPLES OF PROGRESSIVE TENSE FORMS OF VERBS

An earthquake *is rocking* this building. [The italicized *present progressive tense* verb includes the present participle form *rocking*, formed by adding *ing* to the present form *rock*.]

Tremors *were rocking* the building yesterday too. [The italicized *past progressive tense* verb includes the present participle form *rocking*.]

According to geologists, aftershocks *will be occurring* for several more days. [The italicized *future progressive tense* verb includes the present participle form *occurring*.]

Progressive tense verbs may be passive. The passive voice of a progressive tense verb is created using a form of *be* and the auxiliary verb *being* before a part participle form of a verb.

EXAMPLE OF A PASSIVE PROGRESSIVE TENSE VERB

The building *was being shaken* by a passing convoy of military supply trucks. [The italicized verb is in the passive voice; it is a past progressive tense verb.]

EX 12–20   Rewrite each of the following sentences so that the *past, present,* or *future tense* verb is in the corresponding *past, present,* or *future progressive tense.* Underline each present progressive tense verb you write; circle each past progressive tense verb you write; draw a box around each future progressive tense verb you write. Do your writing on another sheet of paper.

> EXAMPLE: The raft moves toward the huge boulder in the middle of the stream.
>
> *The raft is moving toward the huge boulder in the middle of the stream.*

1. Now the paddlers row faster.
2. The guide calls for a left turn.
3. The paddlers practiced this maneuver earlier in a calm stretch of water.
4. Soon the boat will head into a series of difficult rapids.
5. The paddlers joked about one person's ungraceful rowing style.
6. Suddenly the boat is spun around by the swirling current.
7. The paddlers expected a trip free from mishaps.
8. They will talk about this river run for years.

Perfect progressive tense verbs are also used in English. *Present perfect progressive tense* verbs are created by using *has been* or *have been* with the present participle (*ing*) form of a verb. *Past perfect progressive tense* verbs are created by using *had been* with the present participle form. *Future perfect progressive tense* verbs are created by using *will have been* with the present participle form.

EXAMPLES

Critics *have been writing* about the fall TV lineup. [The italicized verb is in the present perfect progressive tense.]

Viewers *had been hoping* for some provocative entertainment. [The italicized verb is in the past perfect progressive tense.]

By next fall faithful viewers *will have been watching Emotional Tideflats* for seventeen years. [The italicized verb is in the future perfect progressive tense.]

EX 12-21   Rewrite each of the following sentences so that the *past, present,* or *future perfect* tense verb is in the corresponding *past, present,* or *future perfect progressive* tense. Underline each present perfect progressive tense verb you write; circle each past perfect progressive tense verb you write; draw a box around each future perfect progressive tense verb you write. Do your writing on another sheet of paper.

EXAMPLE: The medical student had listened to a lecture on kidney diseases.

The medical student (had been listening) to a lecture on kidney diseases.

1. The lecturer has discussed a particularly serious condition.
2. She had stressed the importance of early diagnosis of this illness.
3. In five minutes she will have discussed this condition for an hour.
4. The medical student has applied herself energetically to her studies.
5. This afternoon, though, her mind had wandered to subjects unrelated to the practice of medicine.
6. She has forced her mind back to the subject at hand every five minutes or so.

D. RECOGNIZING MOOD OF VERBS

You have seen that verbs are classified as to their tense (indication of time) and voice (active or passive). Verbs also express *mood.* The great majority of verbs are said to be in the *indicative* mood. Occasionally, though, a writer will use a verb in the *subjunctive* mood, either in discussing a condition that is contrary to fact or specifying an action following from someone's command. Or a writer will give an order or make a request, using the *imperative* mood.

EXAMPLES OF MOOD

I am glad that I *am* a commoner. [The italicized verb tells of a *factual* condition and is in the *indicative* mood.]

If I *were* a prince, I would have to be on good behavior all the time. [The italicized verb tells of a condition *contrary to fact*: the person is not a prince. Notice that *were* is used with *I* in this sentence instead of *was*; this expresses the subjunctive mood.]

She suggested that we *be* present at the tea. [The subjunctive form *be* follows the command *she suggested that.*]

Hold my crown for a moment. [This command begins with a verb in the imperative mood.]

EX 12-22   Complete each of the following sentences; use your imagination. Underline each verb you write that is in the indicative mood; circle each verb you write that is in the subjunctive mood; draw a box around each verb you write that is in the imperative mood.

> EXAMPLE: If *it (were) Halloween today*, I would feel comfortable wearing this outfit.

1. If _____ , I would order the royal baker to have a coffee crunch cake ready for my midnight snack.

2. _____ so I can get some sleep!

3. I have been studying for my biology mid-term for twenty solid hours and
_____ !

4. If _____ , I would not have to worry about trifles like biology tests.

5. On Friday the professor requested that _____ .

6. _____ while I make myself another pot of green tea.

E. MAKING VERBS AGREE WITH SUBJECTS

With the exception of the verb *be*, only one form of any verb changes to show agreement with the subject. The form that changes is the third-person present form used with a singular subject.

EXAMPLES
I *clean* basements. [first-person present tense, singular subject]

You *clean* basements. [second-person present tense, singular subject]

We *clean* basements. [first-person present tense, plural subject]

BUT
Roger *cleans* basements. [The third-person present tense form of a verb used with a singular subject adds *s* to show agreement.]

EX 12-23   Underline the correct verb of each pair given in parentheses. Circle each verb that is third-person present tense and has changed form to show agreement with a singular subject.

> EXAMPLE: A professional football scout (analyze, (analyzes)) the potential of hundreds of young athletes every year.

1. Most scouts (use, uses) a numerical evaluation system.

2. One team's form (call, calls) upon scouts to assign ratings from 1 to 9 in various categories.

3. The number 5 (represent, represents) average ability or quality.

4. Numbers from 6 to 9 (indicate, indicates) increasing levels of skill.

5. Speed and strength (earn, earns) a player high marks in the performance categories.

6. The strengths and weaknesses of a player's character also (enter, enters) into an evaluation of his pro potential.

7. A player with a quick mind, an aggressive personality, and a cool head (interest, interests) many scouts.

8. Nevertheless, physical attributes (loom, looms) large in a scout's final assessment of a player.

9. The college senior with a sheet full of 7s, 8s, and 9s frequently (begin, begins) his pro career with an annual salary in excess of $200,000.

10. College standouts with the curse of 3s and 4s (enter, enters) training camp with only a faint hope of joining the elite.

When a present tense verb is used with two or more subjects joined by *or*, the verb shows agreement with the part of the subject closest to it.

EXAMPLE

The fence or the signposts still *have* termites. [*Have* shows agreement with signposts, a plural noun, since *signposts* is the part of the subject nearer to the verb.]

BUT

The signposts or the fence still *has* termites. [Here *fence* is closer, so *has* is used to show agreement with this singular noun.]

A gerund phrase that functions as a subject is considered third-person singular.

EXAMPLE

Calling two exterminators for estimates *makes* good sense. [*Makes* is the form used to show agreement with a third-person singular subject.]

A present tense verb changes form to show agreement with a pronoun that stands for a *singular* noun. A present tense verb does not change form to show agreement with a pronoun that stands for a plural noun.

EXAMPLES

A publicist who *tells* lies loses credibility quickly. [Here *who* stands for the singular noun *publicist*, so *tells* must be used.]

Publicists who *tell* lies lose credibility quickly. [Here *who* stands for the plural noun *publicists*, so *tell* is the form that must be used.]

A verb must agree with the subject to which it relates.

EXAMPLES

The ax which generations of woodcutters have used to chop willows and scrub pines for firewood and fenceposts and children's lean-tos *hangs* just outside the front door of the cabin. [*Hangs* relates to the singular noun *ax*, not to any of the plural nouns that come between.]

The smell of drying leaves on the ground and overripe fruit on the trees *pulls* you forward along the rutted gully of a driveway. [*Pulls* relates to *smell*, not to *leaves*, *ground*, *fruit*, or *trees*; *smell* is the simple subject, and the other nouns are objects of prepositions.]

EX 12-24   Seven of the following sentences have verbs that do not agree with their subjects. Rewrite these sentences so that their verbs correctly show agreement. Do your writing on another sheet of paper.

> EXAMPLE: Dipping the tips of artichoke leaves into mayonnaise or melted butter make the leaves taste wonderful.
> *Dipping the tips of artichoke leaves into mayonnaise or melted butter makes the leaves taste wonderful.*

1. The leaves of the artichoke takes practice to eat.
2. Boiling artichokes until they become mushy rob them of their flavor and texture.
3. Cooking fresh young artichokes for three minutes in a pressure cooker produce a succulent first course.
4. A novice cook or an experienced chef win praise by serving artichokes to guests.
5. Hearts of artichoke add elegance and character to any salad.
6. The flavor of fresh-picked artichokes far exceeds that of two-week-old artichokes.
7. Throwing away the inner leaves of a properly cooked artichoke constitute a crime against nature and civilization.
8. Gardeners who, when they plant young artichokes, takes the time to mix a little ash in the soil are rewarded with larger, juicier chokes.
9. Each of us get two chokes tonight.
10. The dishwasher or the front cupboards hold the dishes for the artichokes, the butter, and the mayonnaise.

EX 12-25   Complete each sentence by writing the correct present tense form of the verb in parentheses.

> EXAMPLES: Thousands of asteroids *circle* the sun. (circle)

1. Most of these minor planets _____ orbits between Mars and Jupiter. (maintain)

2. Observing asteroids _____ a telescope of considerable power. (require)

3. Ceres, which is the largest of the asteroids, _____ a diameter of about 480 miles. (has)

4. Pallas, Vesta, and Juno _____ as the next largest. (rank)

5. Not all asteroids _____ names. (has)

6. Astronomers concentrating on these floating chunks of rock _____ the orbits of newly discovered asteroids. (calculate)

7. Some scientists theorize that Ceres and its small relatives _____ the remains of a planet that disintegrated long ago. (represent)

8. Unlike a star, which _____ as a dot of light on a photographic plate exposed for a period of time, an asteroid leaves a short line. (appear)

9. Two mysterious groups of asteroids known as the Trojan asteroids

_____ the sun in Jupiter's orbit. (circle)

10. Either asteroids or a meteor shower _____ trouble in just about every space-fiction film. (cause)

Several past and present tense forms of the verb *be* change form to show agreement.

PARTIAL CONJUGATION OF THE VERB *BE*

Present Tense

	Singular	Plural
First Person	I *am*	we *are*
Second Person	you *are*	you *are*
Third Person	he (she, it) *is*	they *are*

Past Tense

	Singular	Plural
First Person	I *was*	we *were*
Second Person	you *were*	you *were*
Third Person	he (she, it) *was*	they *were*

EX 12-26 Underline the correct form of *be* in each of the following sentences.

EXAMPLE: I (was, were) assigned to interview the president of the Grosco Development Company.

1. The company (is, are) planning a high-rise housing development on the edge of campus.
2. Owners of small businesses (is, are) being evicted.
3. The idea of luxury condominiums casting shadows on the main plaza outside the student union (is, are) not very popular on campus.
4. Although I (am, is) a fierce competitor in sports, I am not good at confronting people.
5. You (is, are) probably wondering why I (was, were) assigned this story.
6. It (was, were) my idea to do the interview.
7. I (are, am) aware that I must develop a more effective interviewing style if I (is, am) to succeed as a journalist.
8. The telephone that I will use to make an appointment to see the president of the development company (is, are) right here in front of me.
9. The pad with my notes about the controversy (is, are) next to the telephone.
10. Being prepared for a discussion on the telephone (is, are) always a wise idea.

EX 12-27 The following letter contains several errors in subject–verb agreement. Rewrite the letter to eliminate the errors. Do your writing on another sheet of paper.

Dear Neighbor,

I am associated with the real estate firm of Dale & Co., which have recently opened a Foster County office at 100 Oak Valley Place in the township of Whistle Glen. We be pleased that we will now are able to provide Foster County homeowners with the same conscientious, professional representation we has given to residents of Gibbonville for so many years.

Our firm come to Foster County not as strangers but as old friends. We counts among our salespeople several who lives in Foster County. I myself has lived in Whistle Glen for eighteen years.

What we brings to Foster County are an active, professional pace of handling property that our clients has found most satisfactory. The salespeople here at Dale & Co. has long experience with fine residential properties in areas of strong neighborhood values. We also has many clients who is now seeking houses in Foster County.

I welcome the opportunity to serve you. Please call if I can be of assistance in finding a buyer for your house.

Sincerely,
William Huskisson

F. WRITING CONTRACTIONS

A contraction is a word form that uses an apostrophe to indicate missing letters. Many contractions are combinations of a verb form and the adverb *not*; many others are combinations of pronouns and forms of *be* or *have*.

EXAMPLES
The new musical comedy that everyone is talking about *hasn't* come to Chicago yet. [*Hasn't* is a contraction of *has* and *not*.]

We'll be in the front row on the night of its Chicago premiere. [*We'll* is a contraction of *we* and *will*.]

EX 12-28 Write contractions of the following items.

EXAMPLES: it is   *it's*

1. has not	_____	11. there is	_____
2. we will	_____	12. had not	_____
3. do not	_____	13. will not	_____
4. cannot	_____	14. I am	_____
5. I would	_____	15. he had	_____
6. you had	_____	16. she is	_____
7. are not	_____	17. they will	_____
8. they are	_____	18. could not	_____
9. I will	_____	19. have not	_____
10. you are	_____	20. did not	_____

Most Americans use contracted forms in everyday speech. Writers therefore employ contractions when writing dialogue and when they want to achieve a natural, informal tone.

EX 12-29 On a separate sheet of paper, rewrite the following story. Substitute contractions for word pairs wherever such a substitution would make the dialogue sound more natural.

> Because his employer had been complaining that he had not been digging his holes deep enough, the gravedigger was determined to make the last hole of the day a really deep one. Before he realized it, he had dug the pit so deep that he could not climb out. The sky was dark; all the other gravediggers had gone home. The poor fellow did not know what to do.
>
> "It is no use," he said to himself after hollering for help for several hours. "There is no one to hear me. I will have to spend the night in this cold, miserable hole."
>
> But one of the town's 2:00 A.M. pedestrians happened to take a wrong turn into the cemetery. Hearing mutterings, he staggered over to the marooned gravedigger's hole and looked in. "What is the matter?" he bellowed.
>
> "It is cold down here," the gravedigger yelled back.
>
> "I cannot understand you. You had better speak more clearly," sputtered the pedestrian.
>
> "I said I am cold!"
>
> "Of course you are cold," said the pedestrian, kicking some earth and gravel into the hole. "They forgot to put the dirt on you."

The contraction *ain't* should not be used in written work. The contraction *don't* should not be used with a third-person singular subject.

**SENTENCES CONTAINING CONTRACTIONS THAT
SHOULD NOT APPEAR IN WRITTEN WORK**

Ain't it a shame that the California condor is nearly extinct?

He *don't* realize that this canyon is a nesting ground for those big birds.

CORRECTED VERSIONS

Isn't it a shame that the California condor is nearly extinct?

He *doesn't* realize that this canyon is a nesting ground for those big birds.

EX 12-30 Rewrite the following sentences, substituting acceptable contractions for unacceptable ones. Do your writing on another sheet of paper.

> EXAMPLE: If Pat don't arrive with his pickup soon, I'll have to get mine.
> *If Pat doesn't arrive with his pickup soon, I'll have to get mine.*

1. Don't someone else live closer than you?
2. Pat ain't the kind of person who forgets important jobs.
3. Ain't that he coming down the hill now?
4. He don't seem to be in any hurry; there must be something wrong with the truck.

Contractions give written work an informal, conversational feel. Some authorities on style hold that contractions should be used sparingly, if at all, in formal communications such as business letters, research papers, and reports.

G. CHOOSING APPROPRIATE VERBS

Look at the following sentences.

> a. First we cover the gold rings.
> b. Then we uncover the white rabbit.
> c. Now we recover this watch, which was lost by a member of the audience ten days ago!

What meaning does the prefix *un* add to the verb *cover*? _____

What meaning does the prefix *re* add to the verb *cover*? _____

A prefix is added before the root of a word and usually affects its meaning.

EXAMPLES
Your willingness to work *pleases* me.

Your inability to concentrate *displeases* me. [The prefix *dis* gives a negative meaning to *please*.]

EX 12-31 Use your dictionary to help you match these prefixes with their meanings.

1. re	inside, very, or not
2. in	not
3. pre	again
4. pro	before

EX 12-32 Write eight original sentences about moving. Use the words given in parentheses in the sentences you write.

> EXAMPLES: (inquire) *Most landlords inquire about the tenant's ability to pay the rent.*
> (require) *Many landlords require a rather large security deposit.*

1. (inscribe) _____

2. (proscribe) _____

3. (incur) _____

4. (recur) _____

5. (prepay) _____

6. (repay) _____

7. (inhibit) _____

8. (prohibit) _____

The English language includes many verbs whose shades of meaning differ only slightly from those of other verbs. Choosing the right verb to express your intended meaning is a skill you can develop. A good thesaurus or dictionary of synonyms can help you find the proper word for a particular action. Look at the following sentences.

a. Little Pete *walked* onto the baseball diamond.
b. Roberta *walked* toward the barbecue pit.
c. Leon *walked* toward the kissing booth.
d. Odbert *walked* over to the corn dog booth.

Now look at these versions of the preceding sentences.

e. Little Pete *toddled* onto the baseball diamond.
f. Roberta *trudged* toward the barbecue pit.
g. Leon *strode* toward the kissing booth.
h. Odbert *sauntered* over to the corn dog stand.

The four italicized verbs are just a few of the many synonyms for *walk*. Notice how much clearer a picture the revised sentences give, thanks to the substitution of specific action verbs.

EX 12-33   Rewrite the following paragraph from a children's story. Replace noncommunicative action verbs with verbs that precisely describe actions. Do your writing on another sheet of paper.

The white fox ran along the edge of the crack in the ice for some distance. Then it ran up a great snow-covered ice hill. After stopping a moment at the top, the fox made itself into a ball and began going in somersaults down the slick icy bank toward the open water. This ice slide had an upward curve near the bottom, so when the swiftly moving fox reached this part of the slide, it went traveling through the air well above the dark water. The little white animal came down in a soft snowbank on the other side of the crack, picked itself up, and ran on toward the ice hills that stood in the distance.

A number of verbs are used with adverbs to create idiomatic expressions. These verb–adverb combinations are considered by many linguists to function as two-word verbs. Look at the following sentences.

a. You may *turn in* your ticket stubs for a refund.
b. Today *turned out* to be cold and rainy.
c. Who will *turn off* the stadium lights?
d. If you find yourself in trouble, you can *turn to* your one true friend.

What does the two-word verb *turn in* mean in sentence *a*? _____

What does *turned out* mean in sentence *b*? _____

What does *turn off* mean in sentence *c*? _____

What does *turn to* mean in sentence *d*? _____

Because most dictionaries do not list many two-word verbs, these verbs can cause confusion, especially for people whose native language is not English. Fortunately, several good dictionaries of idiomatic expressions, including two-word verbs, are available. Any of these dictionaries can help you determine the meaning or proper usage of a two-word verb that is unfamiliar to you. Note that many of these idiomatic expressions are not appropriate for use in college composition.

EX 12-34   Underline the correct two-word verb of each pair given in parentheses.

> EXAMPLE: The city editor has told Ho to (<u>tear up</u>, tear down) his first draft
> of a feature story on the Maxilla Hotel arson case.

 1. Ho must (turn up, turn in) a better source.
 2. He has been told to (turn up, turn in) a final draft tomorrow night.
 3. Now he must (make up, make out) for lost time.
 4. He (sets up, sets out) to find someone who knows members of the arson gang.
 5. The first person he finds is afraid she is being (set up, set out).
 6. She (comes up, comes through) with the information Ho needs once he assures her that he will not reveal her identity.
 7. "Have you (come up, come through) with anything yet?" Ho's editor hollers as he charges back to his desk.
 8. "I've (smoked off, smoked out) a hot source," Ho shouts, unaware of his foul play on words.
 9. "I thought she'd (clam up, clam out) on me, but she really (opened out, opened up) and gave me what I needed."
10. The city editor (goes into, goes through) her desk to find a phone number.
11. "Why don't you (call up, call down) this guy?" she says to Ho.
12. "He's (tied in, tied down) with one of the gangs in that neighborhood."
13. "I was going to (go with, go for) what I already have," replies Ho.
14. "Until you learn to (go after, go with) every available fact," snaps the editor, "you'll never be anything but a third-rate reporter."

Writers frequently enliven their prose by using verbs that describe actions *figuratively* rather than *literally*. Look at the following sentences.

> a. Ridgely *rocketed* the paper onto Mrs. Terbovic's roof.
> b. Ridgely *threw* the paper onto Mrs. Terbovic's roof.

Which italicized verb specifies what Ridgely really did with the newspaper?

_____ What does the use of the verb *rocketed* tell the reader about how

Ridgely threw the newspaper? _____

Figurative language generally describes something by comparing it to something that normally has little relation to it. In the example above, the toss of the paper is compared to a rocket launching.

EX 12-35   Write six sentences about a conflict between the imaginary nations of Leucadia and Zirconia. Use each verb in two sentences—once with its literal meaning and once with a figurative meaning.

> EXAMPLE: (*poison*—literal) *A spy poisoned the defense minister by dropping a chemical into her potato soup.*
> (*poison*—figurative) *This treacherous act poisoned the friendship between Leucadia and Zirconia.*

1. (*explode*—literal) _____

_____

2. (*explode*—figurative) _____

_____

3. (*cower*—literal) _____

_____

4. (*cower*—figurative) _____

_____

5. (*collapse*—literal) _____

_____

6. (*collapse*—figurative) _____

_____

The suffixes *fy* and *ize* are added to some root words to create verb forms.

EXAMPLES

She has obtained a *false* nose; when they *falsify* her passport, they will photograph her with the bogus beak. Agents of the secret police *scrutinize* all travelers returning from Zirconia; will close *scrutiny* result in the discovery of her true identity?

Many tradition-conscious speakers of English object to the current tendency—especially prevalent among bureaucrats and advertisers—to create new verb forms by tacking *fy* or *ize* onto whatever nouns are at hand. Words such as *finalize* (meaning "to put into finished form"), *winterize* (meaning "to make resistant to winter weather"), and *scarify* (a combination of *scare* and *terrify*), though they do appear in a number of dictionaries, are considered unacceptable by many of these language purists. This presents a bit of a dilemma: how can you tell which *fy* and *ize* verbs are acceptable to purists and which are not acceptable if some of the unacceptable verbs have made their way into dictionaries? One way you can avoid trouble is to see whether the *fy* and *ize* verbs you use appear in a pre-1960 dictionary. (Someone you know will have one—no one ever throws away a dictionary until its covers fall off.) If a *fy* or *ize* verb is listed in one of these old editions, it should pass muster.

EX 12-36   Rewrite each of the following sentences that contains a *fy* or *ize* verb not listed in your dictionary; eliminate the offending verb. Do your writing on another sheet of paper.

> EXAMPLE: Only an expert should be allowed to colorize your valuable home or office building.
> *Only an expert should be allowed to select the colors of paint for your valuable home or office building.*

1. Haskell Home Improvement Co. will weatherize your ranch-style home at a surprisingly low cost.
2. Our landscaping department can countrify your yard in just a few short weeks.
3. You can modernize your entire living space with our help.
4. Our home protection experts can securify your home and yard.
5. We will identify your design, landscape, and security needs during a free home inspection.
6. Haskell Home Improvement Co. will budgetize costs to fit your ability to pay.

H. PRACTICING CORRECT USAGE OF PROBLEM VERBS

May and *can* are auxiliary verbs that are frequently misused in verb phrases. *Can* means "is able to." *May* means "is allowed to." *May* is also used to express possibility.

EXAMPLES
Some sprinters *can* cover one hundred meters in less than ten seconds.

Yes, you *may* borrow my stopwatch.

The track *may* be slow today as a result of yesterday's rain.

EX 12-37   Underline the correct word of each pair given in parentheses.

> EXAMPLE: "You (can, <u>may</u>) see Dr. Okuno now," said the receptionist.

1. "I assume that I (can, may) bring this magazine into the waiting room with me," said Marva.
2. "Certainly," said the receptionist, "if you (can, may) read in the dark."
3. "How (can, may) the doctor treat me if there is no light in the room?" asked the patient.
4. "He (can, may) have to use a flashlight," replied the receptionist.
5. "(Can, May) I discuss this with the doctor?" the patient asked.
6. "It (can, may) surprise you to learn that I was only kidding," said the receptionist to the bewildered patient.

Some writers make the mistake of writing *could of, should of,* or *would of* in a verb phrase. The proper expressions are *could have, should have,* and *would have.* When the expression *could have* is said quickly, it sounds like *could of; should have* spoken quickly sounds like *should of,* and *would have* sounds like *would of;* this may explain the confusion. Nevertheless, *could of, should of,* and *would of* are never correct in written English.

EX 12-38 On a separate sheet of paper, rewrite the paragraph below, correcting the errors in verb phrases.

> John Fitch should of been given credit for building the first steamboat in America. Fitch certainly would of been a happier person if he had been granted more recognition at the time; perhaps he could of gone on to build other innovative and practical machines. The trial run of Fitch's first steamboat in 1786 was only a partial success; nevertheless, it should of been recognized by nineteenth-century historians as the first voyage of a steamship in the United States. How they could of given Robert Fulton credit for constructing the first steamer is hard to understand; Fulton launched his *Clermont* twenty-one years after Fitch's first steamboat took to the water. A simple check of Delaware newspapers from the years 1786 and 1787 would of given historians enough information to give Fitch the credit he deserved.

The following pairs of words often cause problems.

Accept/except. Accept is a verb meaning "take" or "receive." *Except* is usually used as a preposition meaning "other than" or "leaving out."

> **EXAMPLES**
>
> These machines *accept* quarters.
>
> They offer everything *except* pizza.

Burst/bust. Bust should not be used as a verb to mean "break" or "explode." *Burst* is a verb that means "explode."

> **EXAMPLES**
>
> These balloons *burst* when you hold them too near the heater. [NOT *bust*]
>
> Two *burst* yesterday and one has *burst* today. [NOT *busted*; NOT *bursted*]

Imply/infer. Imply means "suggest that something has additional significance." *Infer* means "come to the conclusion that something has additional significance." A writer or speaker *implies* something; a reader or listener *infers* additional meaning from the words.

> **EXAMPLES**
>
> Your pauses *imply* that you are unsure of the wisdom of your suggestions.
>
> We can *infer* from your vigorous protestations that you are doubly unsure of your proposal's worth.

Lay/lie. Lay (past form *laid*; past participle form *laid*) is a transitive verb meaning "put down." *Lie* (past form *lay*; past participle form *lain*) is an intransitive verb used to indicate that some living thing is reclining.

> **EXAMPLES**
>
> *Lay* your credit cards on the nightstand.
>
> When you *lie* on this waterbed, you will feel as if you are floating on an island of gelatin.

Learn/teach. Learn means "take in knowledge." *Teach* means "instruct."

> **EXAMPLES**
>
> Comedians *learn* stage presence by observing other comedians.
>
> Velma and Luz *teach* juggling at the rec center.

Precede/proceed. Precede is a verb that means "come before." *Proceed* is a verb meaning "go forward or continue."

EXAMPLES

F and *G precede H* in the alphabet.

Entrepreneurs often *proceed* with new enterprises before securing adequate funding.

Prescribe/proscribe. Prescribe is a verb meaning "call for" or "specify." *Proscribe* is a verb meaning "forbid because of harmful qualities."

EXAMPLES

Pediatricians *prescribe* Benadryl for relief of itching.

They *proscribe* coffee for children, except in treatment of hyperactivity.

EX 12-39   Underline the correct word of each pair given in parentheses.

EXAMPLE: Edie, don't (lay, lie) your head on the dinner table.

1. Some medicines that physicians (prescribe, proscribe) for relief of hay fever cause drowsiness.
2. You may (lay, lie) down right after dinner.
3. Why did you eat everything (accept, except) your zucchini?
4. Should we (except, accept) the Nakais' invitation to their Sunday picnic?
5. Edie, you cried last year when your mouse balloon (bursted, burst).
6. If you (lie, lay) your fork down for a moment, I will serve you some rice pudding.
7. Am I to (imply, infer) from your wrinkled nose that you don't like rice pudding?
8. I don't mean to (imply, infer) that you have to eat the pudding.
9. Dinner must always (proceed, precede) dessert.
10. Jack, you may now (proceed, precede) with your explanation of why you tied the telephone cord in knots.
11. Edie, Dr. Vukovich has (prescribed, proscribed) your wearing dark glasses inside at night.
12. You won't (learn, teach) how to speak German by watching *Laverne and Shirley*, Jack.
13. Do you want me to (learn, teach) you how to use litmus paper?
14. Jack, it was on the evening of May 6, 1937, that the dirigible *Hindenburg* (bust, burst) into flames.

I. REVIEWING CHAPTER CONCEPTS

EX 12-40   Underline the verbs in the following sentences. Identify the tense of the verb on the line following the end of the sentence.

> EXAMPLE: Colonel George James had been practicing law in the little
> settlement of San Francisco. *past perfect progressive*

1. He heard talk of gold discoveries in the foothills of the Sierra.

   _____

2. Boredom had made James hungry for adventure. _____

3. Soon he was buying mining tools and supplies. _____

4. The first leg of his journey eastward was by wagon. _____

5. James then rode a horse along the dusty trails. _____

6. Horses balk at steep trails with no firm footing. _____

7. James walked the last few miles. _____

8. He had seen several rich discovery sites by then. _____

9. James made his camp near Wood's Creek, a stream with a considerable

   amount of gold in its bottom sands. _____

10. Soon many miners were working the creek. _____

11. Settlers called the new town on the banks of Wood's Creek Jamestown in

    honor of Col. James, its first resident. _____

12. James, however, was finding mining-camp life not to his liking.

    _____

13. He left Jamestown poor and angry. _____

14. A few stone buildings from the early years still stand in Jamestown.

    _____

15. The town has not become a ghost town. _____

16. The population of this attractive, historic town will probably increase with

    the passage of time. _____

EX 12-41   Write the correct form of the verb in parentheses.

> EXAMPLE: James Reid's father had *come* west to central Illinois. (come)

1. He had _____ seed from the corn he had grown in southern
   Ohio. (bring)

2. Robert Reid had _____ a day in early spring to plant his seed.
   (choose)

3. Not all of the seeds _____ in this colder climate. (grow)

4. He _____ that native corn grew well in the region, though it
   produced only small ears. (know)

5. He _____ native corn seed into the mounds where his Ohio seed had not survived. (stick)

6. The two varieties cross-pollinated, and Reid's cornfield produced the best

yield that anyone in the region had yet _____ . (see)

7. The new variety was _____ the name "Reid Yellow Dent." (give)

8. James Reid _____ higher yields and better-quality corn. (seek)

9. He _____ seed from large ears of high-yielding plants for the next year's planting. (choose)

10. James Reid's corn _____ prizes at fair after fair. (win)

11. Farmers _____ large sums of money for this "World's Fair Corn." (pay)

12. James Reid never _____ wealthy from farming or from seed royalties. (become)

13. Nevertheless, farmers throughout the upper Midwest _____ of his marvelous corn. (know)

14. Although James Reid was not a scientist, he had _____ the most learned agriculturists of his day in breeding high-quality corn. (outdo)

EX 12-42   Rewrite the following paragraphs as if the events described had happened in the past. Do your writing on another sheet of paper.

It is a Tuesday morning, a few minutes past 7:00 A.M. Brenda Wilson has just left her apartment and is passing a corner grocery on her way to the bus stop. Her gaze happens to fall upon the weed patch to the side of the store; she notices something dark among the beer cans and pie wrappers. Becoming curious, she looks closer at the dark object. Yes, it is what she thought it might be: a wallet had been dropped by someone. Brenda picks it up; as she straightens up, she remembers the last time her purse was snatched. "There won't be any money in it," she tells herself as she opens the wallet, "but maybe there are still some cards in it that the owner will want back."

Brenda has guessed wrong. The wallet happens to be full of crisp new twenty-dollar bills. She stares at the money and wonders what to do. Curiosity will not be overruled; she decides to count the money. As she reaches fifteen, Brenda suddenly becomes nervous. Three hundred dollars is a lot of money. What if someone has been watching her? She tucks the money deeper into the wallet. As she does this, she sees that the owner's driver's license is in the wallet. The owner is a young woman who lives on Thirty-Sixth Avenue. Realizing that she now has to hurry in order to avoid missing her bus, Brenda stuffs the wallet into her handbag and begins moving toward the bus stop at a controlled trot. A voice inside her head is telling her that she would be a fool to return the money: people don't expect to get their money back when they lose wallets. But another voice is asking Brenda how she would feel if *she* lost her wallet with that much cash in it. Brenda knows the answer to that one: she would feel suicidal. But, says the first voice, perhaps if she returns *most* of the money and just keeps a *few* of the twenties. Brenda continues listening to this inner dialogue as she steps off the bus and strides toward the office building where she works.

EX 12-43   Underline the correct verb form of each pair given in parentheses.

> EXAMPLE: The tree known as the southern red oak (grow, <u>grows</u>) in the South Atlantic and Gulf States.

1. Mature trees of this variety often (reach, reaches) twenty-five meters in height.
2. Some of the other names by which this tree is known (is, are) spotted oak, turkey oak, Spanish oak, Spanish water oak, and red hill oak.
3. The southern red oak's bark (has, have) a dark-brown or gray hue.
4. The bark of these graceful trees (show, shows) wide ridges, which (is, are) created by numerous shallow fissures.
5. Attaining a trunk diameter of more than one meter (is, are) unusual for southern red oaks.
6. The leaves of this tree, a member of the black oak group, (is, are) smooth and glossy and dark green in color.
7. Which of the other common oaks (belong, belongs) to the large group known as the black oak group?
8. Two general types of leaves on southern red oaks (have, has) been classified and described by dendrologists.
9. All (have, has) a rounded or wedge-shaped base.
10. One type, the finger-shaped leaf, (has, have) pointed lobe tips and a scythe-shaped terminal lobe.
11. The other leaf type (appear, appears) bell-shaped and (has, have) tooth-tipped lobes.
12. A bell-like leaf or a leaf with finger-shaped lobes (has, have) appeared as a symbol of an organization.
13. A pollen-bearing flower or several acorn-producing flowers (make, makes) an attractive study for a photograph.
14. Boards milled from southern red oak (have, has) strength and solidity but (deteriorate, deteriorates) rapidly when in contact with the soil.

EX 12-44   Read the following advertisement for a mail order course. Circle each word or pair of words that could be written as a contraction. On the lines following the advertisement write these words as contractions.

ARE YOU NOT ASHAMED OF YOURSELF!
You *should* be.
You *could* be a *terrific person.* You have been blessed with *all the tools,* all the *potential* to be an *outstanding human being*!
But you *are not terrific.* You *are not even "okay."* Frankly, you are a *miserable failure.* You are a *loser,* a *clown,* a *good-for-nothing bum*! Some days you *cannot even stand* to *look at yourself* in the mirror!
So what is *wrong* with you? What is *holding you back* from becoming the *superstar* you were *born* to be?
Fear.
You are a *loser* because you are *afraid*—afraid to start *developing* into a *walking miracle.* You are *stubborn as a mule* when it comes to *self-development.* You say to yourself, "I am so *messed up* that it would take me a *thousand years* to *get my act together."*
Hogwash.

In just *SIX* to *EIGHT WEEKS* you can change yourself from a *lowly worm* into a *soaring eagle. If you want to . . . .*

Yes, my friend, I am *ready* to *help you.* But it is *up to you,* and *you alone.*

Now you ask, "Will *tomorrow* be too late?' I *do not want* to pressure you, but, to be totally honest, *yesterday* would not have been *any too soon.* If you do not believe it, *look in the mirror.* Then mail your *coupon* and your *cashier's check* immediately . . and *give yourself* the *gift* of *new life* today!!!

EX 12–45   On another sheet of paper, rewrite the following paragraph. Correct usage errors you find. Not all verbs misused in the paragraph were discussed in this chapter.

Lisette frequently writes to a newspaper columnist for advise. She agrees with virtually all the advise the columnist gives but has never once done as the columnist has adviced. You might imply from what I have just said that Lisette has a great many personal problems; I did not mean to infer this. True, she has problems from time to time, as we all do. But if she were to wait for a problem to arise before writing each letter, she would have to limit herself to two or three letters a year, rather than the fifty or so she composes that come to lay on the columnist's desk annually. So what has the advise columnist learned Lisette about life? For one thing, she has taught Lisette that the best proscription for combating boredom is to write something that will let you see yourself in print. Why, just the other day Lisette was practically busting with pride; the advise columnist had printed the letter she had signed EVERYTHING ACCEPT LOVE. In this letter Lisette had made herself out to be a wealthy matron whose frequent social companion refused to except her subtle invitations for a deeper, more personal relationship. The appearance of her letter in the paper proceeding a pithy, witty reply pleased Lisette so much that she immediately sat down and preceded to dash off two more heartfelt letters crying out for thoughtful advise.

WORKSHOP

1. Find in a novel or short story a long narrative paragraph that describes actions taking place in the past. Rewrite the passage so that the actions take place in the present.

2. Spot-check one example of each of the following types of writing; see whether its writer used many, few, or no contractions.
   - a newspaper editorial
   - a consumer-product advertisement
   - an article in an academic journal
   - a case review in a law book
   - an article reporting on a sporting event
   - a city or county ordinance

3. Find a magazine article about a sport or leisure activity you enjoy. Find three verbs that give a precise and vivid literal description of particular actions. Then find three verbs that figuratively describe actions.

4. List twelve synonyms for one of the following verbs: *walk, eat, talk, laugh.* Make sure you know the meaning of each; then use each of these twelve verbs in a sentence about someone you know whose actions epitomize the particular meaning of the verb.

5. Use a dictionary to find the meaning and principal parts of each of the irregular verbs listed below. Then write a narrative paragraph in which you retell a familiar folk tale; use forms of at least two of the listed verbs.

abide	*beseech*	*bid*	*chide*
cleave	*forbear*	*rend*	*smite*

6. Find a paragraph you have written that could benefit from revision. This can be from any paper you have written this year. Rewrite the paragraph. As you do so, ask yourself these questions:
   - Have you correctly used the simple past tense verbs by themselves?
   - Have you correctly used past participle forms either with auxiliary verbs (such as *have* or *has*) or as modifiers?
   - Do all present tense forms of action verbs agree with their subjects?
   - Do all present and past forms of the verb *be* agree with their subjects?
   - Do verbs appear in the proper tenses for the time frames created?
   - Are all contractions written correctly?
   - Should more (or fewer) words and word pairs be written as contractions?
   - Could some verbs be replaced with more precise synonyms?
   - Would the inclusion of one or more figurative verbs increase the impact of the paragraph?

   By using these questions to make sure a composition has no problems in the area of verb usage, you give it a better chance of making a positive impression on those who read it.

Working with Modifiers and Connecting Words

13

A. SELECTING ADJECTIVES

Adjectives usually modify nouns or pronouns. Most adjectives are descriptive words. Some adjectives give quantitative information. Others specify which item is being discussed. The words *a*, *an*, and *the* are a special class of adjectives called *articles*.

EXAMPLES

Miles Davis speaks in *a raspy* whisper. [*Raspy* is an adjective that describes *whisper*.]

Davis is *a brilliant* trumpet player, probably *the greatest* soloist on *this* instrument that jazz has yet known. [*Brilliant* modifies the two-word noun *trumpet player*; *greatest* modifies *soloist. This* specifies that the instrument being discussed is the one that was just mentioned.]

At least *twenty* albums featuring Miles Davis remain *available.* [*Twenty* tells *how many* about the noun *albums. Available* is a subjective complement in this sentence; it too modifies the noun *albums.*]

EX 13-1 In the following sentences all adjectives except articles appear in italics. Draw an arrow to the noun that each italicized adjective modifies.

   EXAMPLE: Guayale is a *short, ugly* shrub in *southwest* Texas and *northern* Mexico.

1. Its seeds are a *good* source of *natural* rubber.

2. *Natural* rubber has become quite *expensive.*

3. *High* demand for *this* substance has allowed producers to raise prices far above *former* levels.

4. *Synthetic* rubber is produced from petroleum; it has become very *costly.*

5. *Experimental* plots of guayale are being established and cultivated by *hopeful* entrepreneurs.

6. Perhaps rubber from the seeds of *this scruffy* plant someday soon will be *competitive* in price with rubber obtained from *other* sources.

260

EX 13-2 Underline the adjectives in the following sentences. (Do not underline *a, an,* or *the.*)

> EXAMPLE: The original *King Kong* once included a particularly scary sequence involving giant spiders.

1. This great film was first released in 1933.
2. Three subsequent releases were distributed; the final release was sent to theaters in 1952.
3. In each release some scenes from the original version were cut.
4. All censored scenes but one were restored in a special release that was distributed in 1971.
5. The single missing scene was part of the film when it was first screened in January, 1933.
6. In this scene King Kong causes four sailors to fall from a wooden bridge.
7. The hapless sailors land in a creepy ravine.
8. There they are eaten by hungry giant spiders.
9. According to one source, this sequence terrified many viewers.
10. They were unable to concentrate on the ensuing action in the film.
11. The producer, Merian C. Cooper, was unhappy with the disruptive effect of the scene.
12. He himself snipped out the footage of the grisly banquet; no copy of the lost footage exists.

EX 13-3 Write descriptive adjectives in the blanks to complete the following sentences. Note that *a(n)* has been used to indicate that either *a* or *an* may appear, depending on the adjective you choose to use.

> EXAMPLE: Flying a kite may seem *childish* to some.

1. A(n) _____ day in spring is the _____ time to return to childhood.

2. A(n) _____ ball of _____ string will be needed, and so, perhaps, will a(n) _____ strip of shirt material.

3. A(n) _____ store in your _____ shopping center or business district will have the ideal kite for you.

4. As you make a(n) _____ run across a(n) _____ field holding your kite's lifeline, a(n) _____ smile will pin itself to your face.

5. The _____ feeling of controlling a(n) _____ object that is two hundred feet in the air is too _____ for words.

6. You will watch with the eyes of a(n) _____ child as your kite soars among _____ kites, _____ kites, kites of every imaginable color and shape.

EX 13-4 Some words you have written in the blanks in EX 13-3 as noun modifiers may actually be nouns modifying nouns (*kite* string) rather than adjectives modifying nouns (*thin* string). Circle any of these that appear. Other words you have written may have created two-word nouns (*box* kite). Draw a box around any two-word nouns you created.

In Chapter 11 the demonstrative pronouns *this, these, that,* and *those* were discussed. Each can also function as a demonstrative adjective.

EXAMPLES OF DEMONSTRATIVE ADJECTIVES
These tires are recaps.

This tire is on sale.

That tire looks to me to be defective.

Those tires are overpriced.

**THESE ARE DEMONSTRATIVE PRONOUNS,
NOT DEMONSTRATIVE ADJECTIVES**
These are mine; *those* are yours.

This is our finest hour!

Use *this* and *these* to refer to things close at hand and to events that are occurring at present. Use *that* and *those* to refer to things far away and to events that have already happened.

In informal speech some people use the word *them* and the expressions *this here, these here, that there,* and *them there* where demonstrative adjectives would properly be used. Avoid these expressions in your written work.

EXAMPLES OF EXPRESSIONS TO AVOID
This here screwdriver is worthless.

Them bargain-bin tools aren't worth five cents.

CORRECTED VERSIONS
This screwdriver is worthless.

Those bargain-bin tools aren't worth five cents.

EX 13-5 On another sheet of paper, rewrite the following sentences. Replace incorrect demonstrative adjectives and articles with correct ones.

> EXAMPLE: That there lady is buying one of them bottles of doggie soda pop.
> *That lady is buying one of those bottles of doggie soda pop.*

1. Them there dogs of hers seem to know that they will be getting a treat.
2. This here poster says that the beverage tastes just like liver.
3. Them marketing students that thought up this product are either geniuses or nuts, or maybe both.
4. This here dog of mine won't ever get to taste any of that there puppy pop.
5. He gets all them there vitamins in the dry food and meat I feed him.
6. The day I pay a buck and a half for a bottle of doggie soda pop is the day you can call them fellows in the white coats to come and take me away.

A proper adjective is an adjective formed from the name of a place; proper adjectives are capitalized.

EXAMPLES OF PROPER ADJECTIVES

spicy *Hungarian* food [*Hungarian* is an adjective related to the proper noun *Hungary*.]

ancient *Chinese* bronzes

a *Canadian* official

the *Martian* year

EX 13–6   In the following sentences underline each word that should begin with a capital letter.

> EXAMPLE: John Metaxas was a greek general and dictatorial ruler.

1. Joseph Pilsudski was a polish general who later ruled his nation with a firm hand.
2. Henry Pu-Yi was the last emperor of China; he was installed as the emperor of the japanese puppet state of Manchukuo in 1934.
3. Mahmud of Ghazni, an afghan emperor, was a conqueror of legendary ferocity.
4. The japanese physicist Hideki Yukawa predicted the existence of the nuclear particles known now as mesons.
5. The writings of english feminist Mary Wollstonecraft have been an inspiration to a number of people seeking equal rights for women.
6. Margaret Thatcher, a leading british conservative, became prime minister of her nation in 1979.

Two or more adjectives may precede a noun or pronoun. If two adjectives specify similar qualities, a comma should separate the pair.

Two tests can be used to determine whether a comma is needed. First, check to see whether the word *and* could sensibly be used between the adjectives. If it could, then a comma is needed. Second, check to see whether the sentence would sound right if the order of the adjectives were reversed. If it would, then a comma is needed.

**EXAMPLES OF THE USE OF A COMMA TO SEPARATE
ADJECTIVES OF THE SAME CLASS**

An *intense, abrasive* clerk sat at the front desk. [*Intense* and *abrasive* both specify personal attributes. The expression *intense and abrasive clerk* sounds fine, as does the expression *abrasive, intense clerk*; therefore, according to both tests, a comma is needed.]

The *hard, rickety* chairs in the waiting area fit in with the ambiance of the office. [*Hard* and *rickety* both specify aspects of the comfort of the chairs.]

If the adjectives specify distinctly different qualities, or if one adjective is more closely linked to the noun than the other, no comma should be used.

EXAMPLES OF ADJECTIVE PAIRS BETWEEN WHICH NO COMMA SHOULD BE USED

They tied a *worn red* t-shirt to the longest stick. [*Worn* and *red* describe different qualities of the t-shirt. The expression *a worn and red shirt* does not sound right; the expression *a red worn t-shirt* is also awkward; so, according to both tests, a comma is *not* needed.]

A *huge commercial* vehicle kept flashing its lights at them. [*Commercial* is closely related to the noun *vehicle*; together the words form a phrase that names a type of vehicle. *Huge* is merely a descriptive word.]

EX 13-7   Insert commas between adjectives that describe similar qualities.

> EXAMPLE: Betsy Erickson is an experienced, accomplished ballerina.

> 1. She has danced with the high-powered prestigious American Ballet Theatre.
> 2. Many great dancers never give a thought to any other career.
> 3. Erickson, a serious talented individual, studied piano and painting as well as dance.
> 4. She also spent two years learning to be a medical illustrator, a precise demanding vocation.
> 5. Her love of ballet drew her back to dance classes, and her considerable physical talent eventually enabled her to make a living as a ballerina.
> 6. Erickson has recently begun a new challenging career as a choreographer.
> 7. Her first ballet uses the second third and fourth movements of Béla Bartók's Fifth Quartet.
> 8. The quick irregular rhythms of the music make the ballet a real challenge for dancers.

Pairs of adjectives can be placed after the nouns they describe. Such adjective pairs normally are linked by a coordinating conjunction and set off from the rest of the sentence by a pair of commas.

EXAMPLES
The wind, *cold and gusty*, gave the badminton players fits.

The white-hatted player, *elderly but cagey*, kept his younger opponent off-balance throughout the match.

An exception to this punctuation rule arises when the adjectives function as a *compound objective complement*; that is, when they say *how* a verb changes its direct object, no comma is needed.

EXAMPLES OF COMPOUND OBJECTIVE COMPLEMENT
Edna painted the crib *blue* and *pink*.

The new cuckoo clock made the baby's room *bright* and *cheerful*.

EX 13-8   Rewrite each of the following sentences so that a pair of adjectives follow the noun they modify Do your writing on another sheet of paper.

> EXAMPLE: A fearless, curious four-year-old may decide to investigate bottles of chemicals stored in the home.
> *A four-year-old, fearless and curious, may decide to investigate bottles of chemicals stored in the home.*

> 1. Useful but dangerous household chemicals are a part of almost everyone's life nowadays.

2. The cluttered, disorganized garage is often the primary storage area for products used for home maintenance.

3. All caustic, poisonous, or flammable dangerous liquids must be kept well out of reach of small hands.

4. The sensitive and unprotected young eyes can be permanently affected by even seemingly safe household cleaning products.

5. Handy and fresh-smelling aerosol cleaning and waxing products not only can cause eye damage; they also may be flammable.

6. Some wise and wary parents conduct periodic safety checks not only of their own house but also of the houses of relatives with whom their children spend time.

Use *a* before words that begin with consonant sounds; use *an* before words that begin with vowel sounds.

EXAMPLES

a house, *a* nasty cut, *a* history, *a* uniform [*Uniform* begins with the sound of the consonant *y*.]

an apricot, *an* urgent message [*Urgent* begins with the short *u* vowel sound.]

EX 13-9 Write the correct article before each item.

EXAMPLE: ___*a*___ useless tool

1. _____ feather duster

2. _____ apple corer

3. _____ inconsiderate relative

4. _____ anemone

5. _____ high mountain pass

6. _____ swordfish

7. _____ obscure fact

8. _____ utility pole

9. _____ yipping pup

10. _____ unfortunate mistake

B. WRITING COMPARISONS USING ADJECTIVES

Adjectives change form or add *more* or *most* to show comparison. Almost all one-syllable adjectives—as well as many of two syllables—add *er* to their *positive* (noncomparative) form to show comparison with one thing; this form is called the *comparative* form. To show comparison with two or more things, these adjectives add *est*; this is called the *superlative* form. Some two-syllable adjectives and almost all adjectives with three or more syllables show comparison with one item by placing the word *more* before them; they show comparison with two or more items by placing the word *most* before them.

EXAMPLES OF POSITIVE, COMPARATIVE, AND
SUPERLATIVE FORMS OF SHORT ADJECTIVES
The Punts are a *flashy* band. [*positive*; *flashy* is a two-syllable adjective that ends in *y*]

The Wolverines are a *flashier* band than the Punts. [*comparative*; note that the *y* at the end of *flashy* changes to *i* when a suffix is added]

No Sisters are the *flashiest* band in San Francisco right now. [*superlative*]

U-2 has a *big* sound. [*positive*; *big* is a one-syllable adjective]

Echo and the Bunnymen have a *bigger* sound. [*comparative*; note that *big* doubles its final *g*] when a suffix beginning with a vowel is added]

Which band has the *biggest* sound of all? [*superlative*]

EXAMPLES OF POSITIVE, COMPARATIVE, AND SUPERLATIVE FORMS OF LONG ADJECTIVES

Berlioz composed several *majestic* symphonies. [*positive*; *majestic* is a three-syllable adjective]

Is *Requiem* a *more majestic* work than *Symphonie Fantastique*? [*comparative*]

Perhaps *Romeo and Juliet* is the *most majestic* of Berlioz' symphonies. [*superlative*]

That music sounds *dated*. [*positive*; *dated* is a two-syllable adjective that is a participial form and so requires *more* and *most*]

I cannot imagine a song sounding *more dated*. [*comparative*]

What is the *most dated* expression you can think of? [*superlative*]

DO *NOT* USE BOTH *ER* AND *MORE* IN THE SAME EXPRESSION

The music of Bach is *more lovelier* than the music of Buxtehude. [SHOULD BE The music of Bach is *lovelier* than the music of Buxtehude.]

NEVER USE A SUPERLATIVE WHEN A COMPARATIVE IS CALLED FOR

The *best* boxer in this match is Duran. [SHOULD BE The *better* boxer in this match is Duran.]

EX 13-10 Write comparative and superlative forms in the blanks.

	Positive	Comparative	Superlative
EXAMPLE:	red	*redder*	*reddest*
1.	old		
2.	kind		
3.	short		
4.	wily		
5.	crazy		
6.	crushed		
7.	careful		
8.	ancient		
9.	gloomy		
10.	magnificent		
11.	tidy		
12.	repulsive		
13.	effulgent		
14.	unsanitary		
15.	forgetful		

A few adjectives have irregular comparative and superlative forms: *good (better, best);* *bad (worse, worst); little (less or lesser, least); many (more, most); much (more, most);* and *old (older or elder, oldest or eldest)* are among these.

EX 13-11   Write the correct comparative or superlative form of the adjective given in parentheses to complete each sentence.

> EXAMPLE: Are there *hardier* city dwellers anywhere else than in Helsinki, Finland? (hardy)

1. A great many Finns feel that nothing is _____ than a sauna. (healthful)

2. A Finnish sauna room is the _____ place imaginable. (hot)

3. Temperatures in these rooms occasionally go _____ than 180°F. (high)

4. According to the people of Helsinki, a sauna is _____ when bathers flick themselves and each other with birch boughs in the sauna room. (invigorating)

5. Some people are _____ of high temperatures than others are. (tolerant)

6. The heat inside the sauna room is greatest on the _____ step. (high)

7. When a bather can take no _____ heat, he or she dashes outside and dives into a frigid pool or a snowbank. (much)

8. The colder the air, water, or snow temperature the _____ . (good)

9. What could be a _____ shock to the body systems? (cruel)

10. Nevertheless, the health of the residents of Helsinki is in general

   _____ than that of the residents of most other cities in the world. (good)

11. The salubrious effect of saunas is not the _____ explanation for the residents' radiant health, though. (logical)

12. Swedes share the Finns' fondness for saunas; of the two, the Finns seem to

   be _____ to head for the hot, steamy shed. (quick)

C. SELECTING ADVERBS

Adverbs are words that tell *how, when, where, how much,* or *how often* about verbs, adjectives, and other adverbs. Many adverbs end in *ly*.

EXAMPLES OF ADVERBS

A taped voice *automatically* tells the time *nowadays*. [*Automatically* is an adverb that answers the question *how* about the verb *tells*. *Nowadays* is an adverb that answers the question *when* about the verb *tells*.]

For *quite* a long time live operators gave the time to Los Angeles callers. [*Quite* is an adverb that tells *how much* about the adjective *long*.]

Regular operators took turns sitting in a soundproof room and announcing *very clearly* the time to the nearest quarter-minute. [*Clearly* is an adverb that tells *how* about the participle *announcing*; *very* is an adverb that tells *how much* about the adverb *clearly*.]

It is *not* easy *constantly* to recite phrases that give time information. [*Not* is an adverb that modifies the adjective *easy*; *constantly* is an adverb that modifies the infinitive phrase *to recite*.]

THESE *LY* WORDS ARE *NOT* ADVERBS

Merle is a *kindly* person. [*Kindly* is an adjective; it modifies the noun *person*.]

I am making my *weekly* visit to the bakery. [*Weekly* is an adjective; it modifies the noun *visit*.]

EX 13-12   The adverbs in the following sentences are italicized. Draw an arrow from each adverb to the word it modifies.

EXAMPLE: This apple juice is *very* tart.

1. Our apple trees are *quite* ancient.

2. They bear fruit *very* early in the summer.

3. The apples *usually* are *rather* small.

4. We *almost always* squeeze some into juice.

5. Cold, tart apple juice is *quite marvelously* refreshing.

6. This commercial brand of apple juice is *so often* a disappointment because of its sticky sweetness.

EX 13-13   Underline the adverbs in the following sentences.

EXAMPLE: New homes have become <u>very</u> expensive to build.

1. Builders are constantly looking for ways to make homes cheaper to build.
2. Storage areas that were once routinely included in a home design are missing from contemporary models.
3. Bedroom closets remain fairly large, but closets in other parts of the home have shrunk drastically.
4. The large attic that was easily accessible is not found in many new homes.
5. Large storage rooms off the garage were frequently included in homes built in the 1950s and '60s.
6. Where do homeowners store their stuffed mooseheads and obsolete appliances nowadays?
7. Quite a few people rent space in temporary storage buildings.

8. These buildings are constructed quickly and cheaply in areas where land is relatively inexpensive.

9. Monthly rents are reasonable but hardly cheap.

10. Is it worth paying $300 annually to be able to store 100 square feet of junk?

EX 13–14   Write appropriate adverbs in the blanks to complete the following sentences.

EXAMPLE: It *seldom* rains in the Sonoran desert of Mexico.

1. Poisonous snakes _____ hunt their prey.

2. Scorpions can _____ deliver a jolt of poison to an incautious traveler.

3. Temperatures _____ exceed 100°F.

4. Springs giving forth sweet water are _____ uncommon.

5. When a rainstorm _____ pours water on the hard-baked desert

floor, flash floods _____ occur.

6. Only a _____ foolish person makes camp in a desert ravine.

EX 13–15   On another sheet of paper, rewrite each of the following sentences. Add an adverb to modify the verb in each sentence.

EXAMPLE: The emporium sold its supply of *Cosmic Conflicts* decals.
The emporium quickly sold its supply of Cosmic Conflicts *decals.*

1. Children begged their parents for more *Cosmic Conflicts* toys.

2. TV commercials pushed *Cosmic Conflicts* action dolls.

3. Black-helmeted youngsters battled one another on *Cosmic Conflicts* game boards.

4. Munchkins wore *Cosmic Conflicts* costumes on Halloween night.

5. They read new issues of *Cosmic Conflicts* comics.

6. Each of them saved his or her pennies for the next re-release of the most recent chapter of the fifteen-movie series cumulatively titled *Cosmic Conflicts.*

Not is a negative adverb. To express a negative thought, use either *not* or another negative word. Do not use two negative expressions together to express a negative thought; this creates an expression commonly called a *double negative.*

EXAMPLES OF DOUBLE NEGATIVES

I'm *not no* hero. [SHOULD BE *I'm no hero* OR *I'm not a hero.*]

Ain't no reason to go back there. [SHOULD BE *There's no reason to go back there* OR *There isn't any reason to go back there.* Note that *ain't* is not an acceptable written expression.]

You *haven't* done *nothing* to earn that badge. [SHOULD BE *You haven't done anything to earn that badge* OR *You've done nothing to earn that badge.*]

THESE USES OF TWO NEGATIVES ARE PROPER

No, I *won't* be coming with you tonight. [*No* is a separate item here; it is separated from the sentence by a comma.]

I am *not unafraid.* [This is a *positive* statement created by the negation of a negative expression. It is another way of saying "I am afraid."]

EX 13-16 On another sheet of paper, rewrite each of the following sentences that expresses a negative thought incorrectly. Make sure the revised versions have only one negative word to express each negative concept.

> EXAMPLE: I don't want no trouble.
> *I don't want any trouble.*

1. I didn't do nothing wrong.
2. You ain't got no right to ask me to leave.
3. No, I wasn't insulting any other patrons.
4. I didn't say that your staff was incompetent.
5. I don't get no respect in here.
6. No, I haven't made nobody feel uncomfortable.
7. You aren't getting no more business from me.
8. Don't think I can't take a hint.
9. Don't nobody order none of those hamburgers.
10. They didn't even take none of their saddles off before they ground up those poor nags and fried them.

Look at the italicized adverbs in the sentences below.

> a. *First* place the paper on the glass screen.
> b. *Next* push the blue button.
> c. *Finally*, retrieve the copy and the original.

The italicized adverbs are called *sentence adverbs* because they modify the entire sentence rather than any particular word. Sentence adverbs are quite useful in establishing a sequence of events, as is mentioned in Chapters 2 and 15.

EX 13-17 Rewrite the following paragraph; add sentence adverbs and prepositional phrases to emphasize the order of events. Do your writing on another sheet of paper.

> Remove the old ashes from the bottom of the barbecue. Make a pyramid-shaped pile of charcoal briquets. Saturate the charcoal with lighter fluid. Light the charcoal in several places with a long wooden match. Leave the coals in the pyramid-shaped pile for at least fifteen minutes. Flatten the pyramid of glowing coals so that the bottom of the barbecue is covered with a single layer. Put the grill in place; scrape off any burned-on materials. When the grill is hot, place the foods to be barbecued on it. Cook till done.

D. WRITING COMPARISONS USING ADVERBS

Adverbs can be used to create comparative and superlative statements. Most adverbs add *more* or *most* to show comparison; a small group add *er* or *est*.

> **EXAMPLES OF POSITIVE, COMPARATIVE, AND SUPERLATIVE STATEMENTS FORMED WITH AN ADVERB ADDING *MORE* AND *MOST***
>
> Pat plays defense *aggressively.* [*positive*]
>
> She plays defense *more aggressively* than Lin does. [*comparative*]
>
> Pat plays defense *most aggressively* when the game is on the line. [*superlative*]

Here is a partial list of adverbs that add *er* and *est* in their comparative and superlative forms. (Note that many of these words can also function as adjectives.)

fast	*(faster, fastest)*	*deep*	*(deeper, deepest)*
early	*(earlier, earliest)*	*long*	*(longer, longest)*
late	*(later, latest)*	*loud*	*(louder, loudest)*
high	*(higher, highest)*	*hard*	*(harder, hardest)*
low	*(lower, lowest)*		

EX 13-18 Write the comparative and superlative forms of the adverbs listed.

	Positive	*Comparative*	*Superlative*
EXAMPLE:	insolently	*more insolently*	*most insolently*
1.	rapidly		
2.	gently		
3.	near		
4.	officiously		
5.	quick		
6.	conveniently		
7.	fancily		
8.	slow		
9.	fruitfully		
10.	romantically		
11.	late		
12.	knowledgeably		

EX 13-19   Underline the correct form of each pair given in parentheses.

> EXAMPLE: Series of youth adventure books were far (<u>more widely</u>, most widely) read in the thirties, forties, and fifties than they are today.

1. Of all the series for elementary school children, the Bobbsey Twins books are remembered (more fondly, most fondly).
2. Many Hardy Boys mysteries were written, but no plot gripped its readers (tighter, tightest) than that of *The Tower Treasure.*
3. The Nancy Drew mystery series has made the transition to modern times (more successfully, most successfully) of all the series.
4. Books relating the exploits of Tom Swift, Chip Hilton, Bronc Burnette, and the Sugar Creek Gang are (more often, most often) found in secondhand stores than on library shelves these days.

E. WRITING NEGATIVE COMPARISONS

Negative comparisons are created by placing *less* or *least* before an adjective or adverb.

EXAMPLE OF NEGATIVE COMPARISONS

Squirt City is a *less efficient* car wash than Bubble Heaven. [This statement includes the negative comparative form of the adjective *efficient.*]

Tunnel of Suds is the *least efficient* of all. [This statement includes the negative superlative form of the adjective *efficient.*]

The workers vacuum old cars *less carefully* than they vacuum new cars.

They vacuum old station wagons the *least carefully* of all.

EX 13-20   Write four sentences about washing (or not washing) cars. Use the forms indicated below.

1. (negative comparative form of an adjective) _____

_____

2. (negative superlative form of an adjective) _____

_____

3. (negative comparative form of an adverb) _____

_____

4. (negative superlative form of an adverb) _____

_____

F. WORKING WITH RELATED FORMS OF WORDS

A *suffix* is an ending added to the root of a word, either to create a different part of speech or to create a word with a different but related meaning. Look at the following sentences.

    a. A *vandal* has sawed down the oak tree in front of the library.
    b. Nowadays people *vandalize* even the most splendid of public properties.
    c. *Vandalism* is on the increase once again.

Which italicized word is the root word of the other two italicized words?

_____ What part of speech is this word? _____ Which italicized

word is a verb created from this noun? _____ What part of speech is

vandalism? _____ How does the suffix *ism* change the meaning of *vandal*?

_____

The suffixes *ism, ment, er, or, ty,* and *ness* are used to create nouns.

    EXAMPLES
    cannibal—cannibal*ism*
    refine—refine*ment*
    paint—paint*er*
    edit—edit*or*
    rare—rari*ty*
    neat—neat*ness*

The suffixes *ify* and *ize* are used to create verbs.

    EXAMPLES
    solid—solid*ify*
    vapor—vapor*ize*

(Note that the form of the root word may change when a suffix is added: *liquid* drops its final *d* to become *liquify*.)

The suffixes *ful, ous, y, ish, less, ic,* and *able* are used to create adjectives.

    EXAMPLES
    wonder—wonder*ful*
    vapor—vapor*ous*
    show—show*y*
    self—self*ish*
    thought—thought*less*
    volcano—volcan*ic*
    vary—vari*able*

The suffixes *ly* and *wise* are used to create adverbs.

    EXAMPLES
    desperate—desperate*ly*
    clock—clock*wise*

EX 13-21   Fill the blanks below with related forms of the words that appear. Circle each word that is formed by adding one or more suffixes to a root word.

Verb	Noun	Adjective	Adverb
EXAMPLE: (scandalize)	scandal	(scandalous)	(scandalously)
1. consider	_____	_____	_____
2.(magnetize)	_____	_____	_____
3. _____	(generality)	_____	_____
4. master	_____	_____	_____
5. _____	_____	(ridiculous)	_____
6. _____	_____	_____	(snappily)
7. _____	_____	(fashionable)	_____
8. _____	_____	_____	(markedly)

As a general rule, use adjectives to modify nouns; use adverbs to modify verbs, adjectives, and adverbs.

EXAMPLES OF MISUSED ADJECTIVES AND ADVERBS

Liam *fortunate* escaped injury in the fall. [SHOULD BE *Liam fortunately escaped injury in the fall*; OR *Fortunate Liam escaped injury in the fall. Fortunate*, an adjective, can only be used to modify a noun.]

A *scruffily* passerby stopped to lend a hand. [SHOULD BE *A scruffy passerby* . . . OR *A scruffily dressed passerby* . . .]

EX 13-22   Underline the correct form of each pair given in parentheses.

EXAMPLE: Several of the factors that influence the slope of a beach can be (easy, <u>easily</u>) observed.

1. In summer beach material is more (plentiful, plentifully) than in winter.
2. In winter the beach is (comparative, comparatively) small and steep.
3. Seasonal weather accounts for the (great, greatly) changes in beach conformation.
4. The summer waves have less energy; they are much longer than they are (steep, steeply).
5. Summer waves (efficient, efficiently) transport sand grains onto the beach.
6. These grains are (light, lightly) and are (easy, easily) moved by the (turbulent, turbulently) water.
7. Winter waves also carry sand to the beach, but these (potent, potently) waves take away more than they leave.
8. Winter waves break (powerful, powerfully), depositing some sand to the landward limits of their reach.
9. Then, departing (swift, swiftly), the water pulls grains of sand from the exposed beach down below the surf line.
10. There the sand spreads itself out relatively (even, evenly), forming bars below the tide lines.

11. Beach features also can be affected by (violent, violently) storms.
12. Sudden (severe, severely) storms can carve (vertical, vertically) walls in a cliff face or upon a beach.
13. Greater slopes (characteristic, characteristically) are produced when coarse-grained material is present.
14. California's Half Moon Bay is an (excellent, excellently) example of the (selective, selectively) arrangement of materials.
15. The protected areas slope very (gradual, gradually) and are made up of (fine, finely) sand.
16. The beach area exposed to waves has a (greater, more greatly) slope and a more coarsely grained sand.

Good is an adjective that means "satisfactory," "positive," or "tasty." *Well* is often used as an adverb meaning "satisfactorily."

EXAMPLES

"Maria Elena" is a *good* song. [*Good* is an adjective that modifies the noun *song.*]

Kimberley plays it *well.* [*Well* is an adverb that modifies the verb *play.*]

Real is an adjective that means "genuine." *Really* is an adverb that means "truly."

EXAMPLES

There is no substitute for *real* mayonnaise. [The adjective *real* modifies the noun *mayonnaise.*]

I *really* like this sandwich. [The adverb *really* modifies the verb *like.*]

AN INCORRECT USE OF *REAL*

You are a *real* good counterperson. [SHOULD BE You are a *very* good counterperson.]

EX 13-23 Write four sentences about fruit juices. Use each word in parentheses.

1. (good) _____

2. (well) _____

3. (real) _____

4. (really) _____

EX 13-24 Rewrite the following paragraph on a separate sheet of paper. Eliminate errors in adjective and adverb usage.

Yugoslavia had externally concerns from the beginning. Several nations had clearly designs on Yugoslav territory: both Greece and Bulgaria wanted Yugoslav Macedonia bad; Hungary wanted the northern regions of the Backa and the Banat; and Italy wanted possession of parts of Istria (the land area nearly the northeast bend of the Adriatic Sea) and Dalmatia. Actual most neighboring nations would have been just as happily to see Yugoslavia partitioned into its former sovereign components. Yugoslavia itself, although active supporting the status quo, desired to obtain eventual the rest of Macedonia from Bulgaria and Greece, portions of Thrace (especial the city of Salonica) from Greece and Turkey, and parts of Italian territory in Istria.

G. USING PREPOSITIONS

A *preposition* is a word that expresses a relationship between a noun (or an item that functions as a noun) and some other word or words in the sentence. A noun that follows a preposition is called the *object of the preposition.* The preposition, its object, and any modifiers constitute a *prepositional phrase.* (See Chapter 7, pages 110–15, for additional information on prepositional phrases as well as a list of commonly used prepositions).

EXAMPLES OF PREPOSITIONS
A check arrived *in today's mail.* [The preposition *in* relates the noun *mail* to the verb *arrived;* the entire phrase answers the question *where.*]

The bills *on the desk* now look less threatening. [The preposition *on* relates the noun *desk* to the noun *bills.*]

EX 13-25 Underline each prepositional phrase in the following sentences. Circle each preposition.

> EXAMPLE: The following fable relates (to) the behavior (of) a certain institution (of) higher learning.

1. The alligator had become an enemy of the rest of the animals in the forest.

2. It had forced them out of their homes and had disrupted life throughout the forest.

3. The angry animals said that they would unite against this greedy, heartless neighbor.

4. The alligator, blessed with an instinct for self-preservation, did not want the animal community to become united against it.

5. Therefore it agreed to hold meetings with the other animals.

6. At these meetings it would discuss its plans and listen to the other animals' reactions.

7. At each public meeting it flashed its most charming reptilian smile.

8. The alligator always listened politely to the other animals' comments.

9. After each meeting it went right ahead and did whatever it had wanted to do in the first place.

10. It paid no heed to the expressed needs or wishes of its neighbors.

11. Everything was the same as it had been in former times, with one exception.

12. Now the alligator responded to protests about its doings with burps about community input and belches about its role as a good neighbor.

EX 13-26 Complete the following sentences by writing appropriate prepositions in the blanks.

> EXAMPLE: Pitons once were standard equipment *for* a rock climber.

1. Climbers hammered these metal spikes _____ cliff faces.

2. These artificial aids do damage _____ a cliff's appearance and surface structure.

3. Many climbers now object _____ the use _____ pitons.

4. Free climbers climb _____ any artificial devices.

5. They climb _____ cliff faces using only their hands and feet

   _____ anchors.

6. Most will affix a rope _____ a rock _____ a removable

   chock _____ safety, however.

7. To hang _____ a cliff face _____ just a few fingers and toes is not easy.

8. With a 2,000-foot drop _____ the climber, he or she cannot make a false move.

9. A feeling _____ exaltation comes _____ each climber as he or she completes a difficult climb.

10. Members _____ a free-climbing party leave no marks _____ the rock to indicate that they have made an ascent.

Some prepositions are easily confused and frequently misused. *In* means "inside"; *into* indicates entry. *On* means "over and in contact with"; *onto* indicates movement to a position on something.

EXAMPLES

The slide is *in* place.

Look *into* the eyepiece of the microscope.

Write your notes *on* this ditto sheet.

Be careful when you drip this solution *onto* the specimen.

EX 13-27   Fill each blank with the correct preposition—*in*, *into*, *on*, or *onto*.

EXAMPLE: Look *into* the fish tank.

1. Which fish is swimming _____ circles?

2. That characin has been nibbling _____ its tankmate's fins again.

3. I should move it _____ its own tank.

4. I could move my small tank _____ the kitchen counter.

5. Of course I would then have to move the toaster and blender _____ my bedroom.

6. It's not easy to keep a dozen varieties of tropical fish _____ a small apartment.

Between is used with two objects, people, or groups—never with three or more. *Among* is used with three or more objects, people, or groups—never with just two.

EXAMPLES

The snake slithered *between* two trees.

A battle developed *between* the two leaders.

Now she must choose *among* the many suggestions.

She found herself standing *among* several hefty shot putters.

EX 13-28   Write *between* or *among* in each blank.

EXAMPLE: A mermaid may linger *between* a rock and the sea.

1. Tales of mermaids are _____ the most common tales concerning supernatural creatures.

2. Men who sailed _____ one British isle and another saw many mermaids.

3. Mermaids supposedly lured sailors to gruesome deaths _____ the rocks.

4. The song of a mermaid drifting _____ wisps of fog must have been a heartbreaking sound.

5. Imagine the poor sailor forced to choose _____ loneliness and almost certain death!

6. Many marvelous creatures live _____ the pages of a book of folk tales.

Like is a preposition; it should not be used as a subordinating conjunction. *As* is the word to use as a subordinating conjunction meaning "in the way that." *As* can also mean "at the time when"; in addition, *as* can be used as a preposition meaning "representing."

EXAMPLES

Tundra-Tex feels good, *as* an artificial fur should. [NOT *like an artificial fur should*]

It feels *like* lynx. [Here *like* is a preposition; *lynx* is its object.]

EX 13-29   Underline the correct word in parentheses.

EXAMPLE: The sun stung my eyes (as, like) I tried to read my magazine.

1. Soon my feet were as tender (as, like) overripe tomatoes.
2. The lotion felt (as, like) liquid ice.
3. Robert snickered (as, like) I walked past.
4. His feet looked (as, like) beets.
5. Our feet could star in a science-fiction film (as, like) four strange creatures.
6. With a face (as, like) mine, my best chance to get into films may be to go feet first.

The words *as* and *like* are used in figurative comparisons called *similes*. A simile is a figure of speech that describes something by comparing it with something it does not literally resemble.

EXAMPLES OF SIMILES

His lies circled the room *like* moths.

He was *as* devious *as* a middle-aged gopher, and harder to trap.

EX 13-30 Write an original simile to describe each item below. Be sure to use *like* only as a preposition. Your similes may remain fragments or be included in complete sentences. Do your writing on another sheet of paper.

> EXAMPLE: a bleak city neighborhood
> *a city neighborhood as bleak as the dreams of a beaten child*

1. a filthy waiting room
2. memories of a past romance
3. echoes of soldiers' marching feet
4. cold beans
5. delicate wild roses
6. tears of joy

Another type of figure of speech is a *metaphor.* A metaphor also figuratively compares unlike things, but it does so without using *as* or *like.*

EXAMPLES OF METAPHORS

The worry was a mad relative, constantly demanding attention and confounding everyone's efforts at rational behavior.

His conscience was a toy once played with but now forgotten.

Tonight the moon is a rotting grapefruit.

To some, the boomtown of Victor was a festering sore.

Metaphors can be written as similes.

EXAMPLES OF METAPHORS TRANSFORMED INTO SIMILES

The worry was *like* a mad relative who demanded constant attention while confounding everyone's efforts at rational behavior.

His conscience was *like* a toy once played with but now forgotten.

Tonight the moon is *as* fat and bilious *as* a rotting grapefruit.

To some, the boomtown of Victor was *as* needful of cleansing *as* a festering sore.

EX 13-31 On another sheet of paper, write an original metaphor to describe each item below. Use your imagination freely.

> EXAMPLE: flat, barren valley
> *The flat, barren valley was an empty dinner table.*

1. the first day of summer vacation
2. a vandalized abandoned warehouse

3. a white rat
4. Mount St. Helens
5. the first cold winds of fall
6. a jack-o'-lantern

EX 13-32   Rewrite each of your metaphors in EX 13-31 as similes. Be sure to use *like* only as a preposition. Your similes may remain fragments or be written in complete sentences.

EXAMPLE: *The flat, barren valley was as empty of promise as a dinner table without food on it.*

H. CHOOSING CONJUNCTIONS AND INTERJECTIONS

Coordinating conjunctions connect items of equal rank. *And, but,* and *or* are the most common single-word coordinating conjunctions. *Either . . . or, neither . . . nor,* and *both . . . and* are correlative coordinating conjunctions.

EXAMPLES OF COORDINATING CONJUNCTIONS
Snag *and* Dawson are towns in the Yukon Territory. [The coordinating conjunction *and* links the two nouns that form the compound subject of the sentence.]

Neither Snag *nor* Dawson is lively in winter. [The correlative coordinating conjunction *neither . . . nor* links the two nouns that form the compound subject of the sentence.]

Dawson's population is about 800 at present, *and* Snag's population is considerably less. [The coordinating conjunction *and* links two independent clauses to form a compound sentence.]

Subordinating conjunctions connect clauses of different rank. To review subordinating conjunctions and dependent clauses, see Chapter 8, pages 140-44.

EXAMPLE OF A SUBORDINATING CONJUNCTION
Theodore Dreiser's novel *Carrie* was considered scandalous *when* it was first published. [The subordinating conjunction *when* subordinates the clause *it was first published* to the independent clause *Theodore Dreiser's novel* Carrie *was considered scandalous* in this complex sentence.]

EX 13-33   Underline each coordinating conjunction in the following sentences. Circle each subordinating conjunction. Not all sentences contain a conjunction; some contain several.

EXAMPLE: The first page of James Joyce's *Portrait of an Artist as a Young Man* is unusual (because) it is written to approximate the thought patterns of a child.

1. The words are simple, and the sentences are simple in structure.

2. The sentences take the form of statements, since observations and assertions make up a child's inner dialogue.

3. Nonsense words are treated as other words are treated; they are neither italicized nor placed in quotation marks.

4. They are treated as real words because that is what they are to the child.

5. The punctuation serves to animate rather than to limit and connect.

6. Joyce's skillful presentation allows the reader to consider the phenomenon of a child's usage of words.

7. A child has not been trained to think of words as they must be ordered for acceptable written sentences.

8. Whereas writers normally use words to explain, a child may use words as sounds or as nonlogical elements of unconscious utterances.

EX 13-34   Complete the following sentences by writing appropriate conjunctions in the blanks. Circle each subordinating conjunction you write.

> EXAMPLE: _*If*_   you are interested in antique farm equipment, you should make a point of traveling to Merced County in central California.

1. _____ you reach LeGrand, ask for directions to Arthur Bright's place on South Plainsburg Road.

2. You should visit his place _____ the world's largest tractor collection is there.

3. Bright has the oldest tractor in the western hemisphere on display

   _____ also a once-brightly-painted tractor used for hauling circus animals.

4. Tractors are bulky, _____ Bright has made room for more than 1,000 of them in his museum.

5. _____ you notice a similarity between some tractors and old steam engines, don't be surprised.

6. _____ Bright has been keeping his museum open most weekdays, weekends, and holidays, it would be a good idea to call before setting out for a visit.

When correlative coordinating conjunctions are used to join phrases or clauses, care must be used in their placement. Misplaced coordinating conjunctions can create awkward sentences.

EXAMPLES OF SENTENCES WITH MISPLACED COORDINATING CONJUNCTIONS
Either you must come to the wedding *or* send a telegram.

Not only is she a sculptor *but also* a violinist.

CORRECTED VERSIONS
You must *either* come to the wedding *or* send a telegram. [The conjunctions are now placed properly before the two parts of the compound predicate *come to the wedding* and *send a telegram.*]

She is *not only* a sculptor *but also* a violinist. [The conjunctions now appear before the two parts of the compound subjective complement.]

EX 13-35   Rewrite each of the following sentences so that the correlative conjunctions are no longer misplaced. Do your writing on another sheet of paper.

> EXAMPLE: You both are an adroit diplomat and a scholar of some promise.
> *You are both an adroit diplomat and a scholar of some promise.*

1. Neither do I have time nor money for such an undertaking.
2. Either the wall will stay standing or crumble of its own accord.
3. Not only am I soaked to the skin but also dangerously close to foaming at the mouth.
4. Either you should change your attitude or leave immediately.

An *interjection* is an expression of emotion that is not part of any independent or dependent clause.

EXAMPLES OF INTERJECTIONS

Ow! You stepped on my toe.

Oh, so you think you're pretty smart.

Hurrah!

EX 13-36   Write an interjection to fill each blank.

> EXAMPLE: *Oof!* What a body punch that was!

1. _____! The champion is down!

2. _____! He's up again!

3. _____! The challenger throws another hard right to the body!

4. _____! My television screen has gone black!

I.   REVIEWING CHAPTER CONCEPTS

EX 13-37   Underline each adjective in the following sentences. (Do not mark articles.) Circle each adverb.

> EXAMPLE: The Arabian Desert is large and (quite) inhospitable.

1. Western mapmakers have only recently learned about some regions of this desert.

2. The desert covers nearly a million square miles of the Arabian peninsula.

3. The Red Sea forms its western boundary, and the Persian Gulf forms its eastern boundary.

4. People usually think of deserts as seas of sand; quite a few great deserts—for example, the Gobi—actually have few sandy areas.

5. The Arabian Desert comes closest to the ideal.

6. Some dunes rise 700 feet in the air.

7. The *shamal* is a fierce hot wind that blows almost constantly across the peninsula.
8. The sands shift gradually under the relentless influence of this wind.
9. Most sectors of this empty desert receive only three to four inches of rain in an average year.
10. When rain does fall, lakes are formed in low-lying areas; the waters in these lakes are very salty.
11. Nomadic peoples have lived here for several thousand years.
12. The first European explorer to cross the Arabian Desert was H. St. John Philby; his trek took place during the 1930s.

EX 13-38   On another sheet of paper, write a paragraph of description about the most desolate natural area you have visited. Underline each adjective you write. (Do not mark articles.) Circle each adverb you write.

EX 13-39   Rewrite the following paragraphs from this student essay about characters in Charles Dickens' novel *Our Mutual Friend*; eliminate usage and punctuation errors.

Silas Wegg is public disgraced. His claim to Boffin's money is dissolved by Harmon (whom he hates) in front of all the people over whom Wegg had hoped to gain power. This extensive and completely humiliation of Wegg does not represent no chance event: several characters join forces to bring Wegg to his knees. In the scheme of the novel Wegg is made a morally example.

Wegg fancies himself deserving of a gooder social position than birth has given him, and thus he ain't content when well fortune allows him to live more comfortable than he had been able to manage through his own efforts. The way in which Wegg is humiliated shows that Wegg loves money too good, and covets money as a means to overt manipulate individuals. First the individuals over whom Wegg has been holding the threat of financially ruin refuse to be cowed. Then these here individuals show Wegg that his scheme can't never succeed. Final they reveal their conspiracy against Wegg, showing how determined they all are to prevent Wegg from becoming wealthily: Dickens makes it real clear that these characters do not react to money in the same way Wegg the coward does.

EX 13-40   Underline the correct item of each pair given in parentheses.

EXAMPLE: The (more recent, <u>most recent</u>) observations of the planet Uranus confirm that it has at least nine rings.

1. These rings are (less clearly, least clearly) visible than those of Saturn.
2. Some scientists believe that the law of orbital mechanics provides the (better, best) explanation for the existence of the rings.
3. Several moons far (smaller, smallest) than ours may have created the rings of Uranus.
4. Two such bodies orbiting a planet can keep in a ring those particles with (less, least) mass than their own.
5. A satellite in a (higher, highest) orbit goes (more slowly, most slowly) than a satellite in a (lower, lowest) orbit.
6. The gravity and velocity of the two moons are the forces that work (more strongly, most strongly) to keep the small particles circling, thus forming a visible ring.

EX 13-41   Complete the following sentences by writing appropriate prepositions and conjunctions in the blanks.

> EXAMPLE: Is Salvador Dali a masterful painter, an egomaniac *with* a keen eye for self-promotion, *or* both?

1. _____ Dali will never be accused of modesty, his sense _____ self-importance can be quite entertaining.

2. _____ his autobiography Dali shares his pre-birth memories _____ his readers.

3. _____ you find it hard to believe that anyone has true memories of life _____ birth, you are not alone.

4. Dali, _____ he tells _____ the day of his birth, writes that "the Mediterranean Sea is motionless and on its back."

5. _____ he was seven, young Salvador was dragged off _____ school, kicking and screaming, _____ his father.

6. _____ he began attending school, he could recite the letters _____ the alphabet and write his name.

7. _____ a year in school Dali had learned nothing new _____ in fact had forgotten what he had known the year before: he could _____ recite the alphabet _____ write his name.

8. Even _____ that tender age Dali was already demonstrating his ability to avoid the commonplace.

9. _____ Dali decided to write his autobiography, he spurned the offers of large publishers _____ chose instead Dial Press to bring out the volume.

10. Dali reportedly chose Dial only _____ its name happens to contain the same four letters that are _____ his last name.

11. _____ many people find Dali's imagery gruesome _____ frightening, Dali does not apply these words _____ what he paints.

12. _____ the subject of horrors, Dali has remarked that he considers Bugs Bunny the most terrible and frightening image to come _____ public view.

WORKSHOP

1. List five adjectives that you guess would appear often in advertisements for luxury consumer products. Then examine ten or more such advertisements; list all adjectives used in the copy in these ads. Compare this list with your list of five adjectives. Note which of the adjectives you listed were used in the ads you examined.

2. Select a descriptive paragraph you have written. Cross out every adjective and every adverb in this paragraph. Reread the paragraph; note where vital information has been deleted and reinsert words or phrases to reincorporate this information. Now compare the altered version with the original paragraph. Which sounds better? What does this tell you about the use of modifiers?

2. Choosing the correct preposition to follow a verb form is one of the hardest tasks a writer of English faces. For example, do you know when to use *compared to* and when to use *compared with*? (Here the answer is that *compared to* should be used when two quite different things are being compared, and *compared with* should be used when two quite similar things are being compared.) To improve your ability to choose correct prepositions, keep a list of preposition problems on a page in a notebook. Each time you come to a situation in your writing where you have to struggle to decide on the proper preposition to follow a particular verb, make a note of the situation. When you have listed at least ten such situations, obtain from the reference section of a library an English usage guide that lists which prepositions are required after particular verbs; check your listed prepositions against those specified in this reference book.

4. Show five different ways of writing the following pair of sentences as a single sentence. Underline each coordinating conjunction you write; circle each subordinating conjunction.

   We see the enemy approaching. We do not show fear.

5. Examine an action comic book. List each interjection that appears in it.

6. Find a paragraph you have written that could benefit from revision. This can be from any paper you have written this year. Rewrite the paragraph. As you do so, ask yourself these questions:
   * Do the descriptive adjectives characterize precisely the nouns or pronouns they modify?
   * Have the correct demonstrative adjectives been used?
   * Have all the proper adjectives been capitalized?
   * Are commas used to separate pairs of adjectives specifying different types of qualities? Are commas used where required to set off pairs of adjectives?
   * Are the adjective forms used in comparative and superlative statements correct?
   * Have adverbs been used to answer essential questions of *how, when, where, how much,* and *how often*?
   * Has only one negative expression been used to convey each negative idea?
   * Have sentence adverbs been used as needed to establish order?
   * Are the adverb forms used in comparative and superlative statements correct?
   * Are negative comparisons properly written?
   * Have usage errors resulting from confusion between adjective and adverb forms been avoided?
   * Does each prepositional phrase begin with the preposition that accurately expresses the relationship between its object and the word that the phrase modifies?
   * Has the use of *and* been limited to situations where elements of equal rank require linkage?
   * Are subordinating conjunctions used effectively to make clear the relationships between linked thoughts?

   By using these questions to make sure a composition is properly expressive as well as free from usage errors, you give it a better chance of making a positive impression on readers.

Composition Writing

Developing and Composing the Body of the Essay

14

This chapter presents fundamental principles for writing a composition or essay. By now you have the writing skills to compose essays, but you also need to bring other ingredients to bear on this task: discipline, forethought, some imagination, and plenty of concentration— the same qualities you need to perform any task well. In particular, this chapter will discuss and practice some simple, sensible concepts and methods for applying your skills and self-discipline to successful writing of the *body* of the essay. In Chapter 15 you will study and practice such special-purpose paragraphs as introduction and conclusion—paragraphs that frame the body, or main part, of the composition.

A. FINDING A SUBJECT

Several considerations should help you to decide what to write about. First, for the sake of authority, you must write about what you know: what you know either from study or from experience. Second, you will write best—most vividly and most persuasively—about subjects you have feelings about, whether positive or negative feelings. But third and some- times most important, you cannot always just write about anything; audience and circum- stances often restrict or, as in school, assign subjects. So here are the three criteria or stan- dards by which to select a subject:

1. your knowledge of a subject
2. your interest and involvement in a subject
3. restrictions of audience, situation, or assignment

When the assignment and occasion are wide open, you can find your own audience and voice. But when the assignment is fixed—as on a test question or job report—you must instead work and study to develop within yourself the necessary authority and interest.

EX 14-1   List five subjects about which you believe you *know* more than the average person. After each, write whether your knowledge comes mostly from study or from practical experience.

1. _____

2. _____

3. _____

4. _____

5. _____

EX 14-2   List five subjects about which you believe you have *stronger feelings* than the average person. After each, write whether your feelings are positive or negative.

1. _____

2. _____

3. _____

4. _____

5. _____

EX 14-3   List five subjects for writing that have been assigned or dictated to you by the situation within the last year. These assignments may have come from applications or interviews as well as from classwork.

1. _____

2. _____

3. _____

4. _____

5. _____

B. NARROWING THE SUBJECT

When you find a subject that you are genuinely knowledgeable about and interested in, you will probably have to narrow or restrict it to suit a particular guideline, occasion, or audience. Hang-gliding enthusiasts, roller skaters, dancers, and nuclear physicists can and do talk for hours about their specialties, when they are talking to one another. But most audiences and assignments will demand briefer, more concise, more carefully focused discussion. If you really have some knowledge and authority, you must be selective and not fall prey to the old wisecrack that says, "Tell me everything you know; I've got five minutes." Furthermore, a wisely restricted subject will help to prevent superficiality—treating an interesting and complex subject in a shallow, detached, or abrupt way.

Some writers can narrow and define a subject mentally in a disciplined thought process. Other writers "freewrite" on a subject (see Chapter 1) and then study the particular drift of their thoughts to see which way their strengths and interests lie. Use the method that you find effective and stimulating.

EX 14-4   "Freewrite" on *one* of the following subject areas to see where your pen leads your thoughts. Do not second-guess or edit yourself, if you can avoid it. Do your writing on another sheet of paper.

> schools
> the family
> the media
> fashion

EX 14-5   Now try to narrow subjects with disciplined, deductive thought. Restrict each of the following subjects to a narrower subject that you think *you* could write sensibly about in two to three pages. Narrowing a subject in stages, as in the example, is sometimes helpful.

EXAMPLE: Sports   *basketball*   *women's intercollegiate basketball*

1. Entertainment _____

2. Schools _____

3. Relationships _____

4. Media _____

5. Crime _____

6. Fashion _____

7. Politics _____

8. Age _____

C. FINDING THE QUESTION

Find your exact purpose for writing by pinning down your narrowed subject with a question—the particular question that your essay will try to answer. Suppose, for example, that a writer has narrowed the large subject "Media" to "Movies" and has narrowed "Movies" to "Horror Films." The writer has thereby reduced the subject to writable size, but "Horror Films" all by itself as a subject is still somewhat loosely defined. This looseness might confuse or mislead a writer if he or she began to write with something so general as "Horror Films" in mind.

See how much more manageable a specific question makes the task of setting out to write about "Horror Films": "How has the Hollywood horror film changed in the last twenty years?" Such a question is likely to help (1) stimulate a writer's thoughts, (2) keep a writer's study and work relevant to the practical matter of turning out a paper focused on a limited purpose, and (3) tap a writer's built-in drive to answer questions, a much stronger drive than most writers' desire to compose essays on loosely defined subjects.

EX 14-6   Narrow each of the subjects you listed in EX 14-1 and EX 14-2; then pin down each of these narrowed subjects with a question that you think *you* might be able to answer in two to three pages of writing.

1. _____

    _____

2. _____

    _____

3. _____

    _____

4. _____

    _____

5. _____

    _____

6. _____

    _____

7. _____

    _____

8. _____

    _____

9. _____

    _____

10. _____

    _____

Workable essay questions usually concern *matters of opinion* (as, for example, in interpretive or cause–effect formats) or *matters of information* (as in descriptive or process writing). Simple *matters of fact* are not usually complex enough to be readily developed into several-page discussions, although facts are, of course, important in the development of matters of opinion and information. For example, a question like "Who won the Academy Award last year for Best Supporting Actress?" will take barely a sentence or two to answer adequately and authoritatively, so it would make a very poor *essay* question.

Similarly, yes-or-no questions do not really suit full compositions, because such questions can be answered with one word—"yes" or "no." When a writer asks, "Is watching television a beneficial pastime for children?" the writer usually means to answer a question like "Why is—or why isn't—watching television a beneficial pastime for children?" Strive to reach through your thoughts to the real question that you wish to answer.

EX 14-7   Rewrite any of your questions from EX 14-6 that concern simple matters of fact or that ask for only a "yes" or "no" answer. Do this on another sheet of paper.

D. EXPLORING THE TOPIC

Once you have found a good question, you have effectively defined your paper's purpose: what goal it will try to accomplish, what need it will try to fill. But before you write and rush off toward that goal, it is a good idea to do some exploratory thinking—to pull ideas and information out of your head and to make sure, before you commit too much time and energy to the writing, that you really have enough to say to answer your question.

Some writers explore a topic by freewriting; others do it entirely in thought. (Such mental exploring can be the solitary person's equivalent of the group activity known as *brainstorming*, which involves the free generation of ideas as its first phase and the evaluation of the ideas as its second phase.) A good, economical compromise between these two methods involves first phrasing the question, then listing quickly on paper as many one-sentence answers to the question as you can think up or dream up—*any* answers. Save editing and analysis of your list of answers till later.

EXAMPLE OF LISTING ANSWERS AS A WAY OF EXPLORING A TOPIC
Question: How has the Hollywood horror film changed in the last twenty years?
1. Frankenstein is funny nowadays.
2. The films are more violent and more graphic today than they used to be.
3. The stories now seem more unreal.
4. In his most recent appearance, Dracula was an elegant, romantic man.
5. In current films more money and screen time are devoted to special effects.
6. There is now more science fiction and black magic where there used to be more complex stories.
7. Today's movies and audiences frequently do not identify with victims; also, they sympathize less with such monsters or madmen as the Wolfman or Frankenstein. The viewer's relationship with the action on the screen is colder, more detached, visual rather than heartfelt.
8. Camera angles nowadays often show events from the monster's point of view.
9. Victims are now usually women and teenagers, whereas they used to be whole communities.
10. Film quality and production values are much better these days, even in low-budget films.
11. There are no more great horror-film actors or directors.

EX 14-8   Take two of your questions from EX 14–6 and freewrite about them one at a time. Answer each with complete sentences as quickly and as thoroughly as you can. If answers fail to come quickly to you, choose another of your questions. Do your writing on another sheet of paper.

After you have come up with a list, take a few moments to study what you have written. First, see that you have framed all your answers as complete sentences, so that each thought will be complete for future reference. Perhaps you have repeated the same point two or three times, or perhaps you have supplied an irrelevant answer to the question. If so, condense your list. Perhaps some points are very similar, or perhaps one point is an example of another. In the sample series on the horror films, answers 1, 4, 7, and 8 seem closely related. (What do they have in common?) Also related are answers 2, 3, and 6. Items 5 and 10 seem related, too. Numbers 9 and 11 seem to stand alone.

EX 14-9   Survey your answers to questions in EX 14-8. Try to associate or cluster similar or related answers to determine just how many different points you might actually be making. On another sheet of paper, list similar groups, and say what idea, point, or thing they have in common. These groups should be somewhat *parallel*: they should cover points of similar scope, importance, and generality. (In the sample, answers 1 and 9 are not very parallel; 1 is far less significant and general than 9.)

Once you have committed some ideas to paper, you have come to a time of decision, with three possibilities before you: (1) You may have plenty to say from your knowledge and experience to answer the question. (2) You may have very little at all to say in answer to your question. (3) You may have something to say, but not enough to cover an interesting question adequately and authoritatively.

In the first case, you are ready to plan, compose, and write. In the second case, unless you are committed to the question by interest or by an assignment, you should explore alternate essay questions about which you have more to say. In the third case, you probably need to do additional reading or research to bolster your learning and experience so that you can successfully cover your question. This flow chart shows your choices and your recourses:

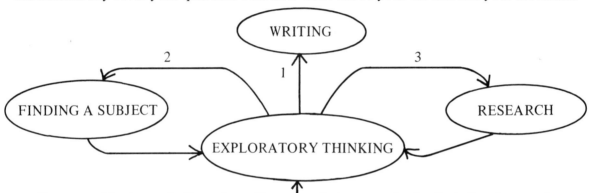

For now, this chapter's discussion will assume that you are in the first situation, ready to plan, compose, and write. Later the chapter will suggest some resources for research to acquire the ideas and information necessary to write a good essay if you find yourself in the second or third situation.

E.   TOPIC-SENTENCE OUTLINING

Most writers find a brief plan or outline a useful guide and reference for composing. An outline can help you manage your task so that you do not lose sight of the whole while working on the parts.

Your freewriting has already produced a rough outline—a question followed by a series of answers—that can be worked up into a very useful plan commonly called a *topic-sentence outline*. Each item of a topic-sentence outline represents the topic sentence of one paragraph of the body of a composition. For a two- to three-page composition, a list of three to five items—and three to five body paragraphs—is customary.

In the case of the horror-film example, freewriting yielded five apparent clusters or categories of answers:

a. Answers 1, 4, 7, and 8 all concerned the monster or villain as *central character* in the film.

b. Items 2, 3, and 6 concerned various changes in the *stories*, or plots, of the films.

c. Numbers 5 and 10 concerned changes in film *production.*

d. Answer 9 concerned the *victims* of the monster or villain.

e. Answer 11 concerned actors, actresses, and directors—*people making these movies.*

Seeing these relationships and generalizations requires concentration and imagination, so don't lose patience too quickly. Besides, if you have a good, clear question, it is relatively easy to find help and advice in answering the question and in organizing your answers into a simple, helpful topic-sentence outline like the following.

EXAMPLE OF A TOPIC-SENTENCE OUTLINE
Question: How has the Hollywood horror film changed in the last twenty years?

A. The central characters have changed and become less worthy of sympathy.

B. Stories are now much less complex than they were twenty years ago.

C. Victims of the monsters' assaults have changed to reflect today's movie audience and its fears and values.

D. With few exceptions, horror films no longer draw the big-name directors and actors that they used to attract.

E. Production values and special effects now frequently get top billing in horror films.

Study the following topic-sentence outline for flaws in logic and relevance that might frustrate a writer's attempts to work from it efficiently.

EXAMPLE OF A FAULTY TOPIC-SENTENCE OUTLINE
Question: Why do young people go so eagerly to rock concerts?

A. They go to enjoy the music.

B. They go to escape from everyday routines.

C. They go to experience the power that comes from the volume and rawness of the music.

D. They go because of powerful peer pressure; attending is a fad.

E. They go to get close to their idols—the rock stars.

"Why Young People Go to Rock Concerts"—a subject perhaps narrowed from "Entertainment"—makes a potentially very interesting subject, especially for those who *don't* go, for those who wonder why anybody would go to such an event voluntarily.

But this writer may have some problems with this topic-sentence outline. Can you see where and why? For one thing, don't answers *A* and *C* seem nearly the same—both concerned with the *experiencing of music at rock concerts*? These two answers should be combined. And item *B*, though it does in a way answer the question, does not directly answer this particular question; it does not *specify* why people "escape" to rock concerts rather than to the movies, the beach, or a hamburger stand. So what is the specific escape value of the rock concert? Perhaps answers *B* and *D* might be combined and improved to assert that the rock concert is a kind of youth circus or carnival where young people, getting away from a more adult world, celebrate their identity as a group in our society; they do something, unlike going to movies or the beach, that adults are not supposed to do or to like.

The revised topic-sentence outline now looks like this:

Question: Why do young people go so eagerly to rock concerts?

A. They go to experience the power of loud volume and live music.

B. They go to participate with peers in a carnival of youth—a renewal of Woodstock.

C. They go to celebrate their idols and heroes.

Do these answers cover the question adequately and authoritatively, in your view? What important points, if any, do you think the writer has overlooked? Would you be interested in reading this essay about "Why Young People Go to Rock Concerts"?

EX 14-10   Study the following topic-sentence outline for flaws in logic and relevance.

> Question: Why is the sun a better energy source than other fuels?
> A. Solar energy is an unlimited resource, so we can avoid the planned obsolescence of nuclear power.
> B. We need cheap fuel, and sunlight is free.
> C. Oil pollutes the earth and sky when burned, but solar energy is pollution-free.
> D. We have tremendous potential for solar power in the Sunbelt states, but in some forms it would be economical even in New England; Alaska, though, is a different story.
> E. Solar energy can belong to every nation, so no one country can monopolize it and use it as a means for controlling world politics.
> F. Wind and geothermal energy can also help us avoid oil use.
> G. The problems associated with the production, transportation, and storage of oil do not exist with solar energy.

Revise this topic-sentence outline by eliminating irrelevant and illogical answers and by combining repetitious or overlapping answers. Note that the writer really seems to have *four* topics—and therefore four paragraphs of the essay's body—to develop. What are they? Write your revised outline on another sheet of paper.

EX 14-11   Study the following topic-sentence outline for flaws in logic and relevance.

> Question: In what important ways does college dating differ from high school dating?
> A. Both parties are more mature.
> B. Both parties are more independent.
> C. At college there is a greater variety of people to date.
> D. Intimacy is more central to dating in college.
> E. College dates more often involve "grown-up" activities—dinner, dancing, night clubs.
> F. College relationships tend to be more serious.
> G. Many college students are actively seeking lifelong mates.
> H. The more open and relaxed college environment encourages personal relationships of all kinds, unlike high school's emphasis on relationships based on mutual participation in particular school activities.
> I. For some people, the size of their college and the importance of study make dating harder than ever.

Revise this topic-sentence outline by eliminating irrelevant and illogical answers and by combining repetitious or overlapping answers. The writer really seems to offer four or five main points or topics in answer to the question. What are they? Write your revised outline on another sheet of paper.

EX 14-12   Polish one of your freewriting lists from EX 14-9 into a finished topic-sentence outline. Write your question. Then follow your question with statements that qualify as paragraph topic sentences. Do your writing on another sheet of paper.

EX 14-13   On a separate sheet of paper, develop one of the topic sentences from your topic-sentence outline into a paragraph of from four to ten sentences. Remember the importance of detail and illustration to this body paragraph. Check to see that your paragraph fits both topic sentence and main question. Check to see that your paragraph has not wandered from one topic sentence into areas covered by other topic sentences.

EX 14-13A   *Optional extension to EX 14-13*: On a separate sheet of paper, develop the rest of your topic sentences into paragraphs so that you have a rough draft of the body of the composition—a main question followed by a series of relevant, thorough, effectively developed answers.

F. DEVELOPING COMPOUND ESSAY QUESTIONS

Some important and interesting composition-writing projects involve answering a compound question or a series of questions. By perceiving all the questions, a writer can bring into better focus the precise extent of his or her task. This clearer focus greatly improves the writer's chances for making an adequate and relevant response to an assignment. Here are some of the types of compound questions that writers meet in college-level writing assignments.

PROBLEM-SOLUTION WRITING
What is the problem? (This question calls for a description.)

What is the solution? (Again, a description is called for.)

Why should the solution you discuss be adopted? (This question calls for an argument or a list of reasons.)

EXAMPLE OF PLANNING A PROBLEM-SOLUTION PAPER
USING QUESTIONS AND ANSWERS
What is the problem? Plastic waste is a problem.

What is the solution? We should recycle plastic the way we recycle metal and glass.

Why should this solution be adopted? Recycling is (a) economical, (b) technically possible, (c) aesthetic, and (d) public-minded and patriotic.

CONTROVERSY WRITING: PRO *OR* CON
What is the controversy? (This calls for a description.)

What do your opponents say? (This calls for a description or list of reasons or arguments.)

What do you say? (Here you should present a list of refutations of your opponents' points and a list of points in support of your position.)

EX 14-14 Supply specifics for an example of controversy writing similar to the specifics provided for the example of problem-solution writing. The subject of the controversy is supplied.

What is the controversy? People continually debate whether or not to abolish grades.

What do your opponents say? _____

_____

_____

_____

What do you say? _____

_____

_____

_____

APPRAISAL WRITING

This is an assessment of strengths and weaknesses or advantages and disadvantages. It is a variation of controversy writing; instead of pro *or* con, you discuss pro *and* con.

What are the strengths of something? (A list or description is needed.)

What are the weaknesses of something? (A list or description is needed.)

This order of questions emphasizes weaknesses by putting them last. To emphasize strengths, reverse the order. This listing of pro and con often leads to two further, optional questions:

What causes this particular arrangement of strengths and weaknesses? (This should be answered by cause–effect development.)

How might this balance be altered to create more strengths (or more weaknesses)? (Again, cause–effect development is needed.)

EVALUATION

What is some person or group trying to do? (This should be answered with description.)

How well does this person or group succeed in this aim? (This question calls for comparison or contrast between the *intention* and the *actual achievement.* A negative evaluation will *contrast* intention with achievement to emphasize the difference; a positive evaluation will *compare* intention with achievement to emphasize the success of the person or group in reaching a goal.)

EX 14-15   Supply a brief example of evaluation writing using some project or goal that you attempted in the last year.

What did you try to do? _____

_____

_____

_____

How well did you succeed in your aim? _____

_____

_____

_____

_____

SOCIAL STUDIES ANALYSIS

This type of writing project is similar to evaluation writing in its study of intention, motive, success, and failure in human action. Think of political, social, or historical essay questions in this light:

What was something? (Answer with description.)

What did this try to achieve? (Answer with description.)

How well did it succeed? (Use comparison or contrast, as with evaluation.)

What were the main causes of its success or failure? (Employ a list of causes.)

(Optional) *What lessons, if any, stem from this success or failure?* (Answer with a list of lessons or conclusions.)

EX 14-16   Using your knowledge of history, political science, or social science, list eight institutions, events, or pieces of legislation that would make suitable subjects for the series of questions above. Write on another sheet of paper.

BIOGRAPHY AND INTERPRETATION

Who was X? (Answer with a description of the person *X*.)

Or *What did* X *do or experience?* (Answer with narration.)

Why was or is X *important?* (Answer with a list of reasons or influences.)

EX 14-17   List five persons you would be interested in writing about in this way.

1. _____

2. _____

3. _____

4. _____

5. _____

TEXT ANALYSIS

What is the text (or the part of the text—word, line, character, event, image) you are focusing on? (Answer with description.)

Why is it important, powerful, or successful? (Answer with a list of reasons or causes.)

EVALUATION OF AN EXPERIMENT

What is the experiment? (Answer with a description.)

What is expected to happen? (Use narration or process development to answer.)

Why is this expected to happen? (Answer with a list of reasons or causes.)

What did actually happen? (Answer with narration.)

Why did this happen? (Answer with a list of reasons or causes or with a process description.)

EXAMPLE OF PLANNING AN EXPERIMENT—EVALUATION PAPER USING QUESTIONS AND ANSWERS

What is the experiment? The experiment involves toasting bread.
What is expected to happen? The bread should become brown and warm in a few minutes.
Why is this expected to happen? The resistance coils in the toaster bake—chemically alter—the surfaces of the bread.
What did actually happen? Nothing happened.
Why did this happen? The experimenter neglected to plug the toaster into the wall outlet.

EX 14-18 Here is a series of college-level writing assignments in the brief form in which such assignments are often given. Recast each assignment as the sequence of questions it is really asking you to answer. Use a dictionary or encyclopedia for reference if you are unfamiliar with a subject or with what kind of writing it might call for. Do your writing on another sheet of paper.

1. Discuss the Declaration of Independence.
2. Discuss behavior modification.
3. Evaluate President Lyndon B. Johnson's War on Poverty.
4. Rate the arrangement of letter keys on the current typewriter keyboard.
5. Discuss Malcolm X.
6. Rate pass-fail grading.
7. Take a stand and discuss capital punishment.
8. Discuss the Planned Parenthood organization and its relation to overpopulation and other problems.
9. Discuss Galileo's legendary dropping of two unequal weights from the leaning tower of Pisa.
10. Discuss the food stamp program.
11. Discuss the Eighteenth Amendment to the U.S. Constitution.

EX 14-19   Take one of the assignments from EX 14-18 that you are most familiar with and interested in and read an encyclopedia article about it. Then, working from your series of questions, develop a topic-sentence outline that you might expand into an essay. Study the following example before you begin. Then write your outline on another sheet of paper.

> **EXAMPLE: DISCUSS THE COUNCIL OF TRENT**
> Questions: What was the Council of Trent? What did it try to do? How well did it succeed? What were the main causes of its success?
> A. The Council of Trent (1545–47, 1551–52, 1562–63) was an assembly of Catholic officials convened to reform the Church in the wake of the Protestant Reformation.
> B. This council sought to oppose Protestantism, to curtail worldly abuses in the Catholic Church, to clarify doctrine, and to reform clerical practices.
> C. The council was a spectacular success that both effectively rebutted Protestant attacks and established the way of modern Catholicism.
> D. Reform-minded popes and a resurgence of religious feeling in Catholic Europe help account for the eventual influence of the council's decrees.

G. CARRYING OUT RESEARCH

Very few people have enough information in their heads to sit down and write successfully about all the topics listed in EX 14-18. Most people use information stored in books, libraries, tapes, and computers, not in their own memories. But you must be able to retrieve information if you are going to use this form of memory and information storage effectively.

The ability to use the library effectively can put all the brain power, experience, and genius of the ages at our disposal, no matter how limited our own powers of reasoning and personal experience may be. In the library, your most important research resource is the reference librarian, a person usually more than willing to answer your serious, considerate questions and to aid you in finding the information you need to write authoritative papers. But college students are also expected to acquaint themselves with the basics of library use—with the card catalog, with book and magazine circulation procedures, and with basic reference tools.

Here is a brief survey of basic library research and reference materials that you might find helpful for researching answers to essay questions.

A. General encyclopedias like the *Britannica* or *Americana* contain comprehensive articles for the nonspecialist on nearly everything under the sun.

B. Specialized encyclopedias (sometimes called "dictionaries" in their titles) contain brief yet thorough accounts of particular areas of human thought and action. Examples are the *Encyclopedia of the Social Sciences*, the *Oxford Classical Dictionary* (concerning ancient Greece and Rome), and the *Encyclopedia of World Art*, among many others.

C. Dictionaries provide much intriguing information about language in addition to correct spellings. The *Dictionary of Slang* offers unique glimpses of sociology and social history, for instance. And the *Oxford English Dictionary* and the *Dictionary of American English on Historical Principles* contain word histories—what words meant at different moments in the history of English.

D. General indexes can refer you to newspaper and magazine articles on particular topics, just as indexes in the backs of books refer you to pages in these books where words or topics appear. The most widely used index, *The Readers' Guide to Periodical Literature*, lists thousands of topics and where more than a hundred general-audience periodicals have covered them Most libraries subscribe to many of these periodicals, so you can turn from the *Readers' Guide* to the library shelves to find helpful information. As you gain practice in using indexes, you will be better able to judge the likely content and relevance to you of magazine articles by inspecting title, name of journal, and number of pages.

E. Specialized indexes like the *Social Sciences Index, Humanities Index,* and *New York Times Index* catalog articles in specific publications, some professional, some technical.

F. Biographical references like *Who's Who* supply concise accounts of the lives of contemporary and historical personages.

G. Atlases provide compact geographical information.

H. A library's main card catalog is, of course, your index to the library's entire collection, in which you will find books about nearly every imaginable subject.

EX 14-20   Here is the list of assignments from EX 14–18 followed by a list of titles of reference sources. In the blank following each topic, fill in the letters of reference sources from the list below that are likely to provide you with useful information in your research of the particular assignment.

    1. Discuss the Declaration of Independence. _____

    2. Discuss behavior modification. _____

    3. Evaluate President Lyndon B. Johnson's War on Poverty. _____

    4. Rate the arrangement of letter keys on the current typewriter keyboard.

    _____

    5. Discuss Malcolm X. _____

    6. Rate pass-fail grading. _____

    7. Take a stand and discuss capital punishment. _____

    8. Discuss the Planned Parenthood organization and its relation to overpopulation and other problems. _____

    9. Discuss Galileo's legendary dropping of two unequal weights from the leaning tower of Pisa. _____

  10. Discuss the food stamp program. _____

  11. Discuss the Eighteenth Amendment to the U.S. Constitution. _____

    A. *Encyclopedia Britannica*
    B. *Dictionary of American Biography*
    C. *The New Oxford History of Music*
    D. *McGraw-Hill Encyclopedia of Science and Technology*
    E. *Dictionary of American History*
    F. Card catalog
    G. *Readers' Guide to Periodical Literature*
    H. *New York Times Index*
    I. *Social Sciences Index*
    J. *Humanities Index*
    K. *Encyclopedia of the Social Sciences*

    L. *Encyclopedia of Philosophy*
    M. *Cyclopedia of American Government*
    N. *Education Index*

WORKSHOP

1. To review this chapter, start with a general subject area and work it through the following composing steps to arrive at a draft of the body of a composition.
   a. Find a subject area.
   b. Narrow the subject.
   c. Find the question or questions that define what you wish to say.
   d. Freewrite a list of answers to your question(s). Research answers to your question, if necessary.
   e. Polish your list of answers into a topic-sentence outline.
   f. Research your paragraph topics if necessary.
   g. Develop each of your topic sentences into a four- to ten-sentence paragraph that includes relevant specifics.

2. Develop your sketches of papers in EX 14–14 and EX 14–15 into fully developed essay bodies.

3. Watch a network television newscast. Note the various subjects illustrated by each story or item and, for each item, prepare a relevant essay question suggested by the report.

4. Find the letters-to-the-editor section of a major newspaper. (Your local library will subscribe to several.) Select a letter in which the writer seems to have composed well-reasoned arguments in support of an opinion, and try to write a topic-sentence outline for this letter in the form of questions and topic-sentence answers. On the basis of this outline, determine how well the letter writer has organized the body of his or her argument.

5. Set a day to be curious. On this day take careful note of, and list, any person, word, event, concept, or item that you hear or see mentioned but that you do not know about. Take this list to the library and research and write brief explanations of at least ten items on your list.

6. Employ the processes described in this chapter to plan a written response required in a situation not directly related to your school coursework. Choose from among the following situations, or devise one of your own:
   a. You are seeking an entry-level position with a corporation you would very much like to work for. Respond to the following item that appears on the application form: *Describe your reasons for wanting to work for XYZ Corporation.*
   b. You receive an argumentative letter from a relative. Respond to this line in the letter: *The only thing worth studying nowadays is how to program or repair computers.*
   c. You are working for an advertising agency. You have been asked to come up with several paragraphs of copy to follow this headline: *What you should know about O'Leary Space Heaters and the so-called "safety tests" by a consumer magazine.*
   Use your imagination as you develop your plan into a complete written response.

Expanding and Polishing the Essay

15

A. EXPANDING A PARAGRAPH INTO A COMPOSITION

In the first half of Chapter 14 a step-by-step method for building the body of a composition was presented. The second half of that chapter covered ways of ensuring clear focus when following this procedure; it also discussed how the facts that provide the substance of a composition's body can be obtained from reference materials. Before moving on to consider methods for preparing the introduction and the conclusion of a composition, we will explore an alternate method of composition development—expanding a paragraph into a composition. This method of development is made possible by the similarities in structure between certain types of paragraphs and certain types of essays.

The paragraph-expansion method proves especially helpful in the case of such paragraphs as comparison, contrast, and listing. These paragraphs usually comprise a series of items, each of which can be isolated as a topic sentence and developed into a separate paragraph. The original topic sentence is then promoted to a "thesis statement," or statement of the overall purpose of the essay. The following diagram illustrates the method of constructing a composition by enlarging a paragraph.

PARAGRAPH TOPIC SENTENCE $\longrightarrow$ THESIS STATEMENT
FIRST ITEM OF SPECIFICS $\longrightarrow$ FIRST PARAGRAPH'S TOPIC SENTENCE
SECOND ITEM OF SPECIFICS $\longrightarrow$ SECOND PARAGRAPH'S TOPIC SENTENCE
THIRD ITEM OF SPECIFICS $\longrightarrow$ THIRD PARAGRAPH'S TOPIC SENTENCE
FOURTH ITEM OF SPECIFICS $\longrightarrow$ FOURTH PARAGRAPH'S TOPIC SENTENCE

EX 15–1   Rewrite the following contrast paragraph as a topic-sentence outline for a whole composition. In place of an overall question heading the outline, use an *answer* to this question—a "thesis statement"—to head your outline.

A car buyer who chooses between full-sized and compact cars does not simply choose between big and little versions of the same thing; these cars differ in subtler ways that the car buyer would be wise to think about. First, the high gas-mileage compact car is obviously more economical in one respect, but its price tag—nearly as high as that of its full-sized cousin—is a reminder that the small car is fully as complex and unpredictable a machine. This complexity makes it almost as expensive to manufacture and repair as a full-sized luxury sedan. Second, the savings that come with small size and lighter, often less expensive materials may be offset by the inherent safety factors of the large, heavy automobile. In some cases plastic proves a stronger, more durable material than metal, but on the whole one price of smallness is a reduction in safety. In addition to economy and safety, a third useful point of contrast between big and small is the ride. Drivers of small cars must sacrifice the famous American cruising ride for handling and ride characteristics that most people associate with sports cars; the compact car rides like a Lotus, even if it scarcely performs like one. Finally, differences between big and small cars are quite pronounced in the case of engines. Small cars, beginning with the very sophisticated, air-cooled Volkswagen, have always relied on "high tech" engineering and on such innovations as front-wheel drive, fuel injection, and transverse-mounted motors, whereas Detroit when building big cars has been able to go with the proven and reliable but inefficient and bulky overhead-cam engines perfected thirty years ago. The small-car driver runs a state-of-the-art machine, with all the performance benefits and repair risks that such innovative, finely tuned technology entails.

Thesis statement: _____
Topic sentences for an essay based on this paragraph:

_____

_____

_____

_____

_____

_____

_____

_____

_____

_____

_____

EX 15-2   Rewrite the following process paragraph as a topic-sentence outline. In place of an overall question heading the outline, use an answer to this question—a "thesis statement"—to head your outline. Write your thesis statement and topic sentences on another sheet of paper.

Painting the wall of a house—whether inside or outside—is relatively easy to do well if you take care to follow all the necessary steps. Surface preparation is particularly important. You must, first of all, clean and scrape the surfaces if old paint is peeling or if the wall has accumulated dirt, mildew, or spider webs. Special but inexpensive tools can make scraping manageable, and special but inexpensive cleansers can help solve mildew problems. The second phase involves patching with a spackling compound or putty any noticeable cracks, holes, or flaws you wish repaired in the wall. Third, if bare wood or masonry has surfaced during your cleaning and repair, you will need to paint these exposed surfaces with a base or "primer" paint to ensure a good bond between the wall and the finish coat of paint. If you are painting new construction, you may have little, if any, work to do on steps one and two, but step three becomes important and time-consuming. Finally, when the surface is clean, patched, and primed, you can stir up your finish paint and brush, roll, or spray it on. Follow the paint manufacturer's application directions. There is no economy in spreading paint on too thin in the hope of stretching paint and money; your surface will simply break down sooner. Work in the shade to ensure good adhesion and even drying, and do a good job, since you do not want to have to go through the process again for quite a while.

EX 15-3   Rewrite the following descriptive paragraph as a topic-sentence outline, again heading the outline with a "thesis statement" instead of with a question. Write your thesis statement and topic sentences on another sheet of paper.

> Sigmund Freud was a restless, curious scientist who developed a number of schemes for describing the human mind as he observed it in his clinical practice of psychology. According to the best-known of his descriptions, the human personality consists of three powers or systems. The power we are most familiar with Freud called the *ego* (Latin for "I"). This is the aspect of our personality that negotiates our business with the outside world and with the daily demands and pressures of reality. The power we know least in ourselves Freud called the *id* (Latin for "it"). The id strives for pleasure or rest or well-being; it tries to protect the personality from uncomfortable or anxious stimulus or excitation. Should needs or desires arise, the id urges their immediate satisfaction so that the organism can return to a state of calm. The third power in this description is the *superego* (Latin for "over-I"). This superego is the source of our ideals, our moral sense, and our conscience. But the superego is an idealist, not a realist like the ego, and in some cases it can be as brutish as the id—for instance, when it insists on one's punishing oneself for desiring or doing something immoral.

The method of composing the body of an essay by expanding a paragraph depends on an analogy between essay and paragraph, an analogy that you have just been exploring. The validity of this analogy allows in-class or workbook paragraphs or paragraph-length freewriting, when reviewed and edited with some care, to inspire and guide whole essays. It is still important, however, for the sake of control and efficiency, to use a brief, simple topic-sentence outline to plan your task.

EX 15-4   Here is an essay assignment: contrast something of your own choosing, some X, at two distinct times in its history. For your subject, your X, you might choose automobiles, hockey, films, fashion, stenography, or some similar thing as it is *now* versus how it was, say, twenty or thirty years ago.

1. Rephrase the assignment as a question.

   _____

   _____

2. On another sheet of paper, answer the question in a short paragraph that enumerates an adequate number of points of contrast. Begin your paragraph with a suitable topic sentence. Adjust and revise your paragraph as you see fit.
3. Now transform your paragraph into a topic-sentence outline that begins with a thesis statement (which should answer the question), followed by specific answers, or topic sentences.
4. State any questions or points of information you would have to research in order to write this paper with authoritative detail and accuracy.

B. INTRODUCING THE BODY OF THE ESSAY

The body of a composition is the largest, most important, most informative, most demanding part of the essay. Therefore you should work longest, hardest, *and first* on the body. Most papers that go wrong go wrong at their openings, so you should, if you can, hold off on your introduction until you have developed and written enough to know just what you have to introduce. This order of composition will also help you keep the task of *developing* a thesis distinct from the task of *introducing* it. Confusing these two tasks is the single most common cause of frustration among essay writers trying to begin their essays.

If you feel a compelling need for prewriting, for warming up to writing the body of the essay, try freewriting or try the exploratory thinking and outlining procedures you practiced in the last chapter. These procedures demand more discipline and concentration than just picking up your pen in an offhand manner with a vague sense of direction. But teachers of writing have developed these procedures over the years to save writers time, energy, and frustration in the long run and to improve student performance on such assignments as in-class essay tests. The essay test is, by the way, hardly a mere school exercise; rather, it is typical of most writing assignments everywhere. Usually you must methodically and cogently present what you know according to essay-writing conventions, without trusting to luck, inspiration, or a reader's willingness to do your work or organization for you.

C. WRITING THE THESIS STATEMENT

When the body of your essay is fleshed out into a rough draft, you can begin to think about introducing it to your intended audience. Some "rules of thunb," or customary guidelines, can help you write this introduction.

First, the introduction to an essay usually includes a statement of your paper's purpose; this statement is customarily called a *thesis statement*, or *thesis.* Such questions as "In what important respects has stenography changed over the last thirty years?" are one form of such a thesis, and you could simply include such a question in your introduction. But many people regard such questions, particularly when they are over-used, as inelegant or clumsy. So instead think of a thesis statement as a comprehensive but concise *answer* to the question that you used to freewrite and develop the body of your essay. This answer will inform the reader generally but accurately what your essay will say, argue, assert, report, or describe.

EXAMPLE OF A THESIS STATEMENT
According to Sigmund Freud's best-known description of the human personality, the mind is divided into three powers or systems.

Or: Sigmund Freud theorized that the human personality is composed of *ego, id*, and *superego*.

Or: Sigmund Freud was probably the single greatest explorer of the human personality. His explorations produced very influential views of the human mind. [Note that, as here, a thesis statement need not be just one sentence.]

Each of these three statements is adequate as a thesis; each informs a reader of what is to follow. (Which do you prefer and why?) Differences among the statements are matters of style and polish that need not delay your completion of the draft of a composition.

EX 15-5   The following thesis statements, which are based on paragraphs in this chapter and Chapter 14, are flawed. Rewrite them so that they reflect more clearly the content of the compositions you have outlined in previous exercises.

1. Question: In what important ways does the making of small cars differ from the making of big cars?
   Thesis: Small cars are overtaking big cars in sales, and manufacturers will soon make only compacts.

   What is wrong with this thesis statement? _____

   _____

   Rewrite it. _____

   _____

2. Question: How does one paint the surface of a house?
   Thesis: The cleanliness of the surface is the most important point to consider in housepainting.

   What is wrong with this thesis statement? _____

   _____

   Rewrite it. _____

   _____

3. Question: In what important ways has the Hollywood horror film changed in the last twenty years?
   Thesis: Horror films have become more fantastic and mind-blowing in the last twenty years, but they remain a great place to take a date.

   What is wrong with this thesis? _____

   _____

   Rewrite it. _____

   _____

EX 15-6   Using information supplied in examples in Chapter 14, write thesis statements in answer to the following questions.

1. Why do young people go so eagerly to rock concerts?

   _____

   _____

   _____

2. Why is the sun a better energy source than other fuels?

_____

_____

_____

3. In what important ways does college dating differ from high school dating?

_____

_____

_____

EX 15-7   Revise your own questions from Chapter 14 into thesis statements.

1. From EX 14-12: _____

_____

_____

_____

2. From EX 14-19: _____

_____

_____

_____

D. INTRODUCING THE THESIS

Customarily, the thesis statement appears as the last sentence or two of the introduction. The rest of the introduction may be said to introduce the thesis. As a whole, the introduction transfers your reader from his or her world into the world of your essay. Thus the introduction is *transitional*, a bridge between worlds or people. It is helpful to think of the analogy of inviting someone into your room or house. Introducing someone into your space demands some formality, some pleasantries, some mutual assurances of fair purposes. Even a strictly business visit is usually preceded by a "hello." This analogy rightly suggests that the purpose of the introduction is more psychological or rhetorical than informative. Where psychological or rhetorical considerations are not important, you may begin a composition directly with a thesis statement.

In other cases, to build a bridge, you should back up a ways from your thesis statement, which may seem too firm, too weighty, or too abrupt a beginning. Instead begin with a sentence more general or more casual or more commonplace or more descriptively vivid and catchy than your thesis statement. Once you have laid down a beginning, steer your way through necessary bridging sentences to reach the thesis that concludes the introduction.

Introductions do not need to be masterpeices, since they are merely a prelude to the body of the essay and to what you really have to say there. When you invite someone into your house, the greeting—clever as it may sometimes be—is not expected to compare with the real entertainment.

EXAMPLE OF AN INTRODUCTORY PARAGRAPH

People like to be scared by art. Art's realistic but artificial terrors let people have high excitement without risking more than a few bad dreams. Popular arts, like film, have regularly fed this appetite and supplied this market. But the diet has also changed over the years. In the last twenty years, horror films have become more popular as escape fare at the same time as they have become less real and less human.

This is a successful introduction, but probably not a perfect introduction; the writer counts on the paper to get better as it moves into the body. But the introduction is fully adequate. It starts with a very general statement, a truism that few people would disagree with, but this truism nonetheless begins to point a reader into the specific concern of the essay. Succeeding sentences narrow down the discussion toward the subject (art ⟶ popular art ⟶ film ⟶ horror film) and thesis. Unlike the opening statement, the thesis is a statement that some people probably would disagree with. Such potential disagreement makes this thesis much more deserving of an essay than the opening sentence. This introduction gives the thesis an assist: it may well persuade many readers to entertain a thesis they would have dismissed outright if it had come straight at them without a preface.

This introduction, then, is funnel-shaped.

The funnel-shaped introduction allows you to pin down your reader to your thesis gently rather than abruptly.

Note other ways—limited only by wit and ingenuity—in which the sample introduction might have begun.

EXAMPLES OF ALTERNATIVE APPROACHES FOR THE INTRODUCTORY PARAGRAPH

The door creaks painfully open, dim moonlight seeps into the gloomy foyer . . . .

Or: Few people who have heard it once can forget the unique way Alfred Hitchcock had of intoning "Goood Eeev'ning." His manner and appearance, at once bizarre and reassuring, matched the inviting, personal tone of his films and television shows—a tone imitated and shared by many of the horror stories of his era. But now, twenty years later, horror films have become more popular as escape fare at the same time as they have become less real and less human.

These are only a few of thousands of ways such a paper might be introduced. Remember that an introduction is in large part a necessary formality, however, and do not get lost among the possibilities.

EX 15-8 Here are six introductions to descriptive essays written in response to the question "What is the stereotype of X?" where X might stand for any of the dozens of social caricatures—bikers, jocks, hippies, housewives, cowboys—that the popular imagination of our culture has dreamed up. Study these introductions for flaws in strategy, flow, or thesis. Use your built-in sense of introduction to help your criticism. Underline the thesis statement in each introduction. Then rewrite defective introductions on a separate sheet of paper; be sure to put the thesis statement last in the paragraph. If an introduction is effective as it is, briefly say why.

1. The word *cowboy* conjures up an image of a man wearing a Stetson hat riding a horse on a ranch. It is natural to classify a stranger and put him or her in a certain group or, in other words, to stereotype him or her. The human mind tends to organize and label. Cowboys, librarians, jocks, and teachers are a few groups of people who are often stereotyped.

2. The stereotype of a single girl is of an appearance-conscious, fun-loving, independent person. A single girl, they say, is constantly seeking a perfect husband to share her life with, just like in the fairy tales. Every single girl lives for today since she is affected by fewer obligations than most other people have.

3. There he is—sitting at his desk for the last nine hours, racking his brain, memorizing every page of his book. He hears no rock music, gossips with no roommate, munches no popcorn, daydreams about no weekend. All silence and concentration, the "A" student is living up to his reputation.

4. If someone were to say the words "books," "study," "quiet," "refined," and "introverted," what would come to mind? How about a typical librarian? If that was the response, then you have just started on the road to making a stereotype of a librarian. To continue with this stereotype, it is logical to start with his or her appearance, which is refined, then his or her personality, which is introverted, and his or her mannerisms, which in general are intellectually oriented.

5. Every stereotype has distinguishing qualities. Susie Sorority always carries her nose in the air. Jocks are always surrounded by cheerleaders. And a cowboy is never without his chew and his pickup truck. The same is true of the typical politician.

6. In every school there is a person that is picked on by the other kids. He or she usually has some sort of unusual behavior that draws notice from classmates. One such person is the class brain, who for no apparent reason seems to have the odd behavior necessary to be the butt of all jokes.

EX 15-9 Write introductions for two of the three thesis statements that you wrote in EX 15–6. Make these introductions three to six sentences long, suitable for a two- to three-page paper. Do your writing on another sheet of paper.

In summary, here are the rules of thumb, or guidelines, that govern the writing of introductions:

- Proportion the length of the introduction to the length of your essay: about one to two sentences per page of body in the paper.
- Conclude your introduction with a thesis statement describing what your essay will argue, assert, or report.
- Match the tone of your introduction to the tone and point of view of the body. Do not, for instance, introduce something frivolously that you later take seriously; do not shift from a personal standpoint to an impersonal standpoint.

- Mention, if you have not successfully implied it, an answer to the question "So what?" That is, your introduction should, in so many words, suggest why your thesis and essay are important, useful, or worthwhile. Look back at sample and exercise introductions in this section to see how answers to "So what?" are usually implied or written between the lines.

E. CONCLUDING A COMPOSITION

Just as most people have a well-developed sense of beginning or introduction, they also have a keen sense of ending or conclusion. These intuitive senses of beginning and ending can be a powerful help to a writer who must decide how to begin or end an essay. As with the introduction, the value of a conclusion is largely rhetorical and psychological rather than informative or substantive.

A writer, when faced by the problem of conclusion, has a number of options:

- The writer may conclude by summarizing the main points of the essay or by restating the thesis.
- The writer may, in a short essay where a summary would seem repetitious and flat, simply strive for a definitive sentence—a strong last sentence of the last paragraph of the body.
- In cases where psychological or rhetorical considerations are not important, the writer may skip the conclusion altogether.
- The writer may point the essay off, not toward some entirely new subject, but toward some implication of the paper—for instance, toward an answer to the "So what?" question implied by the introduction.

Like the introduction, the conclusion is transitional; it says farewell, in so many words, as you lead a reader away from your thoughts back to his or her own.

Here are some sample conclusions to the paper on Hollywood horror films outlined earlier.

EXAMPLES OF TYPES OF CONCLUSIONS
- Conclusive last sentence to the last paragraph of the essay's body (refer to the topic-sentence outline on page 295 of Chapter 14):

For the time being, anyway, moviegoers are preferring cheap visual thrills to expensive, glamorous stars.

- Restatement of thesis or summary of discussion:

Twenty years have changed the Hollywood horror film. Where it used to portray the dark side of human nature by emphasizing story and personality, it now offers something of an amusement park ride that enables an audience to escape, fantasize, and refresh itself ghoulishly for a couple of hours.

- Ending with emphasis on an implication:

These twenty years seem to have changed horror films for the worse. The films have sacrificed literary and artistic values to the entertainment values that a mass audience— particularly a young, television-spoiled audience—is willing to pay for.

● Or the same with a different twist:

> These twenty years, some will say, have changed horror films for the worse. But film makers, in their own restless way, continue to explore the frontiers of their medium. Not content with the achievements of the past, they now explore new realms of entertainment, production, and special effects. No doubt this praiseworthy spirit of experimentation will change the horror film—indeed all film—in the next twenty years.

EX 15-10 Here are three flawed conclusions to an essay on Sigmund Freud's description of the human personality (refer to EX 15-3). This exercise includes one of each kind of conclusion—the strong last sentence, the summary or restatement of thesis, and the emphasis on an implication. On another sheet of paper, revise these endings to make them more conclusive.

1. Freud thought that the superego develops as a result of a person's internalizing— constructing inside the self—an image of the expectations of outside authority figures like parents.

2. In conclusion, Freud's description is interesting.

3. With three such people inside you, maybe it is no wonder that inner conflict is so common and so fierce. Or if Freud is right—and science does still study his theories—it is surprising more people don't have breakdowns, right? Maybe this is all related to another of Freud's descriptions of a life-wish and a death-wish in people.

EX 15-11 Now try some independent work on these various types of conclusions. Refer to the imaginary papers you have worked on in EX 15-6 and EX 15-9. For each of the two thesis statements that you wrote in EX 15-9, write one of each kind of conclusion: a strong last sentence of the last paragraph (consult the appropriate topic-sentence outline in Chapter 14 for the topic of that last paragraph), a restatement of thesis, and a conclusion that points the thesis off toward some relevant consequence or implication. Do your writing on another sheet of paper.

F. ARRANGEMENT OF PARAGRAPHS

Think about the drama and emotional appeal of the following advertisement.

> The 1982 Whippet comes equipped with a fuel-injected, turbocharged four-cylinder engine, AM-FM radio, air conditioning, vinyl top, white-sidewall tires, and front and rear bumper pads.

Can you see what is weak—needlessly weak—about this list of featured equipment?

The principle of saving the best for last is called *climactic order*, a phrase that comes from the word "climax," as in the climax of a drama. This principle of climactic order is worth a writer's attention when the time comes to arrange paragraphs of an essay. The introduction and conclusion, of course, are easy to set in order; one is first, the other last. But the arrangement of the paragraphs of the body sometimes offers various possibilities. Use this rule of thumb: *Unless logic dictates some other order, arrange your essay's body paragraphs in climactic order; save the best, most vivid, most interesting, or most emphatic point for last.* In narrative or process development, for example, *logical* sequence overrules this guideline; but elsewhere writers usually employ it to keep papers from trickling away into insignificance as does the advertisement for the 1982 Whippet.

EX 15-12   On another sheet of paper, rearrange and rewrite the description of the 1982 Whippet using the principle of climactic order.

Opinions may differ about the most important feature of the Whippet, so several different climactic orders are possible. Probably everyone would agree, however, that bumper pads do not deserve the climactic position; probably the engine or radio or air conditioning does.

You can *tentatively* arrange items in a topic-sentence outline in climactic order. You must be tentative because your actual development and writing of these paragraphs may turn up unexpected ideas and arguments that will change the relative importance and arrangement of paragraphs. Here is a topic-sentence outline. What would be the sequence of paragraphs according to climactic order? Why?

Question: Why should capital punishment be banned?
A. It is legally cruel and unusual punishment.
B. It is morally wrong.
C. Contrary to popular belief, it is not always cheaper to kill criminals than to keep them in prison.
D. Contrary to popular belief, capital punishment is not a deterrent to crime.
E. The spirit of revenge should not be encouraged in a democratic society based on public law.
F. Capital punishment cannot be revoked in the event of judicial error.

Here is one way of reasoning out a climactic order of paragraphs. The weightiest points of the argument seem to be A, B, and E, perhaps in that order. In comparison, points C, D, and F seem more mundane, less dramatic and ringing. Besides, points C and D seem to rebut views on the opposite side of the controversy, so they make better logical sense coming early in the argument, when the writer is describing and setting up the controversy (see the controversy format of pages 297–98 of Chapter 14). In short, this sequence—C, D, F, A, B, and E— makes a reasonably logical and climactic order for this essay's points.

EX 15-13   List a reasonably logical and climactic order for points in the following topic-sentence outline. Then write a short explanatory paragraph defending your arrangement. Do your writing on another sheet of paper.

Question: Why should capital punishment be reintroduced?
A. It helps deter crime, especially so-called heinous crime.
B. It would reduce overcrowding in courts and prisons.
C. Everyone can understand the principle of capital punishment much better than current sentencing practices, so it would help end public disenchantment with our criminal justice system.
D. It would provide some satisfaction to victims and survivors of violent crime.
E. The principle of equal justice or retribution is a very moral, time-honored part of our Western heritage.
F. Speedy death is often a less cruel and unusual punishment than lifelong incarceration.

EX 15-14   Here is another topic-sentence outline for you to arrange and justify. List a reasonably logical and climactic order for the points in the following outline. Then write a short explanatory paragraph defending your arrangement. Do your writing on another sheet of paper.

Question: What does one experience at a county fair?
A. The sights of the fair, especially at night, are phantasmagoric.
B. The sounds of the carnival—of crowd, barker, and calliope—come and go in waves of excitement.
C. The taste of the fair is sweet—too sweet.
D. The touch of the fair includes dust, sweat, sticky fingers, and the crush of the crowd, but also the tingle of excitement.
E. The complex smell of a fair may best be reckoned from its ingredients.

EX 15-15   Study the topic-sentence outlines that you polished in EX 14-10, EX 14-11, and EX 14-12. Arrange each of these outlines in reasonably logical and climactic order; be prepared to justify your arrangements.

1. EX 14-10: _____

2. EX 14-11: _____

3. EX 14-12: _____

G. WRITING TRANSITIONS BETWEEN PARAGRAPHS

When polishing and arranging the paragraphs of an essay, a writer often senses gaps between paragraphs. Just as a writer bridges gaps *within* the paragraph, a writer needs to bridge these gaps *between* paragraphs to ensure flow, coherence, and reader comprehension.

Sometimes separate, brief transitional paragraphs provide these bridges. Usually, however, briefer words, phrases, or constructions attached to regular body paragraphs can ensure the clear flow of thought. These transitional elements can often be added to the sentence in a topic-sentence outline.

EXAMPLE OF A TOPIC-SENTENCE OUTLINE WITH TRANSITIONAL ELEMENTS ADDED
How did Freud describe the human personality?
A. First, he identified what he called the *ego*, or reality principle.
B. His second component was the *id*, or pleasure principle.
C. Third, he asserted the existence of a *superego*, a moral, counter-id principle.

The technique of enumeration here—*first*, *second*, and *third*—will probably provide sufficient continuity between these paragraphs. The writer might have written instead *in the first place*, *secondly*, and *finally*. Here are some other possible transitional patterns to bridge paragraph gaps:

EXAMPLES OF INFORMATIVE TRANSITION SENTENCES
In addition to the ego and the id, Freud asserted the existence of a superego.

Freud not only asserted the existence of an id; he *also* claimed the existence of a sort of opposite to the id—a superego.

Besides the ego, he found the id.

Because of the imbalance created in the personality by the id, Freud felt compelled to patch up or balance the whole with a counter-principle—the superego.

When the id strives for quiet, according to Freud, the superego counters this striving.

Here is the topic-sentence outline for an essay expressing opposition to capital punishment; the outline has been rewritten with transitions in the topic sentences, which have been set in climactic order. Can you identify these transitional elements?

> Why should capital punishment be banned?
> A. Contrary to popular belief, it is not always cheaper to kill criminals than it is to imprison them.
> B. Nor is capital punishment actually a deterrent to crime.
> C. More important than such practical concerns, however, is the fact that capital punishment cannot be revoked in the event of judicial error.
> D. In addition, it is cruel and unusual punishment in defiance of the U.S. Constitution.
> E. Not only is capital punishment illegal; it is *also* morally wrong.
> F. Finally and most importantly, the spirit of revenge must not be tolerated in a democratic society or we will revert to practices of the Dark Ages.

Working with outlines rather than with fully developed paragraphs, one can only approximate final, polished transitions. Nevertheless, the transitions in this example would probably hold up in a finished work and would ensure the flow and coherence of the whole essay.

EX 15-16   Rewrite the topic-sentence outlines from EX 15-13 and EX 15-14; add transitional elements that will ensure flow and coherence from one point to the next. Do your writing on another sheet of paper.

H. TITLING YOUR ESSAY

Your last polishing task is one of your most challenging and inviting. You should give your paper a title. Like the thesis, the title should advertise what is to follow and should match your paper in tone and viewpoint. Witty or imaginative titles, if appropriate to the subject, are as welcome as direct, informative titles. Use your well-practiced, well-developed sense of what makes a title. Remember, however, these customs:

- Capitalize first and last words of your title and all important words in between (not *and, a, of, the,* and similarly inconspicuous words).
- Do not underline your title.
- Do not set your title in quotation marks unless it really is a quotation. (You might title a pro *and* con paper about euthanasia, for instance, "To Be or Not to Be.") Note, though, that this custom applies only to the title at the beginning of a paper. If you, or anyone else, mentions your title in paragraph context, it must appear in quotation marks.
- Do not use someone else's title for your title. (*Macbeth* as a title, for instance, has already been taken; you will have to find another, like "The Witches' Revenge.")

EX 15-17   Write titles for the following imaginary papers developed in this chapter. If you can, use some ingenuity to write titles that are catchy and inviting as well as honest and accurate.

1. On cars large and small: _____

2. On housepainting: _____

3. On Freud: _____

4. On horror films: _____

5. For capital punishment: _____

6. Against capital punishment: _____

7. On county fairs: _____

WORKSHOP

1. Watch a local television newscast and note introductions, conclusions, and transitions.
   a. Write down opening statements of introductions to news features and human interest stories.
   b. Write down interesting transitional remarks that move the newscast from one story to the next.
   c. Write down strong last lines, morals, or conclusions offered by reporters in the field.

2. Write three different introductions to the same composition, if possible using three distinctly different openings. Then poll classmates or friends to see which they prefer and why. Summarize your findings in a paper that answers the question, "What do people look for in an introduction?"

3. Inspect a collection of short stories, borrowed either from the library or from your instructor. Write down the last sentences of ten of these stories—ten last sentences that seem to you particularly conclusive (even though you have not read the story). Then try to figure out what it is about those ten sentences that causes them to impart a feeling of conclusiveness. Summarize your views in a paper that answers the question, "What factors contribute to the conclusiveness of a sentence?"

4. Make a list of ten titles of articles, books, songs, movies, albums, products, or businesses that strike you as especially fine. Then try to figure out and explain in a paragraph what caused you to like those titles. You can extend this experiment to include the opinions of friends and acquaintances. If you do, summarize your findings in a paper that answers the question, "What makes a title effective?"

5. List all the examples of climax, of saving the best for last, that you encounter in a day—in conversation, in entertainment, at meals. Write a paper that describes how widely the climactic principle affects our daily life. After describing the extent of the principle, try to explain its wide use and acceptance.

6. Develop and write an essay on some genre or kind of Hollywood film other than the horror film. You may find it helpful to use the exercises about the horror film in this chapter as a guide or model for your essay. Other Hollywood genres or kinds you might choose from include science-fiction films, westerns, detective films, romances, historical epics, screwball comedies, musicals, and spy films.

7. Improve some previous paper of yours by revising and rewriting its introduction, thesis, and conclusion, and adding paragraph transitions; use the skills you have practiced in this chapter.

Getting the Most from Your Composing Skills

16

The material in this final chapter is intended to help you derive maximum benefit from the skills you have worked throughout the course to develop. Section A presents a list of the twelve steps involved in writing a composition. Turn to this page for guidance when you begin work on any writing assignment. The next six sections (B to G) deal with the tasks that *follow* the final step of writing the draft of a composition. If you properly attend to these tasks—proofreading, providing references, checking logic—you can make successful papers into excellent ones. The final sections of this chapter (H, I, and J) will give you a sense of how you can put your newly developed skills to work for you in the world outside the classroom. With a few adjustments and a slight change of perspective, college writing skills become life writing skills—skills that will remain useful to you throughout your years.

A. REVIEWING THE STEPS IN WRITING A COMPOSITION

When you begin a writing assignment, use the following list to help you develop your plan of action; let the list assist you in keeping track of your progress. For more detailed guidance on how to accomplish particular tasks, refer to the text pages or chapters indicated in parentheses.

1. Choose a subject. (See pages 289–90.)
2. Narrow the subject, if necessary, to suit your time, your knowledge, your audience, or the length and scope of the assignment. (See pages 290–91.)
3. Pin your purpose down to a question worth answering in an essay. (See pages 291–92.)
4. Try writing various complete-sentence answers to your question. (See pages 293–94.)
5. Research answers to your question, if necessary. (See pages 301–02.)
6. Cluster and polish these answers into a brief topic sentence outline. (See pages 294–97.)
7. Develop each answer or topic sentence into a body paragraph of four to ten sentences, using a suitable method of paragraph development and providing necessary transitions. (See Chapters 2–4.)
8. Write a thesis by answering your question from step 3 in the form of a concise but comprehensive statement. (See pages 307–09.)

9. Write an introduction to your composition that opens invitingly and concludes with the thesis statement from step 8. (See pages 309–12.)
10. Arrange the paragraphs of your composition's body in a logical or climactic order; add transitional phrases or constructions to bridge gaps between paragraphs. (See pages 313–16.)
11. Write a conclusion to your composition, if necessary. (See pages 312–13.)
12. Write a title for your composition. (See pages 316–17.)

(Note that although these steps cover the entire *writing* process, two more tasks—*proofreading* and *supplying reference notes*—must be completed before the written work is ready to be turned in. The next six sections of this chapter (sections B to G) will instruct you on how to carry out these tasks.)

EX 16-1   Which three of these composing steps give you the most difficulty? List the problem or problems that each of these three steps tends to cause you. In the case of each problem you refer to, cite a task or technique that might help you solve or overcome the composing problem. Write the problem and your proposed solution in opposite columns.

PROBLEM   SOLUTION

1. _____   _____

   _____   _____

   _____   _____

   _____   _____

2. _____   _____

   _____   _____

   _____   _____

   _____   _____

3. _____   _____

   _____   _____

   _____   _____

   _____   _____

B. EMPLOYING REFERENCE MECHANICS: CITING AUTHORITIES

Often writers enhance their own accuracy and authority by citing sources and authorities other than themselves—sources and authorities whom they have researched and whose ideas and facts they have woven into the texture of their own papers. Special rules and mechanics govern the use and acknowledgment of such sources in essay endnotes or footnotes and in bibliographies.

When you quote or paraphrase the particular words or ideas of another author, you incur a debt that you repay with a note or citation of that author's work. Customarily the quote or paraphrase is marked at its conclusion by a raised, or *superscript*, number, like this.[2] The number refers a reader to the corresponding note at the *foot* of the page (thus *foot*note) or to the notes collected in a list at the *end* of the paper (thus notes or *end*notes). The form in which these notes are presented, though it can vary from discipline to discipline, should be regular within a single paper.

Here are a few of the most common forms of the many kinds of references you may need to note or footnote in a researched essay.

- For a book with one author:

[1] James Broderick, *Galileo: The Man, His Work, His Misfortunes* (New York: Harper & Row, 1964), p. 112.

- For a book with a translator or editor:

[2] Galileo Galilei, *Dialogue Concerning the Two Chief World Systems*, trans. Stillman Drake (Berkeley: Univ. of California Press, 1953), pp. 66–67.

- For a magazine article:

[3] Stillman Drake, "Galileo and the Rolling Ball," *Science Digest*, October 1978, p. 76.

- For an essay or article in an edited collection or anthology:

[4] Winifred Lovel Wisan, "Galileo's Scientific Method: A Reexamination," in *New Perspectives on Galileo*, ed. Robert E. Butts and Joseph C. Pitt (Boston: D. Reidel Publishing Co., 1978), pp. 11 and 14.

- For a newspaper article:

[5] "Vatican May Lift Censure of Galileo," *New York Times*, 2 July 1968, Sec. 1, pp. 1 and 10.

- For an encyclopedia article:

[6] Ernan McMullin, "Galileo Galilei," *Collier's Encyclopedia*, 1972, X, 543.

- For additional mentions of a previously noted source:

[7] Broderick, p. 110.
[8] Wisan, p. 12.

Some additional points: The roman numeral X in note 6 refers to the volume number of the encyclopedia. Some magazines are also indexed by volume number instead of by month or by date as in note 3. And for anonymous newspaper, encyclopedia, or magazine articles, simply begin your note with the article's title, as in note 5.

Remember to consult these various forms while you do research, so that you will remember to jot down in an orderly way all the specifics that footnoting requires about a source before you put the source away. When writing or typing your footnotes or endnotes for your finished paper, pay special attention to indentation, punctuation marks, quotation marks, and parentheses: follow prescribed formats conscientiously. Research references need the painstaking accuracy of computer programs, and for the same reason: readers want the information to be where you say it is when they go to seek it.

For additional questions of note format and mechanics, consult your instructor or a reference librarian. No one expects you to know or memorize all the recipes for all situations, but you can reasonably be expected to know where to seek necessary help or advice.

If you have only one or two references in a paper, you may—with the permission of your instructor—find it more appropriate to use parentheses in your text to cite sources. Instead of using numbers and notes, simply follow your quotation or summary with parentheses containing the information you would otherwise footnote (Kenneth Burke, *A Rhetoric of Motives* [Berkeley: Univ. of California Press, 1969], p. 41).

EX 16-2   Here is a rough draft of citations for the endnotes of a researched paper. On another sheet of paper, write them in correct order and correct form, using the earlier examples as guides.

- First reference is to a book called *Frankenstein: Or, the Modern Prometheus* written by Mary Wollstonecraft Godwin Shelley and published in 1923 in New York by Brentano Publishing Company. The paper has quoted pages 34 and 35 of this book.
- The fourth reference is to an anonymous article in the *Encyclopedia Americana* entitled "Shelley, Mary Wollstonecraft Godwin." This is the 1979 edition and the article is on page 693 of Volume 24.
- The fifth reference is to a book by Mary Shelley's mother, Mary Wollstonecraft, entitled *Mary: A Fiction* and *The Wrongs of Woman.* This is two works in one book, edited by Gary Kelley and published in London in 1976 by Oxford University Press. The paper quotes page 109.
- The third reference is to an essay by Albert J. Lavalley in a collection of essays edited by George Levine and U. C. Knoepflmacher. The title of the book is *The Endurance of Frankenstein: Essays on Mary Shelley's Novel*, and the title of the essay (on pages 243 to 289) is "The Stage and Film Children of *Frankenstein*: A Survey." The University of California Press in Berkeley published this collection in 1979. The paper summarizes pages 287 to 289.
- The second reference is to a magazine article by Joan Baum published in Volume 12 of *Rendezvous: Journal of Arts and Letters* in 1977 on pages 5 to 8. The article's title is "The Lessons of *Frankenstein.*" The essay quotes page 8 of this article.
- The seventh reference is to a book by William Godwin, edited by W. Clark Durant. It is entitled *Memoirs of Mary Wollstonecraft.* It was published in New York in 1969 by Haskell House. The essay quotes page 33.
- The sixth reference is to the *Collected Letters of Mary Wollstonecraft* by Mary Wollstonecraft, edited by Ralph M. Wardle for the Cornell University Press of Ithaca, New York. The essay quotes page 198 of this 1979 book.
- The eighth reference is to page 6 of the *Rendezvous* essay by Baum.

Recast all this information into the eight notes that would appear at the end of the essay.

C. EMPLOYING REFERENCE MECHANICS: PREPARING A BIBLIOGRAPHY

A bibliography is sometimes required by instructor, audience, discipline, or assignment. The bibliography is an alphabetically arranged list of all reference works used in researching a paper. It follows the endnotes. Like the list of notes, the bibliography observes a strictly consistent format; however, the form for bibliographic entries differs somewhat from foot-note form, as you can see from this sample bibliography.

EXAMPLE OF A BIBLIOGRAPHY
Broderick, James. *Galileo: The Man, His Work, His Misfortunes.* New York: Harper & Row, 1964.

Drake, Stillman. "Galileo and the Rolling Ball." *Science Digest*, October, 1978, p. 76.

Galilei, Galileo. *Dialogue Concerning the Two Chief World Systems.* Trans. Stillman Drake. Berkeley: Univ. of California Press, 1953.

McMullin, Ernan. "Galileo Galilei." *Collier's Encyclopedia*, 1972, X, 543.

"Vatican May Lift Censure of Galileo." *New York Times*, 2 July 1968, Sec. 1, pp. 1 and 10.

Wisan, Winifred Lovel. "Galileo's Scientific Method: A Reexamination." *New Perspectives on Galileo.* Ed. Robert E. Butts and Joseph C. Pitt. Boston: D. Reidel Publishing Co., 1978, pp. 1–58.

Once more, pay special attention to indentation, punctuation, quotation marks, and word and item order.

EX 16–3　　Convert your list of endnotes in EX 16–2 into bibliography format, using the bibliography above as a model. Do your writing on another sheet of paper.

D. EMPLOYING REFERENCE MECHANICS: AVOIDING PLAGIARISM

When a writer fails to note debts to other authorities, he or she has committed *plagiarism*, or literary theft. When you directly quote words not your own, you must put quotation marks before and after them and note or cite your source. When you summarize or para-phrase ideas not your own, you must also note or cite your source. By *paraphrase*, further-more, most people mean very loose rephrasing or summarizing quite independent of the original phrasing and syntax.

Failure to give proper credit to sources is a serious academic or professional offense that jeopardizes any educational or business system that is based on individual performance and rewards. Plagiarism may result in failing the course, being expelled from school, or losing a job. So it is essential that you know and practice good, careful research habits.

You do not need to note or cite sources of general knowledge or of information in the *public domain* (not copyrighted), like the date of the Spanish Armada or of the factors gen-erally known to have given rise to fascism in Italy during the 1930s. But you should note or cite sources of information and ideas that are not general knowledge, particularly sources of ideas, information, or interpretation that are debatable or controversial. All the same, timely mention of a source like the United States Bureau of the Census can impart credibility to your facts, even if these facts are generally known or available.

When in doubt about the need to cite or note a source of words, facts, or ideas, ask an instructor or reference librarian for advice.

EX 16-4   Which of the following items should be accompanied by a note identifying the source of all or part of the item? Briefly justify your decision in each case.

1. Martin Van Buren was the eighth U.S. President; he was probably not the best President.

   _____

2. T. S. Eliot has written, "The past should be altered by the present as much as the present is directed by the past. . . ."

   _____

3. Mary Shelley, the daughter of famous parents, William Godwin and Mary Wollstonecraft, and the wife of the famous poet Percy Shelley, wrote *Frankenstein.*

   _____

4. President Franklin D. Roosevelt knew of Japan's plan to attack U.S. forces somewhere in the Pacific but cruelly held back warning of a possible surprise attack such as the one that would be made on Pearl Harbor.

   _____

5. A famous anthropologist writes that the difference between so-called primitive peoples and us is not their use of symbolism and our use of science. We too use symbols all the time. Rather, she stresses how our symbols derive from many fragmentary, unrelated contexts, while their symbols tend to refer to one large, coherent, all-embracing cosmos.

   _____

6. Because "all that is beautiful is difficult," according to the philosopher, people often settle for easier, inferior forms of beauty.

   _____

7. Plato has often been called the "father of philosophy," even though he seems like a son to his teacher Socrates.

   _____

8. Rome, at its peak, was the largest, most populous, richest city the world had yet seen.

   _____

E. PROOFREADING FOR MECHANICAL ERRORS (REVIEW)

Though everyone makes mistakes, educated, responsible writers are expected to catch and correct their own mistakes by carefully proofreading their work for misspellings, punctuation faults, and obvious grammatical errors. The inconvenience of consulting a dictionary or grammar handbook cannot compare with the poor impression that negligently proofread papers make on their audience.

Here is a paragraph that, although well-written, caused problems for its writer thanks to shoddy proofreading; the handwritten marks were made by the instructor who graded the essay.

> *cap   cap*   *number apostrophe*
>
> The ancient (r)oman (e)mpire did in fact witness a wom(a)n's liberation movement. But
>
>   *cap   cap*
>
> historians who like to blame this movement for the fall of the (r)oman (e)mpire are being very
>
>   *number*   *sp*   *sp*
>
> unfair. True enough, those wom(a)n who became poets, bus(i)nessmen, and even ath(e)letes lost
>
>   *sp*   *sp*   *sp*
>
> some int(e)rest in b(e)aring and raising children for the priv(a)ledged classes of tomorrow. And true
>
> enough, the population declines of these ruling classes led to a series of crises in leadership.
>
>   *number*
>
> But if wom(a)n were so essential to the state, why had they been treated like cattle—bought
>
>   *apostrophe*
>
> and owned and sold—for hundreds of years? And why coul(d)n(')t the men invent some other
>
>   *sp*   *pct*
>
> method besides a corrupt(a)ble and fragile aristocratic elite for the governing of the empire( )

This writer should have caught and corrected the circled mistakes in this paragraph. This lack of care on the writer's part could cast doubt on the accuracy of his or her information and on the carefulness and acuity of his or her thinking and arguing in the minds of some readers—readers that the writer may be trying to reach, inform, and persuade.

EX 16-5 Proofread the following letter to the editor of a local newspaper. It contains twelve careless mistakes. Circle those mistakes. Then rewrite the paragraph accurately, and proofread your own rewrite to make sure that it is free from new mistakes. Do your writing on another sheet of paper.

To the Editor:

As a taxpayer, I strongly object to the carelesness of the repaving project just completed on High Street. As the old joke says, the contracters crews may have worked slowly, but they sure did a sloppy job. When they oiled the street, to begin with, they spiled oil all over lawns, plantings, and sidewalk. And after graveling the street, instead of sweeping and trucking off the excess gravel, crews simply swept and shoveled them onto the property of residence. Then when crews cut out the asfalt on the manhole covers, instead of trucking it off, they threw it again on private property for children to play with. I sincerly hope the city doesnt contract with this firm again I dont want my tax money helping pay someone to be a thoughtless slob.

John Peoples

F. CHECKING FOR ERRORS IN LOGIC

Errors in reasoning are called *fallacies*, and these lapses in logic can be as embarrassing to writers as mechanical flaws. Here are a few of the more common kinds of fallacies.

- *Ad hominem* argument: The Latin means "against the person" and refers to an argument aimed, not against an opinion, but against a person who holds the opinion.

    ### EXAMPLE
    Ezra Pound's poetry is weakened by his becoming a fascist sympathizer during World War II. [There is no necessary connection between a person's politics and the quality of his or her poetry.]

- Begging the question or circular reasoning: A writer unwittingly assumes as proved the assertion that he or she sets out to prove.

    ### EXAMPLE
    The Italians finally wouldn't tolerate a dictator because they are a freedom-loving people. [Not tolerating a dictator and loving freedom are two ways of expressing a single attitude, so the sentence "circles" instead of advancing the argument.]

- Oversimplification: A writer falsely frames, limits, or simplifies a problem or dispute.

    ### EXAMPLE
    As Mussolini rose to power, Italians faced a choice of either communism or fascism. [Either-or thinking often leads to *false dichotomies* that ignore other views or alternatives.]

- Faulty generalization: A writer bases a universal statement on too few cases or examples.

    ### EXAMPLE
    The case of Ezra Pound shows how politically naive and corruptible literary people are. [Pound may in fact have been exceptional in this regard.]

- *Ad populum* argument: The Latin means "to the people" and refers to arguments that play on *popular* prejudices, beliefs, superstitions, or trust in heroes—things that are supposedly capable of winning over average folk.

    ### EXAMPLE
    Mussolini argued, in effect, support me and you will support the return of Italy's glorious Roman Empire. [This appeal of Mussolini's aimed to take advantage of feelings of nationalism and nostalgia held by Italians, the descendants of the once all-powerful Romans.]

- Equivocation: A writer uses the same word in different senses.

    ### EXAMPLE
    Fascism favored the superior individual and therefore appealed to Pound, who was a superior individual. [Actually, fascism favored those who were "superior" in strength, not those like Pound who were "superior" in poetic or intellectual talent.]

- *Non sequitur*: The Latin means "it does not follow" and refers to conclusions that do not logically proceed from premises or starting points.

  EXAMPLE

  Their past history with Popes, kings, and dictators shows how incapable Italians are of democratic rule. [The writer assumes, but does not state, the unlikely premise that "All nations with tyrants in their past are incapable of democratic rule." This premise is easily disproved from history.]

- False authority: Here a writer cites an authority in one specialty to make a statement about another specialty, in which the authority has no real competence.

  EXAMPLE

  Having closely studied nearly all of literature, myth, and culture, Pound was qualified to endorse Mussolini's attempted renewal of ancient Roman glory. [Literature is no qualification for politics; study of *theory* is no guarantee of success or skill in *practice*.]

EX 16-6   Here is an assortment of assertions. Most are fallacious; only one is logical. Evaluate each assertion. Where reasoning is illogical, briefly state in a sentence or two why the logic is faulty. If you wish, identify the fallacies by name.

1. Europeans have not yet learned how to make entertaining movies; no one I know enjoys European films.

   _____

2. *Saturday Night Fever* was a first-rate movie, thanks to an outstanding sound track.

   _____

3. Studying English is helpful because it improves your language skills.

   _____

5. Those who can, do; those who can't, teach.

   _____

5. The Secretary of State is a peace-loving person, but he knows that nowadays peace comes only from the armed strength to intimidate one's enemies.

   _____

6. Since you have used and practiced English all your life, you excel in it.

   _____

7. "Good fences make good neighbors," goes the proverb, so we should build a partition between the two sides of our room.

_____

_____

8. Part of the problem with Senator Kennedy's health plan comes from his being a Catholic.

_____

_____

9. Army recruiting is hindered by the army's low pay scales.

_____

_____

10. If Robert Young says it's good coffee, that's good enough for me. You know what they say: "Father knows best."

_____

_____

G. REVIEWING THE COMPOSITION: A WRITER'S CHECKLIST

Here is a list of questions, in approximate order of importance, to help you check your compositions. If your paper can withstand such a review, you can avoid most of the unpleasant surprises that greet many writers the day their work is handed back.

Any *nos* turned up by the following checklist should send you back to rethink, revise, and rewrite your paper according to skills and techniques practiced earlier in this workbook.

1. Is your essay's thesis clear and accurate for your paper? Does your introduction clearly indicate why the thesis is worth writing about?
2. Are your topic sentences clear and accurate? Are they really important to your thesis? Do your topic sentences adequately cover your thesis statement? (In other words, have you said enough in your paper? Do your topic sentences sufficiently answer the central question you worked with?)
3. Are all sentences in each body paragraph relevant to the topic sentence of that paragraph? Have you developed the whole topic sentence and avoided developing only one part of the topic sentence?
4. Does the illustration, detail, or example in each paragraph really illustrate the topic sentence? Does the illustration really make the idea of your paragraph clearer?
5. Have you defined, clarified, or explained all important concepts, phrases, and words for your intended audience?
6. Have you used transition words and phrases as necessary to bridge the gaps between sentences and between paragraphs?
7. Have you used pronouns (*it, which, this*) cautiously and sparingly, so that your meaning is clear?
8. Have you avoided unnecessary passive sentences? Have you avoided overuse of such flat formulas as "There are," "He is the one who," and "It is important to realize that"? Have you done your best to streamline and beautify sentences that violate your sense of style and your ear for English?

9. Have you checked each doubtfully spelled word in a dictionary, checking too that the definition fits your use of the word? Have you punctuated your essay as correctly as you can? Have you questioned the proper authorities—tutors, handbooks, instructors—about knotty problems of punctuation, mechanics, diction, and spelling?
10. Have you properly cited published sources from which you have taken direct quotes, paraphrases, and particular ideas?

EX 16-7   Reread and study this checklist. Underline the questions that apply most closely to your personal writing habits and hurdles. On another sheet of paper, copy the questions you have underlined, in the order in which they occur in the foregoing checklist. After each question, write a sentence telling yourself what to do or where to turn when, in reviewing a particular paper, you must answer the question with a *no*.

H. USING COMPOSING SKILLS OUTSIDE THE CLASSROOM: WRITING A BUSINESS LETTER

Some people claim that the three-page composition is only a school exercise—a form they will never use again after graduation. On the surface, this claim may prove true for many people. But in a deeper sense, features of the three-page composition are everywhere present in the educated, literate world. The skills of organization, argument, and style that you use to compose an essay apply to most formal communication situations in our society. Though you may never again write a three-page essay, you will use essay composing skills *constantly*.

Common formats for composition besides the essay include the business letter, the résumé, and the report or memo. It is important to appreciate how these formats differ from the essay, but you should also be aware of how they resemble the essay.

The relation of writer to audience or reader is always important in writing. But in letter writing this relation is crucial in deciding style, point of view, tone, and level of diction and sophistication. Though they sound difficult, adjustments in these elements of style are easy for experienced English speakers to make if they take the time to assess their purpose and audience. Think, for instance, of differences in how you would write a letter applying for a job, a letter to your parents requesting a gift or loan of money, a letter of advice to a younger brother or sister, and a love letter to a special friend. In any of these cases, badly misjudging the relation of writer to reader—as shown by style, tone, diction, point of view—could result in the complete failure of the letter's purpose (or thesis).

A formal business letter should strive to embody the following rules of thumb:

- It is well-organized, like an essay.
- It is brief and to the point, focused on some specific outcome, something the writer would like done.
- It is alert and sensitive to the reader, aware of the reader's self-interest and self-respect.
- It is confident and self-assured in tone without any bullying or complaining.
- It is accurately written; it contains no typographical, spelling, or mechanical mistakes.
- It follows formal letter conventions: it is laid out on the page in acceptable, recognizable fashion.

EXAMPLE OF A BUSINESS LETTER

1886 Geneva St.
Rockhead, MN 55052
June 15, 198–

Dr. Marcie Taylor
Registrar
Hazey State College
Rockhead, MN 55050

Dear Dr. Taylor:

I write to inquire about a grade change on my college transcript.

College policy permits a student to retake a course for a higher grade, provided certain guidelines and procedures are followed.

In accord with this policy, I re-enrolled for Fall Term, 198–, in Biology 103, a course I originally passed with a grade of *D* in Spring Term, 198–. This second time, I received a *B*. But this change has not yet appeared on my transcript.

I will soon apply for jobs and send prospective employers my transcript. You can imagine my desire to show them a *B* instead of the *D* that does not reflect my true ability.

Will you look into my petition for grade change, filed on February 23 of this year, to see what is holding up the transcript change? And will you kindly call me to notify me of your findings? My telephone number is 442-6845. Thank you.

Yours truly,

Susan Iverson

Susan Iverson

This is a simple, direct, and effective letter. Its thesis or purpose is stated in its first sentence. The next three paragraphs support and develop this purpose by explaining the inquiry: because of the policy, because of my compliance with it, because of my pressing needs, you should investigate the lack of grade change since you are overseer of grades and transcripts. This is a letter, but it also follows good, clear, essay structure.

Here is a less successful formal or business letter. As you read it, study where and why it falls short of success.

EXAMPLE OF A FLAWED BUSINESS LETTER

Hiring Dept.
Alpine Instruments
Salt Lake City

Dear sirs,

A friend told me that you have summer jobs for college kids. If this is true, I would like one.

He also said that many of these jobs were in your quality control labs where you test the medical research instruments you make.

I've always liked lab sciences in fact I'm thinking of changing my major back to bio. from business. (I was bio. originally.) Anyway, I have lots of school experience with lab equipment and procedures and have never received lower than a *B* in science, and I'm already a second-semester junior.

I also like the mountain west. Actually I chose to write your company because this year I'll spend the summer in Salt Lake City. I was hoping to hike, camp, and fish some of the time, but mostly I'm coming to stay with my aunt and uncle. They were both in an auto accident last spring and need someone to help them around the house for an hour or two each day (in exchange for room and board) while they continue to recover. They invited me of all my cousins, I guess, knowing I've always been responsible this way.

Let me know if my friend was right—his name's Jerry Reinwalt, son of one of your employees—because I sure could use the money. I'm paying my own way through school.

Respectfully submitted,

Steve Iverson

Steve Iverson

P.S. Is there anything else you need to know about me? Should I file an application form or send some character references?

EX 16-8   Rewrite the letter so that Steve Iverson will get the job, which he really does seem to deserve. In particular, organize the letter around its most important and relevant points, and remove the letter's chatty irrelevances. Do your writing on another sheet of paper.

EX 16-9   Write a letter applying for a summer job in response to the following advertisement. In the letter, feature your actual qualifications and experience. Do your writing on another sheet of paper.

HIRING FOR SUMMER JOBS The Atlantic Service Corporation has a number of summer job openings for college students. Some jobs involve technical skills in laboratory procedures, typing, stenography, and computer operation, but the company also has openings in shipping and receiving, on the plant assembly line, in food service, and in the plant day-care center. Applicants should submit letters stating need and qualifications to Summer Hiring Officer, Personnel Office, Atlantic Service Corp., Yourtown, ST 00001.

I. USING COMPOSING SKILLS OUTSIDE THE CLASSROOM: PREPARING A RÉSUMÉ

The résumé is an important part of most real job searches. It supplies in concise form personal, educational, and vocational information about you for convenient reference and study by prospective employers.

Here is a sample résumé that Steve Iverson might send along with his letter of application to Alpine instruments.

EXAMPLE OF A RÉSUMÉ

RÉSUMÉ: Steven Charles Iverson

Applicant for a position as a laboratory technician

RR2
Seaside, MN 55046   Birthdate: June 16, 1962
(507) 885-6332   Health: Excellent

PROFESSIONAL EXPERIENCE
Management Intern, Gable Manufacturing Corporation, Red Wing, Minnesota, summer 1982.
   Responsibilities: Under a special program for qualified business students, assisted manage-
   ment personnel in sales, accounting, and plant supervision.

Laboratory Tutor, Biology Department, Hazey State College, Rockhead, Minnesota, Sept.
   1982–June 1983. Responsibilities: Assisted beginning biology students with lab work.

EDUCATION
Currently a junior at Hazey State College, majoring in Business.
Graduated from Rockhead High School, Rockhead, Minn., June 1980.

REFERENCES

Dr. Loren Reser	Edward Silkie
Professor of Biology	Assistant Vice President
Hazey State College	Gable Manufacturing Corp.
Rockhead, Minnesota	Red Wing, Minnesota
Terry Hance	Alvin Reinwalt
Professor of Accounting	Alpine Instruments
Hazey State College	Salt Lake City, Utah
Rockhead, Minnesota	

There are several acceptable formats for a résumé. But every format should organize and convey information at least as clearly and directly as does this sample. The résumé, like the essay, follows a clear topic outline.

Purpose or thesis: To apply for a specific position
   I. Personal data
   II. Professional experience
   III. Educational experience
   IV. References

As with essays, additional topics or a different order of topics is possible. Furthermore, résumés like Steve Iverson's can and should be tailored to the particular job one is applying for.

EX 16-10   Compose a personal résumé to accompany the letter of application you wrote in EX 16-9. Write your résumé on another sheet of paper.

J. USING COMPOSING SKILLS OUTSIDE THE CLASSROOM: WRITING MEMORANDA AND REPORTS

Like letters, memos and reports usually have verly clearly defined recipients and purposes that force changes from the general-audience orientation of an essay. Memos and reports are like news stories circulating within organizations and businesses, so your information-sorting technique of *who-what-when-where-why-and-how* can help you develop successful memo and report writing skills. The term *report* loosely covers a wide range of formats adapted to many different information purposes; the résumé, in fact, is a specific form of report. For the sake of illustration, this chapter will focus only on the memorandum, one form the report often takes.

EXAMPLE OF A MEMORANDUM

MEMORANDUM

TO: Students in First-Term English Composition Classes
FROM: Alice Reynolds, Director of Composition
DATE: November 30, 198–
RE: Final Exam Schedule for English Composition Classes

The university has established a special exam period for all English Composition classes. This time is 9:00 A.M. on Monday, December 13. Room assignments are posted at all department offices. With only a very few exceptions, your room for the final exam will be *different* from your regular classroom, so please check the room assignment sheets to avoid last-minute confusion. Prompt attendance at the final exam is your responsibility.

The following memo, on the other hand, is less concise, thorough, and successful.

EXAMPLE OF A FLAWED MEMORANDUM

MEMORANDUM

TO: Residents of Fogg Hall
FROM: Larry Davis, Resident Head

Once more the semester and school year come to an end and we all get ready for summer and for catching up on some sleep. As you move things out of your rooms, remember that you are responsible for restoring dorm rooms to clean condition. Any damages will be deducted from your security deposit of $75. Missing room keys will cost you $5. To clear your record and get your money, be sure to check out on schedule and according to guidelines.

EX 16-11   Rewrite the previous memo more successfully by eliminating irrelevances and including the following important information, which Larry Davis neglected to mention: The date of the memo is June 7, 1983, and the deadline he refers to falls at noon on June 17. Each dorm resident must bring to the dorm office a completed check-out list—a survey of room condition and an inventory of furniture—signed by a resident assistant. The dorm resident can get such a check-out list from the dorm office or from an R.A. R.A.s will be on duty to sign between 9:00 A.M. and 4:00 P.M. during the week of June 12 to June 17. Upon receiving the completed, signed list, the dorm office can authorize a deposit refund.

Memos can run anywhere from one paragraph to several pages. For speedy reference, longer memos are sometimes presented in a format similar to that of the résumé, with paragraph or section headings in distinctive type. Despite such variations, your experience with composing essays should give you a good handle on writing even long memos, which are, after all, little more than streamlined, concise, informative essays.

WORKSHOP

1. Write a formal memo to a friend or roommate proposing changes in living arrangements, routines, or relationship. Then list ways in which the memo—in tone, point of view, level of diction, style—differs from how you would actually convey ideas informally to a close acquaintance.

2. Go to the library and research what a *syllogism* is and what an *enthymeme* is. Write a report defining and exemplifying each.

3. Select a suitable argumentative letter to the editor of a large urban newspaper and list all of this letter's logical assertions—statements that involve reasoning from one point to another. (Such words as *because, therefore, so that, since,* and *as a result* can help you spot such reasoning.) Then evaluate each of these statements as you did in EX 16–10, confirming valid logic and explaining fallacious logic.

4. Select a suitable paragraph, freewriting, or composition of yours from earlier in the term and research its thesis in at least five relevant library sources. Then revise and rewrite your previous work, adding and footnoting your new ideas and information.

5. Try using your composing skills as an aid to self-awareness. Make a list of all your personal, educational, and professional strengths. Then list all your weaknesses under the same headings on a different piece of paper. Write a paper assessing your important strengths and weaknesses, but in this paper strive to portray yourself as a confident, self-controlled, self-aware person who is wise as to strengths *and* manageable weaknesses.

6. Find the "Situations Wanted" section of a large newspaper's classified ad section. Focus on one job classification, such as engineer, secretary, or accountant. Which of the ads that you see there are most effective and appealing? Why? Which ads are least appealing and effective? Why? Translate your findings into a paragraph of process writing that instructs a reader how to write a "Situations Wanted" advertisement.

Index